*Encyclopedia of the Alamo and the Texas Revolution*

# Encyclopedia of
# the Alamo and
# the Texas Revolution

*by* Thom Hatch

McFarland & Company, Inc., Publishers
*Jefferson, North Carolina, and London*

Cover photograph © 1999 Index Stock Imagery

**Library of Congress Cataloguing-in-Publication Data**

Hatch, Thom, 1946–
    Encyclopedia of the Alamo and the Texas revolution / by Thom
Hatch.
      p.   cm.
    Includes bibliographical references (p.   ) and index. ∞
    ISBN 0-7864-0593-7 (illustrated case binding : 50# alkaline paper)
    1. Alamo (San Antonio, Tex.) — Siege, 1836.   2. Texas — History —
Revolution, 1835–1836 — Encyclopedias.   I. Title.
    F390.H33   1999
    976.4'03 — dc21                             99-35608
                                                   CIP

British Library Cataloguing-in-Publication data are available

Manufactured in the United States of America

*McFarland & Company, Inc., Publishers*
  *Box 611, Jefferson, North Carolina 28640*
   *www.mcfarlandpub.com*

For Lynn and Cimarron

# CONTENTS

# INTRODUCTION

The Texas Revolution shares many similarities with the American Revolution. Just as the "Intolerable Acts" committed by the British government had compelled American colonists to take up arms and fight for independence, intolerable acts by the Mexican dictator, Antonio Lopez de Santa Anna, were the reason Texas colonists rebelled. The Texans, most of whom had immigrated from the United States, were protesting taxation without proper representation, the quartering of soldiers, civil law enforced by the military, trial by military tribunal rather than by a jury, and the lack of religious freedom. In other words, after being for the most part ignored for many years by the Mexicans, the Texans, who were self-reliant individualists and accustomed to self-government, resented the heavy handed authority suddenly wielded by a powerful centralist government. One dissimilarity between the two revolutions was that this time the participants were of different races, each of which regarded the other as inferior. From the Mexican perspective, the Texans were invaders who had settled on Mexican land, sworn allegiance to Mexico, yet refused to abide by its rules. The Texans, on the other hand, did not initiate the revolution for the purpose of seeking independence, but rather fought as Mexican citizens to restore the provisions of the Mexican Constitution of 1824 that had been voided by Santa Anna.

This encyclopedia acts as a comprehensive guide to assist the reader in understanding the people; places; battles; and significant social, political, cultural, and historical events spanning the early settlement of Texas by Americans to the forming of the Republic. The Texas Revolution, however, is not simply the story of battles, or politics, or a debate about which side was right or wrong, for each side could justify its actions. Rather, the Texas Revolution stands in history as a testament to the courage, honor, and determination of common people who could not resist the inherent urge to seek freedom from tyranny and were willing to sacrifice their lives for the privilege. The one event of this revolution that demonstrated those qualities like no other was without question the Siege and Battle of the Alamo. For that reason, particular attention has been given to this immortal battle, perhaps the most heroic in American history. The names of other engagements of the Texas Revolution may have become obscure footnotes in history, but as long as courage, honor, and determination are valued, we will always "Remember the Alamo!"

## How to Use This Encyclopedia

Entries are listed in alphabetical order. The keyword or phrase, which represents the form most familiar to the reader, appears in bold type at the beginning of the entry. Common abbreviations are never used as the keyword. A detailed index has been provided in the event no appropriate keyword exists for a topic that the reader wishes to locate.

In order to place events in proper perspective, as well as to refer the reader to associated entries, a chronology based on the in-depth TEXAS REVOLUTION entry appears below as well as throughout the book at each keyword contained therein.

## *Chronology of the Texas Revolution*

- June 29, 1835: Battle of ANAHUAC
- October 2, 1835: GONZALES SKIRMISH
- October 3, 1835: MEXICAN CONSTITUTION OF 1824 officially voided
- October 9, 1835: GOLIAD SKIRMISH
- October 28, 1835: Battle of CONCEPCION
- November 3, 1835: TEXAS CONSULTATION OF DELEGATES
- November–December, 1835: Siege and Battle of SAN ANTONIO
- January–February, 1836: The MATAMOROS EXPEDITION

- February 23–March 5, 1836: The ALAMO SIEGE
- March 1, 1836: TEXAS CONSTITUTIONAL CONVENTION
- March 2, 1836: TEXAS DECLARATION OF INDEPENDENCE
- March 6, 1836: The ALAMO BATTLE
- March 20–27, 1836: Surrender and Massacre at GOLIAD
- April 21, 1836: Battle of SAN JACINTO
- May 14, 1836: Treaties of VELASCO

# THE ENCYCLOPEDIA

## A

**ABAMILLO, Juan** (?–March 6, 1836) Sergeant; SEGUIN'S CAVALRY COMPANY; Alamo defender from Texas. This native of San Antonio participated in the Siege and Battle of SAN ANTONIO, and was killed in the ALAMO BATTLE.

**ALABAMA RED ROVERS** (aka Shackleford's Red Rovers) This group of 60–70 men from Courtland, Alabama (pop. 300), whose name was derived from the red-dyed hunting shirts that comprised their uniforms, volunteered as a unit to fight for Texas independence. The Rovers had been organized and financed by surgeon Dr. John "Jack" Shackleford — although rifles and military supplies had been furnished from the Alabama state arsenal. The unit landed at Copano, Texas on January 19, 1836, and were accepted into the service on February 3. The Red Rovers were garrisoned at Goliad under Col. James W. FANNIN, and their ranks were decimated during the Surrender and Massacre at GOLIAD.

**ALAMO, BATTLE OF** (March 6, 1836) This battle, considered among the most dramatic and heroic in history, was the final assault of a standoff waged over a period of 13 days (see ALAMO, SIEGE OF for the first 12 days) between about 188 American volunteers who had taken refuge within the walls of a compound known as the ALAMO MISSION located in San Antonio, Texas (aka San Antonio de Bexar or Bejar) and the attacking MEXICAN ARMY which was comprised of 1,800–2,100 troops commanded by General Antonio Lopez de SANTA ANNA. The battle, which lasted approximately 90 minutes, resulted in the capture of the Alamo by the Mexican Army, the death of every American defender, and the loss of about 500–600 Mexican soldiers killed and an undetermined number of others wounded.

### Chronology of the Texas Revolution

- June 29, 1835: Battle of ANAHUAC
- October 2, 1835: GONZALES SKIRMISH
- October 3, 1835: MEXICAN CONSTITUTION OF 1824 officially voided
- October 9, 1835: GOLIAD SKIRMISH
- October 28, 1835: Battle of CONCEPCION
- November 3, 1835: TEXAS CONSULTATION OF DELEGATES
- November–December, 1835: Siege and Battle of SAN ANTONIO
- January–February, 1836: The MATAMOROS EXPEDITION
- February 23–March 5, 1836: The ALAMO SIEGE
- March 1, 1836: TEXAS CONSTITUTIONAL CONVENTION
- March 2, 1836: TEXAS DECLARATION OF INDEPENDENCE
- **March 6, 1836: The ALAMO BATTLE**
- March 20–27, 1836: Surrender and Massacre at GOLIAD
- April 21, 1836: Battle of SAN JACINTO
- May 14, 1836: Treaties of VELASCO

### Sunday, March 6, 1836

Mexican officers awakened their troops at just after midnight, and preparation for a massive assault on the Alamo Mission commenced. By order of Gen. Santa Anna, the army would be divided into 4 columns, each with a specific area of responsibility. The 500-man column commanded by Gen. Martin Perfecto de Cós, which was composed of the Aldamas battalion of regulars and 3 companies of the volunteer battalion of San Luis, would attack the west wall, which faced the city. Cós's unit would lead the attack, which was perhaps intended by Santa Anna as an honor that would permit his brother-in-law, who had once commanded the Alamo, to regain his reputa-

tion. Col. Francisco Duque would lead the 3 remaining companies of the San Luis volunteers—about 500 men—and would hit the north wall. Col. José María Romero with the Matamoras and Jimines infantry regulars—about 300 men—would attack the east wall where the chapel was located. The final column of around 100 soldiers composed of cavalry companies of the Matamoras and Jimines regulars and the San Luis Battalion of volunteers under the command of Col. Juan Morales would strike the wooden-stake palisade and south gate. The cavalry—about 300 horseman under Gen. Joaquín RAMÍREZ Y SESMA—would remain on the east to guard the camp and prevent any attempt at escape. A detachment of about 400 men comprised of *Zapadores*—the elite corps of engineers—along with 5 companies of grenadiers would be held in reserve. This battle would be fought by ground troops; the artillery batteries would remain silent.

Grenadiers and cavalry companies would be supplied with six packs of cartridges, and the infantry companies four. Santa Anna ordered that arms, particularly bayonets, be in the best condition. The columns under Gen. Cós and Col. Duque were each provided 10 scaling ladders, 2 crow bars, and 2 axes. The other 2 columns received 6 and 2 respectively. The men who carried ladders were ordered to sling their rifles.

At about 1 A.M. the columns began stealthily crossing the San Antonio River, two men abreast over the narrow wooden bridges. By 4 A.M. the Mexican Army had fanned out in position

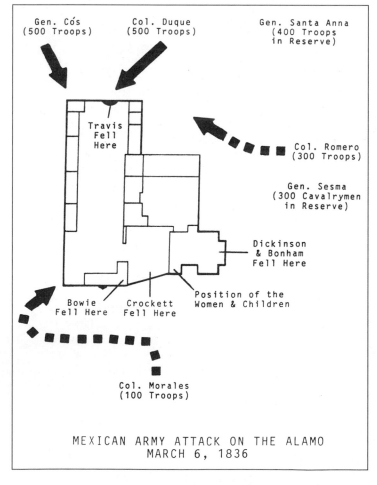

Gen. Cós
(500 Troops)

Col. Duque
(500 Troops)

Gen. Santa Anna
(400 Troops
in Reserve)

Travis
Fell
Here

Col. Romero
(300 Troops)

Gen. Sesma
(300 Cavalrymen
in Reserve)

Dickinson
& Bonham
Fell Here

Position of the
Women & Children

Bowie
Fell Here

Crockett
Fell Here

Col. Morales
(100 Troops)

MEXICAN ARMY ATTACK ON THE ALAMO
MARCH 6, 1836

some 200–300 yards from the Alamo to lie on the cold ground exposed to a brisk north wind and wait under the cloudy sky. Smoking had been forbidden, and overcoats and blankets had been left behind because Santa Anna considered them a hindrance during a charge. The silent men huddled together for warmth, and nervously checked over their weapons and equipment one final time.

Faint streaks of light began to appear on the horizon, and the anticipation of the men became apparent when — somewhere between 5 and 5:30 A.M. — one of them could no longer contain himself, and yelled, "Viva Santa Anna!" This cry was picked up by others, and soon hundreds of voices rose from the darkness with "Viva Santa Anna!" Gen. Santa Anna took that as a sign that the precise time had arrived to send his inspired men into combat. From his position at the north battery, he gave his personal bugler, José María Gonzalez, the order to sound the attack. The signal was immediately echoed by other buglers. The officers screamed "*Arriba!*" (attack), and more than 1,400 determined Mexican soldiers rose to their feet and charged the Alamo. The military band began playing *Deguello*, the "fire and death call," the musical equivalent of the red flag that had been raised atop the belfry of the San Fernando Church that first day that stood for no quarter, no mercy, no prisoners — total annihilation of the enemy.

No alarm was sounded by the 3 sentries that had been stationed outside the mission to warn of an attack. Evidently they had either been sleeping and had failed to detect the advance of the Mexican Army or had been bayonetted to death by advance scouts. Inside the Alamo, officer of the day and second-in-command Capt. John BAUGH had been making his rounds when he heard the bugles and observed the commotion. Baugh yelled "The Mexicans are coming!" to sound

the alarm that called the volunteers to arms. The men scrambled to the walls and immediately opened fire on their onrushing enemy. Col. William TRAVIS, who had been sleeping in his room until roused by Capt. Baugh, rushed to the north parapet, his slave, JOE, close behind. Travis, armed with a sword and double-barreled shotgun, shouted encouragement to his men. The Mexicans, although little more than a dark blur on the dark landscape, were within rifle range, and the volunteers fired, reloaded, and fired again, aiming at the flash of the distant muskets. Some of them had 3 or 4 loaded rifles at their disposal, and fired them all before stopping to reload. Artillery at every position opened up in force, the grapeshot whistling through the pre-dawn to rain down on the sea of soldiers.

The Mexican attack soon wavered, and lost any semblance of military uniformity and discipline as it approached the Alamo. The formations broke apart under the barrage, and detoured around foliage, or fallen comrades, or to conform to the terrain. A number of soldiers panicked and began to retreat, but officers turned them around and directed them toward the Alamo. David CROCKETT and his sharpshooters successfully held back the disorganized lines of running soldiers who stormed the low stockade that ran from the chapel to the south wall. Jim BONHAM and Almeron DICKINSON exhorted the artillery crews that worked the cannon atop the chapel and pinned down the column advancing from the east while the northwestern battery wrecked havoc on Gen. Cós's men. Many Mexican soldiers turned to retreat, but were re-formed by officers who drove them forward with the flats of their sabers to attack in a second full-scale assault.

The Alamo cannons at the north wall could not be aimed below a certain angle, and this offered a sanctuary of sorts at the base of the wall from the grapeshot that had been decimating the Mexican ranks. Soldiers by the hundreds sought out this blind spot to escape the brunt of the cannon barrage, and squeezed themselves against the wall and each other. Col. Francisco Duque was struck in the leg by a bullet and fell, but continued to rally his troops. They ignored him, and trampled his body in their haste to reach the north wall. Gen. Manuel CASTRILLÓN assumed Duque's command as the soldiers milled about in confusion at the base of the wall. This was an ideal location to place ladders, but few had made it that far intact. Many had been discarded or dropped and crushed underfoot, and the chaos created by so many men packed together thwarted any quick effort to locate and employ those ladders that had survived. Hundreds of Mexicans were virtually trapped against this wall, and, although successfully avoiding the cannon, were susceptible to small arms fire. Heavy casualties were sustained both from above and especially from their fellow troops who were indiscriminately firing in the direction of the fortress as they advanced.

Col. Travis leaned over the north wall, aimed his shotgun point-blank into the mass of Mexican soldiers, and fired both barrels. He had raised the weapon to reload when a bullet struck him in the head. Travis reeled backward and tumbled down the dirt embankment. He landed in a sitting position, his sword clutched in his hand, and remained there stunned until dying a few minutes later. William Travis, the man who had vowed "Victory or Death," was likely the first American casualty of the battle. His slave, Joe, fled to seek refuge in one of the rooms. The command of the Alamo had now passed on to Capt. Baugh.

The Mexicans continued to storm the walls, seeking out vulnerable spots that could be breached. But the Texans main-

tained their intense fire, and caused a devastating amount of enemy casualties. Col. Romero's men were repelled at the chapel by grapeshot from the artillery mounted there, and moved to their right to avoid the direct fire. At the same time, Gen. Cós's detachment was under a withering barrage at the west wall. His men panicked and dodged away to their left to assemble with the second column. In a matter of moments, three columns of Mexican soldiers had joined to become one beneath the north wall.

Santa Anna — from his position safely in the rear — then unintentionally made matters worse for his men. He ordered the reserves, accompanied by his entire general staff, to reinforce the attack. More than 400 additional men raced toward the Alamo — blindly firing their weapons as they approached. The friendly fire from Santa Anna's third assault wave blasted into the ranks of soldiers both in the immediate front and those bunched at the wall. Many bullets ricochetted off the stone masonry to cause further casualties. Mexican Gen. Vincente FILISOLA estimated that up to this point — about 15 minutes into the battle — three-quarters of the 400–500 Mexican casualties had been the result of friendly fire. Meanwhile, 1,300–1,500 troops remained trapped at the base of the north wall.

On the other side of the Alamo walls, the Texas volunteers had sustained many casualties as well. Although there was certainly no quit in these men, most knew in their hearts that it was simply a matter of time before they were overrun by the Mexicans or that their ammunition would be depleted.

The lone Mexican column that had not massed at the north wall — 100 men under Col. Morales — had struck the palisade at the south wall. This attempt initially faired no better than the others. David Crockett and his companions at that position had forced Morales to retreat and regroup just out of the field of fire of the Alamo's huge 18-pounder cannon. The assemblage of enemy troops at the north wall, however, drew many of those Texas volunteers away from their assigned posts as they rushed to reinforce that position. Morales and his men were benefactors of that movement of troops, and on a second charge encountered little resistance at the south wall and easily entered to capture the 18-pounder. Morales then deployed his men on a sweep across the plaza toward the north wall just as his comrades were poised to pour over that structure en masse.

Recovered ladders had been brought forward and placed in position, and, by utilizing exposed Alamo timbers and wooden braces of a redoubt, Gen. Juan V. Amador led soldiers up the ladders while others grasped hand and footholds found in the walls and scrambled toward the top. By sheer willpower and overwhelming numbers of men, the Mexicans, often climbing over one another or falling backward and starting over, surged upward and over the top of the wall.

The Texans met their enemy at the parapet along the 54-yard wall with bayonets, rifle butts, knives, and pistols, and briefly delayed the inevitable by repulsing many of the first to appear. But those Mexicans below who were desperate to escape the horde were not deterred by the bodies of their comrades falling upon them from above, and jostled for position to scale the wall. The scene was a chaotic mixture of sound and fury of unimaginable proportion. The smoky air was filled with rifle and pistol retorts, the boom of artillery, bugle calls blown in vain, the clamor of frantic voices — cursing their enemy, officers shouting orders, the groans and cries of the wounded. Waves of bodies pressed the attack against those outnumbered defenders

who perched atop the north wall. The Mexican soldiers were not to be denied, and soon managed to swarm over the parapet and into the Alamo compound. Those volunteers who had not been killed or wounded at the wall fell back into the open plaza to engage the Mexican soldiers in hand to hand combat.

While the north wall was being breached, Gen. Cós managed to turn his troops toward the west wall and, without an effective defense to deter them — only about 20 or 30 defenders manned the 500 foot long wall — poured inside faster than the Texans could fire. The first Mexicans inside opened the northern postern, and a flood of their comrades were freed of their confinement against the wall and surged into the Alamo with malice on their minds.

Capt. Baugh ordered those within earshot to retreat to the long barracks. The Texans fell back and opened fire from the barracks and officer quarters that rimmed the plaza, and cannons were spun around and aimed down at the stream of Mexicans. Steady charges of grapeshot and rifle fire devastated the invading soldiers — as did friendly fire from Col. Morales's men firing from the south. Morales was maneuvering his troops toward the main gate from the rear to join the columns scrambling over the walls and through the gate that were originally led by Duque and Romero but now were commanded by Gen. Castrillón. Many of the volunteers who had fled their positions at the walls to retreat toward the long barracks were caught in the open and shot or hacked to death by the rampaging Mexican soldiers who now had been joined by the cavalry.

At about this point in time, artillery captain Almeron Dickinson, the man who had fired the first shot of the revolution with the Gonzales cannon, departed his position and raced into the sacristy where his wife

Susannah and daughter Angelina were huddled. "Great God, Sue!" he was said to have cried, "the Mexicans are inside our walls! If they spare you, save my child!" He then kissed his wife, hugged his daughter, drew his sword and returned to the fray.

David Crockett and his men at the south palisade were too far removed from the barracks where Travis had planned to make a last stand, and were eventually overwhelmed at that position. Crockett's individual last stand has been the subject of much controversy. Popular belief has always portrayed that Crockett died bravely, clubbing the soldiers with his rifle when his ammunition had run out until finally being killed. Later accounts by Mexican eyewitnesses have suggested that Crockett surrendered and subsequently was executed. (See CROCKETT, David for more.)

The defenders holed up in the barracks that had been earlier prepared for the possibility of a last stand. The doorways that faced the plaza were blocked by semicircular parapets made of dirt packed inside stretched cowskins. Trenches had been dug in many of the rooms, and holes had been punched through the walls from which to shoot or to pass from room to room. The volunteers kept up volleys of fire at the attacking Mexican soldiers, but there were simply not enough of them left alive to fend off the superior force. Col. Romero turned the huge 18-pounder cannon on the rooms, and, along with concentrated musket fire, began blowing them apart. Soldiers methodically burst into each room and killed the entrenched occupants. Others prowled the Alamo compound as if drunk on blood, and took no prisoners as they searched room by room for survivors.

In a room near the low barracks lay Col. Jim BOWIE, who had been too ill to participate in the battle. Mexican soldiers broke down the door, and found a ghost-white Bowie propped up in his cot with pistols in each hand and others at his side said to be provided by Crockett. Bowie discharged his weapons and held off his enemy for a few moments, but was finally killed. The soldiers reportedly tossed Bowie's body on their bayonets until his blood covered their clothes and dyed them red.

Bowie's sister-in-law Juana ALSBURY, her infant son, and her sister, Gertrudis NAVARRO, were hiding in a room along the west wall adjoining the officers' quarters. Gertrudis opened the door and was accosted by Mexican soldiers, one of whom ripped the shawl from her shoulders. She fled back into the room. Defender Edwin T. MITCHELL attempted to protect the ladies and was bayonetted to death. The soldiers entered the room and began looting their belongings, which included items left for safekeeping by the garrison officers. In time, a Mexican officer appeared to escort the women safely outside to a position near one of the cannon. Another officer soon approached, and warned them to stand clear — the cannon was about to be turned and fired on the defenders. The terrified sisters were saved by Juana's brother-in-law, Manuel Perez, who took them to the chapel to join the other women.

The artillery crew of Almeron Dickinson and Jim Bonham continued to fire nails and scrap iron from the 12-pounders at their location on the high platform in the back of the Alamo church. About 11 men had joined them there to make their last stand. They were finally silenced when Col. Morales turned the 18-pounder on them and fired salvo after salvo that destroyed the cannons as well as everything else in the immediate vicinity. The one member of this crew who remained alive was Robert EVANS. Although severely wounded, Evans bravely crawled toward the powder room with a torch in his hand, but was shot and killed before he could ignite the magazine.

The explosion, had Evans been successful, would have certainly taken the lives of Susannah DICKINSON, her daughter, and the Mexican women who were inside the chapel near the magazine. Despite her secluded position, Susannah was witness to many horrible deaths as the Mexican soldiers closed in on the defenders. In one case, a teenaged acquaintance from Gonzales, Galba FUQUA, came to her room and made an effort to speak. But his jaw been shattered by a bullet, and, unable to say a word, he silently returned to the battle. Later, a gunner named Jacob WALKER entered her room followed by 4 Mexican soldiers. The soldiers shot and wounded Walker, then hoisted him several times on their bayonets like a bale of hay on a pitchfork until he died in convulsions. An officer, possibly Gen. Castrillón, arrived and asked, "Is there a Mrs. Dickinson here? If you value your life, speak up." She presented herself, and was accosted by the soldiers who had killed Walker. Castrillón prevented them from harming her or her baby, and escorted her into the plaza where an errant gunshot struck her in the right calf. Susannah and her child were then escorted to the chapel to join the Mexican women and children, and her wound was eventually dressed by a Mexican surgeon.

There are differing stories regarding the death of artilleryman Anthony WOLFE and his two young sons. An account related by young Enrique Esparza, son of defender Gregorio ESPARZA, states that one of the Wolfe boys was killed beside him in the room where he huddled with his family, his body falling upon him. The elder Wolfe then grabbed the remaining boy, and both of them leaped off the high chapel wall. They were either killed by the fall or shot dead by Mexican soldiers. Susannah Dickinson claimed that the only man to ask for quarter was named "Wolff," and he was killed on the spot. His two little boys were then killed, she said, and the Mexican soldiers carried the bodies out of the room on their bayonets.

Apparently some volunteers attempted to escape, several over the low palisade at Crockett's position, but with so many Mexican soldiers in the vicinity few, if any, of those who fled the compound lived for long. One escapee was said to have made it as far as the river and hid for several hours until a woman washing clothes reported his presence to the Mexicans and he was located and killed.

A Mexican army deserter named Brigido GUERRERO who had left his unit the previous year hid from his former comrades inside the Alamo. He was eventually found, and saved his life by lying about being captured by the Texans and held against his will.

Joe, William Travis's slave, was huddled in a room when an accented voice asked, "Are there any negroes in here?" Joe answered, "Here's one," and was immediately threatened by several soldiers until an officer chased them away. Gen. Cós allegedly forced Joe to identify the body of his master. Cós then drew his sword and brutally mutilated the face and limbs of William Travis.

Cós's action was typical of the Mexican soldiers. These men who had seen so many of their comrades fall during the initial assault had complete lost control of their senses and had gone berserk. While mopping up after the battle, they combed every nook and cranny of the Alamo in a killing frenzy. Any Anglo found alive was brutally killed and mutilated. They even located the makeshift hospital, and killed all the helpless sick and wounded. When no Alamo defenders remained alive to kill, these soldiers made their way through the compound stabbing and re-stabbing the dead with their bayonets, firing their muskets into the corpses, and stripping and mutilating these bodies.

Mexican officers, who were appalled by the savagery of their men, finally managed to muster what remained of their units for a roll call. The battle that Santa Anna termed "but a small affair" had lasted about 90 minutes in duration. Every Alamo defender—188 men—had been killed, and a dozen or so noncombatants had been captured. Casualty totals for the Mexican Army are more difficult to estimate. Numbers range from Santa Anna's official report to the Mexican government of 70 killed and 300 wounded, which is quite low, to Susannah Dickinson's estimate of 1,600, which would have left only 200–500 Mexicans alive. The correct number is more likely about 500–600 Mexican soldiers killed and many others wounded, some of whom would later die and be included in the total.

Gen. Santa Anna addressed his assembled troops, and told them how proud he and Mexico was for their courageous actions. The troops, whose ranks had been decimated, reportedly were not receptive to the general's eloquent words, and instead were resentful of the human price that had been paid for his victory. The general then toured the battlefield with the acting mayor of San Antonio, Francisco Ruiz, and requested that the bodies of Travis, Bowie and Crockett be pointed out to him. Apparently satisfied that the leaders of the rebels were dead, he retired to the north side of the plaza and ordered his Black servant, Ben, to brew him some coffee. Santa Anna then assigned Ruiz the task of disposing of the dead bodies—both Mexican and American—that littered the area (see DISPOSITION OF DEAD FROM THE ALAMO BATTLE for more). The general sipped his coffee while Travis's slave, Joe, and the women and children prisoners were presented to him for interroga-

tion. Each one was released after receiving two pesos and a blanket. (See SURVIVORS OF THE ALAMO BATTLE for more.)

The conqueror of the Alamo then began to formulate his strategy for a three-pronged invasion of Texas designed to annihilate the remainder of the rebel forces. His army may have lost an enormous number of troops at the Alamo, but he was assured that 5000 more were at his disposal to fight whatever battles may lay ahead.

See also ALAMO GARRISON; ATROCITIES COMMITTED DURING THE TEXAS REVOLUTION; MEXICAN ARMY; WEAPONS OF THE ALAMO DEFENDERS; and WEAPONS OF THE MEXICAN ARMY.

**ALAMO GARRISON** Following the Siege and Battle of SAN ANTONIO in December, 1835 which had forced Mexican Gen. Martin Perfecto de CÓS and his army to abandon the ALAMO MISSION and return to Mexico, most of the colonists from volunteer militias returned to their homes and farms. The 300 men who remained in San Antonio to garrison the Alamo, which was under the command of Col. James NEILL, were mainly volunteers from the United States, including many from the NEW ORLEANS GREYS. This number was greatly reduced in early January, 1836 by a proposed invasion of Mexico, which was little more than an excuse to plunder the countryside to compensate the volunteers for their service. Col. Frank JOHNSON and Dr. James GRANT had received approval from the General Council of the TEXAS PROVISIONAL GOVERNMENT to organize the MATAMOROS EXPEDITION under the command of Col. James W. FANNIN. In spite of opposition from Sam HOUSTON and Governor Henry SMITH, the organizers began to recruit volunteers anxious for action, and in the process pillaged the Alamo of men and supplies.

Col. Neill, who was of the (correct) opinion that the Mexican Army would soon return and the Alamo would be directly in its path, wrote Governor Smith to protest the action. Neill, who had requested reinforcements and supplies, reported that 200 men had departed to take part in the expedition and most of the food and medicine had also been confiscated. The Alamo would be virtually defenseless against an attack. Smith was outraged, but his efforts to halt the expedition were useless. He then decided to abolish the General Council. The council responded by deposing Smith, who refused to leave office. This would render the government ineffective until the election of new officials at the March, 1836 TEXAS CONSTITUTIONAL CONVENTION. That, however, was of little concern to Neill compared to the armed threat of Mexican Gen. Antonio Lopez de SANTA ANNA. Neill wrote Houston on January 14, 1836 that 20 more men were leaving for the Matamoros Expedition, and those who remained behind were desperate for clothing and food. Perhaps for this reason, reports have indicated that the volunteers regarded the property of local Mexicans to be fair game, and had a habit of plundering cattle and other necessities for their own use without any fear of retribution. In fact, many had made themselves at home by taking up temporary residence in a slum called La Villita on the outskirts of San Antonio across the San Antonio River from the Alamo.

Houston responded to Neill's message by dispatching Col. Jim BOWIE to San Antonio with orders to evacuate and destroy the Alamo. Bowie arrived on January 19 with 20–30 men — including the dashing lawyer James BONHAM, who would bravely return to the Alamo after duty as a COURIER in spite of the knowledge that he was riding to his death. Bowie consulted with Neill about conditions, and the decision was made to spare the mission. Bowie dispatched a message that read in part: "Col. Neill & myself have come to the solemn resolution that we will rather die in these ditches than give it up to the enemy. The salvation of Texas depends in great measure in keeping (San Antonio) out of the hands of the enemy. It serves as a frontier picquet (sic) guard and if it were in the possession of Santa Anna there is no strong hold from which to repel him in his march towards the Sabine." He also advised that an informant had told him that 2,000 Mexican soldiers were at the Rio Grande River and 5,000 more behind them en route from Mexico. Bowie made a plea for reinforcements, food, other supplies, and pay for the soldiers. The men were then put to work repairing the damage that had been done in the previous month's battle and building fortifications under the direction of Alamo chief engineer, lawyer Green B. JAMESON. The conduct of Jim Bowie at the Alamo in the ensuing days has been widely reported in less than flattering terms. He was said to have been drunk much of the time, quarreled constantly with Col. Neill, and became a tyrant to those civilians residing in San Antonio. This behavior apparently escalated when Lt. Col. William B. TRAVIS and 25–30 men rode into town on February 3. Bowie and Travis had become acquainted the previous fall during the Siege and Battle of San Antonio. Bowie had been involved in much of the fighting, while Travis for the most part rode around the countryside setting fires to prevent the Mexicans from finding forage for their horses. Travis had avoided the battle — in which Bowie had fought — by departing for San Felipe in early December. Travis, who was 14 years Bowie's junior, had been a mere lieutenant during that conflict but in the meantime had managed to gain an appointment to lieutenant colonel. Bowie held the unsanctioned rank of colonel.

Friction between the two strong-willed men was inevitable.

National celebrity and former congressman David CROCKETT and about a dozen men who called themselves the TENNESSEE MOUNTED VOLUNTEERS arrived in San Antonio on February 8, which was cause for celebration. The 49-year-old Crockett obliged the men with a speech, and entertained them with his traditional backwoods anecdotes. He concluded by declining any military status other than that of a "high private, in common with my fellow-citizens." A dance was held in his honor two nights later, and the whole town of San Antonio — Mexicans and Americans — joined in the festivities to officially welcome this legendary man whose presence instilled confidence in light of rumors that the Mexican Army was approaching Texas.

On February 12, an election was held among the garrison to choose a commander. Bowie, who was extremely popular with the men, easily won. Many of the volunteers, however, had not been afforded the opportunity to vote, which caused split loyalties in the garrison. Col. Neill found an excuse to leave — illness in his family has been cited — and rode out of the Alamo the following day on furlough. Neill had apparently designated Travis as his successor. Travis began firing off letters to the government in San Felipe complaining about Bowie's high-handedness, drunkenness, and general bad behavior. Bowie was said to have turned San Antonio into one giant party, a drunken orgy designed to demonstrate his power over both his men and the civilians to the point of martial law. He proceeded to free from jail convicted thief Antonio FUENTES, a Mexican who was loyal to Texas. The judge in the matter, Capt. Juan SEGUIN, returned the prisoner to jail. Bowie protested by parading a group of drunken soldiers through town. Other accounts contradict this harsh assessment of Bowie's behavior, and claim that he was not "roaring drunk all the time." Evidently Bowie and Travis managed to negotiate a tentative truce between them. On February 14, a letter was dispatched to Governor Smith that stated in part: "By an understanding of today Coln J. Bowie has the command of the volunteers of the garrison, and Col. W. B. Travis of the regulars and volunteer cavalry. All general orders and correspondence will henceforth be signed by both until Col. Neill's return."

By the time Gen. Antonio Lopez de Santa Anna and the Mexican Army arrived in San Antonio on February 23 to begin the ALAMO SIEGE, the garrison numbered about 150 men. Local Tejano (a native Mexican residing in Texas) rancher Juan Seguin had assembled a small company of his countrymen — called SEGUIN'S CAVALRY COMPANY — who had chosen to fight on the side of the Texans. Artillery captain Almeron DICKINSON, the Gonzales blacksmith who had fired the first shot of the TEXAS REVOLUTION during the GONZALES SKIRMISH, had brought his wife, Susannah DICKINSON, and daughter into the Alamo for safekeeping. Susannah would be the sole white woman inside, and one of the SURVIVORS OF THE ALAMO BATTLE. Jim Bowie had likewise escorted the nieces of his Mexican father-in-law, Juana ALSBURY and Gertrudis NAVARRO, into the mission. Perhaps as many as 25 local Tejano women and children, some related to Alamo defenders, also entered to escape the enemy. A number of these Tejanos would surreptitiously depart during the siege; the remainder were spared following the battle.

Then there were the determined men who would crouch behind the walls with rifles in hand during the 13-day siege, waiting to kill or be killed, standing firm against overwhelming odds. Among these volunteers were those who had been trained as doctors or lawyers, or worked with their hands at some trade or on the family farm, or were merchants or businessmen, or were simply young men who had ventured to Texas in search of adventure. Each of them, however, had one common trait. They had of their own free will decided to put their lives on the line in return for the opportunities that would be available to them should Texas be free of the Mexican tyrant Santa Anna. As best as can be determined, they had originally come to Texas from 22 states (Tennessee, 30; Kentucky and Pennsylvania, 15; Virginia, 13), and 6 different countries (England, 11; Ireland, 9). About 55 percent were permanent residents of Texas; the remainder were mercenaries from the United States. There was Micajah AUTRY, a farmer and lawyer who had come to Texas with David Crockett and was said to be a sensitive man — a poet, musician and painter. Lawyers Peter BAILEY and Daniel CLOUD were also members of the Tennessee Mounted Volunteers, and had intentions of establishing a law practice together. Adjutant John BAUGH would be the first to spread the alarm as Mexican troops streamed toward the Alamo, and would take command of the garrison following the death of Travis in the battle. Surveyor David CUMMINGS had travelled from Pennsylvania to present a letter of introduction and a box of rifles to army commander in chief Sam HOUSTON from his father, who was an old friend of Houston's. Tejano defender Gregorio ESPARZA, whose wife and children were huddled in the Alamo chapel, had a brother who was a soldier in Santa Anna's army. Samuel EVANS was carrying on the family tradition; his grandfather had been a general in the Colonial Army during the American Revolution. A business disagreement with his father compelled John FLANDERS to strike off on his own and journey from Massachusetts to the Alamo. Ohio born Tapley HOLLAND was

the first man to step across the line in the dirt when Col. Travis asked for allegiance on the night before Santa Anna attacked. Native Pennsylvanian Gordon JENNINGS, a farmer from Austin's Colony, Texas, held the distinction at age 56 of being the oldest defender. Travis's slave, JOE, would survive the battle and be treated with unaccustomed respect by Santa Anna. Scotsman John McGREGOR would play his bagpipes and accompany Crockett's fiddle in musical duels that kept up the spirits of the men during the siege. Capt. Albert MARTIN would carry Travis's heroic message "to the People of Texas and all Americans in the world," and return again to the Alamo to face certain death. William MALONE, an 18-year-old from Georgia, had run away from home because he was afraid to face his father after becoming drunk. Robert MUSSELMAN had served in the Seminole Indian War in Florida as a soldier in the U.S. Army. James ROSE, who had arrived with Crockett, was the nephew of James Monroe, the 4th president of the United States. Asa WALKER had stolen a gun and overcoat on his way to Texas, and was guilt-ridden enough to write a letter of confession to the owner. Asa's cousin, Jacob WALKER, was the brother of famous mountain man Joe Walker. Indian scout and interpreter Anthony WOLFE was accompanied by his 2 young sons, both of whom would suffer a horrible death. Charles ZANCO, a painter and farmer from Denmark, had designed the first Texas flag that had portrayed a lone star. And there were a number of men trained in medicine who could have provided assistance to chief surgeon Dr. Amos POLLARD, including John FORSYTH; William HOWELL; Edward MITCHASSON; John REYNOLDS; William SUTHERLAND; and John THOMPSON. The spiritual needs of the garrison could have been attended to by Baptist preacher William GARNETT or Methodist minister James NORTHCROSS.

These men were joined on March 1, the 8th day of the siege, by 29 volunteers who resided in the vicinity of the town of Gonzales — 70 miles away — who called themselves the GONZALES RANGING COMPANY. Their commander was Capt. George KIMBELL, who owned a hat factory and had left behind a pregnant wife. Others included merchant Thomas MILLER, the richest man in town; and John KELLOGG, who had recently stolen away Miller's young bride, Sydney Gaston, whose brother, John GASTON, had also volunteered. James GEORGE and his brother-in-law William DEARDUFF had volunteered, as had 16-year-old Galba FUQUA. Fifteen-year-old William KING, who had persuaded Kimbell to take him instead of his father who was needed at home, would be the youngest to die. One man, Louis ROSE, was said to have escaped on the night before the battle; and nearly two dozen couriers were dispatched, several of whom would return.

When Santa Anna ordered the attack on the morning of March 6, the 188 volunteers who comprised the Alamo garrison would be killed to a man.

**ALAMO MISSION** (Mission San Antonio de Valero). "The Shrine of Texas Liberty." This first mission ever established in San Antonio, Texas was the site of the November–December, 1835 Siege and Battle of SAN ANTONIO, and the famous March, 1836 ALAMO SIEGE and ALAMO BATTLE. The mission was founded in 1718 by Father Antonio Olivares, a Franciscan Friar, and originally named San Antonio de Valero in honor of the viceroy of Mexico, the Marquis de Valero. It was located on the San Antonio River across from the village then called San Antonio de Bexar or Bejar — named for the Duke of Bejar, Marquis de Valero's brother — as part of an effort to

bring Christianity to the Indians of the Yanaguana (the San Antonio River area) including the Apaches, Cocos, Jarames, Karankawas Payayas, Tops, and Zanas. The stick-and-straw buildings were moved from the west bank to the east bank of the San Antonio River in 1724, and moved once more until being partially completed in 1756 with a convent, a large chapel, and whitewashed outer walls around the compound. A statue of the patron saint stood in front of the chapel. Irrigation ditches that distributed water were lined with stone, and a granary stored harvests of corn and beans. By 1762, the mission was a thriving community, and provided Indian living quarters, including necessities such as beds and household utensils, stone for grinding corn, and pots and pans. Various European crafts were taught, such as sewing, spinning, carpentry, farming, and likely tanning and blacksmithing. The mission was abandoned by the Franciscans and secularized in 1793, and the land was divided among the Indian residents.

How the mission became known as the "Alamo" is open to debate. Some contend the name was derived from the groves of cottonwood trees, or *los alamos*, that lined the nearby water ditches. Others have theorized that when it was occupied in the 1820s by a detachment of Mexican troops that had been moved from a post in Mexico called *Pueblo de San Carlos del Alamo de Parras* (present-day Viesca) — "Alamo" for short — these homesick soldiers nicknamed it the Alamo in memory of that previous place.

The mission compound at the time of the two battles in 1835 and 1836 could not be considered a fortress in spite of military alterations. The chapel of stone-masonry construction was 75 feet long and 62 feet wide with walls 4 feet thick and a little more than 22 feet high. Windows had been walled over, and the structure was roofless except for portions over the west end and northern transept. The rectangular plaza was 150 yards long and 54 yards wide — about three acres — and surrounded by stone walls 3 feet thick and varied from 9 to 12 feet high. Small adobe rooms that faced the plaza were built into three sides. The barracks — 5 two-story structures, 18 feet by 18 feet — were built along the eastern wall. Behind the barracks was a small area enclosed on two sides by walls 5 feet high. To the north of this was a cattle pen surrounded by a picket fence. Four stone rooms were located on the west side; on

North Wall

Rammed Earth

Plaza

Officers' Quarters

Command Post

Long Barracks

Picket Fence

Stock Pen

Courtyard

Hospital

Powder Magazine

Chapel

Well

To San Antonio River

Irrigation Ditch to La Villita

Low Barracks

Main Gate

Bowie's Room

Crockett's Position

Position of the Women & Children

THE ALAMO MISSION, 1836

the south was a one-story barracks that was 17 feet wide and 114 feet long and divided by a porte-cochere, a second gateway. These rooms had flat roofs made of cement supported by planks and beams. Platforms of earth for riflemen to shoot from lined the inside of the walls, and dirt had been piled into sloping embankments to fortify the walls.

The army returned the Alamo to the Roman Catholic Church in 1842, and five years later leased the property from the church for use as a supply depot. The army at that time repaired much of the ruins, in-

cluding the adding of a scroll at the top of the entrance wall and the replacement of the roof on the chapel in 1849. At the outbreak of the Civil War, federal troops that had been stationed at the Alamo surrendered to local Confederate soldiers. A San Antonio military group known as the "Alamo City Guards" occupied the site without opposition until Lee's surrender to Grant in 1865 when the mission was once again returned to the control of the U.S. Army.

The army abandoned the Alamo in 1876, and it was sold to a local merchant named Honore (Hugo) Grenet who opened a general store in the long barracks and leased the chapel for use as a warehouse. Grenet constructed a wood-framed structure topped by several castle-like towers, which caused the store to be known by local people as "Grenet's Palace." By this time, the area around the Alamo was a thriving commercial center with businesses such as the Alamo Beer Garden, Saloon, Restaurant and the City Meat Market, as well as other stores, eating establishments, and boarding houses.

The chapel was purchased by the State of Texas from the Catholic Church for $20,000 in 1883, and given to the city of San Antonio. When Honore Grenet died in 1885, the long barracks was sold to the Hugo & Schmeltzer department store. The company ran their store at that location until deciding in 1903 to sell the property. The local chapter of the Daughters of the Republic of Texas, an organization that had been formed in 1891 for the purpose of preserving Texas history, began a fund-raising campaign to buy the Alamo, which had an asking price of $75,000. Unfortunately, the effort led by Adina de Zavala, whose grandfather, Lorenzo de ZAVALA had been the first vice-president of the Republic of Texas, fell short of its goal. In 1905, however, the daughter of a local rancher, Clara Driscoll, whose grandfathers had fought in the Battle of SAN JACINTO, offered a no-interest loan for $65,000 to hold the property. The Texas State Legislature reimbursed Driscoll the amount she had paid, and entrusted the care and maintenance of the Alamo to the Daughters of the Republic of Texas, who have to this day preserved the site according to Texas law "as a sacred memorial to the heroes who immolated themselves upon that hallowed ground." In 1960, the Alamo was named a national historic landmark.

The Alamo today is the most visited tourist attraction in the state, and the cen-ter of San Antonio's business district. For Anglo-Americans, the Alamo stands as the cornerstone of Texas Independence and statehood. Mexican-Americans, however, consider the site a symbol of imperialistic expansion.

The 4.2 acre grounds and buildings are presently home to a Shrine dedicated to the Alamo defenders; the Long Barrack Museum, which was constructed from remains of the original Long Barrack, and houses exhibits and the Clara Driscoll Theater; the Daughters of the Republic of Texas Library, which contains books and documents on Texas history; a sales museum offering exhibits and the gift shop; Cavalry Courtyard, which was used as a stock pen during the siege; and other interesting features such as an outdoor Wall of History that explains the past and present story of the Alamo.

**ALAMO, SIEGE OF** (February 23–March 6, 1836) This 13 day standoff was waged between approximately 188 American volunteers who had taken refuge within the walls of a compound known as the ALAMO MISSION located in San Antonio, Texas (aka San Antonio de Bexar or Bejar) and the attacking MEXICAN ARMY which was comprised of about 1,800–2,100 troops commanded by General Antonio Lopez de SANTA ANNA. The final assault on the 13th day of the siege, March 6 (see ALAMO, BATTLE OF), resulted in the capture of the Alamo by the Mexican Army, the death of every Alamo defender, and the loss of about 500–600 Mexican soldiers killed and an undetermined number wounded.

### Chronology of the Texas Revolution

- June 29, 1835: Battle of ANAHUAC
- October 2, 1835: GONZALES SKIRMISH
- October 3, 1835: MEXICAN CONSTITUTION OF 1824 officially voided
- October 9, 1835: GOLIAD SKIRMISH

- October 28, 1835: Battle of CONCEPCION
- November 3, 1835: TEXAS CONSULTATION OF DELEGATES
- November–December, 1835: Siege and Battle of SAN ANTONIO
- January–February, 1836: The MATAMOROS EXPEDITION
- **February 23–March 5, 1836: The ALAMO SIEGE**
- March 1, 1836: TEXAS CONSTITUTIONAL CONVENTION
- March 2, 1836: TEXAS DECLARATION OF INDEPENDENCE
- March 6, 1836: The ALAMO BATTLE
- March 20–27, 1836: Surrender and Massacre at GOLIAD
- April 21, 1836: Battle of SAN JACINTO
- May 14, 1836: Treaties of VELASCO

## DAY ONE

### *Tuesday, February 23, 1836*

The day dawned relatively clear, partly sunny and chilly. An ominous mass exodus of the Mexican (or "Tejano" as native Mexicans residing in Texas were called) townspeople of San Antonio had begun just before daybreak. The town was alive with the sounds of squeaking oxcart wheels, horse whinnies, mule brays, the clanging of pots and pans, and obvious signs of excitement and animated conversation. This steady stream of men, women, and children, many on foot and carrying their burdens on their backs, was noted with great interest by the defenders of the Alamo, many of whom resided within the town proper.

Col. William B. TRAVIS, who along with the ailing Col. James BOWIE shared dual command of the Alamo defense force, was greatly disturbed by this unusual activity. His inquiries as to the reason for such an action were answered by the absurd excuse that the people were simply going to the country in order to prepare for the upcoming crop planting.

Travis issued orders for the populace to remain in town, which merely increased the commotion associated with the hectic flight. He attempted and failed for some time through arrest and interrogation to uncover the true cause of this unexpected departure.

Finally, at about 11:00 A.M., a friendly Tejano revealed that a messenger had brought word the night before informing them that San Antonio would be attacked by the Mexican Army that day, and all loyal civilians should evacuate at dawn.

Travis had been advised on earlier occasions that Santa Anna and his mighty army was advancing, but had dismissed those reports as false rumors. This latest threat, taking into consideration its seriousness to the townspeople, was viewed in a skeptical but more apprehensive manner.

Travis and Bowie had neglected to deploy a system of patrols around the vicinity, and therefore had no ready manner with which to confirm or debunk the rumor. Travis, in the company of Dr. John SUTHERLAND, quickly made his way up to the octagonal belfry tower of the San Fernando Church, which offered a commanding view of the surrounding area. The two men intensely studied the landscape, but observed nothing but the rolling prairie.

Travis appointed a sentinel, identified in at least one report as Pvt. Daniel W. CLOUD, to remain in the belfry tower with orders to ring the bell if anything suspicious was noticed.

It was about 1 P.M. when the bell wildly clanged, and Pvt. Cloud called out, "The enemy are in view!"

Travis and several others hurriedly scrambled up the wooden steps to the belfry and anxiously scanned the terrain. The vast prairie revealed nothing out of the ordinary.

Travis dressed down the lookout for reporting a false alarm. But Pvt. Cloud swore that he had witnessed a large force of

Mexican troops and speculated that they had likely withdrawn to a hiding place behind clumps of brushwood beyond the distant hills to the west.

Dr. Sutherland volunteered to ride out on horseback and reconnoiter, and was accompanied by John W. "El Colorado" SMITH, the future mayor of San Antonio. The two men told Travis that if they could be seen returning in any gait other than a walk, he would know that the sentry's report had been confirmed. Travis ordered that Cloud immediately ring the bell to alert the other Texans should their worst fear be realized.

The two scouts headed west along the Laredo branch of the Camino Real and up the Alazan Hills about a mile and a half from town. They topped the rise to come within 150 yards of a line of nearly 400 — Sutherland later estimated the number at 1,500 — mounted and well-equipped troops of the Mexican Cavalry from the command of Gen. Juan José Andrade poised there apparently awaiting further orders.

Sutherland and Smith wheeled their mounts and retreated toward town. The road was muddy from recent rains, and Sutherland's horse lost its footing. The doctor was thrown from the saddle, and the horse fell across his legs, pinning him beneath for several frightening minutes. The animal was able to revive itself and they resumed their ride, galloping hell-bent for town, hearing the bell in the church tower wildly clanging as they approached.

David CROCKETT, who, as a member of Capt. William HARRISON's company, had been assigned the task of guarding the town while the garrison moved to the Alamo, greeted the two scouts. He informed them that Travis had moved his headquarters from town to an adobe house along the west wall inside the Alamo and that the entire garrison was in the process of taking up defensive positions. Sutherland, who had injured his knee in the fall from his horse, was assisted by Crockett across the San Antonio River to report to Colonel Travis. Smith hastily returned to town to close up his house.

Word of Santa Anna's advancing army spread like a wildfire throughout the town of San Antonio. Native Mexican townspeople paused to watch the hasty preparations, many admiring the pluck of the defenders but some patriots nonetheless silently hoping that Santa Anna's forces would rule the day. Most locals departed with intentions of taking refuge at outlying ranches, but a number remained in town to display their loyalty to Mexico, protect their homes, and perhaps make plans to profit from providing for Santa Anna's army.

Many of the American volunteers who had pledged to defend the cause (see ALAMO GARRISON) dashed to the Alamo to commence shoring up the fortification, molding bullets, and readying weapons. Others detoured to ransack local homes and businesses for provisions. Sacks of grain and other equipment and vital supplies were carried to the Alamo, and stored in the compound's long barracks. Thirty head of cattle were rounded up and herded into the corral. Water would be provided by the outside irrigation ditches and the inside well.

A small number of Mexican refugees — perhaps only 20–30 of the town's 2000 population and mostly women and children — who sided with the rebellious Texans also sought the protection of the Alamo.

Jim Bowie visited the Vermanedi house in town and packed off to safety in the Alamo the adopted sisters of his late wife, Gertrudis NAVARRO and Juana Navarro de ALSBURY and Alsbury's infant son.

Captain Almeron DICKINSON, the blacksmith from Tennessee and member of the Texas artillery, likewise retrieved his wife,

Susannah, and their 15-month-old daughter, Angelina, from the family living quarters in town and carried them behind the walls of the compound. Susannah DICKINSON would be the sole white woman inside.

Colonel Travis was dismayed that his prior requests for reinforcements had gone unheeded, and now dispatched courier William P. JOHNSON to implore Colonel James W. FANNIN at Goliad, Texas — 95 miles away — to respond quickly with troops. The message was signed by both Travis and Bowie, and read: "We have removed all our men into the Alamo, where we will make such resistance as is due our honour, and that of our country, until we can get assistance from you, which we expect you to forward immediately. In this extremity, we hope you will send us all the men you can spare promptly. We have one-hundred and forty-six men, who are determined never to retreat. We have but little provisions, but enough to serve us till you and your men arrive. We deem it unnecessary to repeat to a brave officer, who knows his duty, that we call on him for assistance."

The Alamo commander then scribbled another message, first addressed to "Andrew Pondon, Judge, Gonzales, (Texas)." He then crossed that out and wrote "To any of the inhabitants of Texas." This message read: "The enemy is in sight. We want men and provisions. Send them to us. We have 150 men and are determined to defend the Alamo to the last. Give us assistance."

The second message was entrusted to the injured Dr. Sutherland who rode out of town with John Smith, who was also heading to Gonzales to request reinforcements. The two men paused at a small ford to wait for shopkeeper Nat Lewis who later claimed he fled because "I am not a fighting man, I'm a businessman."

It was about 3 P.M., and the three of them glanced back toward town to view a most disturbing sight. The advance units of the Mexican Cavalry had arrived in Military Plaza. Sutherland and Smith took leave of Lewis, who was on foot, and decided to avoid the Goliad road and cut across the prairie in an effort to conceal themselves from probable Mexican Army scouting patrols. Lancelot SMITHERS also departed the Alamo at about this time and rode to Gonzales to spread the alarm, possibly without orders to do so.

Before long, Mexican General Antonio Lopez de Santa Anna entered the plaza in San Antonio. He was accompanied by his general staff; his military band; the standard-bearers; three companies of light infantry commanded by Col. Juan Morales; three grenadiers under Col. José María Morelos; two mortar pieces, and detachments of Gen. Joaquín RAMÍREZ Y SESMA's cavalry — perhaps less than one-thousand fighting men. The remainder of the Mexican Army continued to straggle along behind this advance detachment, and would arrive as conditions permitted.

Santa Anna's first official act was to order his men to hoist a large red flag from the belfry of San Fernando Church — some 800 yards distant from the Alamo. The blood-red banner was the traditional Mexican symbol signifying no mercy for their enemy. There would be no quarter — no mercy — no surrender for those Santa Anna termed "perfidious foreigners."

Travis, without consulting Bowie, fired the 18-pounder cannon in response to Santa Anna's taunt, which evoked a chorus of cheers from the Alamo defenders. The cannon ball fell harmlessly in town, but accomplished its purpose as a message of defiance.

Santa Anna was outraged by the brazen retort, and answered with four grenades fired from a 5-inch howitzer that landed inside the Alamo compound but caused no damage or casualties.

Meanwhile, James Butler BONHAM, who was on the road returning to San Antonio from Goliad where he had met with Col. Fannin, also heard the boom of the artillery pieces. He quickened his pace, and later reported to Travis that there would be no assistance from Goliad. Col. Fannin had decided that duty dictated that he remain at that place with his more than 400 troops.

Jim Bowie considered the impulsive action by Travis a waste of cannon shot and a threat to possible negotiation, and dispatched a messenger, Green B. "Benito" JAMESON, to town. Bowie's intention was to explore an honorable truce, but had in his own way of defiance ended his note with the salutation "God and Texas" after crossing out "God and the Mexican Federation."

This insult irritated Santa Anna to the extent that he directed his aide, Colonel José Batres, to make an appropriate response. Batres informed Jameson that the "rebellious foreigners" who had taken refuge in the Alamo "if they wished to save their lives, to place themselves immediately at the disposal of the Supreme Government from whom alone they may expect clemency after some considerations are taken up." There would be no terms other than unconditional surrender.

One account suggests that Bowie's messenger was dispatched when the Mexican Army, either by accident or on purpose, raised a white flag requesting a parley. Santa Anna's demand in this instance was for all practical purposes the same. The lives of the Texans would be spared if they laid down their arms within one hour and promised to never fight again.

Travis was angered that Bowie would send a message signed only by Bowie without consulting his co-commander—inasmuch as the two had agreed to make all decisions together. He was of the opinion that

the attempted parley had sent all the wrong messages to the enemy.

Travis then dispatched his own emissary, Albert MARTIN, who presented himself to Santa Anna's aide-de-camp, Col. Juan N. ALMONTE, who spoke fluent English. Martin advised Almonde that Travis was desirous of a meeting to discuss matters and would receive him "with much pleasure." Almonde explained that he was not the one to consider any propositions, and that the Alamo defenders should lay down their arms and surrender should they wish to save their lives.

Travis was reported by some accounts to have answered the surrender demand with another blast from the 18-pounder cannon.

Santa Anna and his staff set up headquarters in the Yturri house, a flat-roofed, one-story building on the northwest corner of the Main Plaza. The general, impatiently waiting for the arrival of his straggling army, immediately began formulating his plans for an attack on the Alamo.

As darkness approached, the Mexican Army was busy setting up camp, readying their weapons, caring for their horses, looting nearby homes for supplies, and constructing earthen fortifications for their artillery. Two batteries consisting of a 5-inch and 9-inch howitzer and an 8-pounder cannon were positioned bearing on the west and southwest walls of the Alamo—some 400 yards distant.

The Mexicans fired on the Alamo intermittently throughout the night with both small arms and the light cannons, but failed to accomplish any serious damage. The only casualty inside had been a horse wounded earlier in the afternoon.

It has been documented that the Mexicans lost one man that first day. A soldier had approached the river beyond the Alamo's west wall, and was brought down by a shot from the rifle of legendary marksman David Crockett. Crockett had asked for and received the assignment of protecting the most exposed position in the entire fortress — the south stockade wall connecting the chapel and the low barracks.

The determined Alamo defenders manned their posts, worked on fortifying their positions, waited for reinforcements, and speculated about what Santa Anna would decide to throw at them. The last of their local comrades was welcomed when Gregorio Es-PARZA and his wife and children entered to join the company of the Tejanos commanded by ranchero Captain Juan SEGUIN.

## DAY TWO

### Wednesday, February 24, 1836

The controversy surrounding the joint command agreement between Travis and Bowie was settled in the wee hours of morning. Bowie, who had been ill for weeks, took a turn for the worse and became incapacitated. The precise diagnosis of the illness that rendered Bowie too weak to walk has been a matter of speculation — pneumonia, typhoid fever, typhoid-pneumonia, or tuberculosis, "hasty consumption" as it was called in its day, have all been blamed. Critics have claimed that his drinking binges finally caught up with him. Regardless of the nature of the illness, Bowie was compelled to surrender his authority to Travis, and was carried to a small room in the low barracks where he was attended to by a *curandero* — a Mexican folk healer — named Andrea Castanon Ramirez Villanueva. The services of Senora Canaleria, as she was known, had possibly been requested by Bowie's Mexican relatives. And Bowie himself, who had been baptised and married into Mexican culture, was likely comfortable with this woman who would combine medieval Spanish medicine, Native American remedies, and psychiatry — especially

since the American doctors inside the Alamo had nothing available with which to treat him. Bowie was troubled, however, that he had assumed responsibility for his sisters-in-law and now could provide little protection. He beckoned Juana Alsbury to his bedside, and assured her by saying, "Sister, do not be afraid. I leave you with Colonel Travis, Colonel Crockett, and other friends. They are gentlemen, and will treat you kindly."

The morning dawned warm and cloudy to reveal the Mexicans digging an entrenchment on the opposite bank of the San Antonio River only some 350–400 yards distant from the Alamo — just out of normal rifle fire range. By early afternoon, two 9-pounder cannons, each of which could fire two rounds of solid shot per minute to a range of 1,400 yards, had been settled into the earthworks.

Santa Anna returned to town following a scout of the vicinity in the company of a small cavalry unit, and ordered his artillery to bombard the Alamo. Just before dusk, the Mexicans opened up with a furious barrage from the two 9-pounders and a 5-inch howitzer.

Most of the shells burst harmlessly inside the Alamo compound, accomplishing little more than showering the huddled defenders with dirt and debris — no one was killed or injured. The Mexicans did, however, score direct hits on the Alamo's 18-pounder, that covered the town from the southwest parapet, and on a 12-pounder. Travis upon occasion fired a round in response, but for the most part conserved his ammunition.

At dark when the firing had ceased, Travis decided to dispatch his messenger, Albert Martin, who previously had been injured in a wood-cutting accident and was less than able-bodied. This time Martin would not approach the Mexicans with truce entreaties, rather would carry by horseback a message from Travis addressed "To the People of Texas & all Americans in the world." This letter appealing for help has been considered one of the most heroic in American history.

Travis wrote:

Fellow Citizens & Compatriots — I am besieged by a thousand or more of the Mexicans under Santa Anna. I have sustained a continual bombardment and cannonade for 24 hours & have not lost a man. The enemy has demanded a surrender at discretion, otherwise, the garrison are to be put to the sword, if the fort is taken. I have answered the demand with a cannon shot, & our flag still waves proudly from the walls. *I shall never surrender or retreat.* Then, I call on you in the name of liberty, of patriotism & every thing dear to the American character, to come to our aid with all dispatch. The enemy is receiving reinforcements daily & will no doubt increase to three or four thousand in four or five days. If this call is neglected, I am determined to sustain myself as long as possible & die like a soldier who never forgets what is due his own honor & that of his country. VICTORY OR DEATH.

Travis added: "P. S. The Lord is on our side — When the enemy appeared in sight we had not three bushels of corn — We have since found in deserted houses 80 or 90 bushels and got into the walls 20 or 30 head of beeves."

Martin departed the Alamo and galloped through the surprised, sparsely deployed Mexican troops and out across the prairie in an effort to seek reinforcements.

That evening, while Santa Anna's band serenaded the Alamo with blaring horns and trumpets in an effort to unnerve them, those on both sides within earshot occasionally filled the musical lapses by exchanging insults. In fact, some local Tejanos wandered freely to the Alamo to converse with those inside. Several volunteers snuck from be-

hind the walls to forage for firewood among nearby shacks.

Perhaps due to that lax atmosphere, a Mexican Army scouting party comprised of five or six troopers under the command of Col. Juan Bringas attempted to cross a footbridge with intentions of probing Alamo defenses. The Mexicans were observed — one was shot dead and Col. Bringas toppled into the water in his haste to escape.

Santa Anna then ordered his artillery batteries to shell the Alamo with grenades, cannister and grape shot. This sporadic bombardment continued throughout the night, but was not accompanied by any further attempts by troops to penetrate the Alamo defenses.

## DAY THREE

### *Thursday, February 25, 1836*

Santa Anna, encouraged by the steady arrival of additional troops, chose to become bolder and test the Alamo defenders with a more direct course of action. To that end, at daylight he ordered the Battalion of Cazadores to bombard the Alamo, targeting the main gate, while his soldiers assembled at the river below the fortress in preparation for an attack. The bombardment was intended as a diversion designed to enable the soldiers to ford the river. The Alamo defenders were not fooled by the tactic, and hastily readied their weapons and braced for the first real challenge to their position.

It came at 10 A.M. when the Mexican president-general ordered a frontal assault by 300 soldiers backed up by another cannon barrage of grape shot, solid shot, and canister.

The Mexican troops crossed the river, and advanced from the edge of town through scattered ramshackle adobe huts and wooden shacks of a slum area and purported red light district where some Alamo families had lived which was known locally as La Villita. When their approach brought them to within 90–100 yards of the Alamo, they stormed the southern wall.

The defenders practiced fire discipline, and patiently waited until the troops were exposed at point blank range before unleashing grapeshot from the cannon and deadly accurate small arms fire. The Mexican attackers retreated to the protection of the buildings of La Villita — while sustaining 2 dead and 6 wounded.

The La Villita position, Travis deemed, still placed the Mexicans too close for comfort. The situation could be remedied if a number of the wooden shacks could be burned to the ground. Travis called for volunteers, and, while Crockett and other sharpshooters provided a covering base of fire, Robert BROWN and Charles DESPALLIER, and perhaps several others raced out the south gate of the Alamo and torched the nearest shacks.

The Mexican soldiers futilely shot at the arsonists and continued their attempt to advance, but were kept at bay by the withering rifle fire of the defenders and grape and cannister shot from the 8-pounder cannons commanded by Capt. Dickinson.

The battle raged for the remainder of the morning as both sides opened up with artillery and small arms fire. Several additional forays out the south gate by volunteers set more shacks and surrounding fields on fire. Col. Travis singled out David Crockett later in a letter by writing that the frontiersman "was seen at all points animating the men to do their duty." The Mexicans were eventually forced to retreat as the buildings of La Villita burned and provided greater fields of fire for the sharpshooting Alamo defenders. Around noon, as mugginess replaced the morning drizzle, the entire Mexican attack force withdrew.

The skirmish served to lift the spirits of most of those within the Alamo. The defenders had displayed their courage and determination, and had escaped relatively unscathed. The only casualties were minor scratches caused by flying debris.

The exception to this exhilarant attitude was Col. William Travis. The Alamo commander was guardedly elated that his men had held their own against the superior army, but likely understood at this point that the probing attack by a small force had demonstrated that a full-scale assault would be disastrous for his undermanned group of defenders. Nevertheless, Travis used the victory to bolster the confidence of his men, and paraded throughout the Alamo speaking in terms of victory and offering congratulations and encouragement.

Santa Anna, on the other hand, was not necessarily disappointed by the result of the action. He, too, was aware that with more troops he could likely overpower the defenders of the mission should he so desire. A frontal assault would without question cost many Mexican lives, but would be an alternative should patient and continuous bombardment fail to enact a surrender.

The president-general at this point dispatched Col. Bringis to locate Gen. Antonio GAONA, who was marching from Presidio de Rio Grande, and encourage Gaona to make haste. In addition to his 1600-man 1st Infantry Brigade, Gaona was hauling two 12-pounder cannons, the army's largest pieces of artillery.

Santa Anna rode around the area on horseback to personally advise his commanders about locations to dig trenches for troops and gun emplacements in an effort to surround the Alamo. A battery of 9-pounders were positioned at the River; artillery along with troops covered the road to Goliad from La Villita; and additional troops had been deployed on the eastern hills and on the road to Gonzales.

Despite this impressive perimeter, the terrain was too extensive to completely prevent any individual escape attempt or messenger from the Alamo from successfully penetrating the defenses, but was certainly adequate to thwart a retreat of the entire garrison or to discourage a large force of reinforcements from reaching the mission. This porous perimeter was evidenced when Travis dispatched another courier, John W. BAYLOR Jr., to Goliad with instructions to hurry reinforcements and Baylor had little trouble avoiding capture.

The idea of the Alamo defenders contemplating a mass retreat was not that farfetched. The citizen-soldiers inside were for the most part rugged individualists, and not accustomed to playing the role of garrison troops. They complained constantly and vehemently about being trapped behind the walls — especially when the temperature fell into the 30s that night accompanied by a blistering barbed wire wind. David Crockett was particularly agitated about his predicament, and remarked to Susannah Dickinson that he would rather go out the gate and shoot it out with the Mexicans than to be hemmed in.

Travis kept his men alert and focused by challenging each Mexican Army attempt to tighten their grip around the Alamo with barrages of rifle fire and grape shot. The defenders departed the confines of the Alamo on at least two occasions to skirmish with their enemy. One group briefly engaged a detachment of Ramírez y Sesma's troops while another raided La Villita to scrounge for firewood.

Travis was not the only one who believed that the noose was slowly but surely tightening around the mission fortress. Several of the native Mexicans that had sided with the Americans at first now fled the Alamo after darkness and crossed the lines to surrender themselves to their countrymen.

Santa Anna made good use of this cover of darkness as well. In addition to deploying his troops in strategic positions, he managed to install two howitzers, one 5-and-a-half-inch and the other an 8-inch, and one 9-pounder between the Alamo and the bridge to the southwest — some 300 yards distant from the mission, the closest position to date.

The chilly night was interrupted by periodic bugle calls and bursts of artillery as Santa Anna employed his version of psychological warfare designed to unnerve the Alamo defenders.

The worry about his tenuous position and frustration in his inability to dictate the course of action nagged Col. Travis. He composed another message to appeal for reinforcements, and addressed it to the highest possible authority — TEXAS REVOLUTIONARY ARMY Commander-in-chief Sam HOUSTON.

Travis related in detail how Santa Anna's army had surrounded the Alamo with a superior force, and to what depths of desperation the situation of the defenders had deteriorated.

The Alamo commander concluded his message with: "Do not hesitate on aid to me as rapidly as possible, as from the superior number of the enemy, it will be impossible for us to keep them out much longer. If they overpower us, we fall a sacrifice at the shrine of our country, and we hope posterity and our country will do our memory justice. Give me help, oh my Country!"

There was some debate about exactly who would be chosen to depart the Alamo in an effort to deliver this message. Capt. Juan SEGUIN was the logical choice. He was a Mexican who obviously spoke the language in the event of a confrontation at the Mexican lines, and was familiar with the terrain. Travis argued that should further discussions with Santa Anna be held there would be a need for Seguin as an interpreter. In the end, however, Seguin was designated to carry out this important message.

In the wee hours of the night, Seguin — on a horse borrowed from Jim Bowie — and his orderly, Antonio CRUZ Y AROCHA, made their way down the Gonzales road, and were immediately challenged by a Mexican outpost. Seguin coolly conversed with the Mexicans, then, seizing the opportunity, the two men spurred their horses and raced away. The startled Mexicans fired at them, but to no avail. The message was on its way.

Meanwhile, Col. James Fannin in Goliad was undergoing a change of heart. Another message from Travis had arrived, this one carried by courier William P. Johnson, and Fannin was hesitant to ignore the plea for assistance. Perhaps in his vainglorious mind, he viewed himself as the hero who could save the Alamo, or his conscience might have nagged him because he was the one who had recently depleted the ALAMO GARRISON of men and supplies for his ill-fated MATAMOROS EXPEDITION. Regardless, Fannin began organizing a relief expedition. He explained his decision in a letter to Lieutenant Governor James ROBINSON, which read in part: "The appeal of Colonels Travis and Bowie cannot be resisted, and particularly with the description of troops now in the field — sanguine, chivalrous volunteers. Much must be risked to relieve the besieged."

## DAY FOUR

### Friday, February 26, 1836

At daylight, a detachment of Gen. Ramírez y Sesma's cavalry probed the defenses by circling to the rear of the compound. The volunteers scrambled to the northern postern and unleashed a withering barrage of fire that forced the Mexicans to retreat.

The defenders endured the cold, dreary day digging trenches, and reinforcing earthworks along the walls while withstanding sporadic sniper fire and cannon shot. Travis dispatched one squad of men to gather firewood from La Villita and another to carry water from the ditches.

Col. Fannin in Goliad had readied a relief expedition composed of 320 troops, 4 cannons, and several wagons hauled by oxen that contained ammunition and supplies, and set out for the Alamo. His men, however, were ill-prepared for the 95-mile march. Most were under-dressed for the weather; food was in short supply; few saddle-broke horses were available for the men to ride; and ammunition supplies were low. To make conditions worse, a bitter norther had lowered the temperatures to near freezing. The expedition had travelled just several hundred yards when one of the supply wagons broke down. Repairs were made and they resumed their march. Within a mile, two more wagons broke down. At the San Antonio River, Fannin realized that individual oxen were not strong enough to haul the cannons across and the job would require double-teaming the beasts of burden. The process was slow and tedious, and, as night approached, the ammunition wagons still remained on the wrong side of the river. Fannin decided to delay his rescue mission until the following day.

As darkness descended over the town of San Antonio, the sharpshooters at the Alamo continued to spar with their Mexican counterparts. Most notable was David Crockett. He had amazed his companions with unparalleled feats of marksmanship. In fact, his reputation was becoming legendary to the Mexican Army as well. Capt. Rafael Soldona later said of the man believed to be Crockett: "A tall man, with flowing hair, was seen firing from the same place on the parapet during the entire siege. He wore a buckskin suit and a cap all of a pattern entirely different from those worn by his comrades. This man would kneel or lie down behind the low parapet, rest his long gun and fire, and we all learned to keep at a good distance when he was seen to make ready to shoot. He rarely missed his mark, and when he fired he always rose to his feet and calmly reloaded his gun seemingly indifferent to the shots fired at him by our men. He had a strong, resonant voice and often railed at us, but as we did not understand English we could not comprehend the import of his words further than that they were defiant. This man I later learned was known as 'Kwockey.'"

Travis dispatched two more couriers under the cover of darkness. Privates Robert Brown and Charles Despallier, two of the men who had burst from the Alamo and fired the huts at La Villita the previous day, were chosen to separately ride to rally reinforcements.

Santa Anna maintained his psychological warfare throughout the night with bugle calls, frequent artillery and small arms fire, and loud taunts and challenges from his troops. There can be little question that the men inside the Alamo were affected by this unnerving commotion. After all, they were not ignorant to the fact that additional Mexican troops were arriving all the time. They were surrounded by a superior force, and the walls of their fortress were not constructed well enough to withstand a prolonged bombardment. The Alamo could not sustain itself with just those men present, there had been no sign of reinforcements and, worse yet, no word that the outside world was even aware of their predicament.

## DAY FIVE

### Saturday, February 27, 1836

At 3 A.M. that morning, a detachment from Col. Fannin's Matamoros Expedition was attacked by Mexican forces at San Patricio — some 50 miles south of Goliad. Col. Frank JOHNSON and about 50 men had been out attempting to capture wild horses for use in the expedition when they were surprised in a driving rain by Mexican Gen. José URREA and about 100 cavalrymen. The Mexicans killed 16 Americans and captured 24; Johnson and 4 others escaped. Many of the prisoners would eventually be released, but Johnson, who escaped, would spread the word that these men had been executed.

Preparations for Fannin's relief expedition from Goliad were not going well. Several oxen that were needed to haul the wagons and cannons had wandered off during the night, and their capture would be difficult. Fannin sent his men out to round up the missing oxen, and postponed his departure until that task could be completed.

The Alamo defenders awoke to observe a detail of Mexican soldiers attempting to cut off their water supply by blocking the water ditches that sluiced off from the river at an old mill 800 yards to the north. The volunteers opened fire on the workers that were placing timbers across the ditch, and managed to chase them off.

At 2 P.M., the public square in Gonzales, the site of the first shot of the revolution — 70 miles from San Antonio — was the scene of much activity. Albert Martin had arrived with Travis's message of February 24 pleading for assistance, and now about 29 new volunteers led by Capt. George KIMBELL had assembled to ride for the Alamo. They called themselves the GONZALES RANGING COMPANY of mounted volunteers, and would be accompanied by couriers Albert Martin and Charles Despallier. Their scout and guide would be John W. Smith, the San Antonio carpenter who had departed the Alamo in the company of John Sutherland to seek reinforcements that first day of the siege after the two had observed the advance of Mexican cavalry.

Back in Goliad, Fannin had finally rounded up his oxen, and by late afternoon was ready to move out. Fannin, however, had second-thoughts. His men were in desperate need of supplies, and the closest source was 70 miles to the northwest at Juan Seguin's ranch. Besides that, he had left only 100 men to defend Goliad, and the exact whereabouts of the Mexican Army — except for those participating in the Alamo siege — was unknown other than information that a sizeable force was prowling the countryside. Fannin was holding a council of war with his officers when a messenger arrived to inform him that long-awaited supplies had landed at Matagorda Bay, but there were no volunteers present to guard them. Right or wrong, the council was compelled to unanimously vote to suspend the Alamo relief expedition. Fannin hauled his wagons back to Goliad where he learned about Col. Johnson's detachment being decimated by Mexican forces at San Patricio. That disturbing news acted to further justify Fannin's decision to abort the mission to rescue the Alamo.

Col. Travis was unaware that Fannin had decided against bringing relief, and continued to send out messages pleading for help. This time he again chose Jim Bonham, the man he trusted most, who had returned from Goliad on the first day of the siege. Bonham would ride once more to Goliad and attempt to convince Fannin of the urgency of the need for reinforcements. Travis realized that Goliad with its 400 or more volunteers was only 95 miles away, the closest place with enough men to make a difference. Just after dark, Bonham rode out the northern postern on this most important mission, and maneuvered his way through the Mexican troops.

Santa Anna was also concerned about re-inforcements. He dispatched couriers to generals FILISOLA and Gaona with angry orders to speed up the march, send supplies ahead, and hurry the money held by the Commissary General. Another message was sent to Mexico City to boast about his success at capturing San Antonio. He failed to mention that at least 150 armed men remained behind the walls of the Alamo Mission. The general pacified himself with the company of a local young lady while outside his villa the roar of his cannon barrage of the fortress continued. His artillery, most of them planted on the east side of the river, had been brought to bear on the northwest, southwest, and south walls of the Alamo, which left only the east uncovered — perhaps intentionally to invite an escape attempt in that direction. His cavalry was camped on Powder House Hill — on the *east* side of the mission.

## DAY SIX

### *Sunday, February 28, 1836*

James Bonham reached Goliad, and reported to Col. Fannin about the situation at the Alamo. Fannin was heartened by the news that a force of only 150 men had repulsed at least two frontal assaults and were holding 2,000 Mexican soldiers at bay. He had about 420 men assembled at "Fort Defiance," which was far more fortified than the Alamo. In spite of the knowledge that a force under Gen. Urrea was approaching, Fannin believed he could likely hold out indefinitely if necessary. Fannin had been sending out letters requesting that he be relieved of command, partially because he wanted to return home to his wife and children but more so due to what he perceived as unfair treatment by the Texas government by not providing him with vital provisions such as gunpowder, food, and even basic necessities like shoes. He now reconsidered his circumstance, and, perhaps at Bonham's urging, decided that as many as half his garrison — 200 men — could possibly be spared to assist the Alamo. If oxen and saddle-broken horses could be procured, he would personally lead these reinforcements within several days time.

In Gonzales, a message had arrived from Fannin that outlined his earlier plans to march for the Alamo with 300 men, and suggested a rendezvous with the relief force from that town on the Cibolo. The message came too late to inform Capt. Kimbell and the Gonzales Ranging Company, who were already at the Cibolo where they had found 7 more recruits, but some of those men who had remained behind now volunteered to serve. Dr. John Sutherland managed to gather about 12 men and Capt. Juan Seguin assembled about 25 Mexicans, and these two groups set out to meet Fannin at the Cibolo.

Back inside the Alamo, the day was chilly, drizzly and miserable. When they were not working to shore up the fortifications that had been damaged from Santa Anna's incessant artillery, the men would huddle around smoky fires in soggy blankets playing cards, writing letters, and complaining about their lot in life. Meals were cooked and eaten at their positions, and they slept in turns during times of silence from the thunderous guns. Sentries, constantly alert for an unexpected enemy assault, watched as the Mexican soldiers moved artillery emplacements closer and made another attempt to cut off the water supply to the Alamo. Some well-placed musket fire kept the Mexicans alert as well, but Travis was hesitant to fire the cannon very often in order to conserve ammunition.

Jim Bowie was gravely ill, but during those moments when he had a grasp of his senses would have his cot carried out among the volunteers to rally their spirits with encouraging words. He would also make it a point to visit his sisters-in-law, Juana Alsbury and Gertrudis Navarro, on such excursions to reassure the frightened women that they would be protected.

The spirits of the entire garrison also got a lift from the engaging presence of David Crockett. Although the Tennessean continued to grumble about being locked up behind the walls, he had always enjoyed the company of men and was quite adept at entertaining them with outrageous stories and tall tales. In addition to his storytelling, he would perform musical duels with his fellow defender from Scotland, John Mc-Gregor. Crockett, who was an excellent fiddle player, would challenge McGregor's ability with the bagpipes. The two musicians would relish in the unbridled howls and whoops of their companions as they tested each other to see who could create the most noise.

These brief pleasurable interludes predictably would be interrupted by Santa Anna's recurrent artillery, blaring bugle calls, sudden volleys of small arms fire, and taunts from the darkness that reminded the volunteers that the red flag — signifying no quarter, no mercy, total annihilation — that had been affixed to the belfry of San Fernando Church still waved. The beleaguered men would slip back into a mood of brooding and pray that reinforcements — their only hope — would soon arrive to rescue them.

## DAY SEVEN

### Monday, February 29, 1836

San Antonio skies remained gray and dreary on this leap year day, but the norther had blown through and the westerly breeze was mild. Susannah Dickinson, her daughter Angelina, and the Mexican women and children likely ventured outside to enjoy the fresh air. Susannah was a strikingly beautiful young woman, and, as the sole white woman in the garrison, had been the subject of many longing looks and attention over the past week. Her husband, Almeron, would have left his position at the cannon emplacement at the rear of the chapel to briefly share the company of his family. Susannah would have been hurried back inside when the Alamo defenders manning the walls noticed a movement of troops in the distance.

An entire battalion of Mexican soldiers was maneuvering across the ford to the south and would eventually assume a position in that direction. Santa Anna had caught wind of the rumor that Col. Fannin and reinforcements were on their way from Goliad, and he did not intend to allow that force to arrive and support their comrades without a fight. To that end, he busied himself reorganizing his lines, and had ordered Gen. Ramírez y Sesma to prepare the Allende Battalion and the Dolores Cavalry to march down river and head off this threat. Their vacated positions on the east and on the Gonzales Road would be covered by Gen. Manuel Castrillón, who began deploying his men on a line running from the powder house to a new earthwork near the irrigation ditch — 800 yards from the Alamo.

Capt. George Kimbell and the Gonzales Ranging Company — now numbering 32 men — had decided to rest during the day. They had picked up several others, including David CUMMINGS who had been out land prospecting and was anxious to accompany his cousin by marriage and boyhood friend, John Purdy REYNOLDS on the march. These volunteers proudly carried with them the flag that had waved during the GONZALES SKIRMISH when the town had defended their cannon. Naomi DeWitt, daughter of the colony's founder, Green DeWitt, had fashioned the flag from her own silk wedding dress. Above and below the drawing of the cannon at the flag's cen-

ter were the words "Come and Take It!" At sunset, these men from Gonzales moved out with intentions to make the final dash for the Alamo under the cover of darkness.

The night brought to the Alamo the blaring of Santa Anna's military band, and false assaults by groups of soldiers, perhaps to test the alertness of the defenders but more likely as an effort to unnerve them or encourage them to waste ammunition shooting at shadows. One unlucky Mexican soldier on a mission personally ordered by the president-general to reconnoiter the fortress happened to venture too close and was shot and killed by a sharpshooter.

The Alamo had endured one full week of siege and had not suffered even one casualty, but the spirits of the volunteers were becoming lower by the day. Travis had dispatched courier after courier with pleas for reinforcements, but none had yet arrived (see COURIERS DISPATCHED FROM THE ALAMO for more). And every night — this one no exception — periodic artillery bombardments interrupted sleep with the threat that troops would be attacking during each nerve-raking lull. This did not discourage Travis from continuing his attempts to communicate with the outside world. He dispatched Private William OURY with another message urging that men and supplies be hurried to the Alamo before it was too late.

Meanwhile, in Washington-on-the-Brazos — 150 miles from San Antonio and the Alamo — 59 delegates from across Texas were assembling in preparation for the TEXAS CONSTITUTIONAL CONVENTION that would convene in the morning. These men had been assigned the task of forming a government that could effectively oppose the tyrant Santa Anna, who had pledged to annihilate the ideas, much less the lives, of the upstart Texans who had dared to defy his authority over them. Col. Travis's first dispatch had finally reached that town, and some delegates suggested postponing the convention and going to the aid of the Alamo. After some debate, however, it was determined that the business of replacing the ineffective TEXAS PROVISIONAL GOVERNMENT with a more permanent one was more important.

## DAY EIGHT

### Tuesday March 1, 1836

At 1 A.M., with a barbed wire west wind gusting and temperatures well below freezing, the 32 men of the Gonzales Ranging Company approached the outskirts of San Antonio. The sky was cloudless, lit by millions of stars, and the campfires of the Mexican troops were the landmarks that pointed their way. John W. Smith was in the lead as the line of men threaded its way closer to the Alamo. Without warning, an English-speaking voice came from the darkness. "Do you wish to go into the fort, gentlemen?" The silhouette of a man on horseback could be vaguely distinguished. One of the volunteers might have answered in the affirmative. Regardless, the mysterious horseman calmly directed his horse to the head of their column and said, "Then follow me."

John Smith was suspicious. Something was amiss about the sudden appearance of this stranger who had simply materialized from the darkness. Smith heeded his intuition, and called, "Boys, it's time to be after shooting that fellow!" Before anyone could train their gun on him, however, this apparition spurred his horse and vanished into the brush as quickly as he had appeared.

The men from Gonzales intently listened for any hue and cry of warning in the distance that might signal their presence to the Mexican soldiers. After several tense, silent moments, Smith once more cautiously led his men through the brush. Slowly but surely, weaving around heavy foliage, avoiding clusters of campfires, stopping upon occasion to listen, changing direction at the clang of equipment or the sound of voices, the line of horseman eventually edged close enough to view the south wall of the Alamo Mission.

Smith dispatched a man to alert the defenders of their impending arrival. Apparently that man failed to adequately notify the sentries on duty. A shot from the wall rang out, and one of the Gonzales men was struck in the foot. He let out a howl and a string of loud curses — words that could only come from the vocabulary of an American — and the order to cease fire was quickly given. The postern was opened, and the Gonzales Ranging Company dashed triumphantly inside to the welcoming cheers of the volunteers — many of whom were friends. This raised the total representation from the town of Gonzales to about 40, including the regimental surgeon, Dr. Amos POLLARD and artillery captain Almeron Dickinson.

Reinforcements had finally arrived, and, although the men were thrilled by the unexpected appearance, Col. William Travis was disappointed. He had been expecting Fannin from Goliad with hundreds of fresh volunteers and wagonloads of supplies. He had counted only 32 men, and they had not brought along adequate provisions even for themselves. Besides that, the Gonzales men could not confirm that any other reinforcements were on their way. Travis understood that the appearance of the newcomers had served to lift the sagging morale of his men, and for that he was grateful. But on the other hand, he wondered if they would be in as buoyant a mood if this would necessitate the further rationing of food and gunpowder.

The Texas Constitutional Convention was called to order later that morning in Washington-on-the-Brazos inside a partially finished blacksmith building that failed to prevent the near freezing temperatures and gusting wind from invading the interior. That previous November at the TEXAS CONSULTATION OF DELEGATES there had been heated debate about whether to fight for reinstatement of the MEXICAN CONSTITUTION OF 1824 or to declare independence. This time there would be no such debate. The decision to seek independence had been dictated by the presence in Texas of Santa Anna and his army.

The Mexican presence around the Alamo had been progressively creeping closer day by day, and this day was no exception. Mexican artillery batteries had been dragged forward and earthworks had been dug to within 300 yards of the fortress. Patrols became more brazen, but normally were hesitant to approach any closer than 200 yards. After all, Crockett and his sharpshooters had little to do but practice their marksmanship, and any enemy soldier who ventured too close was quickly reminded of that fact.

It was the Alamo artillery, however, that scored the most telling blow on this day. Travis had ordered that the cannon be rarely fired in order to preserve ammunition for the assault — whenever it came. But while Santa Anna was out personally inspecting his perimeter and emplacements, the defenders' artillerymen blasted a 12-pound ball that demolished the Yturri House in San Antonio. It just so happened that the Yturri House was where the president-general had established his headquarters, and had he been at home at that particular time there might have been a change of command ceremony in the Mexican Army. The defenders could not celebrate the destruction of this notable place, however, because it was not yet known that Santa Anna himself was in command of the troops or that the Yturri house had been his headquarters. Santa Anna, who was not amused, demonstrated his wrath by increasing the volume of the bombardment of his defiant enemy's position. Artillery shells soared into and around the compound and slammed against the walls. But, thus far, there had been no casualties and no breach had been opened anywhere in the walls.

The news in Goliad was extremely disappointing to Alamo courier James Bonham. Col. Fannin had in his indecisive manner changed his mind again. Col. Frank Johnson, who had survived the attack at San Patricio, had arrived to relate his harrowing tale of Mexican butchery. The prisoners taken by Gen. José Urrea had actually been sent to Matamoros and eventually released, but Johnson spread the word that his men had been executed. Fannin took this news as further evidence that it was only a matter of time until his position would be the target of an attack, and could not justify weakening his defense of Fort Defiance by sending a detachment — no matter the size — to San Antonio. He urged Bonham to also remain in Goliad where he would be relatively safe. Bonham was disgusted by Fannin's refusal of aid for his beleaguered comrades, and stated that his mission was to find reinforcements and that was what he intended to do. He reportedly rode to Gonzales, and discovered that just about every able-bodied man had already ridden for the Alamo or was attending the convention at Washington-on-the-Brazos. Bonham grudgingly accepted the fact that he had failed in his quest to bolster the Alamo defense force, and spurred his horse in the direction of San Antonio.

## DAY NINE

### *Wednesday March 2, 1836*

Like rats deserting a sinking ship, in the opinion of Col. William Travis, some of the Mexicans who had taken refuge with the volunteers had fled the Alamo — as if they knew something that the defenders did not.

How many had departed could not be accurately determined — probably at least a dozen remained — but their disappearance evoked a condemnation of that entire race by Col. Travis.

Some Mexican officers speculated that Santa Anna had willingly permitted the small relief force from Gonzales to enter the mission in order to have a higher body count total when finally he decided to overrun its walls. The president-general was becoming impatient with the standoff, and was infuriated that his troops under generals Filisola and Gaona were dawdling on the march and had not yet arrived to allow him to move ahead with his plans to capture the Alamo and then continue his effort to destroy the remainder of the Texas army. He had boasted on the march from Mexico that his army would occupy San Antonio by March 2. He had exceeded that projection by a week — San Antonio was his — but also understood that no occupation would be complete until he was in control of the Alamo. And, although his artillery bombardment had failed to cause any significant damage to the poorly-constructed fortress, he was not discouraged and continued to fire his cannons at will.

Thus far that day, the Mexican soldiers had avoided the sharpshooters who manned the Alamo parapets. Santa Anna himself almost had not been as fortunate. He had been inspecting fortifications near the river — well out of rifle range, he believed — when a bullet fired from the Alamo whizzed uncomfortably close to him and he was compelled to make an undignified dash for cover. The incident served to darken his mood for the remainder of the day. The proficiency of the sharpshooters, he reminded himself and his subordinates, would not be underestimated in the future. He did lose one man when a chasseur from San Luis somehow drowned in the San Antonio River.

The president-general was likely also irritated by the arrival of his barely-competent brother-in-law, Gen. Martin Perfecto de Cós, who had come in advance of the reinforcements. It had been Cós who had disgraced himself by surrendering the Alamo in December to culminate the Siege and Battle of SAN ANTONIO. Cós had at that time promised to never again fight the Texans, but Santa Anna had scoffed at that pledge and ordered his general to break it.

While Santa Anna waited out the Texans inside the Alamo, Gen. Urrea, while pushing toward Goliad with his 1,400-man detachment, had set an ambush at Agua Dulce Creek and had annihilated 15 men from the Matamoros Expedition under Dr. James GRANT that had been out capturing wild horses.

One-hundred and fifty miles away in Washington-on-the-Brazos, the Texas Constitutional Convention was taking care of business. The TEXAS DECLARATION OF INDEPENDENCE, drafted by delegate George C. Childress and his committee, was presented to the delegation and unanimously adopted. The next order of business would be the drafting of a constitution.

The Alamo defenders huddled at their positions under cold, cloudy skies to await Santa Anna's next move. These volunteers, many of whom had only recently arrived in Texas, would never know that this historic document declaring independence had been adopted.

## DAY TEN

### Thursday, March 3, 1836

At 11 A.M., James Bonham stealthily maneuvered his way between the Powder House and a Mexican artillery position and galloped into the Alamo. This gallant South Carolinian could have forsaken a return and ridden east to Victoria, San Felipe or Brazoria to seek reinforcements, and, if the Alamo was to fall soon as he might have suspected, would have been saved while on that justifiable mission. But Bonham, the last man who would enter the Alamo before Santa Anna's assault, was not one to run out on a commitment. He immediately reported to an anxious Col. Travis. There would be no reinforcements, Bonham informed him, and explained how the irresolute Col. Fannin in Goliad had started for the Alamo with 320 men then returned to remain at Fort Defiance and prepare for any future attack. He told how Fannin had toyed with the idea of sending half his men, then changed his mind about that as well. In other words, there would be no reinforcements from Goliad, and Bonham had not been able to determine if there would be any additional volunteers coming from anywhere else in Texas. It was his opinion that they were on their own and must fend for themselves for as long as necessary.

Travis was disheartened by the bad news. Had all of Texas abandoned him? he wondered. Was the Alamo and its staunch defenders of no importance to this newly forming government? He intended to find that out. He sat down and composed a letter to the constitutional convention, and, without hiding his contempt for Col. Fannin, stated that he could whip his enemy if only he was provided aid. He boasted about how he had held his position with but 150 men against a force variously estimated from 1,500 to 6,000, and vowed to hold it until he got relief from his countrymen or perished in the attempt. He also requested that any additional reinforcements be supplied with at least ten days' rations — his own provisions were close to being depleted. Travis then stated that he would fire his huge 18-pounder cannon 3 times a day — morning,

noon and night — to signify that his garrison was still alive.

Courier Lancelot Smithers, who carried Travis's famous "Victory or Death" message that had been passed on by Albert Martin, arrived in San Felipe de Austin from Gonzales. Governor Henry SMITH, who no longer held any real authority, called upon the colonists "to fly to the aid of your besieged countrymen and not permit them to be massacred by a mercenary foe." Smith made certain that surrounding towns were informed of the need for reinforcements, but few came forward. His effort to assemble a volunteer force produced just 52 mercenaries from Kentucky commanded by Col. Sidney SHERMAN who marched at once. Word of the Alamo became the main topic of conversation at the convention in Washington-on-the-Brazos. Another message reporting that Col. Fannin was marching to the Alamo from Goliad with more than 300 reinforcements, however, served to diminish any urgency.

Travis's letter writing was interrupted at about noon by wild cheering that originated from the Mexican side of the river. He ran to the wall in time to observe the arrival of a long column of Mexican soldiers. Most of Gen. Gaona's sapper battalions from Aldema and Toluca had finally made their way up from the Rio Grande to boost the number of troops at Santa Anna's disposal to about 2000. An exuberant Santa Anna immediately embarked on a personal deployment of these new men as well as the placement of the 10 guns they had dragged along. The president-general was later informed that a messenger had arrived in San Antonio with word of Gen. Urrea's modest victory at San Patricio. The news was spread among the elated troops, and Santa Anna ordered that the church bell in the belfry of San Fernando Church where the red flag still waved be rung in celebration.

The Alamo defenders were as demoralized as the Mexican soldiers were exhilarated. As darkness descended around San Antonio, a shroud of gloom had replaced the good cheer they had experienced with the arrival of the Gonzales Ranging Company. It was now the Mexicans' turn to festively mark the appearance of their comrades. The periodic Mexican artillery barrages served to remind the defenders about the vulnerability of their makeshift fortress. And the presence of more enemy soldiers likely meant that an assault was imminent. Word was passed that a courier would later be dispatched, and many men solemnly wrote letters to loved ones at home.

Col. Travis could be found in his headquarters room along the west wall finishing his own correspondence. His message to the convention at Washington-on-the-Brazos urging them to respond with men and supplies ended with a scathing condemnation of the Mexican citizens of San Antonio, and advised that they should be declared public enemies and that their land should be confiscated to pay the expenses of the war. Travis scribbled notes to his fiancée, Rebecca Cummings, and a close friend, Jesse Grimes. His final letter was addressed to David Ayers who was boarding Travis's son Charles. "Take care of my little boy," he wrote. "If the country should be saved, I may make him a splendid fortune; but if the country should be lost and I should perish, he will have nothing but the proud recollection that he is the son of a man who died for his country."

Travis selected John W. Smith, the man who had guided the Gonzales reinforcements to the Alamo two days earlier, to carry these important messages and letters. The northern postern was swung open at about midnight, and, under a covering fire from his comrades, Smith vanished into the night.

## DAY ELEVEN

### Friday, March 4, 1836

The Mexican cannon barrage began at dawn. Fortified by the new battery emplacement within 250 yards to the north, the artillery began causing noticeable damage to the walls of Alamo. While Gen. Ramírez y Sesma's howitzers lobbed shells into every corner of the compound, other pieces opened up to batter the stone masonry that had been reinforced by dirt embankments. Mexican batteries and accompanying entrenchments had now completely surrounded the mission. In addition to the new close-in northern position, two 9-pounders had been placed just across the river in San Antonio, 400 yards to the west. Other batteries included one 300 yards away to the south in La Villita; 1000 yards to the south at the powder house; 800 yards northeast on the ditch; and at the old mill, 800 yards north.

The east end of the compound's north wall was the most vulnerable target, and began to crumble from the devastating bombardment. Chief engineer Green B. Jameson frantically rallied a detail of men with shovels and mallets in an effort to shore up that position and other potential breaches. The Alamo, which had held up against the enemy cannon balls for the past 10 days, was presently in serious danger of being pounded into rubble by the incessant shelling.

The volunteers were pinned down by showers of flying debris. Those who had hoped and prayed that Santa Anna would hesitate to storm the Alamo were experiencing second-thoughts — especially when in the distance Mexican soldiers were observed busily building ladders for the obvious purpose of scaling the walls. Jim Bowie, whose illness was painfully evident, was carried from his room, and encouraged the trapped men to carry on. But the sight of more Mexican reinforcements marching into town gnawed at even the resolve of David Crockett, who again voiced his discontent at being hemmed up and that his preference was to march out and die in the open air. Nevertheless, there was no quit in Crockett or the rest of the men, and they remained at their positions and vowed to fight to the end.

Meanwhile, Santa Anna had decided that it was time to hold a council of war, which was unusual because the general rarely asked the opinion of anyone. In early evening, the generals and colonels were summoned to headquarters. Santa Anna stated that the time had come to make an assault on the Alamo, which was greeted with nearly unanimous agreement. The general then asked for suggestions about methods in which to carry out this assault. Gen. Castrillón and colonels Almonte and Romero were convinced that a breach should be made in the Alamo walls before any troops were deployed. That job, they estimated, could be accomplished in probably 8 to 10 hours once Gen. Gaona's two 12-pounders arrived, which should be in 2 days. That advice was taken into consideration, and the artillery commandant was alerted. The other officers were for the most part silent with respect to strategy. Another subject that was presented pertained to the disposition of prisoners taken in the battle or if the Alamo garrison should happen to surrender. Gen. Castrillón and Col. Almonte vented their views that men had certain rights to humane treatment. Santa Anna, however, had the last word and reiterated his earlier dictate that no prisoners would be taken.

The Mexican artillery seemed to get caught up in the enthusiasm for an attack, and continued to bombard the Alamo with renewed fervor.

## DAY TWELVE

### Saturday, March 5, 1836

The day dawned bright, and the temperature rose into the high 60s. By midafternoon, Santa Anna had finalized his strategy for an assault of the Alamo. He was a hands on commander who left nothing to chance. In addition to formulating the overall view of which detachments would attack which locations, he made it a point to personally dictate details that would normally be the responsibility of noncommissioned officers. For example, he outlined instructions about how those soldiers who carried ladders would sling their weapons; and that grenadiers would each carry 6 packages of cartridges; and that the chin straps of their caps would be down; and how it was imperative that bayonets be in perfect order. The afternoon was spent in preparation for this important assault. Santa Anna calmly sat writing orders, dipping his quill in a gold ink pot, and dispatching couriers to each position to make certain that nothing was overlooked by his officers.

Mexican artillery continued to pound the Alamo from positions as close as 200 yards away. The north wall, the weakest point, was specifically targeted. Some officers were disgruntled about the timing of the assault, believing instead that in 2 or 3 days the walls of Alamo would come tumbling down from the steady bombardment and the inhabitants would be impelled to surrender. But once the final order had been issued by Santa Anna, there was no further debate or grumbling, and none doubted that they would be victorious.

The shelling of the Alamo ceased at sunset, and, while the Mexican soldiers slept in prelude to an attack, the Texas volunteers worked feverishly to shore up the north wall where the attack was expected. Eventually, a 10-foot high wall of dirt would support the wall to cushion it against another barrage.

Col. William Travis sought refuge in his headquarters. The idea of a surrender was conceivably on his mind. He understood that it was unlikely that the Alamo could withstand an all out assault by the mass of Mexicans camped across the river, and he could easily raise the white flag and give up. But he would have wondered would become of his men in the event of a surrender. In their defense, the Texans had not killed even one Mexican prisoner — Gen. Cós could attest to that fact after his surrender at San Antonio in December. Could he expect Santa Anna to treat his men with mercy and care for their wounded? He was inclined to think so. After all, Stephen F. AUSTIN had been taken prisoner by Santa Anna in Mexico City, and had been subsequently paroled.

According to both Gen. Vicente Filisola and Col. José Enrique de la Peña, at nightfall, Travis allegedly dispatched from the Alamo a Mexican woman who lived in San Antonio as an intermediary in a effort to seek terms for a possible surrender. She was taken to Santa Anna's headquarters and freely told about how the Alamo was on the brink of collapse, that vital supplies and ammunition was running out, the condition of the walls were deteriorating, and most of all, the will of the men to fight was weakening. Col. de la Peña in his suspect memoirs wrote: "Travis's resistance was on the verge of being overcome; for several days his followers had been urging him to surrender, giving the lack of food and scarcity of munitions as reasons, but he had quieted their restlessness with the hope of quick relief, something not difficult for them to believe since they had seen some reinforcements arrive. Nevertheless, they pressed him so hard that on the 5th he promised them that if no help arrived on that day they would surrender the next day or attempt to escape

under cover of darkness." Santa Anna, however, did not want the garrison to surrender according to de la Peña "because he wanted to cause a sensation and would have regretted taking the Alamo without clamor and without bloodshed, for some believed that without these there is no glory."

Travis then decided to dispatch another courier, and chose James L. ALLEN for the mission. The postern was opened, and Allen galloped away on his mare — the last messenger to leave the Alamo before the Mexican assault.

Apparently Travis could not convince himself to surrender his command en masse to the Mexicans. What Travis was said to have done next has been the subject of much controversy and debate throughout the ensuing years. Detractors have dismissed it as simply legend, a story without definitive proof; others argue that it actually happened, and no proof exists to confirm otherwise (see TRAVIS, William for more).

Col. Travis assembled the entire garrison in a single file and stood before them. He was an effective public speaker, and it was evident that he had rehearsed his speech. In a voice brimming with passion and choked with the emotion of the moment, he told his men that their fate was sealed. Within days or even minutes they all could be dead. Destiny had dictated this fate, and they could do little to change it. Fannin at Goliad as well as the rest of Texas had not responded with reinforcements, and there was an overwhelming number of Mexicans poised to enter and kill them all. He presented the choices that faced them — they could surrender, or try to escape, or, if those options were unacceptable, they could stay and fight. He vowed that it was his intention to stay and fight even if every one of them chose to attempt an escape or surrendered. It was a life or death situation, and each man was entitled to an individual decision.

Travis then dramatically drew his sword, and scratched a line in the dirt as he walked from one end of the compound to the other. Those volunteers who chose to stay and fight, he declared, should step across that line. Those who had chosen one of the other options could remain where they stood.

The first to cross the line was 26-year-old Tapley HOLLAND, an artilleryman from Ohio who had fought in the siege and battle of San Antonio. A stream of men then strode forward, including Jim Bowie and other bedridden volunteers who were carried across on their cots. Within moments, every man in the garrison had crossed the line — except one.

Louis ROSE, a man with an illustrious background that was difficult to document, slumped to the ground and covered his face. Rose ignored the glares of his comrades, gathered his belongings, and disappeared over the wall. He would endure a torturous pathway to freedom, but nonetheless would not be counted among those who had lost their lives at the Alamo.

The moon was almost full and the sky was cloudy when Travis posted 3 sentries outside the walls to sound the alarm. Perhaps seeking some respite from his gloomy thoughts, he paid a visit to Susannah Dickinson and her daughter Angelina who huddled in the chapel. In a gesture that could be interpreted as a premonition of his death and a desire to in some manner be remembered, he removed from his finger the gold cat's eye ring that had been a gift from his fiancée Rebecca Cummings. He then tied the ring on a string and looped it around little Angelina's neck.

The other men remained at their positions, alert for any movement from across the river. They were outwardly subdued, but battled inward emotions that churned with anticipatory dread fueled by the realization that they may never see their loved ones again. (See ALAMO, Battle of for a continuation of this siege.)

**ALLEN, James L.** (January 2, 1818–April 25, 1901) Private, TEXAS REVOLUTIONARY ARMY; Alamo COURIER from Kentucky. Allen, the oldest of 7 children, was a student at Clarion College in Kentucky when he and several others volunteered for service in Texas. He participated in the ALAMO SIEGE as a rifleman, and is notable as the final messenger dispatched from the Alamo (March 5) before the battle and was thereby saved. He later assisted in cutting off the retreat of Mexicans at the Battle of SAN JACINTO by burning bridges behind enemy lines. Allen then went to the United States where he acted as a recruiter for the Texas Volunteers, and returned to Texas as captain of a unit called the Buckeye Rangers. He signed on as a Texas Ranger, and fought in the Indian battle of Corpus Cristi in July, 1844. He married Frederica Manchan in 1849, and they had 7 children. Among his various enterprises, Allen worked in the stock business; was mayor and justice of the peace in Indianola; and owned a 260 acre farm in Hochein, Texas. He was serving as tax assessor/collector for Calhoun County, Texas during the Civil War when he was captured by Union troops but later escaped. Allen died at his home near Yoakum, Texas.

**ALLEN, Robert** (?–March 6, 1836) Private, TEXAS REVOLUTIONARY ARMY; Alamo defender from Virginia. Little is known about Allen other than that he participated in the ALAMO SIEGE as a rifleman with Capt. John H. FORSYTH's cavalry company, and was killed during the ALAMO BATTLE.

**ALMONTE, Juan Nepomuceno** (1803–1869) Colonel, MEXICAN ARMY. Almonte was the illegitimate son of an Indian girl and José Maria Morelos y Pavon, a discontented, revolutionary parish priest. His father was executed in 1815 for his attempt to eliminate the caste system during the War of Independence. Young Juan at that time had been sent to the United States for safekeeping where he was educated at a Catholic school and therefore became fluent in English. He was just a teenager when he returned to Mexico to fight for his country's independence. Following the revolution, he was sent to England to negotiate that country's first commercial treaty with a foreign power, served in the national Congress, and edited a newspaper that came under fire and was shut down after accusing the president of permitting outsiders to meddle in Mexico's affairs. Almonte served on the 1834 commission whose published intention was to establish the border between Mexico and the U.S., and embarked on a fact-finding tour of the region. His actual mission, however, was to infiltrate American colonies and assess the amount of duties that had gone unpaid, take a headcount, as well as determine the political attitude of this area that had gone unpoliced for four years. The Americans were at this time contemplating independence, and, although he was outwardly friendly and glib, Almonte was treated civilly but with some distrust. Almonte returned to Mexico, and recommended in part that friendly Indians be settled in Texas to countercolonize the region. He did not specifically mention using slaves as well, but had been authorized on his trip to encourage them to invoke their freedom and settle in Texas. His most adamant recommendation, however, was that the army should be dispatched without delay or there would be little hope of keeping Texas under Mexican control.

Almonte was a colonel serving as aide-de-camp to Gen. Antonio Lopez de SANTA ANNA when the Mexican Army arrived in San Antonio to begin the ALAMO SIEGE on February 23, 1836. On that day, Col. William TRAVIS dispatched an emissary, Albert MARTIN, from the ALAMO MISSION, who presented himself to Almonte. Martin advised Almonte that Travis was desirous of a meeting to discuss matters and would receive him "with much pleasure." Almonte explained that he was not the one to consider any propositions, and that the Alamo defenders should lay down their arms and surrender should they wish to save their lives. At a war council held on March 4, Almonte suggested to Santa Anna that they wait to storm the Alamo until the arrival of Gen. Antonio GAONA's heavy artillery, which could perhaps encourage a surrender or at the very least minimize Mexican casualties. Santa Anna refused. It should also be noted that Col. Almonte at that time and during the Surrender and Massacre at GOLIAD was outspoken in his opposition to executing prisoners, arguing about the rights of men and the philosophical and humane principles which did them honor. He was consistently overruled by Santa Anna. Late in the ALAMO BATTLE, Santa Anna sent his aides, including Almonte, into the fray for the purpose of encouraging the Mexican troops. It is believed that Almonte was the officer who, following the battle, successfully interceded on behalf of survivor Susannah DICKINSON when Santa Anna was determined to adopt her 15-month-old daughter, Angelina.

On April 11, Almonte used his English to trick a slave into transporting Santa Anna and a small group of soldiers across the Brazos by ferry. Almonte demonstrated his compassion and chivalry a week later when the Texas president, David BURNET, and his cabinet were attempting to escape from Almonte's cavalry. Burnet's small party, which included his wife, were frantically fleeing aboard a rowboat in Galveston Bay — well within rifle range — when Almonte ordered his men to hold their fire because there was a lady in the boat. The gallant Almonte did at that time capture large food stores from warehouses in New Washington. At the April 21 Battle of SAN JACINTO, Almonte realized that the battle was lost and the only way to save his own life and that of any his comrades was to assemble a sizable group of his troops and surrender en masse to the Texans. Almonte rounded up about 400 men, and surrendered to Texas Secretary of War Thomas RUSK, who personally escorted these prisoners to prevent them from becoming victims of atrocities by the angry Texas volunteers. Rusk later said that Almonte's men were treated more kindly by the guards due to the colonel's "philosophic and cheerful temper" about his predicament. Col. Almonte then acted as interpreter for Santa Anna in talks with Sam HOUSTON. He was held prisoner for seven months — some of the time chained to an oak tree. In November, Almonte accompanied Santa Anna to Washington, DC, where on January 26, 1837 the Mexican dictator culminated his visit by attending a dinner party hosted by President Andrew Jackson and his entire cabinet. Almonte returned to Mexico with Santa Anna in mid-1837 aboard a U.S. battleship provided by Jackson.

Almonte was Mexican minister of war from 1839–1841, and appointed ambassador to the United States in 1842. It was while serving in the latter capacity that in 1843 Almonte threatened that Mexico would declare war should the U.S. annex Texas. On three formal occasions in 1844, he reiterated those threats, and responded to President Polk's acceptance of a resolution in 1845 to annex Texas by stating that Mexico would defend its rightful territory. On March 6, 1845, he broke off diplomatic relations between Mexico and the U.S. in prelude to

the Mexican War. He later served as minister to London and Paris, and lobbied for Europe to establish a monarchy in Mexico after Republican forces won the War of the Reform (1858–1861). He returned to his homeland in 1862, and was selected for the Council of Notables and later regent. He was appointed to a cabinet post and as representative of the Mexican Empire to Napoleon III by Emperor Maximillian in 1866. Almonte died 3 years later in Paris.

**ALSBURY, Juana Navarro de** (?–July 25, 1898) Civilian Alamo survivor from Texas. This resident of San Antonio, Texas was the daughter of a former officer in the Mexican Army, and had been married for one month to her second husband, Dr. Horace Alsbury, a Kentucky colonist and Texas Volunteer who was on a scouting mission when the ALAMO SIEGE began. Juana and her sister, Gertrudis NAVARRO, were the nieces of Vice-Governor Juan Martin de Veramendi, who happened to be the father-in-law of James BOWIE. When it was determined on February 23, 1836 that the Mexican Army was approaching San Antonio, Bowie rushed into town and escorted the sisters and Juana's infant son, Alijo Perez, Jr., behind the walls of the ALAMO MISSION. When Bowie became incapacitated, he told Juana, "Do not be afraid. I leave you with Colonel (William) TRAVIS, Colonel (David) CROCKETT, and other friends. They are gentlemen, and will treat you kindly." Several times during the siege, Bowie was carried on his cot to visit her. During the ALAMO BATTLE, the ladies and their companions were hiding in a room along the west wall adjoining the officers' quarters when Mexican troops overran the defenders. When the soldiers appeared at their room, a private named Edwin T. MITCHELL attempted to protect them and was bayonetted to death. Another man sought to use Juana as a shield, but was torn away and stabbed to death. The soldiers accosted the women, but did not harm them. Instead they looted their belongings, many of which had been placed there for safe-keeping by the garrison officers. In time, a Mexican officer appeared to escort them safely from the room to a position near a cannon. Another officer approached, and warned them to stand clear — the cannon was about to be turned and fired on the defenders. The terrified sisters were saved by Juana's brother-in-law, Manuel Perez, who took them to the chapel to join the other women. Juana and her sister were presented to Gen. Antonio Lopez de SANTA ANNA following the battle, and, after a brief interrogation, he gave each of them two pesos and a blanket and released them. Dr. Alsbury was killed in 1847 during the Mexican War, and Juana later married her late husband's cousin. She was awarded a pension from the State of Texas in 1857 for her service at the Alamo.

**ANAHUAC, Battle of** (June 29, 1835) When merchants were arrested after protesting what they considered unfair duties collected by the Mexican customhouse at Anahuac, William TRAVIS, in an action considered rash by most Texans at the time, led a group of 25 men to the Mexican garrison and compelled the commander and his 44 troops to surrender and leave Texas.

### Chronology of the Texas Revolution

- **June 29, 1835: Battle of ANAHUAC**
- October 2, 1835: GONZALES SKIRMISH
- October 3, 1835: MEXICAN CONSTITUTION OF 1824 officially voided
- October 9, 1835: GOLIAD SKIRMISH
- October 28, 1835: Battle of CONCEPCION
- November 3, 1835: TEXAS CONSULTATION OF DELEGATES
- November–December, 1835: Siege and Battle of SAN ANTONIO
- January–February, 1836: The MATAMOROS EXPEDITION
- February 23–March 5, 1836: The ALAMO SIEGE
- March 1, 1836: TEXAS CONSTITUTIONAL CONVENTION
- March 2, 1836: TEXAS DECLARATION OF INDEPENDENCE
- March 6, 1836: The ALAMO BATTLE
- March 20–27, 1836: Surrender and Massacre at GOLIAD
- April 21, 1836: Battle of SAN JACINTO
- May 14, 1836: Treaties of VELASCO

The Texans at this point in time were divided between war and peace, and most hoped to avoid a direct conflict with Mexico. In mid-1835, the Mexicans reopened the garrison and customs post at Anahuac, Texas, the legal port for Galveston Bay, after a 3-year absence with intentions of strictly enforcing the collection of duties. Several merchants, including Andrew Briscoe and De Witt C. Harris, protested that duties should not be collected at that port until collections throughout Texas were equally assessed. It was argued that the practice was rife with corruption, and duties should be more evenly collected. The Mexican Army commander, Capt. Antonio Tenorio, decided to silence Briscoe and Harris by jailing them. Texans in neighboring San Felipe had gathered to discuss the incident, which was considered relatively insignificant, when a Mexican courier approached. The Texans impulsively waylaid the courier and seized his messages. One missive stated that civil government had been suspended, and General Martin Perfecto de CÓS would be in charge upon his arrival; another assured Tenorio that reinforcements had been dispatched; and the third promised that Gen. Antonio Lopez de SANTA ANNA and troops under Cós were on the way to take punitive measures against the Texans. Public opinion now apparently swayed to the side of those promoting war, and it was decided on June 22 that the Mexicans should be removed from the garrison in Anahuac before Gen. Cós arrived. Lawyer William B. Travis assembled about 25 men and a 6-pounder cannon mounted on a pair of sawmill truck wheels, and set out on June 24 from San Felipe on the sloop *Ohio*. The small army arrived in Anahuac on June 29, and rowed ashore. To demonstrate their determination, Travis ordered one round fired from the cannon. Capt. Tenorio sent out a messenger, and Travis demanded that the garrison surrender. Tenorio requested a cease-fire until morning. Travis advanced on the post, and the Mexicans withdrew into nearby woods. Travis fired one aimless round into the trees, which had little effect other than perhaps psychological. The next morning, Tenorio surrendered his 44 troops and weapons, and agreed to leave Texas under parole. Rather than returning to a triumphant hero's welcome, Travis and his army were surprised to learn that public sentiment had now turned against them. The people wrote a letter of apology to Capt. Tenorio, which failed to mollify the Mexicans. Santa Anna, as promised, dispatched Gen. Cós and an army of regular troops to join those already in Texas to arrest Travis and other rebels. This edict evoked concerns of martial law and military occupation, and the Texans considered it unthinkable to turn their people over to a military tribunal rather than have them tried by a jury of peers. Committees began to form all across Texas to protest Santa Anna's actions. For all practical purposes, the TEXAS REVOLUTION had begun (see also PEACE PARTY; WAR PARTY).

**ANDROSS, Miles DeForrest** (aka "Mills D. Andross"; 1809–March 6, 1836) Private,

TEXAS REVOLUTIONARY ARMY; Alamo defender from Vermont. Andross was from San Patricio, Texas, by way of Bradford, Vermont. He participated in the siege and battle of SAN ANTONIO; and served as a rifleman in Capt. William BLAZEBY's infantry company during the ALAMO SIEGE, and in the ALAMO BATTLE where he lost his life.

**ATROCITIES COMMITTED DURING THE TEXAS REVOLUTION** Both sides were guilty of atrocities during the period of this conflict. The MEXICAN ARMY, however, due to the brutality of their commander, Gen. Antonio Lopez de SANTA ANNA, have been condemned for the wanton slaughter of many Texans, which encouraged retaliation. Evidence exits that initial outrages were committed by white mercenaries — volunteers for the army that had been lured to Texas in late 1835 due to the civil unrest and the promise of cheap land. (See UNITED STATES SUPPORT FOR TEXAS INDEPENDENCE for more.) Bands of these barbarians roamed the countryside and terrorized anyone who caught their fancy — stealing, beating innocent people, raping Mexican women, and quartering themselves in private homes. Gonzales was one of the hardest hit towns. In early November, most of its men were in San Antonio — 70 miles away — serving during the Siege and Battle of SAN ANTONIO. A group of newly arrived volunteers from the Ayish Bayou near the Louisiana border came into that town and terrorized the women and children — chasing them from their homes, vandalizing property, taking money and clothing, and feeding their horses in the cornfields. Susannah DICKINSON, whose husband Almeron was one of those in San Antonio, was wary of these strangers. She asked future Alamo COURIER Lancelot SMITHERS to accompany her home for protection. He agreed, and was subsequently dragged into the street and assaulted by men who beat his head "to a poltice" and nearly killed him. Mrs. Dickinson then fled to San Antonio, and thus became the only white woman in the ALAMO MISSION during the ALAMO BATTLE. It has been reported that those volunteers who remained to garrison the Alamo following that siege and battle in December — many of them members of the NEW ORLEANS GREYS — regarded the property of local Mexicans to be fair game, and had a habit of plundering cattle and horses for their own use. The stage was set for military atrocities by the MEXICAN ARMY when Santa Anna issued a circular of the Supreme Government which stated in part "That any foreigners invading the Republic be treated and tried as pirates whenever found armed." This was meant as an order to execute any prisoner. The matter of executing prisoners was argued against by subornites Gen. Manuel Fernandez CASTRILLÓN and Col. Juan ALMONTE in a council of war held by Santa Anna prior to the March 6, 1836, assault of the Alamo. The general, however, reiterated his previous order. In the aftermath of that battle, the Mexican soldiers showed no mercy, took no prisoners, and, in a killing frenzy, went from room to room searching for survivors. The soldiers killed Jim BOWIE, then reportedly tossed his body on their bayonets until his blood covered their clothes and dyed them red. Defender Jacob WALKER — in the presence of Alamo survivor Susannah DICKINSON — was hoisted several times on Mexican bayonets like a bale of hay until he died in convulsions. The two young sons of defender Anthony WOLFE were killed and carried out of the room on bayonets. Gen. Martin Perfecto de CÓS allegedly forced William TRAVIS's slave, JOE, to identify the body of his master. Cós then drew his sword and brutally mutilated the face and limbs of Travis. Cós's action was typical of the Mexican soldiers. These men

had lost control of their senses, and were drunk on blood. Any Anglo found alive was brutally killed and mutilated — even those helpless sick and wounded in the hospital. When no Alamo defenders remained alive to kill, these soldiers made their way through the compound stabbing and re-stabbing the dead with their bayonets, firing their muskets into the corpses, and stripping and mutilating the bodies. Mexican officers, who were for the most part appalled by the savagery of their men, could not stop most of it, but did manage to protect Susannah Dickinson — who was shot in the leg — and the Mexican women and children.

Meanwhile, Mexican Gen. José URREA and 1,400 troops had been sweeping north from Matamoros toward Goliad, and along the way had captured 50 rebels in several separate incidents. Bowing to pressure from his subordinate officers to obey Santa Anna's orders and execute all prisoners, Urrea departed camp while 30 of these men were killed. The remaining 20 — determined to be Mexicans or colonists — were released.

The most outrageous and brutal atrocity of the revolution occurred on Palm Sunday, March 27, 1836 at Goliad. On March 14, Col. James W. FANNIN, commander of the 400-man Goliad garrison, was informed by Gen. Sam HOUSTON that the troops under Gen. Urrea were headed in that direction and Fannin should evacuate immediately. For various reasons, Fannin did not depart until March 19, and was overtaken and surrounded that afternoon by the Mexicans. The Texans fought off Urrea's troops until the following afternoon when Fannin, against the wishes of many of his troops, agreed to surrender. Fannin's men were marched back to Goliad, and joined there by other prisoners captured elsewhere, which brought the total confined to about 500. The Texans were put to work repairing fortifications and building rafts until Santa Anna was informed of their presence. The Mexican dictator was incensed to learn that Gen. Urrea had not already followed orders and executed these men. He dispatched a messenger with orders for Urrea to comply with the circular that called for the execution of all prisoners. Urrea replied with a request for clemency, but Santa Anna was adamant. While Urrea was attending to business in Victoria, Santa Anna had the same order delivered to Col. José Nicólas Portilla, who was temporarily in command of the prisoners. On Palm Sunday, March 27, the prisoners were assembled for roll call at 8 A.M., and informed by way of rumor that they were to be released. The Texans were then divided into three columns, and marched away in different directions. The columns were eventually halted, and the Mexican soldiers opened fire. Some men — perhaps as many as 60 — escaped by running away and hiding near the San Antonio River, but most were killed by Mexican muskets. Col. Fannin was executed separately — the last of at least 400 who were shot down in cold blood that day by direct order of Santa Anna. (See GOLIAD, Surrender and Massacre at for more.)

The TEXAS REVOLUTIONARY ARMY had treated its prisoners humanely throughout the early period of the revolution. In fact, the Texans were surprised to learn that those Mexican soldiers captured and spared in the October 28, 1835 Battle of CONCEPCION were under the impression that they would be executed. And, when Mexican Gen. Cós surrendered more than 1,000 troops to end the December, 1835 Siege and Battle of SAN ANTONIO, these men were not held captive but paroled and sent south of the Rio Grande River. After the butchery that took place at the Alamo and Goliad became widely known, however, the Texans evidently lusted for revenge. That opportunity came at the April 21, 1836, Battle of SAN JACINTO. Sam HOUS-

TON and his men surprised the sleeping Mexican Army, and engaged in a vicious killing frenzy. Mexican soldiers were not permitted to surrender but were shot or stabbed by the Texas volunteers who were inspired by the battle cries "Remember the Alamo!" and "Remember Goliad!" Houston and other officers tried but could not control their troops. The men were so engrossed in their blood orgy that they became vulnerable to a counterattack. At one point Houston feared that if Mexican reinforcements should arrive his men would be easily defeated. One Texan said, "If Jesus Christ were to come down from Heaven and order me to quit shooting Santanistas, I wouldn't do it!" Another said, "We obeyed no command but the impulse of our feelings. We came, we saw, we conquered." Col. Sidney SHERMAN and his 52 Kentucky mercenaries were said to be the most flagrant offenders of this wanton slaughter. One of Sherman's men happened upon a young drummer boy lying on the ground, and prodded him with the point of his bayonet. The boy grabbed the man's legs and begged for mercy. The mercenary shot the boy in the head. The butchery stopped only when darkness descended, and it was 3 days before the wounded Mexican prisoners received medical treatment. These prisoners then served as virtual slaves for local families before being released.

**AUSTIN, Moses** (October 4, 1761–June 10, 1821) Father of Stephen F. AUSTIN. This merchant and founder of the American lead industry was the first *EMPRESARIO* to obtain permission to establish an American colony in Texas. Austin was born in Durham, Connecticut, and orphaned at 15 years of age. He worked for the family dry-goods import business in Middleton, Connecticut and Philadelphia, and in 1784 opened a branch of his own at Richmond, Virginia. That same year, he married Maria Brown who bore him a daughter and two sons. In 1789, Austin gained control of the Chiswell lead mines in southwestern Virginia, the state's richest lead deposit. Within 3 years, he had established the town of Austinville (Wythe County), worked the mines with slave labor, and for all practical purposes created the American lead industry. In 1797, he obtained the richest lead deposit in present-day Potsi, Missouri, and established that town as the first Anglo settlement west of the Mississippi River. Austin's innovative techniques influenced the lead industry until the advent of heavy machinery after the Civil War. He steadily became wealthy from both real estate and his mines. Austin and other investors founded a bank in St. Louis in 1816 — the first bank west of the Mississippi — but its subsequent failure wiped him out. Moses Austin may have been deeply in debt, but he was not without ideas about how to regain his lost fortunes. He was aware that American colonization of Texas was only a matter of time, and that the Spanish would perhaps be receptive to a plan for an orderly settlement. Austin would act as *empresario* — the promoter of a colony — and by assisting the Spanish in their dilemma would in the process restore his financial stability. Part of the panic that had ruined Austin was due to wild land speculation. He would, therefore, offer more generous terms to those who desired to own land in Texas. Austin arrived in San Antonio, Texas on December 23, 1820 and was able to convince the governor to endorse his application to settle 300 families. The application was approved by the provincial deputation in Monterey on January 17, 1821. Austin returned to Missouri, and word of the approval of the petition granting him 200,000 acres of land reached him in May, 1821. Moses Austin, however, died of pneumonia on June 10. He had on his death bed, however, begged his wife to tell his son Stephen that it was his wish that he carry on with the plan to colonize Texas. Stephen obeyed his father's last request, and became the first *empresario* in Texas. (See TEXAS SETTLEMENT BY AMERICANS for more.)

**AUSTIN, Stephen Fuller** "The Father of Texas" (November 3, 1793–December 27, 1836) Founder of the first colony in Texas. Austin has been described as standing about 5 foot 5 or 6, weighing about 135 pounds, with wavy dark brown hair worn long. He smoked, enjoyed music and dancing, and drank in moderation. Austin never married.

### Birth and Early Life

Stephen was the eldest son born to Moses AUSTIN and Maria (Brown) Austin at Austinville, Virginia, the lead mines owned by his father. The family moved to Missouri in 1798, which was populated by mostly the French and Spanish, and settled at present-day Potsi. He attended Colchester Academy in Colchester, Connecticut from ages 11 to 14, and moved on to Transylvania University in Lexington, Kentucky until returning to Missouri in 1810. Austin then went to work under his father's tutelage as a shopkeeper, a manager in the lead mines, as well as in banking, land speculation, and manufacturing. He served in the state legislature from 1814 to 1820, and was an officer in the local militia. When the family business collapsed, Austin moved to Arkansas where in June 1821 the governor appointed him judge of the first judicial circuit. Instead of serving in that capacity, however, he travelled to New Orleans to study law while working as an assistant to the editor of the *Louisiana Advertiser* newspaper.

Meanwhile, his father, Moses, had an idea about how to regain his lost fortunes. He was aware that American colonization of Texas was only a matter of time, and that the Spanish would perhaps be receptive to a plan for an orderly settlement. Austin would act as *empresario*— the promoter of a colony — and by assisting the Spanish in their dilemma would in the process restore his financial stability. Part of the panic that had ruined Austin was due to wild land speculation. He would, therefore, offer more generous terms to those who desired to own land in Texas. Stephen was reluctant to enter into this land speculation, and declined to participate in his father's endeavor. Moses went ahead and convinced the Mexican governor in San Antonio to endorse his application to settle 300 families. Moses returned to Missouri, and informed his son about the good news. Stephen remained apprehensive about the situation, but did agree to accompany his father on his next scheduled trip to Texas. That trip never occurred; Moses Austin died of pneumonia on June 10. Moses had on his death bed, however, begged his wife to tell Stephen that it was his wish that his son carry on with the plan to colonize Texas. Stephen could not refuse such a request.

### Texas

In the company of a small group of Americans, Stephen Austin arrived in Texas on July 21, 1821. This was not by any means a half-hearted attempt on his part to patronize his father's dying request, rather a commitment that he later explained by stating: "I bid an everlasting farewell to my native country, and adopted this, and in so doing I determined to fulfill rigidly all the duties and obligations of a Mexican citizen." Austin set out to explore the country, and discovered in an area 175 miles southeast of San Antonio in the rich river bottoms of the Colorado and Brazos Rivers what he described in his journal as "a most beautiful

situation for a town or settlement. The country back of this place for about 15 miles is as good in every respect as a man could wish for, land all first rate, plenty of timber, fine water." This particular place had access to the gulf, enjoyed abundant rainfall, and would make for fertile farmland. The town of San Felipe de Austin was established on a bluff in the midst this grant, and Stephen Austin had become Texas's first *EMPRESARIO*. His trips to Mexico City during those early years enabled him to learn the language and make friends with those in power. Austin gained additional land grants in 1825, 1827, and 1828, and, until 1828, had absolute rule of this colony as supreme judge and military commander. The importance of his personal efforts in the colonization of Texas cannot be overstated. He had total authority over the admittance of settlers who would benefit the colony; commanded a militia to fight hostile Indians; mapped the land and charted the bays and rivers; encouraged the establishment of schools and diverse businesses such as gins and sawmills; promoted trade with the United States; and influenced people at the state and federal levels with the fair but strict terms of the colonization laws he defined, which were a model for other colonies. Austin reflected on his success at colonizing Texas by saying: "Such an enterprise as the one I undertook in settling an uninhabited country must necessarily pass through three regular graduations. The first step was to overcome the roughness of the wilderness, and may be compared to the labor of the farmer on a piece of ground covered with woods, bushes, and brambles, which must be cut down and cleared away, and the roots grubbed out, before it can be cultivated. The second step was to pave the way for civilization and lay the foundation for lasting productive advancement in wealth, morality, and happiness. This step might be compared to the ploughing, harrowing, and sowing the ground after it is cleared. The third and last and most important step is to give proper and healthy direction to public opinion, morality, and education…to give tone, character, and consistency to society, which, to continue the simile, is gathering in the harvest and applying it to the promotion of human happiness." (See TEXAS SETTLEMENT BY AMERICANS for a detailed account of Austin's efforts to establish his colony.)

Austin had pledged his loyalty to Mexico, and apparently was sincere. In a letter to his sister in 1829 urging her family to immigrate to Texas, he wrote: "This is the most liberal and magnificent Govt. on earth to emigrants — after being here one year you will oppose a change even to Uncle Sam."

He believed that the key to coexisting with Mexico was to abstain from involvement in its politics. He was of the opinion that the political factions in Mexico had no fixed character or permanency of purpose, and if the Texans chose to take part in that system they would be "like children in a mob, and as likely to be trodden upon by friends as by foes. Play the turtle," he advised, "head and feet within your own shell." Texans, if asked, should declare "that they will do their duty strictly as Mexican citizens — that they will adhere to Mexico and to the federal and state constitution, and resist any unjust attacks upon either, by any or by all parties."

His loyalty to Mexico and relationship with the Mexicans paid dividends in 1832 following the first major armed rebellion of the pre-revolution. Some colonists — including William B. TRAVIS — protested the ruling of the Mexican garrison and customhouse commander in Anahuac concerning a land dispute and were arrested. Volunteers from Brazoria responded to assist their brethren, and while en route to Anahuac were intercepted by Mexican soldiers from the garrison at Velasco. In the ensuing June 26, 1832, Battle of VELASCO, 10 colonists and 5 Mexican soldiers were killed, but the Mexicans were forced to surrender and abandon their garrison. The colonists feared retribution for their rash acts, but fortunately for them Antonio Lopez de Santa Anna was at that moment leading a rebellion against President Anastacio Bustamante, and both political leaders were preoccupied with that conflict. An expedition of 400 soldiers under the command of Col. José Antonio Mexia, who was loyal to Santa Anna, did march to Texas. In his company, however, was Stephen Austin, who was returning by way of Matamoros from the legislature of Coahuila and Texas in Saltillo, which he served as a member beginning in 1831-32. Austin alerted the colonists and perhaps influenced the colonel along the way. The colonists greeted Col. Mexia in Brazoria with a lavish dinner and grand ball. Mexia accepted the explanation that the colonists had been fighting not against the Mexican Constitution but against the garrison commander, who happened to be a Bustamante loyalist.

*Politics*

The incident at Anahuac had compelled the colonists to petition Mexico for concessions and assurances that those abuses would not be repeated. The Texans held a convention in October, 1832, which was attended by 58 delegates from 16 districts, and presided over by Stephen Austin. In addition to local business, such as Indian affairs and the organization of a militia, the convention petitioned the Mexican government to repeal the April 6, 1830, law that had cut off immigration; requested a 3-year extension to the tariff exemption on necessities; and asked for the right to establish Texas as a separate state in the Mexican confederation. Mexican authorities ignored the convention, and the petitions were never presented.

The Texans held a second convention on April 1, 1833. The delegates repeated the concerns of the first convention, including a constitution for a new state that Sam HOUSTON helped draft, which was loosely based on the United States Constitution. Stephen Austin was chosen as best qualified to deliver the petitions and constitution to Mexico City. By this time, Santa Anna had overthrown Bustamante and won the presidency. Austin arrived in Mexico City in July, and presented the petitions to Vice-President Valentin Gómez Farías — Santa Anna was said to have been "recuperating" from his political victory at his estate and was unavailable. Austin became impatient at the delay in gaining an audience with Santa Anna, and warned Farías on October 1 that unless Mexico addressed "the evils which threaten Texas with ruin" the colonists were prepared to establish a state government on their own. Farías, as could be expected, became disenchanted with Austin. In a fit of anger, Austin wrote a letter to the predominately Mexican city council in San Antonio that contained such statements as, "The fate of Texas depends on itself and not upon this government," and "The country is lost if its inhabitants do not take its affairs into their own hands." On November 5, Santa Anna finally agreed to a conference with Austin, and was surprisingly sympathetic to the concerns of the colonists. Austin was successful in persuading the president to repeal the April 6, 1830, immigration law, a modification of the tariff, and other requests such as the promise to encourage the government to consider trial by jury. Santa Anna, however, refused to approve a separation of Texas from Coahuila and recognize Texas as a state.

## Prison

Austin started home from Mexico City on December 10, but, on a January 3, 1834, stopover to visit the commandant at Saltillo, was arrested on suspicion of attempting to incite insurrection in Texas. The October letter Austin had written "in a moment of irritation and impatience" had found its way into the hands of Vice-president Valentin Gómez Farías. Austin, the man who had pledged undying loyalty to Mexico, was transported back to Mexico City and incarcerated in the Prison of the Inquisition. He was denied a trial when the matter of jurisdiction could not be settled. Lawyers from the colonies were dispatched — as well as petitions for his release — but those efforts failed to gain his freedom. He was kept in solitary confinement for 3 months until moved to another cell. In spite of his treatment, Austin continued to implore the Texans to avoid revolution and not to hold any more conventions. Stephen Austin would be held until Christmas Day, 1834, when he was released on parole, and finally was permitted to leave Mexico in July, 1835 when a general amnesty law was passed.

## Revolution

During Austin's absence Texas enjoyed improved relations with Mexico in 1833 and 1834. Laws were repealed that prohibited only native-born Mexicans from retail merchandising; Texan representation in the 12-man state congress was increased from 1 seat to 3; the English language was recognized for official purposes; there was more tolerance toward religious worship; trial by jury was established; and land was made easier to acquire. In early 1835, however, rampant land speculation and corruption in Coahuila, which had been going on for some time, came to the attention of Santa Anna. He dispatched troops in June to put a stop to this corruption by arresting known land speculators, the governor, and suspending civil government in favor of martial law.

These actions were propagandized by the so-called WAR PARTY—those Texans promoting independence—as intolerable acts that would lead to martial law and the confiscation of land in Texas. This threat, whether real or imagined, became one factor that encouraged Texans, the majority of whom still favored peace, to openly rebel against Mexico. Santa Anna had also decided in that spring of 1835 that the customhouses and garrisons in Texas that had for all practical purposes been abandoned in 1832 would be reopened and duties would be collected. This led to an incident at Anahuac when several merchants protested to the Mexican commander that the collection of duties was rife with corruption, and should be more fairly collected. These protesters were subsequently jailed. In what became known as the Battle of ANAHUAC, lawyer William Travis raised a company of 25 armed men, and, on June 29, ordered the Mexicans to leave. The commander complied and surrendered his 44 troops. Santa Anna ordered more arrests; an edict evoked concerns of martial law and military occupation.

By the time Stephen Austin arrived back in Texas in September, committees began to form to protest Santa Anna's actions. The various factions among the colonists found common ground with their own particular grievances toward Santa Anna, and for all practical purposes revolution in Texas became a distinct possibility. Austin was a changed man as well and also opposed Santa Anna, but adopted the stance of the so-called PEACE PARTY and encouraged the colonists to fight to restore the provisions of the MEXICAN CONSTITUTION OF 1824 that were rapidly being picked apart by Santa Anna rather than seek independence. On September 8, Austin was guest of honor at a testimonial dinner in Brazoria, and was informed that another convention had been planned for October. He agreed that a consultation was in order, and accepted the chairmanship of the Central Committee of Safety of San Felipe, which for all practical purposes made him the leader of the revolution. And this man who had been a martyr in that Mexican prison did not disappoint those who expected leadership. Austin for all intents and purposes declared war by saying: "Every man in Texas is called upon to take up arms in defence (sic) of his country and his rights."

The first shots of TEXAS REVOLUTION were fired October 2 in the GONZALES Skirmish when townspeople protested a Mexican attempt to seize their cannon. That battle was quickly followed by the Skirmish at GOLIAD, and the news that Santa Anna had annulled the Mexican Constitution. The convention that had been scheduled for October 15 was postponed due to a new threat. Mexican Gen. Martin Perfecto de Cós and about 1,400 troops were garrisoned in San Antonio at the ALAMO MISSION, and about 300–500 volunteers—including many convention delegates—had assembled at Gonzales in preparation to march to that town and expel the Mexicans from Texas. Stephen Austin was summoned and reluctantly accepted command of the ragtag force. Austin disapproved of Sam Houston's heavy drinking and profanity, but nonetheless had offered the position of command to Houston, who declined.

On October 28, in the Battle of CONCEPCION, a scouting party of 92 volunteers killed about 60 Mexicans, while losing only 1 man—the first colonist killed in the revolution. Bolstered by their victory, the volunteer army surrounded San Antonio and, hesitant to attack the superior enemy, settled in to wait. (See Siege and Battle of SAN ANTONIO for more.)

The TEXAS CONSULTATION OF DELEGATES convened on November 3, 1835, in San Felipe—without Stephen Austin who remained in San Antonio with his army. The primary issue facing these delegates was whether Texas would fight for independence from Mexico or remain loyal to Mexico and endeavor to restore the Mexican Constitution of 1824. A vote was taken — which became known as the DECLARATION OF NOVEMBER 7, 1835 — and it was decided that they would fight to restore the Mexican Constitution. The delegates then designed a vague constitution, and elected a TEXAS PROVISIONAL GOVERNMENT. Austin received word on November 18 that he had been relieved of command of the army to be part of a commission that would travel to the United States to seek aid. He departed on November 25. The commission was somewhat successful, although only about $150,000 in loans was procured, mostly from land speculators. Austin would return in June, 1836 after Texas had already gained its independence. (See TEXAS REVOLUTION for events between Austin's departure and return.)

## Republic of Texas

Perhaps Austin's position that called for restoration of the Mexican Constitution rather than seeking independence led to his "honorable exile" in the United States in behind the scenes politicking by the War Party. Regardless, that stance, in addition to his outspoken support for saving Santa Anna from execution and accusations that Austin had not served Texas to the best of his ability while in the United States, had affected his reputation during his absence. He returned to discover that his popularity had plummeted. He became a reluctant candidate in a three-way race for the first presidency of the Republic of Texas. The results: Sam Houston, 5,110 votes; provisional governor Henry SMITH, 743; and Stephen F. Austin, the man who had founded Texas and pro-

vided distinguished and unselfish service, received only 587 votes. Houston evidently respected Austin's skills and accomplishments, and made him secretary of state in his cabinet.

## Death

On Christmas Eve, 1836 Austin developed a severe chill, and died in Columbia, Texas on December 27, 1836 at the age of 43. His last words spoken from a coma: "Texas is recognized! Did you see it in the papers?" The announcement was made by Sam Houston, who said: "The father of Texas is no more. The first pioneer of the wilderness has departed. General Stephen F. Austin, Secretary of State, expired this day." The capital of Texas and a county were named in his honor.

**AUTRY, Micajah** (1794–March 6, 1836) Private, TENNESSEE MOUNTED VOLUNTEERS; Alamo defender from North Carolina. Autry departed Sampson County, North Carolina at age 18 to volunteer for duty in the War of 1812, and was wounded during that conflict. He left the service in 1815 and tried his hand at farming, but due to ill health became a teacher. In 1823, he began studying law in Hayesboro, Tennessee, and the following year married a widow, Martha Wilkinson. They had two children of their own, a boy and a girl, and raised Martha's daughter from her first marriage. Autry was admitted to the bar in 1829, and soon moved to Jackson, Tennessee where he practiced law, dabbled in a dry goods business, which went bankrupt, and became a slave owner. He was also said to have been a sensitive man — a poet, writer, singer and violinist, and artist. Autry heard about opportunities in Texas, and in 1835 boarded a steamboat in Nashville with others headed for the west. On January 14, 1836, Autry was sworn into service in Nacogdoches, and arrived in San Antonio on February 8. Autry was a rifleman in Capt. William B. HARRISON's company during the ALAMO SIEGE, and was killed in the ALAMO BATTLE.'His son, a colonel in the Confederate Army, was killed during the Civil War.

# B

**BADILLO, Juan A.** (aka "Antonio Padillo"; ?–March 6, 1836) Sergeant, SEGUIN'S CAVALRY COMPANY; Alamo defender from Texas. This native Texan fought in the Siege and Battle of SAN ANTONIO, and was killed in the ALAMO BATTLE.

**BAILEY, Peter James III** (1812–March 6, 1836) Private, TENNESSEE MOUNTED VOLUNTEERS; Alamo defender from Kentucky. This native of Springfield, Logan County, Kentucky, graduated with a degree in law from Transylvania University in 1834. He traveled to Texas in 1835 by way of Illinois, Missouri, Arkansas, and Louisiana where, with former classmate Daniel CLOUD, Bailey was seeking a new place to practice law, and arrived with fellow defenders William FONTLEROY, B. Archer M. THOMAS, and Joseph G. WASHINGTON. The five men enlisted with their small unit, which was under the command of Capt. William HARRISON, in Nacogdoches on January 14, 1836, and arrived in San Antonio on February 8. During the ALAMO SIEGE, Bailey was a rifleman defending the wooden palisade that ran from the chapel to the low barracks along the south wall of the ALAMO MISSION, and was serving in that capacity when killed in the ALAMO BATTLE. In addition to land awarded his heirs, Bailey County, Texas is named in honor of his sacrifice at the Alamo.

**BAKER, Isaac G.** (1804–March 6, 1836) Private, GONZALES RANGING COMPANY; Alamo defender from Arkansas. Baker arrived in Texas in 1830, and became a property owner in Dewitt's Colony. He entered the ALAMO MISSION with his unit on March 1, 1836, and was killed in the ALAMO BATTLE while serving as a rifleman.

**BAKER, Moseley** (Mosely) (September 20, 1802–November 4, 1848) Captain, TEXAS REVOLUTIONARY ARMY. This Virginia native and resident of San Felipe was an outspoken leader of the WAR PARTY that advocated Texas independence. His name was on the list of those agitators that Mexican dictator Antonio Lopez de SANTA ANNA ordered arrested in the summer of 1835, but Baker eluded capture. Baker participated in the Battle of GONZALES and in the so-called "Grass Fight" during the Siege and Battle of SAN ANTONIO. He officially entered the army on February 3, 1836, and was elected captain of his company. He accompanied Gen. Sam HOUSTON on what has become known as the "Runaway Scrape" in prelude to the Battle of SAN JACINTO. When this retreating procession finally arrived at San Felipe, Baker refused to retreat any further. Baker was ordered to burn San Felipe ahead of the advancing MEXICAN ARMY, and rejoined Houston after doing so. He participated in the Battle of San Jacinto where he was wounded. Baker became a planter and lawyer in Houston and Galveston, and was also involved in banking. He represented Austin County in the First Congress and Galveston County in the Third Congress. He was elected brigadier general in the army in 1839, and fought against Indians on the Brazos. In 1846, Baker became a Methodist minister, and died of yellow fever in Houston at the age of 46.

**BAKER, William Charles M.** (?–March 6, 1836) Captain, company commander, TEXAS REVOLUTIONARY ARMY; Alamo defender from Missouri. This resident of Mississippi came to Texas as a volunteer in late 1835, and participated in the Siege and Battle of SAN ANTONIO. He was serving as a company commander when he was killed in the ALAMO BATTLE.

**BALLENTINE, John J.** (aka "Voluntine" and "J. Ballentine"; ?–March 6, 1836) Private, TEXAS REVOLUTIONARY ARMY; Alamo defender from Pennsylvania. Ballentine, who had been living in Bastrop, Texas for several years, was an artilleryman with Capt. William CAREY's artillery company when he was killed in the ALAMO BATTLE.

**BALLENTINE, Richard W.** (aka "R. W. VALENTINE"; 1814–March 6, 1836) Private, TEXAS REVOLUTIONARY ARMY; Alamo defender from Scotland. Ballentine was a farm boy in Marengo County, Alabama when he volunteered for service in Texas. He arrived in January, 1836 aboard the schooner *Santiago* in the company of fellow defender Cleveland K. SIMMONS. He was serving as a rifleman when he was killed in the ALAMO BATTLE.

**BAUGH, John J.** (1803–March 6, 1836) Captain, adjutant staff officer, NEW ORLEANS GREYS; Alamo defender from Virginia. Baugh arrived in San Antonio on November 21, 1835, and was a 1st Lt. when he participated in the Siege and Battle of SAN ANTONIO. He was promoted to captain following that battle, and served as executive officer to Alamo garrison commander Col. J. C. NEILL and later to Col. William TRAVIS. On March 6, Baugh was officer of the day, and was the first one to hear the Mexican bugle and observe the assault that signaled the commencement of the ALAMO BATTLE. He sounded the alarm, and assumed command when Travis was killed. Baugh died while directing the last stand in the barracks.

**BAYLISS, Joseph** (1808–March 6, 1836) Private, TENNESSEE MOUNTED VOLUNTEERS; Alamo defender from Tennessee. Bayliss enlisted at Nacogdoches, Texas on January 14, 1836, arrived in San Antonio on February 8, and was serving as a rifleman with Capt. William HARRISON's company when he was killed during the ALAMO BATTLE.

**BAYLOR, John Walker, Jr.** (December, 1813–September 3, 1836) Private, TEXAS REVOLUTIONARY ARMY; Alamo COURIER from Woodlawn on Stone Creek, Bourbon Co., Kentucky. Baylor is notable for his participation in every major engagement of the TEXAS REVOLUTION. He was the son of a United States Army physician, and the grandson of the commander of Gen. George Washington's Life Guard. An appointment to the U.S. Military Academy at West Point in July, 1832 did not last long — he was dismissed after 7 months for a combination of disciplinary problems and class failures. Baylor then studied medicine under his father for 2 years, but left for Texas when his father died. On October 5, 1835, he volunteered for service to Texas under Capt. Philip DIMITT at Matagorda, and participated in the October 9, 1835 GOLIAD SKIRMISH, the Battle of CONCEPCION on October 28, and the Siege and Battle of SAN ANTONIO in November and December of that year. He was dispatched by Col. William TRAVIS as a courier to Goliad on February 25 during the ALAMO SIEGE, and for that reason was absent for the battle. Baylor remained in Goliad, and survived the Surrender and Massacre at GOLIAD because he was scouting ahead when those volunteers were captured and executed. He served in the 4th Company, 2nd Regiment of Texas Volunteers at the Battle of SAN JACINTO where he received a wound to the thigh that was thought to be minor. Following his participation in the seizure of three supply ships headed for the Mexican Army, he traveled to the home of his uncle in Alabama. He soon developed complications from the wound received at San Jacinto, and died.

**BEXAR, Siege and Battle of** See SAN ANTONIO, Siege and Battle of

**BLAIR, John** (1803–March 6, 1836) Private, TEXAS REVOLUTIONARY ARMY; Alamo defender from Tennessee. Little is known about this native Tennessean who was residing at Zavala's Colony, Texas, when he traveled to San Antonio and was killed during the ALAMO BATTLE.

**BLAIR, Samuel B.** (1807–March 6, 1836) Captain, TEXAS REVOLUTIONARY ARMY; Alamo defender from Tennessee. Blair was residing in McGloin's Colony, Texas, when he participated in the Siege and Battle of SAN ANTONIO. He was assistant to the ordnance chief—responsible for the maintenance of all the weapons—when he was killed in the ALAMO BATTLE.

**BLAZEBY, William** (1795–March 6, 1836) Captain, infantry company commanding officer, NEW ORLEANS GREYS; Alamo defender from England. Blazeby was living in New York when he volunteered for service in Texas. He arrived in San Antonio by way of New Orleans on November 21, 1835, and was a 2nd lieutenant while participating in the Siege and Battle of SAN ANTONIO. Blazeby was promoted to captain soon after that engagement, and was commanding an infantry company during the ALAMO BATTLE when he was killed.

**BONHAM, James Butler** (February 20, 1807–March 6, 1836) 2nd Lieutenant, MOBILE GREYS; Alamo defender from Edgefield County, South Carolina. It was perhaps inevitable that this fiery, chivalrous, born-rebellious Southern aristocrat would became part of the TEXAS REVOLUTION; he had a history of opposing any form of authority. His militancy began in 1824 when he was expelled from South Carolina College (later the University of South Carolina) for leading a student protest against the administration that he claimed was serving substandard food, forcing the students to attend class in poor weather, and for his opposition to the school's position on states' rights. Bonham then studied law, and in 1830 set up practice in Pendleton, South Carolina. Two years later, he was named colonel in command of an artillery company in Charleston, which was readied in preparation for secession and a declaration of war against the federal government during what was called the "Nullification Crisis"—another states' rights issue. His courtroom demeanor can be evidenced by his caning of an opposing lawyer whom Bonham claimed had insulted his lady client. When ordered by the judge to apologize for his actions, Bonham refused, threatened to yank on the judge's nose, and was sentenced to 90 days for contempt of court. His chivalry was rewarded by local ladies who visited him in his cell during his period of incarceration and brought food and fresh flowers. He subsequently moved his practice to Montgomery, Alabama. The lure of revolution in Texas—or perhaps at the request of William TRAVIS who had been a college classmate—called Bonham to New Mobile, Alabama, in the fall of 1835 where he helped organize the volunteer unit called the MOBILE GREYS, and was elected to take their resolution of support directly to Sam HOUSTON. Soon after entering Texas in November, 1835, Bonham wrote Houston offering his service without compensation, and was awarded a commission as 2nd lieutenant in the cavalry. He showed up at the ALAMO MISSION— in the company of James BOWIE— on January 19, 1836, and a week later was appointed to a committee charged with drafting a pre-amble and resolutions in support of Gover-nor Henry SMITH on behalf of the garrison. Bonham was an unsuccessful candidate when the San Antonio garrison elected candidates to represent them at the TEXAS CONSTITU-TIONAL CONVENTION. Prior to the ALAMO SIEGE, Col. Travis dispatched Bonham to seek aid and reinforcements from Col. James FANNIN in Goliad. Bonham returned to the Alamo empty-handed on February 23, the first day of the siege. He was dispatched once more to Goliad on February 27 with orders to stress the need for immediate assistance. On March 3, Bonham became the last man to enter the Alamo when he courageously slipped through Mexican lines. He could have forsaken a return and ridden east to seek reinforcements, and, if the Alamo was to fall soon as he might have suspected, would have been saved while on that justifiable mission. But Bonham was not the sort of man to run out on a commitment. Unfortunately, the word he brought from Goliad was bad news for the defenders — there would be no rein-forcements. Three days later in the ALAMO BATTLE, Bonham was killed beside the 12-pounders on the high platform of the church. The town of Bonham, Texas was named in his honor.

**BOURNE, Daniel** (1810–March 6, 1836) Private, TEXAS REVOLUTIONARY ARMY;

Alamo defender from England. Bourne had immigrated to Texas and settled in Gonza-les when he participated in the Siege and Battle of SAN ANTONIO. He was an artil-leryman with Capt. William CAREY's artil-lery company when he was killed in the ALAMO BATTLE.

**BOWIE, James** (1795–March 6, 1836) Colonel, TEXAS REVOLUTIONARY ARMY; co-commander of the Alamo garrison from Kentucky. Slave trader; plantation owner; land speculator. Bowie was just over 6 feet tall, weighed about 180 pounds, had a fair complexion, blue eyes, and reddish-brown hair.

### Birth and Early Years

Bowie's paternal grandfather and name-sake, James, along with 2 brothers emi-grated to America from Scotland — where their ancestry indicates a noble birth and can be traced back to Rob Roy — some time prior to the American Revolution. Two of the brothers settled in Maryland while James moved on to South Carolina where he was married and had 4 sons and a daughter — including a set of twins born in 1762, one of whom, Rezin, was the father of our sub-ject Jim Bowie. Rezin was a member of the famous Swamp Fox Francis Marion's hit-and-run dragoons during the Revolutionary War, and at the storming of Savannah was wounded — his hand nearly severed by a saber — and taken prisoner. His nurse dur-ing confinement was an educated, patriotic local young girl named Elve (also Elvy) Ap-Catesby Jones, the daughter of a Welsh emigrant. Rezin and Elve were married in 1782, and became the parents of ten chil-dren. Twin girls, Lavinia and Lavisia, died in infancy in 1783; David, who was said to have drowned in the Mississippi in his late teens, was born in 1784; John, 1785; Sarah,

1787; Mary, 1789; and Martha in 1791 were likely all born in Georgia, although the last 2 girls could have been born in Tennessee where the family moved somewhere between 1787 and 1793. Rezin Bowie, Jr., was born in Elliot Springs, Tennessee in 1793. The family moved to Logan Springs, Kentucky, soon after, and James was born in 1796 and Stephen in 1797. The year and place of Jim Bowie's birth has been variously noted as early as 1795 and as late as 1805 and the location in Burke County, Georgia as well as Elliot Springs, Tennessee and Logan Springs, Kentucky.

Bowie was about 6 years old when his family moved to Bushley Bayou, district of Rapides, Louisiana, which at the time was under Spanish rule. The children gained an education from both parents — Rezin taught cotton and sugar cane planting, cultivating, and harvesting, lumbering, animal husbandry, firearms, knives, hunting, and woodsmanship; and Elve, who had a "finishing school" education, schooled them in the basic subjects as well as lessons from the Bible. The boys also learned various outdoor techniques, such as how to shoot a bow and arrow, from the local Indians; and were fluent in the French and Spanish languages, which were commonly spoken in that area.

The remote wilderness area had little official law enforcement, and was a magnet for smugglers, slave runners, and others of dubious character. People were compelled to protect their land from squatters, and on one occasion Rezin happened to kill a man. He was subsequently arrested for manslaughter, and incarcerated. Elve, who was aware that the constable was an enemy of her husband, took matters into her own hands. In the company of a Black servant, she visited the wooden jail and demanded to see her husband. She was admitted, and, moments later, both Elve and Rezin emerged and held pistols pointed at the jailer. The Bowies made

their escape, and apparently nothing further came of the incident.

The family moved to Bayou Teche parish in 1809, and on to Opelousas Parish in 1812. Jim and his brother Rezin, Jr., soon became known as "those wild Bowie boys," in honor of their penchant for seeking danger and adventure. It has been said that the two engaged in such activities as breaking mustangs, trapping bear, roping wild deer, and even riding alligators. The latter "sport" evidently came about when Jim became furious after one of the fearsome reptiles had eaten his favorite hound. He reportedly leaped astride the huge alligator with his knife clamped between his teeth, and held on for dear life until finally stabbing the creature to death.

## Slave Trade and Land Speculation

Around 1814, Jim moved away from home, bought a small parcel of land in Bayou Boeuf in Rapides Parish, and made a meager living by sawing and selling lumber. Brother Rezin joined him in 1818 and the two discovered a more profitable endeavor — slave trading in order to accumulate capitol with which to get into land speculation. Bowie sold his land and sawmill in Bayou Boeuf, and was eventually introduced to the privateer Jean Lafitte who wined and dined the two brothers in lavish style. Lafitte made a business arrangement with the Bowies to smuggle slaves to his island stronghold. Brother John, who claimed to have participated, explained how their operation ran: "James, Rezin and myself fitted out some small boats at the mouth of the Calcasieu, and went into the trade on shares. Our plan of operation was as follows: We first purchased forty Negroes from Lafitte at the rate of one dollar per pound, or an average of $140 for each Negro; we brought them into the limits of the United States, delivered them to a custom-house officer, and became the informers (on) ourselves; the law gave the informer half of the value of the Negroes, which were put up and sold by the United States Marshall, and we became the purchasers of the Negroes, took half as our reward for informing, and obtained the Marshall's sale for forty Negroes, which entitled us to sell them within the United States." The legal sale of these $140 slaves brought about $1000 each, and the Bowies amassed $65,000 until their operation was closed down by Lafitte around 1819 — the year that their father, Rezin, Sr., died. Those profits were used to purchase land to establish plantations.

In the ensuing years, Bowie engaged in a number of entrepreneurial endeavors. He reportedly joined an army formed by FILIBUSTER James Long, a merchant from Natchez who was angered by the treaty in 1819 that verified Spain's claim to Texas. Long had established a civil government in Nacogdoches, Texas, and declared independence. While Long was attempting to recruit the aid of Jean Lafitte, his "government" was abolished by a visit from the Spanish army. Long subsequently took his army, which included Bowie and Ben MILAM, to La Bahia in 1821. Mexico had by then gained independence from Spain, and Long was arrested and later shot under mysterious circumstances while on parole in Mexico City. Bowie's actual role in this initial attempt to establish a Texas republic has not been documented.

Bowie returned home to go into land speculation, and became co-owner with brother Rezin in plantations in Arkansas and Louisiana. The brothers set up the first steam mill for grinding sugar in Louisiana. Evidence exists that some of Jim Bowie's land transactions may have been considered shady, and he therefore decided to retire from that business in that region.

## The Bowie Knife and Sandbar Fight

The famous knife which bears Bowie's name was most likely collectively created by Jim and Rezin, although at least one story of its origin points more towards Rezin as the inventor. Rezin apparently cut three fingers when butchering a heifer, and contracted with Louisiana blacksmith Jesse Cliffe to make a knife that he could hold more tightly. Rezin drew a sketch and supplied a file as material for the blade. There exists no accurate description of initial versions of this knife, because it apparently was made in various sizes and shapes and evolved over the years. The knife, as best as can be determined from later models, had more curve than usual on the blade near the point, was balanced for better throwing, and had a strong, protective guard between the blade and handle. This knife became famous and indelibly linked to Jim Bowie for his skillful use, particularly in what has become known as "The Sandbar Fight," a duel on a Mississippi River sandbar (see below). British manufacturers recognized the popularity of the knife, and mass produced the Bowie design in blade sizes varying from 9 to 18 inches and often used horn for a handle. The Bowie Knife quickly became a favorite with frontiersman across the American West. Another version of the knife that had a slender, more pointed blade was called the "Arkansas Toothpick."

The deaths of between 15 and 20 men in fights or duels have been attributed to Jim Bowie. That was not to imply that he was an indiscriminate killer, rather, on the untamed frontier, he was known as someone who would come to the aid of friends, vigorously defend himself, or simply attempt to bring about justice. Bowie was known as fearless, the possessor of an explosive temper, and someone who held a grudge against anyone who crossed him or his family.

The target of one such grudge was a

neighbor named Major Norris Wright. The two men were competitors in the land speculation business, and, among other things, Wright had prevented Jim from obtaining a loan from a bank on which Wright sat as a director. The two happened to meet on the street in Alexandra, Louisiana one day in 1826. Wright allegedly drew his pistol and fired. Legend has it that the bullet struck a silver dollar in Bowie's breast pocket to save his life. Bowie immediately drew his own pistol, and, when the weapon misfired, resorted to fists. He would have beaten Wright to death had not friends intervened. After this unexpected encounter, Bowie was urged by his brother to carry their custom-made knife as insurance against another misfiring pistol.

Bowie was acting as a second for a man named Samuel L. Wells who had arranged a duel against adversary Dr. Thomas H. Maddox on a small island, or sandbar, in the Mississippi River located opposite Natchez on September 19, 1827. One of the men in this group of seconds and supporters that had gathered happened to be Major Norris Wright, who sided with Maddox. Wells and Maddox proceeded to exchange two shots that missed their targets, and stepped forward to shake hands. At that point, one of Well's seconds, Gen. Samuel Cuney, decided to renew a dispute with Col. Robert A. Crain, one of Maddox's seconds. Bowie and Wright viewed that action as an opportunity for them to settle their own differences, and within moments what began as a duel between two men had become a minor battle as a number of the men fired their single-shot pistols at one another. Crain shot and killed Cuney, and wounded Bowie with a bullet through the hip. Bowie drew his knife and attacked Crain, who clubbed Bowie over the head with his pistol. Maddox attacked Bowie while he was down, and was thrown off just as Major Norris Wright

fired his pistol at Bowie then came forward wielding a sword. Bowie might have first shot at the charging Wright, which, if so, did not halt the other man's attack. Regardless, Bowie drew his custom-made knife and plunged it into Wright, killing him instantly. Bowie had been shot twice, once possibly after dispatching Wright. Two men, Wright and Crain, had been killed, and three others — Bowie included — had been seriously wounded. The Sandbar Fight became known as one of the most famous encounters on the frontier, and served to firmly establish Bowie's reputation throughout the region as a skilled fighter.

The stories about his prowess as a man who would fight at the drop of a hat are so numerous and outrageous that it is difficult to separate the tall tale, exaggeration and embellishment from fact. He was said to have fought with knives while his wrist was tied to that of his opponent, and another time when the buckskin breeches worn by he and his foe had been nailed to the log on which they were seated. He fought crooked gamblers on river boats and in taverns; assassins hired by rivals — once killing 3 at one time with his knife; and slashed a man whom he observed mistreating a slave on a plantation near Bayou Rapides. Not all engagements were fought with his famous knife. He shot John Lafitte, the son of his old partner in the slave trade, in a duel on a Mississippi riverboat. Other times, Bowie was said to have battled with bare knuckles — once thrashing a noted actor over a girl in a gambling house. Upon occasion, just the threat of Jim Bowie's wrath was enough to compel men to back out of duels or give this dangerous man a wide berth — to the point of leaving town.

It has been said, however difficult to believe, that Jim Bowie was in reality a charming, kind-hearted, generous man who never fought unless provoked or was protecting his friends or interests. He was considered a gentleman who was no more prone to violence than most men of that era in Louisiana — only perhaps he was more accomplished in its execution.

## Texas

The land speculation business had for all intents and purposes played out in Louisiana, Arkansas, and Mississippi, and, in early 1828, Bowie travelled to Texas in search of property to buy for himself and some of his associates. He bypassed east Texas and arrived in San Antonio de Bexar to discover that his legend had preceded him, and he was immediately accepted in the highest levels of Mexican society. One of these contacts was Don Juan Martin de Veramendi, the most important man in town who would soon become vice-governor of Coahuila and Texas and whose wife was a member of the prominent Navarro family. Veramendi was impressed with Bowie's charm and implied assets, and sponsored the American in 1828 for baptism into the Catholic faith and for citizenship in 1830. Evidently Veramendi's 18-year-old daughter, Ursula, was impressed with Bowie as well. The two were married in San Fernando Church on April 25, 1831, and honeymooned in New Orleans and Natchez. Bowie managed to gain full citizenship through an act of the legislature, which entitled him to buy nearly 50,000 acres of land at a nickel an acre. He also persuaded a number of Mexicans to exercise grants for land, and purchased the titles from them. In a relatively short time, Bowie had acquired about 750,000 acres of land in Texas.

Bowie had apparently searched for treasure in Mexico in the mid-1820's, and in November, 1831 renewed his interest by recruiting 11 men — including his brother Rezin — for an expedition to locate the lost San Saba silver mine. This legendary mine, located in the Guadalupe Mountains northwest of San Antonio, had been operated initially by the Lipan Indians, then by the Spanish who had worked it with Indian labor, and was finally repossessed by the Indians. It has been said that perhaps only one white man, an early 18th-century French-Canadian explorer named Louis Juchereau de St. Denis, had ever found the mine. He had allegedly extracted a fortune from it, but was eventually murdered by the Indians. It has been speculated that Bowie had obtained a map used by St. Denis, or had secured a map through his wife. Regardless of his methods, Bowie had within a week of searching discovered an old log house belonging to St. Denis and a rock that had St. Denis' name and the date, 1714, carved into it. At 8 A.M. on November 21, Bowie and his men were attacked by a superior force of about 160 Comanche Indians and forced to take refuge in a grove of tress. In a battle that lasted 14 hours in duration, Bowie and his men made a stand and reportedly killed about 50 Indians, wounded 35 others, while losing only 1 man killed and 3 wounded. Bowie made future trips to San Saba, carving his name on a gatepost at the St. Denis cabin in 1832, and there has been some speculation — but no proof — that he might have actually found the mine.

In a pre-revolution military action, the Texans revolted against a Mexican garrison at Nacogdoches which was under the tyrannical command of Col. José de las Piedras in 1832. Piedras maintained his allegiance to the old government and had not declared himself in favor of the MEXICAN CONSTITUTION OF 1824. The colonists decided to rid themselves of him, and attacked on July 31. Piedras sustained heavy casualties, and withdrew to the west, but was cut off by a 20-man cavalry detachment under the command of *Colonel* Jim Bowie — the honorary rank originating from his election as such in a Texas Ranger company. Piedras resigned his command and his replacement then surrendered 310 men to Bowie.

That same year, Bowie was said to have accompanied Stephen F. AUSTIN to the convention in San Felipe and later joined the company of Sam HOUSTON on a trip to San Antonio, where Bowie introduced Houston to his father-in-law. He also participated as a delegate in the 1833 convention, and later that year while a cholera epidemic was raging, Bowie returned east on business while his wife and in-laws were at their summer residence at Monclova, Coahuila. Bowie returned home to discover that Ursula and his in-laws had died of cholera within a few days of each other. Some accounts report that 2 Bowie children — a boy and a girl — also died, but the existence of children has never been confirmed. No baptismal record of children born to the Bowies exists in San Antonio, and in 1883 the Texas Supreme Court ruled that Ursula had died without leaving children. Some have pointed to the fact that Bowie's will, which had been drawn up on his 1833 trip and had excluded his wife, and the fact that within a year he had sued the Vermendi estate for property, are evidence that he was not exactly grief-stricken over the death of his wife. Most accounts, however, regard this tragedy as a tremendous shock to Jim Bowie, and that for the following 2 years he was rarely sober.

In the spring of 1835 Bowie was a land speculator, and for that reason was targeted for arrest by Mexican president Antonio Lopez de SANTA ANNA in a sweeping reform that included abolishing the corrupt government of Coahuila, which had been involved in dishonest land dealings. Gen. Martin Perfecto de CÓS and his army were dispatched for that purpose, and several land speculators, including Ben Milam, were arrested, but Bowie managed to elude capture.

He then became an outspoken proponent of revolution, warning that he believed that Santa Anna was preparing for an invasion of Texas.

### Texas Revolution

Bowie's first action in the Texas Revolution came at the Battle of CONCEPCION on October 28, 1835. Mexican Gen. Cós, under orders from Santa Anna to quell the rebel uprising, landed at Copano Bay in September with 400 men, and moved to join those 1,000 troops under Col. Domingo de Ugartecha garrisoned at the ALAMO MISSION in San Antonio. The 300–500-man TEXAS REVOLUTIONARY ARMY, commanded by Stephen F. AUSTIN, embarked on a quixotic quest to remove the Mexican Army. On October 27, Austin ordered Col. Bowie, along with the first division of Capt. James FANNIN's company, to reconnoiter the area around San Antonio. That night, the scouting party of 92 Texans camped south of San Antonio near Mission Purisima Concepcion de Acuna. At dawn on October 28, the fog lifted to reveal that Bowie and his men were surrounded by a force of about 400 Mexican army regulars who also had a 4-pounder cannon. Bowie distinguished himself as he directed his men in repulsing several assaults and finally routing the Mexicans into retreat. A total of 60 Mexicans were killed and about the same number wounded. Bowie lost only one man killed — the first for the volunteers in the revolution.

Bowie, however, was dissatisfied with his relatively unimportant assignments, and that his rank of colonel held no more distinction in the army than that of a private. Bowie resigned on two occasions, but his action was ignored by Austin. He was again disgruntled when Sam HOUSTON, who had been named commander in chief when Austin was sent to the United States on a recruitment mission, passed over Bowie for temporary commander of the troops during the Siege and Battle of SAN ANTONIO in favor of Col. Edward BURLESON. Bowie was placed in charge of a cavalry detachment, however, that chased down an approaching Mexican wagon train that was supposed to be carrying gold. In what has been called the "Grass Fight," Bowie captured the wagons but they contained only forage for the horses penned up inside the Alamo.

Following his participation in the Siege and Battle of San Antonio, Bowie travelled to San Felipe and apparently made an appeal — supported by Houston — for appointment to colonel. Some reports indicate he was successful; others indicate he was not. Regardless, Bowie was chosen to lead the MATAMOROS EXPEDITION, a direct assault into Mexico, but the orders were either rescinded or word failed to reach him before the operation, the leadership of which had been handed to Col. James Fannin, was eventually scuttled. Bowie was then ordered by Houston on January 17, 1836 to raise a company of volunteers and return to San Antonio to oversee the evacuation and demolition of the ALAMO MISSION, which was not considered capable of protecting that town with its present small garrison.

## The Alamo

On about January 19, 1836, Col. Jim Bowie rode into San Antonio in the company of 20–30 men — including James B. BONHAM. Bowie and the commander of the garrison, Col. James C. NEILL, discussed the orders calling for the destruction of the Alamo, and came to the joint conclusion that the mission should not be razed. In what some have termed disobedience of orders by Bowie, he wrote to Governor Henry SMITH on February 2: "The salvation of Texas depends on keeping Bexar [San An-

tonio] out of the hands of the enemy. It stands on the frontier picquet [sic] guard, and if it was in possession of Santa Anna, there is no stronghold from which to repel him in his march to the Sabine. Colonel Neill and myself have come to the conclusion that we will rather die in these ditches than give up to the enemy. The citizens deserve our patriotism, and the public safety demands our lives rather than evacuate this post to the enemy." Bowie requested that men and provisions be sent to San Antonio in order to hold this garrison together.

The conduct of Jim Bowie at the Alamo in the ensuing days has been widely reported in less than flattering terms. He allegedly was drunk much of the time, quarreled constantly with Col. Neill, and became a tyrant to those civilians residing in San Antonio. This behavior apparently escalated with the arrival of Lt. Col. William B. TRAVIS on February 3. Bowie and Travis had become acquainted the previous fall during the Siege and Battle of San Antonio. Bowie had been involved in much of the fighting, while Travis for the most part rode around the countryside setting fires to prevent the Mexicans from finding forage for their horses. Travis had become impatient with the siege, and avoided the battle — in which Bowie fought — by departing for San Felipe in early December. Travis then managed to convince the government to appoint him lieutenant colonel in the cavalry of the fledgling regular army. Bowie remained with the unsanctioned rank of colonel. On February 12, an election was held among the garrison to chose a commander. Bowie, who was extremely popular with the men, easily won. Col. Neill immediately found some excuse to leave — illness in his family has been cited — and rode out of the Alamo the day following the election. Neill apparently had designated Travis as his successor. Travis began firing off letters to San Felipe complaining about Bowie's highhandedness, drunkenness and general bad behavior. Bowie was said to have turned San Antonio into one giant party, a drunken orgy designed to demonstrate his power over both his men and the civilians to the point of martial law. He proceeded to free from jail Antonio FUENTES, a Mexican who was loyal to Texas. The judge in the matter, Capt. Juan SEGUIN, returned the prisoner to jail. Bowie protested by parading a group of drunken soldiers through town.

Other accounts contradict this harsh assessment of Bowie's behavior, and claim that he was not "roaring drunk all the time." Apparently Bowie and Travis managed to negotiate a tentative truce between them. On February 14, a letter was dispatched to Governor Smith that stated in part: "By an understanding of today Col. J. Bowie has the command of the volunteers of the garrison, and Col. W. B. Travis of the regulars and volunteer cavalry. All general orders and correspondence will henceforth be signed by both until Col. Neill's return."

This joint command was tested when on February 23 Santa Anna and his army approached San Antonio to begin the ALAMO SIEGE. Bowie immediately rushed to the Vermendi home in town and escorted his sisters-in-law, Juana ALSBURY and Gertrudis NAVARRO, to the safety of the Alamo. Santa Anna ordered that a red flag — the Mexican symbol for no mercy — be hoisted from the belfry of San Fernando Church. Travis, without consulting Bowie, fired the 18-pounder cannon. The cannonball fell harmlessly in town, but served as a message of defiance. Jim Bowie considered the impulsive action by Travis a waste of cannon shot and a threat to possible negotiation, and, without consulting Travis, dispatched a messenger, Green B. JAMESON, to town to explore an honorable truce. He had in his own manner of defiance ended his note with the salutation

"God and Texas" after crossing out "God and the Mexican Federation." This insult irritated Santa Anna to the extent that he directed his aide, Col. José Batres, to respond that there would be no terms other than unconditional surrender. One account suggests that Bowie's messenger was dispatched when the Mexican Army, either by accident or on purpose, raised a white flag requesting a parley. Travis was angered that Bowie would send a message signed only by Bowie without consulting his co-commander, and dispatched his own emissary, Albert MARTIN, who received more or less the same reply.

The feud between Travis and Bowie was settled in the wee hours of February 24 when Bowie became incapacitated. The precise diagnosis of the illness that rendered Bowie too weak to walk has been a matter of speculation — pneumonia, typhoid fever, typhoid-pneumonia, or tuberculosis, "hasty consumption" as it was called in its day, have all been blamed. Others claim that his drinking binge had caught up with him.

Bowie at that time surrendered his authority to Travis, and was carried to a small room in the low barracks where he was attended to by a *curandero* — a Mexican folk healer — named Andrea Castanon Ramirez Villanueva. Her services had possibly been requested by Bowie's Mexican relatives, or by Bowie himself. He would have been familiar with Mexican culture, and was likely comfortable with this woman who would combine medieval Spanish medicine, Native American remedies, and psychiatry — especially since the Americans doctors inside the Alamo had nothing available with which to treat him. Bowie was troubled, however, that he had assumed responsibility for his sisters-in-law and now could provide little protection. He beckoned Juana Alsbury to his bedside, and assured her by saying, "Sister, do not be afraid. I leave you with Colonel Travis, Colonel Crockett, and other friends. They are gentlemen, and will treat you kindly."

Bowie departed his room with assistance on several occasions during the siege to visit his relatives, but his illness grew progressively worse. On the evening of March 5 when Col. Travis drew his line in the dirt and requested those who wished to remain and fight to cross, Bowie was said to have been carried across on his cot.

### Death

Bowie was in his room propped up on his cot with pistols in each hand and others at his side said to have been provided by David CROCKETT when Mexican soldiers broke down the door during the ALAMO BATTLE on March 6. A ghost-white Bowie discharged his weapons and held off his enemy for a few moments, but was finally killed. The soldiers reportedly "tossed Bowie's body on their bayonets until his blood covered their clothes and dyed them red." Some accounts suggest that Bowie had already died by the time of the battle, but, taking into consideration his participation in crossing the line the previous night, he was likely alive to face his enemy.

His body was burned that afternoon with his comrades in a mass bonfire ordered by Santa Anna (see DISPOSITION OF ALAMO DEAD).

**BOWMAN, Jesse B.** (1785–March 6, 1836) Private, TEXAS REVOLUTIONARY ARMY; Alamo defender from Tennessee. Bowman was born in Tennessee, later moved to Illinois, and in 1824 became the first known settler of Camden in Ouachita County, Arkansas. He and his wife and three children moved to Hempstead, Arkansas in 1828. Bowman was awarded land in Red River County, Texas, during the 1830s, and moved there with his son (who also served

in the army during the TEXAS REVOLUTION), a brother, and several nephews. He was serving as a rifleman when he was killed in the ALAMO BATTLE.

**BROWN, George** (1801–March 6, 1836) Private, TEXAS REVOLUTIONARY ARMY; Alamo defender from England. This Englishman came to Texas from Yazoo, Mississippi, and was serving as a rifleman when he was killed in the ALAMO BATTLE.

**BROWN, James** (1800–March 6, 1836) Private, TEXAS REVOLUTIONARY ARMY; Alamo defender from Pennsylvania. Brown immigrated to DeLeon's Colony, Texas, from Pennsylvania in 1835, and participated in the Siege and Battle of SAN ANTONIO. He was serving as a rifleman when he was killed in the ALAMO BATTLE.

**BROWN, Robert** (1818–?) Private, TEXAS REVOLUTIONARY ARMY; Alamo COURIER residing in Texas. Brown, along with Charles DESPALLIER, brazenly dashed from the ALAMO MISSION on February 25, 1836 during the ALAMO SIEGE and set fire to shacks in the nearby slum called La Villita, which provided improved fields of fire for the defenders. He was dispatched as a courier around February 26, and later served in the SAN JACINTO campaign.

**BUCHANAN, James** (1813–March 6, 1836) Private, TEXAS REVOLUTIONARY ARMY; Alamo defender from Alabama. In 1834, Buchanan settled with his wife in Austin's Colony, Texas. He was serving as a rifleman when he was killed in the ALAMO BATTLE.

**BURLESON, Edward** (1793–December 26, 1851) Colonel, TEXAS REVOLUTIONARY ARMY. This native of Buncombe County,

North Carolina was raised in Tennessee and Alabama. In 1813, he married Sarah G. Owen in Madison County, Alabama, and the couple had 6 children. Burleson moved to Missouri and later Tennessee, serving in local militias in both places. He immigrated to Texas in 1830, and the following year received title to land in Stephen F. AUSTIN's second colony in present-day Bastrop County. He was a delegate from Bastrop to the convention at San Felipe in 1833. Burleson was elected colonel of Stephen Austin's regiment in October, 1835, and assumed command when Austin was sent as emissary to the United States on November 25 during the Siege and Battle of SAN ANTONIO. Burleson wanted his small force of perhaps 500 to storm the city and engage 1,400 MEXICAN ARMY troops commanded by Gen. Martin Perfecto de CÓS, but was overruled in a council of officers who voted to withdraw the volunteers to Gonzales. Many volunteers at that time returned to their homes until Ben MILAM took matters into his own hands, rallied the troops, and attacked San Antonio. Burleson, although for all practical purposes deposed as commander, managed to convince the men who had not accompanied Milam to remain in camp as a reserve force rather than leave. On December 10, Cós surrendered. Burleson then negotiated the terms of this surrender, and chose to accept a pledge from Cós to never again fight against Texas or the MEXICAN CONSTITUTION OF 1824. In return, Cós and his troops were released provided they return to Mexico. Burleson subsequently resigned that command, but was elected colonel of the 1st Regiment of Texas Volunteers on March 12, 1836, at Gonzales. He and his unit then joined commander in chief Sam HOUSTON on his "Runaway Scrape" retreat across Texas in prelude to their participation in the Battle of SAN JACINTO. Following that battle, Burleson and

scout Deaf SMITH carried the message from Gen. Antonio Lopez de SANTA ANNA to his troops at Fort Bend ordering them to leave Texas. Burleson was elected brigadier general of the militia, and colonel in the regular army in 1837. He served as a member of the House of Representatives from 1837-1838, and in the Senate from 1838-1839. Burleson was commander of the regular army in the 1839 Cherokee War, and formed a militia the following year to chase hostile Indians. He was elected vice-president of the Republic of Texas in 1841, and was a losing candidate for the presidency in 1844 against Dr. Anson Jones — 7,037 votes to 5,668. Burleson served as an aid to James Pinckney Henderson during the Mexican War. He was elected senator in 1846, and was serving as president pro tempore at the time of his 1851 death and burial in Austin at age 58. Burleson County, Texas was named in his honor.

**BURNET, David Gouverneur** (April 14, 1788–December 5, 1870) Lawyer; first president, of the Republic of Texas; vice-president, and secretary of state. This New Jersey native was the grandson of William Burnet, governor of New York and New Jersey (1720–1728), and the brother of Jacob who became a justice of the supreme court of Ohio and later United States Senator. At 17, Burnet worked as a clerk in a New York accounting firm. When that company went under in 1806 — taking his inheritance of $1,400 with it — he accepted a commission as a lieutenant and embarked on a failed expedition to free Venezuela from Spain in which Burnet commanded the launch that fired the first shot for South American independence. After a second expedition to Caracas in 1808 also resulted in failure, Burnet resided with his brothers in Ohio until establishing a trading post in Natchitoches,

Louisiana in 1817. He eventually left that business — possibly due to its failure or his developing tuberculosis — and went off to live in the upper-Colorado River region of Texas with the Comanche Indians, who were said to have nursed him back to health. From 1819 to about 1825, he practiced law and engaged in various businesses in Ohio, Louisiana, and Texas. Sometime during the summer of 1826 Burnet travelled to Saltillo, Mexico, and obtained an *EMPRESARIO* grant along with Lorenzo de ZAVALA and Joseph Velein to settle 300 families near Nacogdoches. With the assistance of Sam HOUSTON, the partnership transferred these rights to the Galveston Bay & Texas Land Company on October 16, 1830. On December 30 of that year, Burnet married Hannah Estis of New York, and settled on the San Jacinto River across from the Lynchberg ferry. Burnet was a delegate to the Texas convention in 1833, and distinguished himself by writing a petition proposing the separation of Texas from Coahuila. (Mexico later rejected the petition). He was appointed judge in San Felipe the following year, and served as a delegate from Liberty at the TEXAS CONSULTATION OF DELEGATES in November, 1835. Burnet was a member of the so-called PEACE PARTY and was hesitant to support rebellion, but was won over to the cause of independence when the MEXICAN ARMY invaded Texas in late 1835. He was a member of TEXAS CONSTITUTIONAL CONVENTION at Washington-on-the-Brazos in March, 1836, and was elected president *ad interim* of the fledgling Republic of Texas by a vote of 29 to 23 over Samuel P. Carlson. He immediately fled that city with his government from the advance of the Mexican soldiers. The president and his cabinet were attempting to escape when cavalry troops under Col. Juan ALMONTE caught up with them at New Washington. Burnet's small party, which included his wife, were frantically fleeing aboard a rowboat in Galveston Bay — well within rifle range — when Almonte ordered his men to hold their fire because there was a lady in the boat, thus sparing the Texas government. Burnet — as well as most officers and troops — was critical of army commander Sam Houston's "Runaway Scrape" in which he engaged in a humiliating retreat across Texas instead of fighting the Mexican Army. "Sir," Burnet wrote in a message to Houston delivered by Secretary of War Thomas RUSK, "the enemy are laughing you to scorn. You must fight them. You must retreat no farther. The country expects you to fight." Rusk at that time had the authority to replace Houston, but instead remained with this man that he came to admire. Houston, who in turn criticized Burnet and his government for itself running away, proved his strategy right by winning the Battle of SAN JACINTO. Houston considered Burnet a humorless man, and nicknamed him "Wetumpka," which he claimed was Cherokee for "hog thief." Burnet was perhaps envious of the personable Houston, and disapproved of the general's highhanded style. The Texas president distained profanity and alcohol, and was said to carry a pistol in one pocket and a Bible in the other. On May 14, following Houston's victorious battle, Burnet negotiated the Treaties of VELASCO with Mexican dictator Antonio Lopez de SANTA ANNA, which declared Texas independent of Mexico. Burnet came under fire for his determination to live up to the treaties, and, against the wishes of the army, spared the life of Santa Anna. There was a conspiracy to arrest Burnet, but he resisted any effort to remove him from office and be replaced with a military rule. He attempted to mollify the troops by replacing Houston with Gen. Thomas RUSK, and then Rusk with popular Mirabeau LAMAR. Burnet was critical of the volunteers who continued to arrive in Texas, calling them "mere leeches" and pointing to their 3-month enlistment as a sign of greed not sacrifice. He resigned the presidency on October 22 after the election of rival Sam Houston. In 1838, Burnet was elected vice-president, and later as acting secretary of state in the administration of Mirabeau Lamar. He assumed the presidency after Lamar's resignation in December, 1841. Burnet ran for the presidency in 1841 against Sam Houston, who remained an adversary, but was defeated 7,915 votes to 3,616. He had retired to his farm, but in 1846 and 1847 accepted the post of secretary of state under J. P. Henderson, the first governor after annexation by the United States. His wife died in 1858, and he lost his only son in a Civil War battle at Mobile in 1865. (Burnet had remained neutral about Texas's secession during the Civil War). Burnet was elected to the United States Senate in 1866, but not permitted to be seated because Texas was an unreconstructed former slave state. He retired to his farm in Galveston, and died there at age 82 in 1870. Burnet County, Texas, was named in his honor.

**BURNS, Samuel E.** (1810–March 6, 1836) Private, TEXAS REVOLUTIONARY ARMY; Alamo defender from Ireland. Burns was residing in Natchitoches, Louisiana when he volunteered for service, and was an artilleryman with Capt. William CAREY's artillery company when he was killed in the ALAMO BATTLE.

**BUTLER, George D.** (1813–March 6, 1836) Private, TEXAS REVOLUTIONARY ARMY; Alamo defender from Missouri. Butler came to Texas by way of New Orleans, and was serving as a rifleman when he was killed in the ALAMO BATTLE.

# C

**CAIN, John** (aka "Cane"; 1802–March 6, 1836) Private, TEXAS REVOLUTIONARY ARMY; Alamo defender from Pennsylvania. Cain participated in the Siege and Battle of SAN ANTONIO and was awarded a section of land for his service. He entered the ALAMO MISSION on March 1, 1836, during the ALAMO SIEGE with the relief force from Gonzales, Texas. Cain was an artilleryman with Capt. William CAREY's artillery company when he was killed in the ALAMO BATTLE.

**CAMPBELL, Robert** (1810–March 6, 1836) Lieutenant, TENNESSEE MOUNTED VOLUNTEERS; Alamo defender from Tennessee. Campbell was sworn into service in Nacogdoches on January 14, 1836, and arrived in San Antonio on February 8. He was an officer serving with Capt. William HARRISON's company when he was killed in the ALAMO BATTLE.

**CAREY, William R.** (1806–March 6, 1836) Captain, TEXAS REVOLUTIONARY ARMY; Alamo defender from Virginia. Carey arrived at Washington-on-the-Brazos, Texas, via New Orleans, Louisiana, on July 28, 1835. He participated in the GONZALES SKIRMISH, and soon after on October 28 was appointed second lieutenant. Carey was wounded during the Siege and Battle of SAN ANTONIO, and awarded a field promotion to first lieutenant. He was elected Captain of the artillery company he called "The Invincibles" on December 14, 1835, and was serving in that capacity when he was killed in the ALAMO BATTLE. One report states that it is possible that a slave owned by Carey also died at the Alamo.

**CASTRILLÓN, Manuel Fernandez** Major General, MEXICAN ARMY. This native Cuban, who had served with General Antonio Lopez de SANTA ANNA beginning in 1822, had been imprisoned following the president-general's failed 1832 coup attempt. It was for that reason that Castrillón, who was said to have taken the 1835-36 Texas campaign lightly — calling it a military review and wondering if the Texans would fire even one shot — became one of the most outspoken advisors against the mistreatment of prisoners. Santa Anna, however, chose to ignore the pleas of Castrillón and other officers and issued orders that all prisoners be executed. During the ALAMO SIEGE, this aging general was of the opinion that they should wait for the artillery to arrive before attacking the fortified Texans. His reasoning was again humanitarian — waiting would permit the cannons to decimate the Alamo walls and perhaps impel a surrender, thereby saving the lives of many Mexican soldiers who would die in a frontal assault. Santa Anna predictably refused to wait for the artillery, and Castrillón's concerns became reality. In the ALAMO BATTLE, Gen. Castrillón assumed command of one of the attacking columns when Col. Francisco Duque was wounded and trampled by his own men. According to stories circulated after the battle, Castrillón was the officer who accepted the surrender of a number of Alamo defenders — including David CROCKETT. Castrillón allegedly presented the prisoners to Santa Anna, and argued that they had fought bravely and for that reason their lives should be spared. Santa Anna subsequently executed Crockett and the others. (For an in-depth account of this controversial incident, please see CROCKETT, David.) Castrillón accompanied Santa Anna's force on its sweep eastward through Texas in prelude to the Battle of SAN JACINTO. Castrillón, who had voiced his opposition to the site of their camp, which he believed was vulnerable, was in his tent drinking champagne with a subordinate when the Texans attacked at 4:30 P.M. on April 21, 1836. He rushed from the tent and made a futile effort to control his panicked troops, then managed to fire the 12-pounder cannon several times. He was wounded in the leg and cornered upon an artillery ammunition crate behind the cannon. Castrillón glared at the Texans, and reportedly said, "I've been in 40 battles and never showed my back. I'm too old to do it now." Texas Secretary of War Thomas RUSK attempted to save the Mexican general's life by ordering the men not to shoot him — even going as far as to knock aside rifle barrels. While his commander, Santa Anna, and most of other staff officers ran for their lives, Castrillón refused to flee and was riddled with bullets by the blood-crazed volunteers. Two days later, Texas Vice-President Lorenzo de ZAVALA, an old friend of Castrillón from his career in Mexico, arrived on the battlefield and located the Mexican general's stripped body. He had his servants carry the body of Castrillón across the bayou to his ranch, and buried the general in the Zavala family plot.

**CLARK, Charles Henry** (?–March 6, 1836) Private, NEW ORLEANS GREYS; Alamo defender from Missouri. Clark arrived in Texas on November 21, 1835, and participated in the Siege and Battle of SAN ANTONIO. He was serving as a rifleman when he was killed in the ALAMO BATTLE.

**CLARK, M. B.** (?–March 6, 1836) Private, TEXAS REVOLUTIONARY ARMY; Alamo defender from Mississippi. Clark was serving as a rifleman when he was killed in the ALAMO BATTLE.

**CLOUD, Daniel William** (February 20, 1812–March 6, 1836) Private, TENNESSEE MOUNTED VOLUNTEERS; Alamo defender from Lexington, Kentucky. Cloud graduated from Transylvania University in 1834 with a law degree, and travelled to Texas in 1835 by way of Illinois, Missouri, Arkansas, and Louisiana where, with former classmate Peter BAILEY, he was seeking a new place to practice law. The two arrived in Texas with fellow defenders William FONTLEROY, B. Archer M. THOMAS, and Joseph G. WASHINGTON. The five men enlisted with their small unit, which was under the command of Capt. William HARRISON, in Nacogdoches on January 14, 1836, and arrived in San Antonio on February 8. At least one report identified Cloud as the sentry on duty in the belfry of the San Fernando Church in San Antonio who first spotted the approach of advance troops from the MEXICAN ARMY on February 23, 1836, the first day of the ALAMO SIEGE. Cloud was a rifleman defending the wooden palisade that ran from the chapel to the low barracks along the south wall of the ALAMO MISSION, and was serving in that capacity when killed in the ALAMO BATTLE.

**COCHRAN, Robert E.** (1810–March 6, 1836) Private, TEXAS REVOLUTIONARY ARMY; Alamo defender from either New Hampshire or New Jersey. Cochran had lived in Boston and New Orleans before settling in Brazoria, Texas, and participating in the Siege and Battle of SAN ANTONIO. He was serving as an artilleryman in Capt. William CAREY's company when he was killed in the ALAMO BATTLE.

**COLETO CREEK, Battle of** See GOLIAD, Surrender and Massacre at

**CONCEPCION, BATTLE OF** (October 28, 1835) Col. Jim BOWIE and his 92-man scouting party were attacked south of San Antonio by 400 Mexicans. In the ensuing battle, about 60 Mexicans were killed and likely that same number wounded — the remainder retreated. The Texans lost 1 man — the first casualty of the revolution.

### Chronology of the Texas Revolution

- June 29, 1835: Battle of ANAHUAC
- October 2, 1835: GONZALES SKIRMISH
- October 3, 1835: MEXICAN CONSTITUTION OF 1824 officially voided
- October 9, 1835: GOLIAD SKIRMISH
- **October 28, 1835: Battle of CONCEPCION**
- November 3, 1835: TEXAS CONSULTATION OF DELEGATES
- November–December, 1835: Siege and Battle of SAN ANTONIO
- January–February, 1836: The MATAMOROS EXPEDITION
- February 23–March 5, 1836: The ALAMO SIEGE
- March 1, 1836: TEXAS CONSTITUTIONAL CONVENTION
- March 2, 1836: TEXAS DECLARATION OF INDEPENDENCE
- March 6, 1836: The ALAMO BATTLE
- March 20–27, 1836: Surrender and Massacre at GOLIAD
- April 21, 1836: Battle of SAN JACINTO
- May 14, 1836: Treaties of VELASCO

Mexican Gen. Martin Perfecto de CÓS, under orders from Gen. Antonio Lopez de SANTA ANNA to quell the rebel uprising in Texas, landed at Copano Bay in September with 400 men and moved to join those 1,000 troops under Col. Domingo de Ugartecha already garrisoned at the ALAMO MISSION in San Antonio. The volunteer TEXAS REVOLUTIONARY ARMY, commanded by Stephen F. AUSTIN, embarked on a quixotic quest to remove the Mexican Army. On October 27, Austin ordered Col. Jim Bowie, along with the first division of Capt. James

FANNIN's company, to reconnoiter the area around San Antonio. That night, the scouting party of 92 Texans camped south of San Antonio near Mission Purisima Concepcion de Acuna. At dawn on October 28, the fog lifted to reveal that Bowie and his men were surrounded by a force of about 400 Mexican army regulars who also had a 4-pounder cannon. The Texans took refuge behind a bushy, tree-lined riverbank. At about 8 A.M. the Mexicans opened fire with small arms from their distant position. Bowie ordered that the men conserve their fire. One man would rise above the natural breastworks to shoot, then retired under cover to be replaced by another man while he reloaded. The Mexican rifleman, supported by cavalry, charged several times, but on each occasion were forced to retreat. The 4-pounder cannon was fired at least 5 times from a distance of about 80 yards. After about a half an hour, the Mexicans had failed to penetrate the accurate fire from the volunteer defensive position and executed a final retreat. The Texans seized the opportunity and charged to rout the fleeing Mexicans, then turned their cannon around and fired it at them. A total of 60 Mexicans were killed and about the same number wounded. Those wounded soldiers abandoned on the battlefield pleaded for mercy, which struck the volunteers as odd. The Mexican soldiers were evidently unaware of the practice of "civilized warfare," and were likely surprised that the volunteers did not finish them off. This example of mercy at Concepcion was later used by the Americans in their condemnation of Mexican brutality during the ALAMO BATTLE and the Surrender and Massacre at GOLIAD. One volunteer, Big Dick Andrews, was struck by a bullet and died, thereby earning himself the dubious distinction of being the first American casualty of the Texas Revolution — and the only volunteer killed or wounded in this battle.

**CÓS, Martin Perfecto de** (1800–1854) General, MEXICAN ARMY; brother-in-law of General Antonio Lopez de SANTA ANNA— married to Santa Anna's sister. Cós was described as standing 5 foot 9, with black eyes, a well-groomed mustache, long black sideburns, and a gold earring in each ear. This native of Veracruz joined the army in 1820, and was promoted to general in 1833. Cós was ordered by Santa Anna in April, 1835 to lead a regular army detachment to Saltillo, and break up the corrupt government, expel American settlers, and arrest those rebels who were stirring up the rebellion in Texas as well as those who were dishonestly selling land to undesirable Americans. Cós immediately suspended the government, and arrested the governor and many land speculators, including Ben MILAM. The Texans at this point in time were divided between war and peace, and most hoped to avoid a direct conflict with Mexico. In mid-1835, the Mexicans reopened the garrison and customs post at Anahuac, Texas, the legal port for Galveston Bay, with intentions to strictly enforce the collection of duties which previously had been handled corruptly. This unequal action caused protests by the Texans. Gen. Cós sent messages to the commander at Anahuac stating that civil government had been suspended, that Cós was now in charge, and assuring that reinforcements had been dispatched. These messages fell into the hands of the Texans, who decided that the Mexicans should be removed from the garrison in Anahuac before Gen. Cós arrived. Lawyer William B. TRAVIS assembled about 25 men and a six-pounder cannon, and on June 29 in the Battle of ANAHUAC forced the surrender of the garrison. Some Texans had second thoughts about the battle and sent letters of apology to Cós, but the general refused to be mollified and called for the arrest of the perpetrators.

Cós landed at Copano Bay in September with 400 men, and moved to join those troops under Col. Domingo de Ugartecha garrisoned at the ALAMO MISSION in San Antonio. These 1,400 troops set to work shoring up the walls and repairing the buildings. The news of this build-up of Mexican forces was a call to arms for the Americans who inhabited Texas and considered their futures jeopardized by the action. Some 500 Texas volunteers proceeded to surround San Antonio on October 29, and remained there until — led by Ben Milam — they finally attacked on December 5. On December 9, Cós raised the white flag to end the Siege and Battle of SAN ANTONIO. The following morning, a humiliated Gen. Cós agreed to turn over to the Texans all public property, money, arms and ammunition, and supplies in San Antonio, and promised to never fight against Texas again or to interfere with the restoration of the MEXICAN CONSTITUTION OF 1824. In return, Cós and his troops were permitted to retreat south of the Rio Grande River with arms and ammunition only sufficient enough to protect themselves against possible Indian attack. (The General Cós House, the location of the signing of surrender terms, has been preserved in San Antonio). Cós obeyed the terms of his parole until a rendezvous with Santa Anna on December 26 at Laredo. Santa Anna ordered that Cós violate his word, and turn his troops around and return to San Antonio with the rest of the army. Cós's troops were in poor condition from their ordeal and march south, and many of them soon died.

Gen. Cós was present at the February 23–March 6, 1836 ALAMO BATTLE and SIEGE. When the battle commenced, he commanded a column comprised of a battalion from Aldama and three companies from the San Luis contingent. That column attacked the west wall — facing the city — and sustained heavy casualties from small

arms and grapeshot artillery fire. His men panicked and broke formation in a confused mass to join with the other columns attempting to climb the north wall. Cós organized his troops and directed them back to the west side of the Alamo. When his troops had finally overrun the defenders and continued to randomly shoot, an act that was causing friendly casualties, Cós was unable to control his men and stop the devastating firing. It has been reported that following the battle, Cós made JOE, the slave owned by William Travis, identify his master. Cós then drew his sword and brutally mutilated the face and limbs of Travis.

At 9 A.M. on April 21, the day of the Battle of SAN JACINTO, Gen. Cós reported to Santa Anna's camp with 500–550 reinforcements. Cós's men were asleep when the Texans attacked, and were unprepared to fight. Cós fled on foot when the Mexican troops were routed, then swam the bayou and headed for the Brazos. He was captured late on the 23rd by scout Erastus "Deaf" SMITH close to Dr. Pleasant Rose's deserted farm near the Brazos. Cós, whose identity was unknown to Smith, was said to be carrying a fine china pitcher and an ear of corn. Smith told his captive that he had been looking for Gen. Cós who had once offered $1000 for Smith's head. Smith vowed to cut off Cós's head and send it to Mexico if he should happen to find the general. Cós was returned to San Jacinto, and, much to Smith's surprise, identified. Smith, however, took no action against his nemesis. Prisoner Cós was said to have been a popular sightseeing attraction for the Americans who were surprised that this famous, dapper general was just a "little scrub of a thing."

Following his release from captivity, Cós returned to Mexico and was defeated by the Federalists in the battle at Tampico in 1838 and at Tuxpan in 1839. In 1847, he fought the U.S. Army at Tuxpan. Cós later acted as a government leader for Tehuantepec, and died at age 54 in 1854.

**COTTLE, George Washington** "Wash" (1811–March 6, 1836) Private, GONZALES RANGING COMPANY; Alamo defender from Missouri. Cottle arrived in DeWitt's Colony, Texas from Hurricane Township, Lincoln County, Missouri on July 6, 1829. A marriage to his cousin in 1830 was annulled 11 months later, and he remarried in January, 1835. Cottle participated in the GONZALES SKIRMISH, October 2, 1835, and was a member of the relief force from Gonzales that entered the ALAMO MISSION on March 1, 1836. He was serving as a rifleman when he was killed along with his brother-in-law, Thomas J. JACKSON, in the ALAMO BATTLE.

**COURIERS DISPATCHED FROM THE ALAMO DURING THE SIEGE** A steady stream of couriers were dispatched from the ALAMO MISSION just before and during the ALAMO SIEGE. There has been some difficulty in documenting precise dates of departure and a complete roster of those Alamo defenders who served as couriers. It could be entirely conceivable that some names on the roll of those killed in the ALAMO BATTLE could have been captured and killed as they attempted to ride through the MEXICAN ARMY lines. This listing documents only those who were known to successfully escape from the Alamo to carry their messages. It also should be noted that some returned and were subsequently killed in the battle. The first courier worth mentioning would be 2nd Lt. James BONHAM who left the Alamo on or about February 16 to seek reinforcements and supplies from Col. James FANNIN at Goliad. Bonham returned on February 23, the first day of the siege. Pvt. Benjamin HIGHSMITH was also sent to Goliad somewhere around February 18 to ap-

peal for reinforcements. Capt. William PATTON was dispatched for the same purpose at an unknown date but likely just prior to the arrival of the MEXICAN ARMY troops on February 23. On that first day of the siege, Capt. Philip DIMMIT departed in the company of Lt. Benjamin F. NOBLES, and possibly Capt. Francis L. DESAUQUE, to reconnoiter the approach of the Mexicans. Dimmit met Dr. John SUTHERLAND who was being escorted by David CROCKETT to report to Col. William TRAVIS after observing the advance Mexican cavalry unit. Dimitt apparently told them that he did not believe the Alamo had enough men to adequately defend itself and he and his companions would ride to gather reinforcements. None of the three returned. Sutherland, accompanied by John W. SMITH, was sent later that day by Travis as a courier to Gonzales. He attempted to return but did not make it back before the Alamo had been overrun. There are indications that at the same time Sutherland departed, another courier, William P. JOHNSON, was sent by Travis to inform Col. Fannin at Goliad about the presence of the Mexicans. Sometime that same day, Lancelot SMITHER also rode to Gonzales to spread the alarm, possibly without orders to do so. Capt. Albert MARTIN, who had been an emissary from the Alamo to the Mexican forces in San Antonio that first day, carried Travis's famous "Victory or Death" message to Gonzales on February 24. Martin passed on the message to Lancelot Smither, who headed east to spread the news. Martin returned to the Alamo on March 1 with the GONZALES RANGING COMPANY and was killed in the battle. John W. BAYLOR, Jr., departed the Alamo for Goliad possibly on February 25, and did not return. He was executed the following month during the Surrender and Massacre at GOLIAD. After dark on the night of February 25, Capt. Juan SEGUIN and Pvt. Antonio CRUZ Y AROCHA, managed to sneak past Mexican check points by using their native language. Neither returned before the battle. Possibly on the 26th, privates Robert BROWN and Charles DESPALLIER, the two men who had brazenly set fire to the shacks at La Villita the previous day, separately departed the Alamo as couriers. Despallier returned on March 1 with the Gonzales Ranging Company, and was killed in the battle. James Bonham was dispatched once more to Goliad on February 27 with orders to stress the need for immediate assistance. Pvt. William OURY was said to have been dispatched on or about February 29 to plead for reinforcements. On March 3, Bonham became the last man to enter the Alamo when he courageously slipped through Mexican lines. Unfortunately, the word he brought from Goliad was bad news for the defenders — there would be no reinforcements. That same day, John W. Smith, who had departed the Alamo on the first day of the siege and returned with the Gonzales Ranging Company was dispatched. At some point during the Siege, Mexican Alexandro DE LA GARZA was dispatched, as well as Capt. Byrd LOCKHART and Private Andrew SOWELL who were sent to Gonzales to buy cattle and supplies but were unable to return before the battle. The last courier known to leave the Alamo was Pvt. James L. ALLEN who was able to make it safely through the Mexican perimeter on March 5 — one day prior to the battle.

**COURTMAN, Henry** (1808–March 6, 1836) Private, NEW ORLEANS GREYS; Alamo defender from Germany. Courtman travelled on a Pittsburgh steamboat to join the New Orleans Greys, and arrived in San Antonio on November 21, 1835 to participate in the Siege and Battle of SAN ANTONIO. He was serving as a rifleman when he was killed in the ALAMO BATTLE. His brother

was killed in the surrender and massacre at GOLIAD.

**CRAWFORD, Lemuel** (1814–March 6, 1836) Private, TEXAS REVOLUTIONARY ARMY; Alamo defender from South Carolina. Crawford was serving as an artilleryman in Capt. William CAREY's artillery company when he was killed in the ALAMO BATTLE.

**CROCKETT, David** (August 17, 1786–March 6, 1836) Private, TENNESSEE MOUNTED VOLUNTEERS; Alamo defender from Tennessee. Farmer; hunter; scout; frontiersman; militia colonel; justice of the peace; Tennessee state legislator; 3-term United States Congressman. Crockett stood nearly 6 feet tall, weighed about 190 pounds, had dark blue eyes, a clean-shaven, ruddy face with high cheekbones, and brown hair worn long. He was a generous man who possessed a good sense of humor, did not use profanity, and, although lacking in formal education, expressed himself without depending entirely on backwoods lingo. His common manner endeared him to his constituents and the public, but he refused to compromise his beliefs in the name of "politics," which eventually led to his downfall in that arena. He has been criticized for his frequent absences from his family as he pursued some adventure.

### Birth and Early Years

Crockett's family arrived in America in the late 18th–century by way of Scotland and Ireland, and settled in the New Rochelle, New York vicinity. This extended family then moved to the Pennsylvania-Maryland border, and in the ensuing years some stayed put while others travelled to North Carolina and on to Virginia in what is now present-day Rogersville, Hawkins County in the northeast corner of Tennessee. The family suffered numerous casualties at the hands of the Creek Indians—David's grandmother and grandfather were both murdered in 1777; an uncle was wounded; a brother and two uncles were captured, one uncle remaining captive for nearly 18 years until his freedom was purchased.

David Crockett was born in a wilderness cabin near Rogersville at the confluence of Limestone Creek and the Nolichucky River in Greene County on August 17, 1786, to John and Rebecca (Hawkins) Crockett — the 5th of 9 children that included 6 sons and 3 daughters born in that order. John Crockett was a former Revolutionary War soldier who had fought at King's Mountain, and his wife was a native of Joppa, Maryland. The family raised corn, hogs and cattle, and John served as constable of Greene County in 1783, 1785, and 1789. The Crocketts moved to nearby Cove Creek in 1794, and in an effort to improve their hardscrabble existence began operating a grist mill in partnership with another man until it was destroyed by a flash flood. In 1796, the year Tennessee joined the Union, John again moved his family and opened a 6-room tavern that catered almost exclusively to crude wagoners in Jefferson County, Tennessee on the road from Abingdon to Knoxville. In keeping with the custom of the day to pay debts or reduce mouths to feed, young David was hired out by his alcoholic, abusive father at age 12 to drive cattle 400 miles to Virginia for a man named Jacob Siler. At the end of the drive, David was coaxed into remaining with Siler as an indentured servant, but soon ran away and returned home. Crockett was enrolled in school the following autumn (1799), and within days got into an argument with an older boy. David waited in ambush for his bigger rival, and, in his words, "I pitched out from the bushes and set on him like a wild cat. I scratched his face all to flitter jig, and soon made him cry out for quarters in earnest." David skipped school for several days and was afraid of a whipping from both the schoolmaster and his father, so he fled home to join an older brother on a cattle drive. He subsequently worked at various menial tasks — in Baltimore he signed on as a cabin boy on a ship bound for London but before he could leave was forced to flee from a wagoner who held his money and possessions and threatened to beat Crockett if the boy refused to remain with him. It would be 3 years of odd jobs and wandering before he would return home in 1802 to hire himself out as a farmer to work off a couple of notes owed by his father.

*Marriage*

At 18, Crockett decided to make himself more acceptable to the young ladies and once more attended school. He soon started courting Margaret Elder, who promised to marry him. David purchased the marriage license on October 21, 1805, and called on her parents to formally ask for her hand. He was informed at that time that Margaret was planning to marry someone else the following day. Crockett endured a 9 month depression before meeting a young red-haired lady 2 years his junior named Mary "Polly" Finley (variously spelled Findley, Findlay, Finlay), the daughter of an Irish mother and Scotch-Irish father. According to Crockett: "I was plaguy well pleased with her from the word go. She had a good countenance, and was very pretty, and I was full bent on making an acquaintance with her." Polly had another suitor, one favored by her mother, but that did not stop Crockett from courting her. Finally, Polly agreed to marry him — her father consented but her mother objected. Undaunted, David purchased a marriage license on August 12, 1806, and set out with a group of relatives and friends to collect his bride-to-be. Polly's mother remained adamant against the marriage, and her father was obliged to block the gate. Following 2 days of negotiations, David Crockett and Polly Finley were married on August 16 at the Finley home and departed to celebrate at Crockett's tavern.

David rented some land near his parents, and began farming with the bride's dowry of 2 cows and 2 calves. Polly was an excellent weaver, and her spinning wheel and loom, in addition to David's day labor, provided a meager income. On July 10, 1807, Polly gave birth to John Wesley, and son William was born in 1809. Times were hard, however, and, around October, 1811, the family moved to the Mulberry fork of Elk River in Lincoln County in southern Tennessee. Crockett was a poor farmer, and turned to what he knew best to make a living. He hunted for food and pelts, and quickly gained the reputation as an excellent marksman — consistently winning top prizes at local shooting matches. In 1812, Margaret, who would be called "Polly," was born to the Crocketts. Soon after, the family moved to Indian country in Franklin County just above the Alabama line, and settled on the Rattlesnake Spring branch of Bean's Creek in a primitive cabin David named "Kentuck."

## The Creek Indian War

On September 24, 1813, after the massacre of 36 settlers at Fort Mims, Alabama, Crockett enlisted in the 2nd Regiment of the Tennessee Volunteer Mounted Rifleman for a period of 90 days to fight in the Creek War of 1813-1814 against the Creek Indian "Red Sticks"—so named for the color of their war clubs. He was assigned to scouting duty due to the reputation he had gained as a tracker, woodsman and hunter, and

chose as his companion a man named George Russell, who evidently was the model for the Walt Disney character of the same name. Crockett was initiated into the realities of war by participating in a bloody massacre in the Creek village of Tallussahatchee, Alabama on November 3, 1813. He had embarked with 11 others on a 65-mile reconnaissance that led them through several friendly Creek villages. One night, a runner arrived at his camp with the news that a large war party had crossed the Coosa River near Tallussahatchee, an Indian village, in prelude to attacking the army. The army proceeded to within 8 miles of that village when it encountered a small war party. The soldiers pursued, and drove the Indians back toward their village where many began to surrender. Forty-six warriors had taken refuge in a log house in the center of town. An Indian woman in the doorway fired an arrow from a bow held by her feet, and killed one of the volunteers. That woman was instantly struck by dozens of musket balls. The enraged army then refused to allow any further Indians to give up, and began a wholesale slaughter. The log cabin was set on fire, and those inside were burned to death. A total of 186 men, women, and children were killed and 80 captured. The Americans lost 5 men in the "battle." The following day, the soldiers were scavenging for food when they located a potato cellar beneath the burned lodge. The famished men had no choice but to eat the potatoes. Crockett said: "Hunger compelled us to eat them, though I had a little rather not, if I could have helped it, for the oil of the Indians we had burned up on the day before had run down on them, and they looked like they had been stewed with fat meat." According to official records, David Crockett was discharged on December 24, 1813.

Crockett reenlisted on September 28,

1814 as 3rd sergeant, and served throughout Florida and the south, gaining a great measure of popularity with his comrades in arms. But he eventually grew weary of army life and hired a substitute to complete his term of enlistment. His return to the farm in February, 1815 coincided with what he described as "the hardest trial which ever falls to the lot of a man." His wife, Polly, was gravely ill, and soon died of some unknown disease.

## Marriage and Politics

Crockett began courting a widow named Elizabeth Patton who lived in the vicinity of Rattlesnake Spring with her 2 children (George and Margaret Ann), and the two were married at her farm in the summer of 1815. Elizabeth gave birth to son Robert Patton in 1816, and daughters Elizabeth Jane, 1818; Rebeckah Elvira, 1819; and Matilda, 1821. The substantial dowry of land and cash acquired by this union later afforded Crockett the opportunity to pursue politics — ownership of a minimum of 200 acres of land was needed to qualify for admission to the state legislature. In late 1817, the family moved from Franklin County 80 miles west to Lawrence County at the headwaters of Shoal Creek — 3 miles from present-day Lawrenceburg. Crockett's parents as well as other relatives also made the move. David was informally chosen a magistrate, and later appointed justice of the peace, holding court in his cabin. He became town commissioner in 1818, and was also elected colonel of a local 57th Militia Regiment, which was maintained for protection against the Indians. By 1820, David and Elizabeth Crockett owned 614 acres of land, a gunpowder factory, a distillery, an iron-ore mine, and a water-powered gristmill. Crockett decided to run for a seat in the Tennessee State Legislature in 1821. By spinning comical folk

tales, which became his trademark style, and employing the motto "Be sure you are right, then go ahead," this common man endeared himself to the electorate and was elected by a two-to-one margin. He was occasionally mocked by the more "sophisticated" members of the legislature, but proved himself a champion of the disadvantaged by presenting land issues of interest to squatters and poor farmers. Crockett, however, was suddenly faced with bankruptcy when a flash flood destroyed his gristmill, distillery and powder factory. The family was forced to scramble financially to pay off creditors, but could never be considered destitute or even poor.

Crockett and his son, John Wesley, had explored the wilderness of northwest Tennessee in late 1821, and David decided the following year that it was time to leave Lawrence County. In early fall, the Crockett family, including his parents and some of his in-laws, settled on the east side of Rutherford's Fork, the southernmost branch of the Obion River. It was here that Crockett spent much of his time in the woods hunting — more for pleasure than necessity — while hired hands worked his farm. Wild game was abundant, and David established himself as a premier bear hunter — taking a total of 105 in one season. In 1823, Crockett ran for state legislature from his new home, and despite changing districts easily defeated 3 opponents to become the representative for 11 counties. Crockett made his first run for Congress in 1825, but his opposition to Andrew Jackson's nomination as a presidential candidate and of certain bills favored in western Tennessee played against him. This time even his engaging personality and tall tales could not save him — he was defeated 2,866 to 2,599 by incumbent Adam Alexander. David Crockett returned to the woods and his passion for bear hunting and the companionship of his hounds and drinking buddies.

In the fall of 1825, Crockett had the idea that he could get rich in the lumber business. While he spent his time hunting, a hired crew built 2 flatboats on which he planned to float his cargo of wooden barrel staves down the Obion to the Mississippi and on to market in New Orleans. Crockett and his inexperienced crew finally cast off in the summer of 1827 with 30,000 staves, and upon reaching the Mississippi discovered that the flatboats were overloaded. In an effort to remedy the problem, Crockett lashed the two boats together and became the captain of a runaway barge at the mercy of the current. Crews from nearby flatboats tried to inform them how to land, but, when that was unsuccessful, advised them to keep going on the main channel. That night, after surviving a rough stretch known as Devil's Elbow, Crockett attempted to land — with men waving lanterns on the shore to guide him — but failed. While Crockett retired to his cabin to warm himself by the fire, his craft had turned broadside to the current as it approached Memphis, an area of the river rife with mid-river islands and snags. Predictably, the flatboats hit a snag — an uprooted tree — and threatened to capsize the lumbering craft. Crockett made an effort to escape through the deck hatch, and when thwarted there tried to squeeze through an opening in the hull. As luck would have it, he was firmly stuck with only his arms and head clear. Crockett explained what happened at the last instant: "By a violent effort they (his crew) jerked me through; but I was in a pretty pickle when I got through. I had been sitting without any clothing over my shirt; this was torn off and I was literally skin'd like a rabbit." The men were stranded on a snag of downed timber while the flatboats and cargo continued on down the mighty Mississippi.

They were finally rescued by wealthy merchant Marcus Winchester, who fed and clothed them. Crockett, who was known in Memphis due to his service in the legislature, entertained locals that night with his amusing yarns and charming personality. Winchester took notice of Crockett's popularity, and promised financial support as he urged the failed riverboat captain and would-be timber tycoon to run for public office again.

### Crockett Goes to Washington

With influential men backing him — like Marcus Winchester, who had loaned him campaign costs — Crockett decided to run for the House of Representatives against 2 other candidates in 1827. He travelled throughout the district giving his trademark homespun speeches and campaigning in taverns and at farms, relying on the kindness of strangers for food and lodging. The results of the August election were Crockett, 5,868 votes; incumbent Adam Alexander, 3,646; and William Arnold, 2,417. Crockett had received 49 percent of the vote and was on his way to Washington to serve in the 20th Congress.

Crockett was by no means a statesman, and was frequently ridiculed for his backwoods manner. His bear hunting stories and imaginative language on the floor of Congress did, however, endear him to many who were amused by this conscientious representative from the wilderness of the west, and he was a welcome guest at dinner parties and other social gatherings. Perhaps the worst thing that can be said against him was that in a political climate that was inherently corrupt, David Crockett was honest, possessed with common sense, and was independent — if not frequently absent. He missed 30 roll call votes in the first session and 28 in the second. Crockett, in keeping with his personal agenda of fair land laws for squatters and farmers, introduced a land bill that would award each settler in the Western District 160 acres of land, but the House adjourned without taking action. And that became a trend in his career — he would campaign on a platform promising to fight for land rights, but in his 6 years in office would fail to get a single bill passed.

Crockett was reelected in 1829, receiving 64 percent of the vote — 6,773 to Adam Alexander's 3,641. Crockett had come to Washington as an ardent supporter of President Andrew Jackson, but then voted against a number of Jackson-supported issues, including an Indian Removal Bill in 1830 which would have uprooted tribes from their traditional lands. His star began to fall in Tennessee, but he was a growing celebrity nationally and in Washington. In April, 1831, a popular play by James Kirke Paulding titled *The Lion of the West* opened at the Park Theater in New York that had incorporated many of Crockett's tall tales. The main character of the comedy was Nimrod Wildfire, a crude, eccentric congressman from Kentucky who claimed to be "half-horse, half-alligator, a touch of airth-quake," who had the "prettiest sister, fastest horse, and ugliest dog in the deestrict." The play was so successful that it ran for 2 years then opened in London. It was from this play that Crockett was saddled with the enduring image of a man wearing a coonskin cap — Nimrod Wildfire wore a coonskin or bobcat-skin hat; Crockett never did.

The backlash from his opposition to Jackson, the native son who was an idol in Western Tennessee, was felt in scathing editorials in newspapers and spelled defeat for Crockett in the 1831 congressional election. William Fitzgerald won a close race 8,543 to 7,948. Crockett claimed that libel had been used against him and contested the results of the election, but his petition was tabled by the House Committee on Elections.

The campaign had eroded Crockett's finances, and he set to work restoring them. He also travelled extensively to cull favor with voters and his financial backers whom he asked to continue support for his planned run for office in 1833. In early 1833, a biography called the *Sketches and Eccentricities of Colonel David Crockett of West Tennessee*, was published. Crockett was said to have been offended by this characature that quoted him as bragging, "I'm that same David Crockett, fresh from the backwoods, half-horse, half-alligator, a little touched with snapping-turtle; can wade the Mississippi, leap the Ohio, ride upon a streak of lightening, and slip without a scratch down a honey locust; can whip my weight in wild cats — and if any gentleman pleases, for a ten dollar bill, he may throw in a panther — hug a bear too close for comfort, and eat any man alive opposed to Jackson." The book, however, served to enhance Crockett's popularity, but he was perhaps somewhat naive and bothered by rumors that it had been written as propaganda by a supporter of the Whig Party, which was said to have been courting him to run on that ticket — possibly for vice-president. The ploy may have worked. In the 1833 congressional election, Crockett received 3,985 votes to 3,812 for incumbent William Fitzgerald — a margin of only 173 votes, but enough to send him back to Washington.

During this term in office, he posed for five painted portraits. Four of these that had him wearing formal clothing — which was his normal attire around Washington — greatly displeased him, perhaps because, as he related, they made him look like "a sort of cross between a clean-shirted Member of Congress and a Methodist Preacher." He commissioned a 5th oil-painting, this one by John Gadsby Chapman, in which he wore his genuine backwoods clothing and added hunting dogs. This was the image Crockett wanted portrayed.

In March, 1834, Crockett published an autobiography, *A Narrative of the Life of David Crockett of the State of Tennessee*. This volume, a self-mocking satire, written in part to rebut his previous biography, was filled with his misadventures, backwoods philosophy, such as the rhyme — "I have this rule for others when I'm dead, Be always sure you're right Then Go Ahead." Crockett's work became an immediate best seller, and heightened his celebrity. He became more closely aligned with the Whigs at that time, and the following year that party published 2 books under Crockett's name: *Col. Crockett's Tour to the North and Down East*, which emphasized an anti–Jackson tour by Crockett the previous year; and *Life of Martin Van Buren*. The first of the "Crockett Alamanacs" was also published that year as well as the song "The Crockett Victory March."

This publicity may have served to keep him in high national standing, but his differences with President Jackson by favoring the use of Federal funds for internal improvements and the longheld belief that public lands should be at the disposal of settlers caused him to be a prime target by the president and his powerful allies. The results of the 1835 congressional election were Crockett 4,400 votes; his opponent Adam Huntsman, who was supported by Jackson, 4,652. Crockett lost by 252 votes. David had promised his constituents during the campaign that if elected he would "serve tham to the best of my ability; but if they did not, they can go to hell, and I would go to Texas."

### Texas and the Alamo

Crockett wrote to his brother-in-law on October 31, 1835: "I am on the eve of Start-ing to the Texas. On tomorrow morning myself, Abner Burgin and Lindsy K. Tinkle & our nephew William Patton from the Lower Country — this will make our company. We will go through Arkinsaw and I want to explore the Texas well before I return."

The *Niles Register* was perhaps prophetic when it reported that "Col. Crockett had proceeded to Texas — to end his days there."

The purpose for Crockett's journey to Texas was not by any means compelled by the call for volunteers to fight for Texas independence. He was actually seeking land and business opportunities, and likely more material for another book.

Crockett's party of adventure-seekers caroused their way down the Mississippi beginning on November 1, paused at Memphis, then headed west on the Arkansas River, arriving in Little Rock about November 12. A committee of Little Rock citizens, who had found him skinning a deer behind his hotel, feated him with a shooting match — which Crockett was said to have won by placing a second bullet in his first bull's eye — then treated him to a banquet. Crockett then moved southwest through the Red River Country, then south across the Sabine, and arrived in Nacogdoches, Texas about January 5 where a cannon salute was fired in his honor. He was hailed as a hero wherever he went, which must have been a tonic for his recent political defeat.

Crockett was a Pied Piper to the many men who were drifting around Nacogdoches. He also learned that by joining the army he would be entitled to a grant of land and could vote, which meant he would immediately qualify to run for office. He was sworn into military service on January 14, 1836, with about 17 new "friends" who would call themselves the TENNESSEE MOUNTED VOL-UNTEERS, although only about half of them came from that state — none with whom he had begun his journey. Following a few more honorary banquets, Crockett and his party headed for San Antonio where the ALAMO MISSION was located. Crockett was called "colonel" by these men with respect for his militia rank, but he was in truth merely another private in a company commanded by Capt. William B. HARRISON. The group, with a few men dropping out along the way, arrived in San Antonio on February 8, and a speech was demanded from Crockett, who gladly obliged. He did not disappoint his audience, and entertained them with his traditional backwoods anecdotes and concluded by declining any military status other than that of a "high private, in common with my fellow-citizens." A dance was held in his honor two nights later, and the whole town of San Antonio — Mexicans and Americans — joined in the festivities to officially welcome this legendary man whose presence instilled confidence in light of rumors that the MEXICAN ARMY was approaching Texas.

On the first day of the ALAMO SIEGE (February 23) Crockett, as a member of Capt. Harrison's company, was assigned the task of guarding San Antonio while the garrison fell back into the Alamo. Crockett and his company subsequently received the assignment of protecting the most exposed position in the entire fortress — the south stockade wall connecting the chapel and the low barracks. That night, he was provided an opportunity to display his legendary marksmanship. A Mexican soldier had approached the river beyond the Alamo's west wall, and was brought down by a shot from Crockett's rifle — the first casualty sustained by either side. On the third day of the siege, Mexican Gen. Antonio Lopez de SANTA ANNA ordered a frontal assault which was repulsed by the volunteers. Crockett was singled out for praise in a letter written by Col. William TRAVIS. "The Hon. David Crockett," the Alamo commander wrote, "was seen at all

points animating the men to do their duty." During the Course of the siege, Crockett entertained his companions with his tall tales, and engaged in loud fiddle duels with the bagpipes played by John MCGREGOR. As the siege wore on, however, he occasionally remarked that he would prefer to be killed out in the open rather than hemmed in. When the Mexican Army attacked on March 6, however, David Crockett was prepared to defend his position.

### Death

The most controversial and intriguing part of the Crockett biography centers around the circumstances of his death at the Alamo on March 6, 1836. The enduring image of Crockett's demise was created by Robert Jenkins Onderdonk in his 1903 painting that depicts Crockett using his flintlock rifle like a club to fend off an advancing wave of Mexican soldiers. This portrayal was further popularized by Walt Disney's television version of Fess Parker as Davy Crockett in a 1955 episode titled "Davy Crockett at the Alamo," and by John Wayne in the same role in the 1960 motion picture *The Alamo*. There was little question in the minds of generations that Crockett had gone down fighting bravely until overwhelmed by his enemy. That image, however, has been a matter of contention in recent years.

According to a number of Mexican Army eyewitnesses, six or seven rebels were rescued from the Alamo carnage by Gen. Manuel Fernandez CASTRILLÓN and delivered to Santa Anna shortly after the battle. The most controversial of these accounts was said to have been documented in a diary written by Lt. José Enrique de la Peña in September, 1836. This volume, *With Santa Anna in Texas: A Personal Narrative of the Revolution*, translated and edited by Carmen Perry, and published in 1975 (College Station: Texas A

& M Press), appears to propose serious questions concerning the circumstances surrounding Crockett's heroic death. De la Peña writes about the prisoners:

Some seven men had survived the general carnage and, under the protection of General Castrillón, they were brought before Santa Anna. Among them was one of great stature, well proportioned, with regular features, in whose face there was the imprint of adversity, but in whom one also noticed a degree of resignation and nobility that did him honor. He was the naturalist David Crockett, well known in North America for his unusual adventures, who had undertaken to explore the country and who, finding himself in Bejar (San Antonio) at the very moment of surprise, had taken refuge in the Alamo, fearing that his status as a foreigner might not be respected. Santa Anna answered Castrillón's intervention in Crockett's behalf with a gesture of indignation and, addressing himself to the sappers, the troops closest to him, ordered his execution. The commanders and officers were outraged at this action and did not support the order, hoping that once the fury of the moment had blown over these men would be spared; but several officers who were around the president and who, perhaps, had not been present during the moment of danger, became noteworthy by an infamous deed, surpassing the soldiers in cruelty. They thrust themselves forward, in order to flatter their commander, and with swords in hand, fell upon these unfortunate, defenseless men just as a tiger leaps upon his prey. Though tortured before they were killed, these unfortunates died without complaining and without humiliating themselves before their torturers. It was rumored that General RAMÍREZ Y SESMA was one of them; I will not bear witness to this, for though present, I turned away horrified in order not to witness such a barbarous scene.

Although almost immediately following the battle there had been rumors and newspaper reports of Crockett's surrender and execution, that one paragraph in de la Peña's diary in 1975 served to change history in the minds of many historians. Most scholars — some of whom have too often taken perverse pleasure in debunking heroes based on the thinnest shreds of evidence — were quick to rally around the premise that Crockett was not killed swinging his rifle like a club, fighting to the end, but was a coward who had abandoned his post to hide from his enemy only to be found and executed after begging for his life.

There exists, however, other relevant evidence that may not necessarily completely restore Crockett's reputation in some minds or definitively solve the mystery surrounding his death but clearly casts more than a shadow of doubt on the validity of the de la Peña account.

Reports indicate that among the seven Mexican soldiers who alleged to have witnessed Crockett's execution, several related that the prisoners were not slashed to death with swords but instead were killed by musket fire. It would stand to reason that a witness to such a heinous act would accurately recall whether the execution was carried out in a torturous fashion with swords or with a loud volley of muskets. Additionally, none of these Mexican eyewitnesses, including de la Peña, had ever before laid eyes on David Crockett (nor had Santa Anna), and would not have been able to identify him by sight. For argument's sake, suppose that small group of Alamo defenders had been captured. It would certainly be to the advantage of some clever rebel to assume the identity of a man who had only recently arrived in Texas — one who was a former United States Congressman who could perhaps argue for some sort of diplomatic courtesy if other stories failed to save him. Santa Anna, after all, was not particularly interested in going to war with the United States at that time. The execution of a dignitary from a foreign country could have serious implications. That premise may seem far-fetched, but within the ranks of the Alamo defenders were numerous lawyers, doctors, land speculators, merchants and other well-educated professionals (see ALAMO GARRISON for more). Crockett was known as an excellent spinner of yarns, but a desperate impostor — a lawyer for example — could conceivably have had the presence of mind and been glib enough to portray himself as the celebrity David Crockett in an effort to gain freedom. This theory can be found in another impostor story. This one was inspired by a letter dated February 6, 1840 written by a William C. White to the editor of a newspaper identified as "the Gazette," in which White claimed to have met a man in a Salinas mine near Guadalajara who identified himself as David Crockett. Congressman John Crockett, David's son, received the letter, and requested that the Secretary of State investigate. Apparently nothing substantial was uncovered, and it was presumed that this claimant was merely seeking notoriety to draw attention to his predicament. Another version of Crockett's death told by a Mexican soldier alleged that Crockett and William Travis both had fallen asleep in the midst of their dead comrades. Upon rising from their slumber, they were shot to death by personal order of Santa Anna. Other stories of escape and capture have appeared over the years to further confuse the issue.

One additional speculative notion with respect to combat survivors concerns the behavior of the Mexican troops while mopping up after the battle. These soldiers went berserk, and, in a killing frenzy, combed every nook and cranny of the Alamo for any Anglo and brutally killed them, often committing unspeakable atrocities upon their defenseless prey. They even killed all the helpless sick and wounded in the hospital, and attempted to harm the women until driven away by officers. When no Alamo defenders remained alive to kill, these sol-

diers made their way through the compound stabbing and re-stabbing the dead with their bayonets, firing their muskets into the corpses, and stripping and mutilating these bodies. The odds would be slight that in such an environment as that, 6 or 7 Americans could surrender and be taken to Santa Anna alive.

Other eyewitnesses included two Americans, a Mexican civilian official, a Mexican soldier who participated in the battle, and a young Mexican survivor from the Alamo, each of whom later stated that they had observed Crockett's dead body. One of these was Susannah DICKINSON, who, with the Mexican women and children, had been kept under guard in the chapel during the alleged execution of Crockett. These non-combatants were marched through a maze of dead bodies and presented to Santa Anna shortly after the battle. Susannah claimed that at that time she observed Crockett's dead body lying between the chapel and the barracks building, which had been his assigned defensive position. Susannah said, "I recognized Col. Crockett lying dead and mutilated between the church and the two story barrack building, and even remember seeing his peculiar cap by his side." Col. William Travis's slave, JOE, who also survived, said, "Crockett and a few of his friends were found together with twenty-four of the enemy dead around them." There can be no doubt that Susannah in particular would have been studying the face of each fallen defender she passed — likely with a sense of dread — in an effort to recognize that of her husband, Almeron. She would have known Crockett on sight from their 13 days together, having later remarked about his talent as a fiddle player. A Mexican soldier, Sergeant Felix Nunez, although not mentioning Crockett by name, reported in 1889: "He was a tall American of rather dark complexion and had on a long buckskin coat and a round cap without a bill, made out of fox skin with the long tail hanging down the back. This man apparently had a charmed life. Of the many soldiers who took deliberate aim at him and fired, not one ever hit him. On the contrary, he never missed a shot. He killed at least eight of our men, besides wounding several others. This being observed by a lieutenant who had come in over the wall, he sprang at him and dealt him a deadly blow with his sword, just above the right eye, which felled him to the ground, and in an instant he was pierced by not less than twenty bayonets." Another eyewitness, 12-year-old Enrique Esparza, son of Alamo defender Gregorio ESPARZA, who had been with the women and children, said in 1907: "He (Crockett) fought hand to hand. He clubbed his rifle when they closed in on him and knocked them down with its stock until he was overwhelmed by numbers and slain. He fought to his last breath." Francisco Antonio Ruiz, the acting *alcalde* (mayor) of San Antonio, was assigned the task of disposing of the Alamo dead—both Mexican and American. At one point, Santa Anna asked Ruiz to personally escort him through the carnage and point out the bodies of William Travis, Jim Bowie, *and* David Crockett. The testimony of this Mexican civilian differed only slightly from that of Dickinson and Joe when he recalled viewing Crockett's remains closer to the 18-pounder, which would have been farther to the west than the position designated by the other two.

Notable by its absence is documentation by the alleged perpetrator—General Antonio Lopez de Santa Anna. He certainly would have viewed the cowardice of another famous figure as an opportunity to elevate his own heroic status, and would have embellished a good story. Santa Anna's autobiography, however, makes no mention of the surrender and execution of Crockett or anyone else at the Alamo.

Perhaps the most contradictory piece of evidence, oddly enough, is the one that initiated the controversy in the first place—de la Peña's memoir. The "diary" was self-published in 1955 by Jesus Sanchez Garza, an antiques dealer in Mexico City under the title *La Rebelion de Texas—Manuscrito Inedito de 1836 por un Oficial de Santa Anna* (The Texas Revolution-Unpublished Manuscript of 1836 by one of Santa Anna's officers). This manuscript was purchased by John Peace, Chairman of the University of Texas Board of Regents, and was virtually unknown except by a few scholars until Carmen Perry, archivist and director of the Daughters of the Republic of Texas, translated and published it in 1975. From that year forth, nearly every book on the subject of Crockett or the Alamo has recorded de la Peña's version as fact.

Alamo scholar Bill Groneman, who has written a number of excellent books on the subject, had the opportunity to examine the original, handwritten de la Peña manuscript at the University of Texas at San Antonio. His findings were most interesting—in fact, enough for Groneman to label the memoir a fake and forgery. He discovered that, among other things, the document contained more than one person's handwriting; was written on at least 15 makes, kinds, and sizes of paper; contained errors of fact and used phrases that were common in later years; and included material from sources unknown at that point in time. In addition, it seemed that certain phrases in the de la Peña memoir bear striking resemblance to phrases in a book called *The Journal of Jean Lafitte* by John Andrechyne Laflin, which was published by a vanity press in 1958. The Lafitte book was proven to be a forgery. Charles Hamilton, a handwriting authority who included Laflin's forged work as a chapter in one of his books, viewed photocopies of de la Peña's "diary" and concluded that it was also likely written by John Laflin.

In spite of this evidence casting doubt about the authenticity of the de la Peña diary, the 700-page manuscript was sold at auction in Los Angeles in November, 1998 to two anonymous buyers who outbid the University of Texas by $50,000 and paid (with commissions) $387,000 for the privilege of owning what may or may not be a piece of history.

Common sense, however, should perhaps prevail with respect to the contradictory evidence. Consequently, until more definitive proof than simply the de la Peña diary can be presented, it should be assumed that David Crockett lived up to his legend and was killed fighting to the end beside his comrades somewhere near the south palisade.

Regardless of how he died, Crockett's body was burned along with those of the other Alamo defenders by order of Santa Anna in a giant bonfire on the afternoon of the battle (see DISPOSITION OF ALAMO DEAD for more). The town of Crockett, Texas, and Crockett County, Texas, were named in his honor in addition to two municipal parks; a national forest; the spring where the Tennessee Mounted Volunteers camped on their way to the Alamo; and a county museum. The Davy Crockett Monument stands in the Ozona, Texas city park. Tennessee has also memorialized its native son with a county named in his honor.

*The Legendary Crockett*

The fictional "Davy" Crockett has been the subject of countless books, plays, songbooks, almanacs, motion pictures, television shows — far too many to be completely documented in this volume. For further infor-mation please see *Davy Crockett: The Man, The Legend, the Legacy* by Michael A. Lofaro (Knoxville: University of Tennessee Press, 1985).

**CROSSMAN, Robert** (1810–March 6, 1836) Private, NEW ORLEANS GREYS; Alamo defender from Pennyslvania. Crossman arrived in Texas on November 21, 1835 as a member of the New Orleans Greys, and was wounded in the Siege and Battle of SAN ANTONIO. He was serving as a rifleman in Capt. William BLAZEBY's infantry company when he was killed in the ALAMO BATTLE.

**CRUZ Y AROCHA, Antonio** Private, orderly to Capt. Juan SEGUIN in SEGUIN'S CAVALRY COMPANY; Alamo COURIER from Texas. Cruz y Arocha participated in the Siege and Battle of SAN ANTONIO, then moved into the ALAMO MISSION on the first day of the ALAMO SIEGE. He accompanied Seguin when the captain was chosen on February 25, 1836 during the siege to deliver a message from Col. William TRAVIS requesting reinforcements. The two men left the Alamo on horseback and rode down the Gonzales road where they were soon challenged at a Mexican outpost. Seguin conversed with the Mexicans in his native tongue, then, seizing the opportunity, the two men raced away. The startled Mexicans fired at them, but missed their mark. Cruz y Arocha was a member of Seguin's company at the Battle of SAN JACINTO.

**CUMMINGS, David P.** (1809–March 6, 1836) Private, TEXAS REVOLUTIONARY ARMY; Alamo defender from Lewiston, Pennsylvania. Cummings's father was an acquaintance of Sam HOUSTON, and provided his son with a letter of introduction and a box of rifles which the younger Cummings presented after arriving in Texas in December, 1835 aboard a boat from New Orleans. Cummings proceeded to Gonzales and San Antonio where he became a member of the garrison in late January, 1836. He was out prospecting land on Cibolo Creek when the ALAMO SIEGE began, and entered the ALAMO MISSION with the GONZALES RANGING COMPANY on March 1, 1836. Cummings was serving as a rifleman when he was killed in the ALAMO BATTLE. His childhood friend and cousin by marriage, John REYNOLDS, was also an Alamo defender who perished.

**CUNNINGHAM, Robert** (October 18, 1804–March 6, 1836) Private, TEXAS REVOLUTIONARY ARMY; Alamo defender from Ontario County, New York. Cunningham moved with his family to Indiana and Kentucky before travelling to New Orleans in 1832 as a worker on a cargo flatboat. He immigrated to Texas in March, 1833, and owned one league of land at Skull Creek in Austin's Colony. He joined the army in 1835, and participated in the Siege and Battle of SAN ANTONIO. He was serving as an artilleryman in Capt. William CAREY's artillery company when he was killed in the ALAMO BATTLE.

# D

**DARST, Jacob C.** (aka "Durst or "Dust"; December 22, 1793–March 6, 1836) Private, GONZALES RANGING COMPANY; Alamo defender from Missouri. Darst, accompanied by his second wife and their two children, left their Woodford County, Missouri, farm and immigrated to DeWitt's Colony, Texas, in January, 1831 where he registered for land. He participated in the GONZALES SKIRMISH in September, 1835, and was one of the "Old Eighteen," named in honor of the original defenders of the town cannon. He entered the ALAMO MISSION with his unit on March 1, 1836, where he was killed while serving as a rifleman in the ALAMO BATTLE.

**DAVIS, John** (1811–March 6, 1836) Private, GONZALES RANGING COMPANY; Alamo defender from Kentucky. Davis immigrated from Kentucky to DeWitt's Colony, Texas and received title to land on the LaVaca Creek in late October, 1831. He subsequently gained a reputation for his Indian fighting ability. He entered the ALAMO MISSION with his unit on March 1, 1836 where he was killed while serving as a rifleman in the ALAMO BATTLE.

**DAY, Freeman H. K.** (1806–March 6, 1836) Private, TEXAS REVOLUTIONARY ARMY; Alamo defender from parts unknown. Day participated in the Siege and Battle of SAN ANTONIO, and was awarded a section of land for his service. He was serving as a rifleman with Capt. Robert WHITE's infantry company when he was killed in the ALAMO BATTLE.

**DAY, Jerry C.** (1816–March 6, 1836) Private, TEXAS REVOLUTIONARY ARMY; Alamo defender from Missouri. Day was residing near Gonzales, Texas, when he was killed while serving as a rifleman in the ALAMO BATTLE.

**DAYMON, Squire** (1808–March 6, 1836) Private, GONZALES RANGING COMPANY; Alamo defender from Tennessee. Daymon settled in Gonzales, Texas, and participated in the Siege and Battle of SAN ANTONIO. He returned to the ALAMO MISSION with his unit on March 1, 1836, and was an artilleryman in Capt. William CAREY's artillery company when he was killed in the ALAMO BATTLE.

**DEARDUFF, William** (?–March 6, 1836) Private, GONZALES RANGING COMPANY; Alamo defender from Tennessee. Dearduff settled in DeWitt's Colony, Texas on November 5, 1831, and was residing in Gonzales. He entered the ALAMO MISSION with his unit on March 1, 1836, and was serving as a rifleman when he was killed in the ALAMO BATTLE. His sister, Elizabeth, was married to fellow Alamo defender James GEORGE.

**DECLARATION OF NOVEMBER 7, 1835** This document, influenced by Stephen F. AUSTIN and adopted at the TEXAS CONSULTATION OF DELEGATES (1835), proclaimed the Texans' opposition to the military dictatorship of Antonio Lopez de SANTA ANNA and pledged loyalty to the MEXICAN CONSTITUTION OF 1824.

The preamble and first article read:

DECLARATION OF THE PEOPLE
OF TEXAS
IN GENERAL CONVENTION
ASSEMBLED.

*Whereas*, General Antonio Lopez de Santa Anna and other Military Chieftans have by force of arms, overthrown the Federal Institutions of Mexico, and dissolved the Social Compact which existed between Texas and the other Members of the Mexican Confederacy — Now, the good People of Texas, availing themselves of their natural rights,

SOLEMNLY DECLARE

1st. That they have taken up arms in defense of their rights and Liberties, which were threatened by the encroachments of military despots, and in defense of the Republican Principles of the Federal (Mexican) Constitution of eighteen hundred and twenty-four.

The Texans designed the fifth article with the politically unstable Mexican government in mind. It reads:

5th. That they hold it to be their right, during the disorganization of the Federal System and the reign of despotism, to withdraw from the Union, to establish an independent government, or to adopt such measures as they may deem best calculated to protect their rights and liberties; but that they will continue faithful to the Mexican Government so long as that nation is governed by the Constitution and Laws that were formed for the government of the Political Association.

In other words, Texas would gladly remain a state of Mexico if the Federalists were in power, and the document would serve as a declaration of independence should Santa Anna's Centralist government prevail, which later was the result. The Declaration was translated, and widely distributed to Mexican communities to encourage their support.

**DE LA GARZA, Alexandro** Private, SEGUIN'S CAVALRY COMPANY; Alamo COURIER from Texas. This native Mexican participated in the Siege and Battle of SAN ANTONIO, and, according to Capt. Juan SEGUIN, was dispatched as a courier sometime during the ALAMO SIEGE.

**DENNISON, Stephen** (1812–March 6, 1836) Private, NEW ORLEANS GREYS; Alamo defender from either England or Ireland. Dennison immigrated from Kentucky to New Orleans, and arrived in Texas with his unit on November 21, 1835. He participated in the Siege and Battle of SAN ANTONIO, and was serving as a rifleman in Capt. William BLAZEBY's infantry company when he was killed in the ALAMO BATTLE.

**DESAUQUE, Francis L.** (?–March 27, 1836) Captain, TEXAS REVOLUTIONARY ARMY; Alamo COURIER from Pennsylvania. This merchant from Philadelphia had immigrated to Texas in 1835, and soon after joined the army. DeSauque was in San Antonio just prior to the ALAMO SIEGE, and, after loaning $200 to Col. William TRAVIS for garrison supplies, was dispatched as a courier to Goliad. He was on his way back to San Antonio when word of the ALAMO SIEGE reached him, and he returned to Goliad. He was taken prisoner during the Surrender and Massacre at GOLIAD, and subsequently executed.

**DESPALLIER, Charles** (1812–March 6, 1836) Private, TEXAS REVOLUTIONARY ARMY; Alamo COURIER and defender from Louisiana. Despallier departed Rapides Parish, Louisiana, for Texas soon after his brother Phillipe, who had been wounded in the Siege and Battle of SAN ANTONIO, had returned home. He joined the army, and arrived in San Antonio in mid–February, 1836. Despallier, along with Robert BROWN, brazenly dashed from the ALAMO MISSION on February 25 during the ALAMO SIEGE and set fire to shacks in the nearby slum of La Villita, which provided improved fields of fire for the defenders. He was dispatched as a courier on February 26, but returned March 1 with the GONZALES RANGING COMPANY and was killed while serving as a rifleman in the ALAMO BATTLE.

**DEWALL, Lewis** (aka "Duel" and "Dewell"; 1812–March 6, 1836) Private, TEXAS REVOLUTIONARY ARMY; Alamo defender from New York. This boatman from Manhattan immigrated to Vehlein's Colony on Harmon Creek, Texas in October, 1835 where he worked as either a blacksmith or mason. He participated in the Siege and Battle of SAN ANTONIO, and was serving as a rifleman with Capt. Robert WHITE's infantry company when he was killed in the ALAMO BATTLE.

**DICKINSON, Almeron** (aka "Dickerson" and "Dickenson"; 1810–March 6, 1836) Captain, TEXAS REVOLUTIONARY ARMY; Alamo defender from Hardeman County, Tennessee. (There has been some confusion about the correct spelling of this family name of Almeron, Angelina, and Susannah Dickinson, and to date no definitive verification has been found. His name was reportedly spelled "Dickinson" on his marriage certificate and application for headright land. Therefore, his name and that of his family will be spelled as such in this and related entries.) Dickinson and his wife of two years, Susannah (see DICKINSON, Susannah Arabella), immigrated from Tennessee to DeWitt's Colony, Texas in February, 1831. He opened a blacksmith shop in Gonzales, and entered into a partnership with George KIMBELL in a hat factory. A daughter, Angelina E. DICKINSON, was born in December, 1834. Dickinson was the individual who personally touched off the initial armed confrontation of the Revolution, which became known as the "First Shot of the TEXAS REVOLUTION." He was a member of the original "Old Eighteen," defenders from Gonzales, who refused to turn over their town cannon to the Mexican Army. Dickinson had modified the cannon, and fired the 6-pounder at a detachment of Mexican troops during the GONZALES SKIRMISH. He served in the Siege and Battle of SAN ANTONIO, and soon after moved his wife and daughter into a house in that town due to the threat of rampaging white mercenaries in his hometown of Gonzales (see ATROCITIES for more). On the first day of the ALAMO SIEGE (February 23, 1836), Dickinson escorted his family from town into the ALAMO MISSION where he commanded an artillery company. On February 25, when the Mexican Army executed a frontal assault, Dickinson had his cannons open up with canister and grapeshot to effectively halt the charge. In the final moments of the ALAMO BATTLE, Dickinson dashed to the chapel where his wife and daughter were hiding. He was said to have cried, "Great God, Sue! The Mexicans are inside our walls! All is lost! If they spare you, save my child!" He hastily hugged his child and kissed his wife good-bye, and returned to the battle. Dickinson was killed beside his cannon in the rear of the Alamo chapel. Susannah and Angelina were spared.

**DICKINSON, Angelina Elizabeth** (December 14, 1834–1871) "The Babe of the Alamo" was the infant daughter of Almeron and Susannah DICKINSON, and an Alamo survivor. Angelina and her mother were brought by Almeron to the ALAMO MISSION on the first day of the ALAMO SIEGE. Prior to the ALAMO BATTLE, Col. William TRAVIS visited the child and her mother. In a gesture meant for luck or simply to be remembered by some memento, he tied a string through his gold ring with the cat's-eye stone and placed it around Angelina's neck. The ring is on display at the Alamo. During the Alamo Battle, Angelina and her mother, along with the other women and children, were hidden in the Alamo chapel. Their lives were spared. Following the battle the two surviving Dickinsons were presented to Mexican General Antonio Lopez de SANTA ANNA, who was instantly struck by the beauty of the 15-month-old girl. The Mexican dictator, whose soldiers had just killed Angelina's father, said through an interpreter that he wanted to adopt the child and take her to Mexico where he would raise her like a princess. Susannah refused, and with the intervention of the interpreter, thought to

be Col. Juan ALMONTE, Santa Anna finally was persuaded to give up the notion. Angelina married at age 16, bore three children, divorced, and became a prostitute — a camp follower of Confederate troops during the Civil War. She married again in 1864, and died seven years later of a hemorrhaging uterus.

**DICKINSON, Susannah Arabella** (1814 or 1815–October 7, 1883) This wife of Almeron DICKINSON and mother of Angelina DICKINSON was the sole white woman inside the ALAMO MISSION during the ALAMO SIEGE and BATTLE. Susannah married Almeron on May 24, 1829 — when she was about 15 years of age — and the couple immigrated from Tennessee to DeWitt's Colony, Texas in February, 1831. Her husband opened a blacksmith shop in Gonzales and entered into a partnership with George KIMBELL in a hat factory. She gave birth to her daughter, Angelina, in December, 1834. While Almeron participated in the Siege and Battle of SAN ANTONIO in the fall of 1835, Susannah and her child were threatened by white mercenaries who were rampaging through the countryside and terrorizing women. She asked Launcelot SMITHER to accompany her home for protection. He agreed, and was subsequently dragged into the street and severely beaten (see ATROCITIES for more). For that reason, Susannah and her daughter traveled to join Almeron and settled into a house in San Antonio. On the first day of the Alamo siege (February 23, 1836), Susannah and Angelina were escorted to safety inside the ALAMO MISSION by Almeron, who was an artillery captain. In the final stages of the Alamo battle, her husband rushed to her side, and was said to have cried, "Great God, Sue! The Mexicans are inside our walls! All is lost! If they spare you, save my child!" He kissed her good-bye, and rushed back to his position in the rear of the chapel where he was killed. Susannah was witness to many horrible deaths as the Mexican soldiers closed in on the defenders, but, although wounded by an errant gunshot to the right calf, she and Angelina were spared by a Mexican officer who drove away his men to save them. She claimed to have seen the dead body of David CROCKETT lying between the chapel and the two-story barracks building, which contradicts later testimony from Mexican soldiers that Crockett had been taken alive and subsequently executed (see CROCKETT, David for more). Following the battle, Susannah and her daughter were presented to Mexican General Antonio Lopez de SANTA ANNA, who was instantly struck by the beauty of the 15-month-old girl. The Mexican dictator said through an interpreter that he wanted to adopt the child and take her to Mexico where he would raise her like a princess. Susannah refused, and with the intervention of the interpreter, thought to be Col. Juan ALMONTE, Santa Anna was finally persuaded to give up the notion. Santa Anna gave the grieving widow two pesos and a blanket, and she was dismissed — possibly in the company of JOE, the slave owned by Col. William TRAVIS — and departed on the road to Gonzales. Sam HOUSTON had dispatched scouts from Gonzales to confirm the Alamo defeat. These scouts found Susannah along the road on March 13, and escorted her to Gonzales where she recounted the particulars of the tragedy. She also informed them that a detachment of 700 Mexican troops under Gen. Joaquín RAMÍREZ Y SESMA was on its way to Gonzales — pillaging the countryside as he went — information that compelled Houston to move his small army east. Susannah married 4 more times in the ensuing years — divorced twice and widowed once. Her fourth husband successfully charged her in 1857 with adultery, desertion, and

living in a "house of ill fame" in Houston, Texas. She moved later that year to Lockhart, Texas with her fifth husband, Joseph W. Hanning, a German immigrant, and ran a boardinghouse. Susannah and her husband relocated to Austin in the 1870's, and reportedly did quite well in real estate and other business ventures. She died in Austin at age 68, and was buried in Oakwood Cemetery.

**DILLARD, John Henry** (1805–March 6, 1836) Private, TEXAS REVOLUTIONARY ARMY; Alamo defender from Tennessee. Dillard immigrated from Smith County, Tennessee to Nashville-on-the-Brazos, Texas, and was serving as a rifleman when he was killed in the ALAMO BATTLE.

**DIMITT, Philip** (aka "Dimmitt"; 1801– July 8, 1841) Captain, TEXAS REVOLUTIONARY ARMY; Alamo survivor from Kentucky. Dimitt arrived in Texas in 1822, married a Mexican woman, and set up a trading post called Dimitt's Landing in the LaVaca Bay area. He participated in the GOLIAD SKIRMISH, and afterward became commander of volunteers in that town. At that time, he designed a flag utilizing the Mexican tri-colors and the inscription "1824" in reference to the year the MEXICAN CONSTITUTION was adopted that tradition has it was of the type that flew over the ALAMO MISSION. He participated in the Siege and Battle of SAN ANTONIO. In January, 1836, at the urging of Sam HOUSTON, Dimitt formed a company of volunteer troops and marched to San Antonio. He departed that town on the first day of the ALAMO SIEGE with intentions of reconnoitering the enemy. His plans changed when he encountered David CROCKETT and Dr. John SUTHERLAND on the doctor's return after discovering Mexican troops. Dimitt stated that he did not believe there were enough men to hold the fort and therefore he was going to fetch reinforcements. He never returned, and spent the remainder of the war commanding a company of volunteers. Dimitt began work on a new trading post in Corpus Cristi Bay, and on July 4, 1841, he and his workers were taken prisoner by Mexicans. His workers managed to escape, but Dimitt was held in a Saltillo, Mexico prison where he reportedly committed suicide by overdosing on morphine in order to avoid execution.

**DIMPKINS, James R.** (aka "Dickens"; "Dimkins"; "Dinkin"; and "Dockon"; ?–March 6, 1836) Sergeant, NEW ORLEANS GREYS; Alamo defender from England. Dimpkins arrived in Texas on November 21, 1835 by way of New Orleans, and participated in the Siege and Battle of SAN ANTONIO. He was serving as a noncommissioned officer in Capt. William BLAZEBY's infantry company when he was killed in the ALAMO BATTLE.

**DISPOSITION OF ALAMO DEAD** Immediately following the ALAMO BATTLE, victorious Mexican General Antonio Lopez de SANTA ANNA summoned Francisco Ruiz, the *alcalde* (mayor) of San Antonio, and ordered that he dispose of the dead. Ruiz dispatched some local men to obtain ox carts for the purpose, while he — at the request of Santa Anna — reportedly escorted the president-general around the compound to point out the bodies of Alamo defenders James BOWIE, David CROCKETT, and William TRAVIS. At that time, Santa Anna decided that the dead Mexican soldiers, whose number was perhaps as high as 600, would be given a Christian burial in the Campo Santo Cementerio. The anglo–Americans would be cremated on three pyres — a final insult by denying them a Christian burial. Ruiz

was provided soldiers to cut wood for his pyres while the carts made trip after trip carrying Mexican bodies to a mass grave in the cemetery. In a field southeast of the Alamo, the soldiers busily constructed the cremation pyres by layering the structure with wood, then bodies of Alamo defenders, then more wood, then more bodies. Santa Anna had retired to the north side of the Main Plaza, and sat sipping coffee in preparation for interviewing the SURVIVORS OF THE ALAMO BATTLE, which included Ana Salazar ESPARZA, the wife of Gregorio ESPARZA, and her 4 children. He was approached by one of his troops, Francisco Esparza, who admitted that he had a brother, Gregorio, who had fought with the Americans. Esparza requested, however, that an exception be made to permit him to bury his brother in the cemetery rather than have him burned with the others. Santa Anna granted his request, and Gregorio Esparza became the only Alamo defender who received a Christian burial. The pyres, now stacked with mounds of wood and more than 180 bodies, were set afire at about 5 P.M. The make-shift crematorium burned for 2 days until the fire finally died out to leave ashes and bits of flesh and bones lying exposed to the elements. An eyewitness, Pablo Diaz, was interviewed by the San Antonio *Daily Express* on July 1, 1906, and told about what he had seen as he approached the Alamo from San Antonio 3 days after the disposal of bodies had began: "I noticed that the air was tainted with the terrible odor of many corpses, and I saw thousands of vultures flying over me. As I reached the ford in the river my gaze encountered a terrible sight. The stream was congested with corpses that had been thrown into it." These were bodies of Mexican soldiers that had happened to fall off the oxcarts and into the San Antonio River. It took many days to gather these bodies that had floated away in the quickly polluting river —

the main source of water for San Antonio. Diaz then moved to join the crowd at the pyre. "Fragments of flesh, bones and charred wood and ashes revealed it in all its terrible truth," he said. "Grease that had exuded from the bodies saturated the earth for several feet beyond the ashes and smoldering mesquite faggots. The odor was more sickening than that from the corpses in the river. I turned aside and left the place in shame." About a year after the Alamo Battle, Lt. Col. Juan SEGUIN, who had been charged with protecting San Antonio until a proper government could be restored, gathered some of the exposed ashes and bones that remained from the cremated bodies of the Alamo defenders and placed them in a coffin. A Texas Republic flag was draped over the coffin and upon that a rifle and sword. The coffin lay in state in the San Fernando Church until on February 27, 1837, a military procession of Texas soldiers and local officials buried the ashes with honors, including a firing squad, near a peach orchard. That act led to rumors of apparitions — ghosts with flaming swords — that are said to haunt the Alamo grounds to this day.

**DUVALT, Andrew** (aka "Devault"; 1804–March 6, 1836) Private, GONZALES RANGING COMPANY; Alamo defender from Ireland. Duvalt arrived in Texas by way of Missouri, and settled in Gonzales. He participated in the Siege and Battle of SAN ANTONIO, and then returned home. The precise date that he entered the Alamo remains uncertain, but likely was prior to the arrival of his unit on March 1, 1836. Duvalt was killed in the ALAMO BATTLE while serving as a rifleman in Capt. Robert WHITE's infantry company.

# E

**EMPRESARIOS** The Texas frontier was sparsely populated in the early 1800's — the non–Indian population was likely less than 3,500 in 1821 when Mexico gained its independence from Spain. Those who had settled there had done so against the wishes of the Mexican government which was suspicious of the political intentions of foreigners (see FILIBUSTERS). Therefore, the Mexican Congress enacted the National Colonization Law in August, 1824, which opened up Mexico's state of Coahuila y Texas to controlled settlement by Americans (see TEXAS SETTLEMENT BY AMERICANS). The proprietors, or land agents, of these colonies — those who had received contracts permitting them to establish new colonies under the Mexican law — were called *empresarios*. An *empresario* was entitled to approximately 22,140 acres of grazing land and approximately 885 acres of farmland in a specific location for each 100 families — up to 800 families — and could charge each family a basic fee of $60. The *empresario* contract would remain in effect for 6 years, and became void if at least 100 families had not settled in that period of time. Stephen F. AUSTIN, who had inherited his father's grant, became the first *empresario* in April, 1823 by a special arrangement with the Mexican government. He applied for 3 additional contracts in 1825, 1827, and 1828 under the new law to settle a total of 900 families. Austin also shared a contract northwest of his original colony with Sam M. Williams to settle 800 families, which later became a matter of contention with agent Sterling Robertson of the Nashville Company who had established Robertson's Colony in 1825 for 800 families. By 1831, Robertson had made little progress, and the governor awarded the grant to Austin and Williams. The claim changed hands twice more between the two claimants, and finally ended in up the hands of Austin and Williams. In 1847, a Texas court ruled in favor of Robertson, who had died, and awarded his heirs substantial land as restitution. On April 15, 1825, Green De-Witt (DeWitt's Colony) received a contract for 400 families located on the Guadalupe, San Marcos, and Lavaca Rivers, and with the exception of Austin's was the most successful settlement. The town of Gonzales in this colony, which was the site of the 1835 GONZALES SKIRMISH— the first shot of the TEXAS REVOLUTION— was plagued by attacks from hostile Comanche Indians, and was abandoned once in 1826 but reestablished in 1828. Martin de Leon, a native Mexican, established a predominantly Mexican settlement in April, 1824, near the coast between the Lavaca and Guadalupe Rivers. This contract encroached on territory already granted to DeWitt, which caused another abandonment and re-establishment of Gonzales. David BURNET, who would become the first president of the Republic of Texas, Mexican national Lorenzo de ZAVALA, who would become the first vice-president, and Joseph Vehlein received a contract in 1826 for land on the eastern border of Texas, which, with the assistance of Sam HOUSTON, was later sold to the Galveston Bay & Texas Land Company. An Englishman, Arthur G. Wavell, with associate Ben MILAM, received a contract in March, 1826 for 500 families in northeast Texas. John Cameron obtained grants in 1827 and 1828, but failed to fulfill either of them. Irishman John McMullen and his son-in-law, James McGloin, received a contract in August 1828 for 200 Irish families east of the Nueces River and established the town of San Patricio, but were only able to attract 84 families. Two other natives of Ireland, businessmen James Powers and James Hewetson, received a contract in 1828 to settle 200 Mexican and Irish families between the Nueces and Guadalupe

Rivers. Powers travelled to recruit families from Ireland, but most died of cholera en route.

One particular *empresario*, Haden Edwards, received a grant in 1825 of more than 300,000 acres in eastern Texas, some of which already had been settled. Edwards, against the advice of Stephen Austin, ordered these people off his land. The settlers complained to the President of Mexico, and while Edwards was visiting the U.S., his contract was revoked and he was ordered to leave the country. His brother, Benjamin, however, called for a revolt against Mexico, and in what became known as the Fredonia Rebellion, rallied about 30 colonists, seized an old fort near Nacogdoches, and proclaimed it the "Republic of Fredonia." In late January, 1827, 250 Mexican troops accompanied by about 100 militia members from Austin's colony, set out to expel Edwards from the country. When the expedition arrived at "Fredonia," they found it deserted. Benjamin Edwards had fled to the United States. The Fredonian affair did, however, serve to create further suspicions in the minds of Mexican officials about whether or not the U.S. had intentions of adding Texas as a state.

*Empresario* activity was dealt a severe blow by the Mexican government in a decree on April 6, 1830 that, due to excessive American influence in Texas, prohibited colonists from states or territories adjacent to Texas from settling— meaning the United States. Additional Mexican Army garrisons were established to enforce this edict. Contracts not yet fulfilled were at that time suspended. Mexican General Vicente FILISOLA obtained a contract in 1831 to settle 600 families, but was unsuccessful in doing so. Many *empresarios* failed to fulfill their contracts due to Indian trouble, boundary disputes, questionable business tactics, or ineptitude, and were transferred to others, added to existing colonies, or remained vacant. A few sold their grants to other land speculators without settling even one family. About 25 land grants were made under *empresario* contracts in the decade following the enactment of the law. Mexico began admitting Americans again in 1833, and the population quickly swelled. The land offices were closed with the commencement of the Texas Revolution in 1835, and *empresario* contracts ceased on March 2, 1836, the day of the TEXAS DECLARATION OF INDEPENDENCE.

**ESPALIER, Carlos** (1819–March 6, 1836) Private, TEXAS REVOLUTIONARY ARMY; Alamo defender from Texas. This native of San Antonio was serving as a rifleman when he was killed in the ALAMO BATTLE.

**ESPARZA, Ana Salazar** (?–December 12, 1847) This native of San Antonio, Texas was the wife of Alamo defender Gregario ESPARZA. She entered the ALAMO MISSION with her husband and four children — Maria, 10; Enrique, 8; Manuel, 5; Francisco, perhaps as old as 4 — during the evening on the first day of the ALAMO SIEGE to join her husband. She was afforded the opportunity to leave with her children during the siege, but refused. Gregario was killed in the ALAMO BATTLE; Ana and her children survived sheltered in the Alamo chapel. After being interrogated by Gen. Antonio Lopez de SANTA ANNA, she was given two pesos and a blanket and released to return to her home in San Antonio where she mourned the loss of her husband. Enrique, who claimed to have witnessed several killings — including that of David CROCKETT — during the battle, related his experiences at the Alamo in 1905 and 1906 to the San Antonio *Daily Express*.

**ESPARZA, Gregorio** (March 8, 1808–March 6, 1836) Private; SEGUIN'S CAVALRY COMPANY; Alamo defender from Texas. This native of San Antonio, accompanied by his wife and four children (see ESPARZA, Ana Salazar), entered the ALAMO MISSION during the evening on the first day of the ALAMO SIEGE. His brother, Francisco, was a member of the Mexican Army, but was held in reserve during the siege and battle. Esparza, who was considered a traitor by the Mexicans, was shot and bayoneted in the ALAMO BATTLE, his body found near the chapel where he manned a cannon and where his family was sheltered. Following the battle, Esparza's brother, in respect for his allegiance to Mexico, obtained permission from Gen. Antonio Lopez de SANTA ANNA to remove the body from the Alamo. Esparza was interred on the west side of San Pedro Creek at the present-day site of Milam Square — the only defender to receive a Christian burial.

**EVANS, Robert** (1800–March 6, 1836) Major, TEXAS REVOLUTIONARY ARMY; Alamo defender from Ireland. Evans arrived in Texas by way of New York and New Orleans. He was ordnance chief at the ALAMO MISSION, and responsible for the care and maintenance of all weapons inside the walls. Susannah DICKINSON claimed that during the ALAMO BATTLE, Evans made a valiant effort to blow up the several hundred pounds of gunpowder captured after the Siege and Battle of SAN ANTONIO that had been stored in the antechamber of the chapel. He raced for his objective with a torch in his hand, but was killed by a bullet only a few feet away. The blast, had he been successful, likely would have killed Dickinson and the other women and children sheltered in the chapel.

**EVANS, Samuel B.** (January 16, 1812–March 6, 1836) Private, TEXAS REVOLUTION-

ARY ARMY; Alamo defender from New York. This native of Jefferson County had descended from a line of military men. His grandfather, Samuel, was a general in the Colonial Army during the Revolutionary War, and his uncle, Gen. Jacob Brown, had commanded the United States Army. Evans was serving as a rifleman when he was killed in the ALAMO BATTLE.

**EWING, James L.** (1812–March 6, 1836) Private, TEXAS REVOLUTIONARY ARMY; Alamo defender from Tennessee. Ewing participated in the Siege and Battle of SAN ANTONIO, and later served as secretary to Col. James NEILL. He was killed in the ALAMO BATTLE while a member of Capt. William CAREY's company.

# F

**FANNIN, James Walker** (ca. January 1, 1804–March 27, 1836) Colonel, TEXAS REVOLUTIONARY ARMY; leader of the MATAMOROS EXPEDITION and commander during the Surrender and Massacre at GOLIAD. This son of Dr. Isham Fannin, a Georgia planter, was adopted by his maternal grandfather, James W. Walker, and raised on a plantation near Marion, Georgia. Fannin was only 14-and-a-half years of age when on July 1, 1819 he was admitted to the U.S. Military Academy at West Point under the name "James F. Walker." He stood 60th in a class of 86 when he dropped out in November, 1821 following an argument with a fellow cadet, and returned to Georgia. Fannin married Minerva Fort in about the year 1829, and the couple had two daughters born in 1830 and 1832. In 1834, he moved to Texas and settled at Velasco on the Brazos River. Fannin, who claimed to be a plantation owner, apparently made trips to Cuba

and quickly established a prosperous slave-trading business as well as dabbling in land speculation. By the time of the TEXAS REVOLUTION, Fannin was an influential member of his community and aspired to military leadership.

He participated in the October 2, 1835 Skirmish at GONZALES, the first armed conflict of the revolution. Fannin then distinguished himself as captain of a Georgia militia called the Brazos Guard when, in the company of Col. Jim BOWIE, their scouting party of 92 men was attacked south of San Antonio by 400 MEXICAN ARMY regulars on October 28, 1835. The ensuing Battle of CONCEPCION was a clear-cut victory for the volunteers who subsequently went on to claim another victory in the Siege and Battle of SAN ANTONIO. On December 10, 1835, he successfully led a group of volunteers west of the Trinity River on a mission to secure supplies and additional volunteers. Fannin, whose military ambitions were no secret, applied to Sam HOUSTON for commission to general. Houston refused, but placated Fannin by promoting him to colonel.

Fannin along with Col. Frank JOHNSON and Dr. James GRANT had voiced the opinion that the volunteer soldiers should be paid by plundering their enemy, a practice that Houston angrily forbade. Fannin and other supporters of this idea were not be denied. They made a proposal to the November, 1835 TEXAS CONSULTATION OF DELEGATES to carry the war into Mexico and attack (and plunder) the allegedly wealthy town of Matamoros. Both Houston and Governor Henry SMITH were opposed to this MATAMOROS EXPEDITION, but the General Council finally approved the plan in early 1836 and Fannin was appointed their agent, with dictatorial powers to organize the expedition. In preparation for this expedition, Fannin ordered the ALAMO MISSION garrison in San Antonio stripped of men, in addition to vital provisions such as food, medical supplies, and ammunition, which left the interior of Texas virtually defenseless against the impending attack by the Mexican Army of Gen. Antonio Lopez de SANTA ANNA. Houston believed that Fannin was betraying his country with this undertaking, and took his case directly to the volunteers. He travelled to the places where volunteers were massing, and succeeded in dissuading many of them from participating. On February 12, Fannin grudgingly admitted that a 300 mile march without proper supplies to fight a superior force would be unrealistic. The Matamoros Expedition was abandoned for the time being, and Fannin withdrew to Fort Defiance at the presidio at Goliad with about 450 men.

Fannin was the recipient of a number of messages from Col. William TRAVIS urging assistance for the ALAMO MISSION during the ALAMO SIEGE. On February 25, the third day of the siege, Fannin made the decision to organize a relief expedition and march the 95 miles from Goliad to the Alamo. By the next morning, he had readied a force of 320 troops, 4 cannons, and several wagons hauled by oxen that contained ammunition and supplies, and set out for the Alamo. His men, however, were ill-prepared for the arduous march, and a bitter northerner had lowered the temperatures to near freezing. The expedition had travelled just several hundred yards when one of the supply wagons broke down. Repairs were made and they resumed their march. Within a mile, two more wagons broke down. At the San Antonio River, Fannin realized that individual oxen were not strong enough to haul the cannons across and the job would require double-teaming the beasts of burden. The process was slow and tedious, and, as night approached, the ammunition wagons still remained on the wrong side of the river.

Fannin decided to delay his rescue mission until the following day.

That morning, it was discovered that several oxen had wandered off during the night. Those oxen were rounded up by late afternoon, and the expedition was ready to move out. Fannin, however, had second-thoughts. His men were in desperate need of supplies; he had left only 100 men to defend Goliad; and the exact whereabouts of the Mexican Army was unknown. Fannin was holding a council of war with his officers when a messenger arrived to inform him that long-awaited supplies had landed at Matagorda Bay, but there were no volunteers present to guard them. Right or wrong, the council was compelled to unanimously vote to suspend the Alamo relief expedition. Fannin hauled his wagons back to Goliad where he learned that on February 27, a foraging detachment from his Matamoros Expedition under Col. Johnson had been attacked by Mexican forces under Gen. José URREA at San Patricio — some 50 miles south. That disturbing news acted to further justify Fannin's decision to abort the mission to rescue the Alamo. If that was not enough, another detachment of 15 men under Dr. Grant were killed by Urrea's troops on March 2.

Fannin received orders from Sam Houston on March 14 to abandon his position and fall back to Victoria. It was suspected that about 1,400 Mexican Army troops under the command of Gen. Urrea — one element of Santa Anna's three-pronged strategy to overwhelm the Texas army following his victory in the ALAMO BATTLE — were marching toward Goliad. Instead of obeying orders without question or delay, Fannin assumed an on-again off-again mode of retreat. He directed that preparation for retreat begin by burying a number of the fort's cannons to prevent the Mexicans from capturing them. Then, changing his mind, he ordered that those cannons be dug up and remounted.

Fannin finally departed Goliad at 9 A.M. on March 19. He had waited too long. That afternoon, Fannin's troops were overtaken by Urrea's superior force in an open prairie near Colleto Creek. The Texans held out until the following afternoon when Fannin, who had been wounded in the thigh, unconditionally surrendered against the wishes of many of the volunteers. The prisoners were marched back to Goliad, and set to work rebuilding the fort and constructing bridges. On Palm Sunday, March 27, Fannin was not present when the rest of the prisoners were assembled for roll call at 8 A.M. The men had no inkling of impending disaster. In fact, they were excited. They had been informed by way of rumor that they were to be released and sent to New Orleans where they could return to their homes in America. The prisoners, however, were divided into three columns, and marched away in different directions where they were executed. Fannin was the last to die. He was taken to a spot beside the chapel where he gave the officer attending him a gold watch belonging to his wife and ten pesos. Fannin was then seated in a chair, blindfolded, and executed by a firing squad. His body was later burned. (See Surrender and Massacre at GOLIAD for a detailed account.)

Fannin's wife died in 1837; one daughter in 1847; the other died insane in 1893. Fannin County, Texas and the town of Fannin in Goliad County were named in his honor.

**FAUNTLEROY, William Keener** (aka "Fontleroy," or "Furtleroy"; 1814–March 6, 1836) Private, TENNESSEE MOUNTED VOLUNTEERS; Alamo defender from Logan County, Kentucky. Fauntleroy traveled to Texas in the company of fellow defenders Peter BAILEY, Daniel CLOUD, B. Archer M. THOMAS, and Joseph WASHINGTON. The

five men enlisted with their small unit, which was under the command of Capt. William HARRISON, in Nacogdoches on January 14, 1836, and arrived in San Antonio on February 8, 1836. During the ALAMO SIEGE, Fauntleroy was a rifleman defending the wooden palisade that ran from the chapel to the low barracks along the south wall of the ALAMO MISSION when he was killed in the ALAMO BATTLE.

**FILIBUSTERS** The first Americans ventured across the Louisiana border into Texas in the late 18th-century while that sparsely inhabited land was ruled by Spaniards, and worked for the most part as horse traders who at times provided the Indians a market for horses stolen from Spanish posts. The presence of these intruders or "filibusters" as they were known — traders, land speculators, and others with potential revolutionist interests — was a matter of great concern to Spanish authorities who had ordered Texas off limits to all Americans. One of these early filibusters, Philip Nolan, who had first come to Texas as a trader around 1790, was said to have been the first American to map Texas. He had been granted permission to take horses out of the country, but eventually came under scrutiny by the Spaniards who feared he had ulterior motives with respect to eventual settlement. Spanish authorities dispatched 100 soldiers to arrest Nolan in 1801. He was found near present-day Waco in March, and in the ensuing fight Nolan, who was in the company of 17 armed men, was shot and killed. His ears were sent to the Texas governor as trophies. Nine companions of Nolan were imprisoned in Chihuahua for 6 years, and made to roll dice to determine which one of them would be hanged. Nolan's death, however, did little to discourage other filibusters who had heard about the rich soil, dense forests, and natural harbors in this wilderness.

Minor revolutions designed to gain freedom from Spain became commonplace. Priest Miguel Hidalgo led a revolt in 1810, and captured several cities with a small army made up mostly of Indians; he was later put to death. Juan Bautista de las Casas captured government officials at San Antonio in 1811; he was later executed for his act. An unofficial envoy of the revolutionists, Bernardo Gutierrez de Lara, went to Washington in 1811, and convinced some U.S. cabinet members to assist in organizing a filibustering force and invade Texas. This army comprised of about 100 Americans, Frenchmen, Mexicans, and Indians led by Lt. Augustus W. Magee found little opposition when invading and occupying Nacogdoches in August, 1812. When Magee became ill, Samuel Kemper defeated 1,200 Spaniards and occupied San Antonio in April, 1813. Gutierrez issued a declaration of Texas independence, but soon fell out of favor with the Americans and was replaced with José Alverez de Toledo, a revolutionary Spaniard. This uprising was finally ended by Gen. Joaquín de Arredondo and 1,800 Spanish troops who slaughtered the upstart Texans west of San Antonio on the Medina River on August 18, 1813, in what was known as the Battle of Medina. Lieutenant Antonio Lopez de SANTA ANNA was decorated for his bravery with the royalist army. This began an effort to remove all Americans and liberal Mexicans from Texas. Deserters were shot, their wives and children made slaves, and their property seized.

James Long, a merchant from Natchez, was angered by the treaty in 1819 that gave Florida to the U.S. but verified Spain's claim to Texas. Long formed a filibustering army of 300 men — which included Jim BOWIE and Ben MILAM — and established a civil government in Nacogdoches. Long declared

independence, and invited immigrants to join him. He traveled to Galveston Island and attempted to solicit the aid of Jean Lafitte. While Long was absent, his "government" was abolished by a visit from the Spanish army. Long failed to recruit Lafitte, and subsequently formed another group that went to La Bahia in 1821. Mexico had by then gained independence from Spain, and arrested Long, who was later shot under mysterious circumstances while on parole in Mexico City. During Long's absence, his wife, Jane, survived at frozen Bolivar Point on Galveston Bay throughout the winter of 1821-1822 with only her 6-year-old daughter Ann, a teenage servant, and a dog for company. She subsisted by shooting birds and catching fish, and at one point chased away the savage Karankawa Indians by firing the cannon. On December 21, 1821, while her servant was ill, Jane gave birth to another daughter, Mary. The courageous woman was finally saved by a passing sloop that carried the first men to settle in Stephen AUSTIN's colony. She returned to Mississippi upon learning of her husband's death, but later settled in Austin's colony. Jane Long gained prominence for her actions, and became known as the "Mother of Texas."

The advent of *EMPRESARIOS* in the 1820s with grants to settle law-abiding colonies and establish rules within Mexico's guidelines did not end filibustering. Americans coming to Texas were land-obsessed, and, inasmuch as many *empresarios* failed for a variety of reasons to fulfill their contracts, some were sold to speculators. *Empresario* activity was dealt a severe blow by the Mexican government in a decree on April 6, 1830 that, due to excessive American influence in Texas, prohibited colonists from states or territories adjacent to Texas from settling — meaning the United States. This act was later repelled, but did not stop some enterprising filibusters from rampant land speculation. The governor and state legislature at Saltillo, Coahuila was rife with corruption, and began selling thousands of acres of land at scandalously low rates to undesirables, which troubled those legal settlers who feared that their land rights eventually could be threatened. Mexican dictator Antonio Lopez de SANTA ANNA dispatched his brother-in-law, Gen. Martin Perfecto de CÓS, in June, 1835 to Saltillo to put a stop to this corruption by arresting known land speculators. One filibuster arrested was Ben Milam, who later escaped, and led the colonists in the Siege and Battle of SAN ANTONIO. Jim Bowie managed to elude capture. Cós at that time also arrested the governor and suspended civil government in favor of martial law. These actions were propagandized by the so-called WAR PARTY as intolerable acts that would lead to martial law and the confiscation of land in Texas. This threat, whether real or imagined, became one factor that was seized upon to encourage Texans to openly rebel against Mexico and initiate the TEXAS REVOLUTION (see also TEXAS SETTLEMENT BY AMERICANS).

**FILISOLA, Vicente** (ca. 1789–July 23, 1850) General, MEXICAN ARMY. This native of Rivoli, Italy, emigrated to Spain early in life, joined the army in 1804, and at age 21 attained the rank of second lieutenant for his gallantry under fire. He was sent to Mexico with Spanish royalist forces in 1811, and was in the Mexican army when he supported his friend Agustin de Iturbide's plan for independence. Filisola led 4000 troops into Mexico City on September 24, 1821 to secure it for the arrival of Iturbide. He was rewarded with a promotion to brigadier general and the title Knight of the Imperial Order of Guadalupe. Filisola was then dispatched to Central America, and, in No-

vember, 1822 after that region voted in favor of a union with Mexico, he led an attack against San Salvador, the only city that had resisted the union, and occupied that city on February 9, 1823. Iturbide, however, was overthrown, and Filisola returned to Guatemala and accepted their declaration of independence. Filisola fought against the Spanish invasion in 1829, and tried his hand at being an EMPRESARIO, the promoter of colony in Texas in 1831 when he received a grant to settle 600 foreign families in east Texas. He later returned to Mexico City, and was named commandant of the eastern division in January, 1833. He was second in command of the Mexican Army at the outbreak of the TEXAS REVOLUTION, and accompanied General Antonio Lopez de SANTA ANNA on the march to Texas but did not arrive in San Antonio until 3 days after the ALAMO BATTLE. Gen. Filisola, as well as other officers, had urged Santa Anna to bypass San Antonio and Goliad and instead strike the population center in east Texas, but the president-general chose San Antonio and the ALAMO MISSION as his destination. Filisola also joined other officers in an attempt to talk Santa Anna out of his standing policy to execute prisoners of war, and suggested that they could be put to work and thereby defray the expenses of war. Santa Anna, however, would not waver from his policy. Filisola claimed that he was informed — possibly by Lt. José de la Peña — that on the evening before the Mexican Army assaulted the Alamo (March 5, 1836), Col. William TRAVIS dispatched a woman to propose a surrender of the Alamo garrison. Santa Anna rejected the entreaty, which carried the condition of sparing the lives of the volunteers, and allegedly replied that there would be no guarantees for traitors. Gen. Filisola later estimated that three quarters of the Mexican casualties during the Alamo Battle had been caused by friendly fire. He was extremely critical of Santa Anna's insistence at attacking and sustaining such a great loss of lives rather than starving the Texans out or accepting a surrender. While Santa Anna moved east across Texas in prelude to the Battle of SAN JACINTO, Filisola was placed in charge of troop crossings at the Colorado River. Filisola was moving his forces eastward for a rendezvous at Fort Bend when Santa Anna was defeated in the Battle of San Jacinto on April 21, 1836. Santa Anna signed the Treaties of VELASCO on May 10, which included a provision calling for the Mexican Army to be retired south of the Rio Grande River. Against the wishes of other officers, Filisola, now in charge of the army, chose to obey the president-general's order and withdraw. It was decided by the Texas government, however, to ensure validity of the Velasco Treaties, that Gen. Filisola, who was not a prisoner, should also sign. Emissaries were dispatched, and on May 26, 1836, at the stream of Mugerero secured the signatures of Filisola and two subordinates, Gen. Eugenio Tolsa and Col. Agustin Amat. Filisola was criticized for signing the treaty, but was simply obeying the orders of his superior, Santa Anna, as well as — and perhaps more importantly — discretionary powers granted him by the Minister of War in Mexico City, Gen. José Maria Tornel y Mendivil. Tornel was the dominant member of Santa Anna's government, and was more concerned with the disposition of President Santa Anna and the prisoners than the loss of Texas. Filisola later justified his actions by stating "…only in a war where no quarter was to be given, by an especial and positive order from the government, could I be prohibited the exchange of prisoners. And to what else did I compromise myself in recognizing that treaty (of Velasco) than to retreat and exchange prisoners … Mexico had lost it (Texas) forever, due to the anxiety and indiscretion of the general-in-chief (Santa Anna), who wasn't content with only punishment … but who wanted to exterminate them (the Texans) forever." In 1840, Filisola was imprisoned on charges brought by Gen. Urrea with respect to his actions during the Texas Revolution, but was exonerated at a court martial in June, 1841. He ran for senate in 1843, but was unsuccessful, and later wrote extensively, including *Evacuation of Texas* (Waco: Texian Press, 1965) and *The History of the War in Texas*, translated by Wallace Woolsey; 2 vols. (Austin: Eakin Press, 1985–87). Filisola died of cholera in Mexico at the age of 61.

**FISHBAUGH, William** (aka "Fishback"; ?–March 6, 1836) Private, GONZALES RANGING COMPANY; Alamo defender from parts unknown. Fishbaugh had been residing in Gonzales, Texas, and entered the ALAMO MISSION with his unit on March 1, 1836. He was serving as a rifleman when he was killed in the ALAMO BATTLE.

**FLANDERS, John** (1800–March 6, 1836) Private, GONZALES RANGING COMPANY; Alamo defender from Salisbury, Massachusetts. Flanders impulsively departed his home over a dispute with his father involving John's intention to foreclose on a mortgage held on property belonging to a widow which was opposed by the elder Flanders. He entered the ALAMO MISSION with his unit on March 1, 1836 and was serving as a rifleman when he was killed in the ALAMO BATTLE.

**FLOYD, Dolphin Ward** (aka "Dolphin Ward"; March 6, 1804–March 6, 1836) Private, GONZALES RANGING COMPANY; Alamo defender from North Carolina. Floyd moved from Nash County, North Carolina, to settle in Gonzales, Texas, where on April 26,

1832, he married widow Ester Berry House. He entered the ALAMO MISSION with his unit on March 1, 1836, and was killed on his 32nd birthday while serving as a rifleman in the ALAMO BATTLE. Floyd County, Texas was named in honor of his sacrifice.

**FORSYTH, John Hubbard** (August 10, 1797–March 6, 1836) Captain, TEXAS REVOLUTIONARY ARMY; Alamo defender from New York. This farmer from Avon, Livingston County, New York, briefly studied medicine but never practiced. He departed for Kentucky in 1828 following the death of his wife on Christmas day of that year — leaving his son in the care of his father's family. He travelled to Texas in 1835, and entered the ALAMO MISSION in the company of Col. William TRAVIS on February 3, 1836. Forsyth spent his own money along the way to supply his unit. He was serving as commanding officer of a cavalry company when he was killed in the ALAMO BATTLE.

**FUENTES, Antonio** (1813–March 6, 1836) Private, SEGUIN'S CAVALRY COMPANY; Alamo defender from Texas. Fuentes was a native of San Antonio, who fought in the Siege and Battle of that city in 1835. He was convicted of theft by a jury which included both James BOWIE and William TRAVIS. Judge Juan SEGUIN, his commanding officer, sentenced Fuentes to jail. A drunken Jim Bowie, in his capacity as commander of the volunteers, freed Fuentes, an act that became a matter of contention between Bowie and Travis. Juan Seguin subsequently returned his private to jail. Fuentes entered the ALAMO MISSION with his unit on February 23, 1836, and was serving as a rifleman when he was killed in the ALAMO BATTLE.

**FUQUA, Galba** (March 9, 1819–March 6, 1836) Private, GONZALES RANGING COMPANY; Alamo defender from Alabama. This 16-year-old descendant of French Huguenot refugees whose grandfather was a Revolutionary War veteran accompanied his family from Alabama to Texas in 1828. Fuqua was serving as a rifleman when he entered the ALAMO MISSION with his unit on March 1, 1836. During the ALAMO BATTLE, he rushed into the room occupied by Susannah DICKINSON and attempted to speak to her. His jaw, however, had been shattered by a bullet, and he was unable to utter a word. Fuqua returned to the battle, and was subsequently killed.

# G

**GAONA, Antonio** General, MEXICAN ARMY. This Cuban native was in command of the First Infantry Brigade — which consisted of about 1,540 men and 6 artillery pieces — during the TEXAS REVOLUTION. His detachment trailed about 200 miles behind that of his commander, General Antonio Lopez de SANTA ANNA, on the march to Texas. Gaona's forward units did not arrive in San Antonio until March 7, 1836, one day after the ALAMO BATTLE, which caused a reprimand from the president-general for Gaona's slow progress. He was ordered on March 24 to take 725 men and march toward Nacogdoches by way of Bastrop and attempt to prevent the Texans from forming large groups of fighting men that might offer serious resistance. Gaona's men plundered the Bastrop vicinity, taking whatever suited their fancy from the colonists. His orders were amended on April 15, and he was directed to march for San Felipe to join Santa Anna. Gaona, however, became lost between Bastrop and San Felipe, and failed to arrive before the April 21 Battle of SAN JACINTO. Gaona returned to Mexico under the command of Gen. Vincente FILISOLA in accordance with provisions of the Treaties of VELASCO. He became commandant of the fortress of San Juan de Ulloa, and surrendered that position to the French fleet in November, 1838 in what has been called the Pastry War.

**GARNETT, William** (1812–March 6, 1836) Private, TEXAS REVOLUTIONARY ARMY; Alamo defender from Virginia. This wandering Baptist preacher who had been residing in Falls-on-the-Brazos, Robertson's Colony, Texas was serving as a rifleman when he was killed in the ALAMO BATTLE.

**GARRAND, James W.** (1813–March 6, 1836) Private, TEXAS REVOLUTIONARY ARMY; Alamo defender from Louisiana. Garrand participated in the Siege and Battle of SAN ANTONIO, and was serving as a rifleman in Capt. William BLAZEBY's infantry company when he was killed in the ALAMO BATTLE.

**GARRETT, James Girard** (1806–March 6, 1836) Private, NEW ORLEANS GREYS; Alamo defender from Tennessee. Garrett arrived in San Antonio with his unit on November 21, 1835, and participated in the Siege and Battle of SAN ANTONIO. He was serving as a rifleman in Capt. William BLAZEBY's infantry company when he was killed in the ALAMO BATTLE.

**GARVIN, John E.** (1809–March 6, 1836) Private, TEXAS REVOLUTIONARY ARMY; Alamo defender from parts unknown. Garvin, who was residing in Gonzales, arrived at the ALAMO MISSION on March 1, 1836 with the GONZALES RANGING COMPANY. He was serving as an artilleryman with Capt. William CAREY's artillery company when he was killed in the ALAMO BATTLE.

**GASTON, John E.** (aka John "Davis," his step-father's name; 1819–March 6, 1836) Private, GONZALES RANGING COMPANY; Alamo defender from Kentucky. Sixteen-year-old John Gaston entered the ALAMO MISSION with his unit on March 1, 1836, and was serving as a rifleman when he was killed in the ALAMO BATTLE. His sister, Sidney, had been married to and divorced from fellow defender Thomas R. MILLER, and was at that time married to Alamo defender John KELLOGG—both of whom were also killed in the Alamo Battle.

**GEORGE, James** (1802–March 6, 1836) Private, GONZALES RANGING COMPANY; Alamo defender from parts unknown. George was married to the sister of Alamo defender William DEARDUFF, and was a resident of Gonzales, Texas. A yoke of his oxen were used to haul the cannon that was the subject of the October 2, 1835, GONZALES SKIRMISH. When he departed Gonzales to ride for the Alamo with his unit, George was said to have asked a man named Rowe, who had been renting a room from him, to watch over his wife and children in exchange for free rent. George entered the ALAMO MISSION with his unit on March 1, 1836, and was serving as a rifleman when he was killed in the ALAMO BATTLE. Rowe later married George's wife, Elizabeth.

**GEORGIA BATTALION** This 3-company volunteer unit of about 112 men organized and commanded by Col. William Ward, which carried arms furnished by the state of Georgia, arrived at Velasco, Texas on December 20, 1835, and were sworn into the TEXAS REVOLUTIONARY ARMY on Christmas Day. The unit was garrisoned at Goliad under Col. James FANNIN in February, 1836. On March 14, Col. Ward and about 200 men were dispatched by Fannin to assist

Capt. Amon King who was assisting in the evacuation of settlers around Refugio. Mexican Gen. José URREA surrounded Ward's men, and, in a running battle, killed 16 and captured 31. Ward and about 120 survivors made an effort to reach Victoria, and eluded Urrea for a week before being captured and delivered to Goliad to join Fannin and his men as prisoners. Other than a few who might have escaped, every man from this unit was killed in the Surrender and Massacre at GOLIAD.

## GOLIAD, Skirmish at (October 9, 1835)

### Chronology of the Texas Revolution

- June 29, 1835: Battle of ANAHUAC
- October 2, 1835: GONZALES SKIRMISH
- October 3, 1835: MEXICAN CONSTITUTION OF 1824 officially voided
- **October 9, 1835: GOLIAD SKIRMISH**
- October 28, 1835: Battle of CONCEPCION
- November 3, 1835: TEXAS CONSULTATION OF DELEGATES
- November–December, 1835: Siege and Battle of SAN ANTONIO
- January–February, 1836: The MATAMOROS EXPEDITION
- February 23–March 5, 1836: The ALAMO SIEGE
- March 1, 1836: TEXAS CONSTITUTIONAL CONVENTION
- March 2, 1836: TEXAS DECLARATION OF INDEPENDENCE
- March 6, 1836: The ALAMO BATTLE
- March 20–27, 1836: Surrender and Massacre at GOLIAD
- April 21, 1836: Battle of SAN JACINTO
- May 14, 1836: Treaties of VELASCO

Goliad, Texas, was situated on a hilltop and commanded the road connecting San Antonio to the sea, which made it strategically important by denying landing sites for the MEXICAN ARMY. A detachment of about 25 Mexican Army troops had been left behind in Goliad by General Martin Perfecto

Cós when he moved his main force to San Antonio. A small company of Texas volunteers under the command of Capt. George M. Collinsworth and Col. Ben MILAM entered the city at about 11:00 P.M., stormed into the chapel where the Mexicans were quartered and forced the surprised soldiers to surrender. The action was significant in that the Texans captured vital supplies which enabled them to maintain their army in the field while preventing Gen. Cós from obtaining provisions and reinforcements by sea.

## GOLIAD, Surrender and Massacre at (March 19–27, 1836)

More than 400 Texas volunteers who had been manning the garrison at Goliad, Texas fled from the advance of a superior force of the MEXICAN ARMY. They were overtaken, captured, returned to Goliad, and later executed by personal order of Gen. Antonio Lopez de SANTA ANNA.

### Chronology of the Texas Revolution

- June 29, 1835: Battle of ANAHUAC
- October 2, 1835: GONZALES SKIRMISH
- October 3, 1835: MEXICAN CONSTITUTION OF 1824 officially voided
- October 9, 1835: GOLIAD SKIRMISH
- October 28, 1835: Battle of CONCEPCION
- November 3, 1835: TEXAS CONSULTATION OF DELEGATES
- November–December, 1835: Siege and Battle of SAN ANTONIO
- January–February, 1836: The MATAMOROS EXPEDITION
- February 23–March 5, 1836: The ALAMO SIEGE
- March 1, 1836: TEXAS CONSTITUTIONAL CONVENTION
- March 2, 1836: TEXAS DECLARATION OF INDEPENDENCE
- March 6, 1836: The ALAMO BATTLE
- **March 20–27, 1836: Surrender and Massacre at GOLIAD**
- April 21, 1836: Battle of SAN JACINTO
- May 14, 1836: Treaties of VELASCO

Col. James W. FANNIN, who had been charged by the TEXAS PROVISIONAL GOVERNMENT's General Council with organizing the MATA-MOROS EXPEDITION, an invasion of Mexico, had begun assembling troops and supplies at Capano and then Refugio. Upon hearing on February 7 that Gen. Santa Anna was en route from Mexico to Texas with his huge army, Fannin moved his headquarters and over 400 volunteers to Goliad. Fort Defiance, as Fannin called his position, commanded the road connecting San Antonio to the sea, which made it strategically important by denying landing sites for the Mexican Army. On February 19, James BONHAM arrived in Goliad with a message from Col. William TRAVIS, co-commander of the ALAMO MIS-SION garrison in San Antonio — 95 miles away — encouraging Fannin to relocate his headquarters (and men) to the Alamo. Fan-nin, a West Point dropout with a reputation for indecisiveness, however, chose to remain at Goliad and put his men to work rein-forcing his fort. Another message from Travis arrived on February 25. Fannin had a change of heart and began organizing a relief expedition. He explained his decision in a letter to Lieutenant Governor James ROBINSON, which read in part: "The appeal of Colonels Travis and Bowie cannot be re-sisted, and particularly with the description of troops now in the field-sanguine, chival-rous volunteers. Much must be risked to re-lieve the besieged."

Fannin readied a relief expedition com-posed of 320 troops, 4 cannons, and several wagons hauled by oxen that contained am-munition and supplies, and set out for the Alamo on the morning of February 26. The expedition had travelled just several hun-dred yards when one of the supply wagons broke down. Repairs were made and they resumed their march. Within a mile, two more wagons broke down. At the San An-tonio River, Fannin realized that individual oxen were not strong enough to haul the cannons across and the job would require double-teaming the beasts of burden. As night approached, Fannin decided to delay his rescue mission until the following day.

The following morning, it was discov-ered that several oxen that were needed to haul the wagons and cannons had wandered off during the night. Fannin sent his men out to round them up. It was late afternoon before the relief expedition was ready to move out. Fannin, however, had second-thoughts. His men were in desperate need of supplies, and the closest source was 70 miles to the northwest at Juan SEGUIN's ranch. Besides that, he had left only 100 men to defend Goliad, and the exact whereabouts of the Mexican Army — except for those participating in the Alamo siege — was un-known other than information that a siz-able force was prowling the countryside. Fannin was holding a council of war with his officers when a messenger arrived to in-form him that long-awaited supplies had landed at Matagorda Bay, but there were no volunteers present to guard them. Right or wrong, the council was compelled to unan-imously vote to suspend the Alamo relief expedition. Fannin hauled his wagons back to Goliad where he learned that at 3 A.M. that morning a detachment of 50 men from his Matamoros Expedition commanded by Col. Frank JOHNSON had been attacked by Mexican Gen. José Urrea at San Patricio — 50 miles south of Goliad. Sixteen Ameri-cans had been killed and twenty-four cap-tured. Johnson and 4 others had escaped, and incorrectly spread the word that the re-mainder of his men had been executed. That disturbing news acted to further jus-tify Fannin's decision to abort the mission to rescue the Alamo. On March 2, Fannin once more refused a plea from Travis deliv-ered by James Bonham. That same day, an-other detachment of the Matamoros Expedition-15 men under Dr. James GRANT—had been ambushed and killed by Urrea's troops.

On March 14, a message arrived from Gen. Sam HOUSTON ordering Fannin to abandon his position and fall back to Victoria. It was known that about 1,400 Mexican Army troops under the command Gen. Urrea were marching directly toward Goliad. That same day, Fannin had dispatched Col. William Ward, commander of the GEORGIA BATTALION, and about 200 men to aid Capt. Amon King who was assisting in the evacuation of colonists around Refugio. Unknown to Fannin, the detachment commanded by Gen. Urrea had surrounded Ward's men, and, in a running battle, killed 16 and captured 31. Ward and the remainder of his unit began a desperate march to reach Victoria with Urrea determinedly in pursuit. Urrea also captured couriers dispatched by Fannin, and had learned about Fannin's strength and plans to fall back to Victoria.

Col. Fannin was hesitant to leave without word from Ward. Some questioned the logic of risking his entire command by waiting for men who could have likely later caught up with the main force. Fannin, however, was of the opinion that his position, unlike the Alamo, could likely withstand a Mexican assault almost indefinitely. The fortress, which stood upon a hill and had nearly cannon-proof walls, was well-stocked with supplies and boasted 12 pieces of artillery. Fannin had earlier sworn never to retreat, and now, instead of obeying orders without question or delay, he assumed an on-again off-again mode of retreat. Fannin directed that preparation for retreat begin by burying a number of the fort's cannons to prevent the Mexicans from capturing them. Then, changing his mind, he ordered that those cannons be dug up and remounted. Late on the afternoon of March 17, Fannin learned the fate

of Ward and King, and there was nothing left to keep him in Goliad.

On March 18, Fannin had the artillery he intended to take along hitched to oxen, and was finally ready to retreat when he was surprised to observe a Mexican army reconnaissance patrol in the distance. A small detachment led by Col. Albert Horton, the future governor of Texas, rode out to meet the Mexicans. An inconsequential skirmish ensued, without either side sustaining casualties. Fannin was about to move out when it was brought to his attention that the oxen had remained hitched and had not been properly attended to, which would necessitate another delay. Fannin once more ordered that the cannons be buried; then, in his indecisive fashion, ordered that they be dug up.

The morning of March 19 was foggy, and Fannin slipped away at 9 A.M. He had destroyed any additional serviceable artillery and vital supplies at Fort Defiance, but, in an oversight or blunder, had somehow forgotten to bring along sufficient food for his retreating army.

Gen. Urrea's troops arrived in Goliad at about noon to find the garrison empty, and immediately gave chase.

Fannin was informed after just several miles that the oxen would require time to rest and graze. Then, two miles farther, the ammunition wagon broke down and the oxen appeared on the brink of collapse. Fannin halted his people in the middle of a prairie rather than venturing two or three miles more to reach the sanctuary of timber and water of a forest at Coleto's Creek.

Meanwhile, Col. Horton and several scouts had been serving as rear guard, and had dismounted to relax when the advance of the Mexican cavalry startled them. They galloped away—the Colonel and two of them racing past Fannin's troops to apparently seek refuge in the forest beyond. One man stopped to spread the alarm.

Fannin resumed his retreat, prodding the oxen in an effort to make it into the forest where they would could establish a suitable defensive position. The Mexicans overtook them one-half mile from their objective in a low part of the prairie that no commander would have chosen as a place of defense. The wagons were formed into a square, and the volunteers prepared to make a stand.

Mexican charges were repelled throughout the afternoon with moderate casualties sustained on both sides. The volunteers positioned cannons at corners of the square, and fired grapeshot point-blank into their attacking enemy.

At nightfall, the two sides suspended hostilities. Bodies of dead Mexicans littered the prairie — about 50 killed and 140 wounded. The rebels had to that point suffered 9 killed and 51 wounded, including Col. Fannin who was wounded in the thigh.

There was no food or water in the rebel camp, most of the oxen had wandered off, and the Mexican troops had surrounded the square of wagons shouting taunts while the buglers played an eerie serenade. The volunteers endured the night by creating makeshift breastworks from dead horses, dirt, and the contents of the wagons.

The Mexicans were critically low on ammunition for a period of time following the day's battle, and Fannin and his men might have been able to escape under the cover of darkness. But, to his credit, he refused to abandon his wounded. The Mexicans were replenished by troops arriving during the night. These reinforcements were also hauling additional artillery pieces.

The Mexican artillery opened up at daybreak. Fannin was convinced that the only way to save any of his beleaguered command was to surrender. That proposal was hotly contested, especially by members of the NEW ORLEANS GREYS who forcefully argued in favor of dying fighting rather than turning themselves over to Mexicans whom they termed barbarians who could not be trusted to treat them humanely. The decision was put to a vote. The Greys and ALABAMA RED ROVERS voted to fight, but most of the remaining 200 or so men were in favor of surrendering.

Fannin raised the white flag, and met with three Mexican officers half-way between the two armies in order to negotiate an honorable surrender. Fannin was under the impression that his wounded would be provided medical care, and the rest of the detachment would be treated as prisoners of war.

Gen. Urrea personally visited Fannin's camp, and informed them that he would accept no such terms. He stated that Fannin could surrender at discretion, or unconditionally, otherwise the attack would be renewed. Fannin agreed to the terms dictated.

Mexican soldiers had wandered into the camp to take stock when the rebels' powder magazine exploded. One of the New Orleans Greys had taken a page from the book of Maj. Robert EVANS at the Alamo and made an effort to inflict casualties by detonating the explosive. The resultant blast wounded several men, but only the perpetrator was seriously hurt.

The explosion was heard by Col. Horton, who had ridden to Victoria and was returning with about 30 to 40 reinforcements. Horton, his astonishment evident, discerned from his position secreted in the timber that Fannin had surrendered. Horton understood that his small detachment could make little difference now that the fight was apparently over, and ordered his men to turn their horses and return to Victoria.

Fannin and his volunteers were taken back to Goliad, and imprisoned in the chapel. The quarters were so confining that it was impossible for most of them to even sit down.

Over the next two days, the Mexicans transported about 90 wounded volunteers from the battlefield to Goliad. These men were joined by one of the missing detachments that had been one of the reasons Fannin had delayed their departure in the first place. Col. William Ward and the survivors of Urrea's attack — about 120 men — had eluded capture for a week before Urrea took them all prisoner and delivered them to Goliad. Eighty-two mercenaries from New York that had just arrived at the port of Copano, Texas had been also captured by the Mexicans, and were sent to the makeshift prison. This brought the total to about 500 volunteers that were incarcerated at Goliad.

The prisoners were offered only water the first day, then were provided one steer to share. The men bartered with the Mexican soldiers, trading clothing and personal items for whatever morsels of food they could afford with the inflated prices.

Gen. Urrea was uncertain about the disposition of these prisoners. Santa Anna had ordered that all prisoners without exception be executed — 30 or so had already been killed on the way to Goliad. But Urrea could not comprehend the execution in cold blood of such a large number of people. Therefore, he permitted the wounded to be treated, and put the healthy to work building rafts and repairing fortifications that had earlier been destroyed. He even gained an admiration for Col. Fannin, whom he believed was a man of great courage and worthy of being spared.

Santa Anna, however, was incensed when informed that Gen. Urrea had not already followed orders and executed his prisoners. He dispatched a messenger with a letter to Urrea that read in part: "I have been surprised that the circular of the said supreme government has not been fully complied with in this particular; I therefore order, that you should give immediate effect to said ordinance in respect to all foreigners...."

Gen. Urrea replied to Santa Anna with an request for clemency. The plea, however, failed to change his commander's mind. Santa Anna wrote out an order in triplicate, and had it delivered to Col. José Nicolás Portilla, who was in direct command of the Goliad prisoners. The general also dispatched one of his colonels to witness the executions. Even as Portilla received this order from Santa Anna, Urrea — who was away attending to other business — sent him a message telling him to treat the prisoners well and have them continue rebuilding the fort. Portilla endured a sleepless night, but awoke on Palm Sunday, March 27, understanding which authority held more weight.

Col. Fannin and the wounded were not present when the rest of the prisoners were assembled for roll call at 8 A.M. The men had no inkling of impending disaster. In fact, they were excited. They had been informed by way of rumor that they were to be released and sent to New Orleans where they could return to their homes in America.

The prisoners were divided into three columns, and marched away in different directions. Each column was guarded on either side by a line of soldiers. The separate columns were eventually halted, and the men were ordered in Spanish to kneel down — a language few of them understood. The Mexican soldiers then opened fire at them from a distance of only a few paces away. The volleys of musket fire continued until those who had only been wounded in the initial blast had been killed. Some men — perhaps as many as 30 — escaped by running away in the smoky confusion and hiding near the San Antonio River, but most were killed in cold blood.

The disturbing gunfire was heard by those left behind in Goliad. The wounded were now escorted outside — those who could not walk were carried. These men were either shot, sabered, or bayoneted to death.

Col. James Fannin was taken to a spot beside the chapel. He was well aware of the fate that awaited him. He gave the officer attending him a gold watch belonging to his wife and ten pesos. Fannin was then seated in a chair, blindfolded, and executed by a firing squad. His body — as were those of the others killed — was later burned.

Only certain skilled artisans and doctors that suited the Mexican's needs had been spared. Others lived due to the efforts of Senora Francisca Alavez, the wife of a Mexican officer, who had interceded on their behalf with another officer who was himself opposed to the executions. For this act of compassion, Senora Alavez has been called the "Angel of Goliad."

The sad truth, however, was that over the objections and principles of Gen. Urrea and other noble Mexican officers, more than 400 prisoners had been slaughtered by order of Santa Anna. That total was more than double those who had died fighting at the Alamo.

"Remember Goliad" along with "Remember the Alamo" became a battle cry for the volunteers at the Battle of SAN JAC-INTO.

Fannin Plaza in present-day Goliad is the site of a Texas Revolution cannon and several historical markers. Two miles south of Goliad is a monument that marks the grave of Col. Fannin and his men. A few hundred yards away at Presidio La Bahia can be found the massive stone walls and other structures of the restored mission where Fannin and his men were imprisoned. Memorabilia and artifacts recovered during the restoration have been housed in a museum.

**GONZALES RANGING COMPANY (of Mounted Volunteers)** This group of 29 volunteers was hastily organized from colonists residing in the vicinity of Gonzales — 70 miles from San Antonio. COURIER Albert MARTIN arrived on February 27, the 6th day of the ALAMO SIEGE, with Col. William TRAVIS's message of the 24th pleading for assistance. At 2 P.M., these volunteers led by Capt. George KIMBELL had assembled in the public square to ride for the Alamo. Some were members of the "Old Eighteen," the ones who had participated in the GONZA-LES SKIRMISH the previous October and had protected their town cannon from being seized by the Mexicans in what had been the first shots fired in the TEXAS REVOLUTION. The company included Thomas MILLER, the richest man in town, and John KELLOGG, who had recently stolen away Miller's young bride, Sydney Gaston, whose brother, John GASTON, had also volunteered. James GEORGE and his brother-in-law William DEARDUFF volunteered, as did 14-year-old Galba FUQUA. Outside of town, they picked up 15-year-old William KING, who persuaded Kimbell to take him instead of his father who was needed at home. Alamo couriers Martin and Charles DESPALLIER would accompany the small force, and John W. SMITH, who had departed San Antonio on the first day of the siege, would serve as scout and guide. The unit successfully infiltrated MEXICAN ARMY lines, and entered the Alamo at about 3 A.M. on March 1, 1836 — the eighth day of the siege (see ALAMO SIEGE for more). The arrival of these men, in spite of fact that they had not brought much in the way of ammunition or supplies, served to bolster the spirits of those already inside the compound. Every man was subsequently killed during the ALAMO BATTLE. In addition to those listed above, other members of this unit known to have been killed in the Alamo Battle include: BAKER, Isaac; CAIN,

John; COTTLE, George; DARST, Jacob; DAVIS, John; DAMON, Squire; DUVALT, Andrew; FISHBAUGH, William; FLANDERS, John; FLOYD, Dolphin; HARRIS, John; JACKSON, Thomas; KENT, Andrew; LINDLEY, Jonathan; McCOY, Jesse; MILLSAPS, Isaac; NEGGAN, George; SEWELL, Marcus; SUMMERS, William; TUMLINSON, George; and WRIGHT, Claiborne.

**GONZALES, Skirmish at** (October 2, 1835) This skirmish between American settlers at Gonzales, Texas who refused to surrender a cannon to a detachment of Mexican soldiers was the spark that ignited the TEXAS REVOLUTION. The incident has been called the "The First Shot of the Texas Revolution," or, in a reference to the American Revolution, "The Lexington and Concord of the Texas Revolution."

### Chronology of the Texas Revolution

- June 29, 1835: Battle of ANAHUAC
- **October 2, 1835: GONZALES SKIRMISH**
- October 3, 1835: MEXICAN CONSTITUTION OF 1824 officially voided
- October 9, 1835: GOLIAD SKIRMISH
- October 28, 1835: Battle of CONCEPCION
- November 3, 1835: TEXAS CONSULTATION OF DELEGATES
- November–December, 1835: Siege and Battle of SAN ANTONIO
- January–February, 1836: The MATAMOROS EXPEDITION
- February 23–March 5, 1836: The ALAMO SIEGE
- March 1, 1836: TEXAS CONSTITUTIONAL CONVENTION
- March 2, 1836: TEXAS DECLARATION OF INDEPENDENCE
- March 6, 1836: The ALAMO BATTLE
- March 20–27, 1836: Surrender and Massacre at GOLIAD
- April 21, 1836: Battle of SAN JACINTO
- May 14, 1836: Treaties of VELASCO

The settlement at Gonzales had been provided a 6-pounder cannon four years earlier for the purpose of protecting itself against marauding Indians. The 6-pounder had been crudely mounted on wheels made from tree trunks, and had been damaged and modified to the extent of compromising its ballistic force. Despite its suspect condition the cannon could fire, and, at the least, could make a noise loud enough to chase away Comanches. Col. Domingo de Ugartechea, the Mexican commandant of Texas stationed in San Antonio, 70 miles west of Gonzales, heard about the cannon and was concerned that it could be turned against his army. Ugartecha dispatched a corporal and four other cavalrymen to Gonzales with orders to seize the cannon. Word of this demand reached Gonzales, and the defiant townspeople buried their cannon in a peach orchard. The Mexican troops upon arrival were met by Mayor Andrew Pondon, who claimed that he had no authority to hand over the cannon. The Mexicans returned empty-handed to San Antonio. Pondon, fearing that the Mexicans might take further action, then called for volunteers — reminiscent of the "minutemen" of the American Revolutionary War — from neighboring settlements up and down the valleys of the Colorado and Brazos Rivers to come to the aid of Gonzales.

Colonel Ugartechea was indeed adamant about his intention to remove the cannon from Gonzales. He sent Lt. Francisco Castaneda and about 100 men with orders to capture the 6-pounder by force if necessary. The Mexican troops arrived on September 29, and set up camp on the west side of the Guadalupe River about 4 miles above the settlement of Gonzales.

Meanwhile, Pondon's request for reinforcements brought more than 160 men to arms. The cannon was exhumed from the peach orchard, mounted on ox cart wheels, and loaded with chains, nails, and iron scraps made from old horseshoes. A flag — said to have been fashioned from the white silk wedding dress worn by Naomi DeWitt, daughter of the colony's late founder, Green DeWitt, when she married W. A. Mathews in 1833 — had been affixed to the Gonzales cannon. The words "Come and Take It!" had been inscribed above and below the drawing of a cannon that dominated the center of the flag.

The Gonzales volunteers, under the command of Colonel J. H. Moore, decided to strike the Mexicans before their town was invaded. At dawn on October 2, the Texans approached the Mexican camp — the cannon in question hauled by longhorn steers.

The morning was foggy, which made visibility poor. The volunteers, some in boats, others on foot, snuck to within 350 yards of the camp. Blacksmith Almeron DICKINSON fired the cannon at the surprised Mexicans.

Lt. Castaneda immediately requested a parley, but was rebuffed by the taunt, "Come and take it!"

Dickinson fired the cannon once more, and was accompanied by musket fire from the volunteers. The Mexicans were quickly routed, and abandoned their camp to retreat down the road back to San Antonio — taking with them at least one killed and several wounded.

The Texans, who had not suffered a casualty, returned to Gonzales and staged a huge town celebration that night, perhaps not entirely aware that the revolution had truly begun that day. Those original defenders of the cannon became known as the "Old Eighteen."

Gonzales Memorial Museum in present-day Gonzales features a replica of the cannon that initiated the battle as well as other artifacts. An annual "Come and Take it" celebration includes a reenactment of the battle.

**GOODRICH, John Camp** (1809–March 6, 1836) Cornett, TEXAS REVOLUTIONARY ARMY; Alamo defender from Virginia. Goodrich came to Texas with his brothers by way of Tennessee and settled in Anderson, Grimes County on April 30, 1834. He was serving as a company officer/guidon bearer when he was killed in the ALAMO BATTLE. His brother, Benjamin Briggs Goodrich, was one of the signers of the TEXAS DECLARATION OF INDEPENDENCE.

**GRANT, Dr. James** (July 28, 1783–March 2, 1836) This physician, a native of Killearnan Parish, Scotland, came to Texas as a land speculator in 1823 and settled in Parras, Coahuila. He served as secretary of the Executive Council of Coahuila, and as a member of the Legislature in 1832. He moved to Nacogdoches in 1833, and, in partnership with English surgeon Dr. John Beales, contracted to settle 800 European families in the region between the Rio Grande and Nueces Rivers. A settlement named Delores was established in 1834, but due to crop failure, Indian raids, and later Mexican General Antonio Lopez de SANTA ANNA's invasion of Texas, the colony was abandoned. Grant was serving as secretary of the Congress of Coahuila at Monclova, and was one of the land speculators that had conspired with that corrupt government in shady land deals to invite the wrath of Santa Anna in early 1835. The Mexican dictator dispatched an army under Gen. Martin Perfecto de CÓS to round up known land speculators. Grant was captured, but escaped. He was elected as a delegate to the November, 1835 TEXAS CONSULTATION OF DELEGATES, but had joined the army and declined to attend. Grant became an instigator of controversy in January, 1836 when he and several others, including Colonels Frank JOHNSON and James FANNIN, encouraged an invasion of

Mexico called the MATAMOROS EXPEDITION. The ensuing debate over the propriety of this endeavor led to the impeachment of Governor Henry SMITH, who was opposed because part of the reason for the expedition was to pay its members with plunder. Grant's motives were to restore the MEXICAN CONSTITUTION OF 1824 rather than fight for Texas independence in order to permit him to maintain his questionable land dealings. He prepared for this expedition by pillaging the Alamo garrison in San Antonio of men and supplies, which weakened it in the face of the advancing MEXICAN ARMY. On March 2, 1836, while out attempting to collect horses and supplies for this expedition, which was later scuttled, Grant and 15 other volunteers were attacked by a Mexican force commanded by Gen. José URREA at Agua Dulce Creek. Grant and all his men were killed.

**GRIMES, Albert Calvin** (December 20, 1817–March 6, 1836) Private; TEXAS REVOLUTIONARY ARMY; Alamo defender from Georgia. Grimes had been residing near present-day Navasota, Texas when he was killed in the ALAMO BATTLE while serving as a rifleman. His father Jesse was one of the signers of the TEXAS DECLARATION OF INDEPENDENCE.

**GUERRERO, Brigido** Alamo survivor. This former Mexican soldier came to Texas from Mexico with Col. Domingo Ugartecha, and deserted his unit at the outbreak of the TEXAS REVOLUTION. He was living in San Antonio when he was employed to provide cattle for the Texans that were garrisoned in that town. Guerrero sought refuge inside the ALAMO MISSION when Gen. Antonio Lopez de SANTA ANNA and his army attacked. During the ALAMO BATTLE, he hid from his former comrades, and, when discovered, lied about being captured by the Texans and brought against his will into the Alamo. Guerrero was believed, and his life was spared.

**GUERRERO, José Maria** This man apparently has been confused with Brigido GUERRERO. Although at one time a member of SEGUIN'S CAVALRY COMPANY, it is doubtful that José Maria was present during the ALAMO BATTLE as reported in some accounts.

**GWYNNE, James C.** (aka "Groya," "Groyan," and Gwin"; 1804–March 6, 1836) Private, TEXAS REVOLUTIONARY ARMY; Alamo defender from England. Gwynn came to Texas from Mississippi, and participated in the Siege and Battle of SAN ANTONIO. He was serving as an artilleryman in Capt. William CAREY's artillery company when he was killed in the ALAMO BATTLE.

# H

**HANNUM, James** (aka "Hannan" and "Hanuam"; August 8, 1815–March 6, 1836) Private, TEXAS REVOLUTIONARY ARMY; Alamo defender from Pennsylvania. Hannum was serving as a rifleman when he was killed in the ALAMO BATTLE.

**HARRIS, John** (1813–March 6, 1836) Private, GONZALES RANGING COMPANY; Alamo defender from Kentucky. Harris was living in Gonzales, Texas, participated in the Siege and Battle of SAN ANTONIO and was awarded a section of land for his service. He entered the ALAMO MISSION with his unit on March 1, 1836, and was serving as a rifleman when he was killed in the ALAMO BATTLE.

**HARRISON, Andrew Jackson** (1809–March 6, 1836) Private, TEXAS REVOLUTIONARY ARMY; Alamo defender from Tennessee. Harrison was serving as a rifleman when he was killed in the ALAMO BATTLE.

**HARRISON, William B.** (1811–March 6, 1836) Captain, TENNESSEE MOUNTED VOLUNTEERS; Alamo defender from Tennessee. Harrison was sworn into the service at Nacogdoches on January 14, 1836 as the commanding officer of the Tennessee Mounted Volunteers, and arrived in San Antonio with his unit on February 8. During the ALAMO SIEGE and BATTLE, his company had the responsibility of defending the wooden palisade which ran from the chapel to the low barracks along the Alamo's south wall. He was killed while serving in that capacity.

**HAWKINS, Joseph M.** (aka "M." or "Mark" Hawkins; 1799–March 6, 1836) Private, TEXAS REVOLUTIONARY ARMY; Alamo defender from Ireland. Hawkins arrived at the ALAMO MISSION by way of Louisiana in the company of James BOWIE on January 19. He was serving as a rifleman in Capt. William BAKER's company when he was killed in the ALAMO BATTLE.

**HAYS, John M.** (1814–March 6, 1836) Private, TEXAS REVOLUTIONARY ARMY; Alamo defender from Nashville, Tennessee. Hays was serving as a rifleman when he was killed in the ALAMO BATTLE.

**HEISKELL, Charles M.** (aka "Haskell" and "Huskill"; 1813–March 6, 1836) Private, TEXAS REVOLUTIONARY ARMY; Alamo defender from Tennessee. Heiskell was a member of the ill-fated MATAMOROS EXPEDITION, but returned to the ALAMO MISSION in the company of James BOWIE on January

19, 1836. He was serving as a rifleman when he was killed in the ALAMO BATTLE.

**HERNDON, Patrick Henry** (March, 1802–March 6, 1836) Private, TEXAS REVOLUTIONARY ARMY; Alamo defender from Virginia. Herndon, who had been residing in Navidad, Texas, was serving as a rifleman when he was killed in the ALAMO BATTLE.

**HERSEE, William Daniel** (1805–March 6, 1836) Sergeant, TEXAS REVOLUTIONARY ARMY; Alamo defender from England. Hersee, a married man with 4 children, came to Texas by way of Louisiana. He was wounded in the Siege and Battle of SAN ANTONIO, and was serving as an noncommissioned officer in Capt. William CAREY's artillery company when he was killed in the ALAMO BATTLE.

**HIGHSMITH, Benjamin Franklin** (August 11, 1817–November 20, 1905) Private, TEXAS REVOLUTIONARY ARMY; Alamo COURIER from St. Charles District, Missouri. In 1823 at age 6, Highsmith travelled with his family by wagon train and raft to arrive in Texas and settle near present-day La Grange. At age 15, he participated in the 1832 Battle of VELASCO, and later settled in Bastrop, Texas where he lived for the next 50 years. He participated in the GONZALES SKIRMISH, the Battle of CONCEPCION, and the Siege and Battle of SAN ANTONIO. Sometime prior to the ALAMO SIEGE, Highsmith was dispatched as a courier from San Antonio to Goliad by Col. William TRAVIS. He returned to find the Mexican Army occupying the area, and headed for Gonzales. He then served as a courier for Gen. Sam HOUSTON, and as a rifleman in the Battle of SAN JACINTO. Highsmith, who was wounded in the Mexican War, later became a Texas Ranger, married, and fathered 13 children. He enjoyed showing off his whetstone that he claimed had sharpened the knives of such luminaries as James BOWIE, Sam HOUSTON, Erastus "Deaf" SMITH, and William TRAVIS.

**HOCKLEY, George Washington** (1802–June 6, 1854) Colonel, TEXAS REVOLUTIONARY ARMY. This Philadelphia native was working as a clerk in the War Department in Washington, D.C., when he met Sam HOUSTON. In 1828, when Houston was elected governor of Tennessee, Hockley moved to that state. He followed Houston to Texas in 1835, and served as chief of staff when Houston was made commander in chief of the army. Hockley was commander of artillery — the "Twin Sisters" cannons — at the Battle of SAN JACINTO, and later accompanied Mexican dictator Antonio Lopez de SANTA ANNA to Washington. He was secretary of war in 1838 and again in 1841 in Houston's cabinet, and in 1843 was dispatched to Mexico City on an armistice mission. Hockley died in Corpus Cristi at the age of 52.

**HOLLAND, Tapley** (1810–March 6, 1836) Private, TEXAS REVOLUTIONARY ARMY; Alamo defender from Ohio. This resident of Grimes County, Texas, participated in the Siege and Battle of SAN ANTONIO. On the final night of the ALAMO SIEGE (March 5), Col. William TRAVIS drew a line across the dirt with his sword to distinguish those who wanted to leave from those who wanted to remain and fight. According to Alamo escapee Louis ROSE, Holland was the first man to step across that line to demonstrate his support for staying and fighting. He was killed in the ALAMO BATTLE while serving as an artilleryman in Capt. William CAREY's artillery company.

**HOLLOWAY, Samuel** (1808–March 6, 1836) Private, NEW ORLEANS GREYS; Alamo defender from Pennsylvania. This Philadelphian came to Texas with his unit on November 21, 1835, and participated in the Siege and Battle of SAN ANTONIO. He was serving as a rifleman in Capt. William BLAZEBY's infantry company when he was killed in the ALAMO BATTLE.

**HOUSTON, Samuel** "Sam" (March 2, 1793–July 26, 1863) General, commander in chief, TEXAS REVOLUTIONARY ARMY; 2-term U.S. Congressman; governor of Tennessee; first president of the Republic of Texas; United States Senator; governor of Texas. Houston was about 6 feet 2 inches tall, with a fair complexion, brown hair and gray eyes.

*Birth and Early Life*

The paternal great-grandfather of Sam Houston was an Ulster Scot whose Scottish ancestry could be traced back to the Middle Ages. He immigrated from Northern Ireland to Philadelphia with his Presbyterian church congregation in the early 18th-century, and moved to Virginia near present-day Brownsburg in about 1742. Houston's father, Samuel, served in the American Revolution as a member of the Virginia Rifle Brigade in the Continental Army. His mother, Elizabeth (Paxton), was the Scotch-Irish daughter of the richest man in Rockbridge County, Virginia. Sam was born in a stately columned plantation house built by his grandfather in Rockbridge County — 7 miles from Lexington — the 5th son (after Paxton, Robert, James, and John) of Samuel and Elizabeth. Houston began his education at a small local school and learned the 3 R's, but much of his schooling was performed at home in his father's small library. Sam's father had remained in the army with the rank of major, and was away a good deal of the time. In 1807, Major Houston died suddenly while on an inspection tour of a frontier army post some 40 miles away near present-day Callaghan, Virginia. Elizabeth Houston sold the plantation, and moved her family — 6 sons and 3 daughters — to the vicinity of Marysville in eastern Tennessee to join relatives who already lived in that wilderness pioneer settlement. The Houstons settled on Baker's Creek, 10 miles south of Marysville, 5 miles from the Little Tennessee River which was the border of lands roamed by the Cherokee Indian Nation.

Sam was educated at the Porter Academy, and it was said that his favorite book was Alexander Pope's translation of *The Illiad*, which inspired great dreams within him. He ended his formal education at age 16 in a dispute over the schoolmaster's refusal to teach him Greek and Latin, and was subsequently forced by his brothers into taking a job in the village store. He did not, however, embrace that business, and one day simply disappeared into the nearby forests to live with the Cherokee Indians. Sam professed to his brothers when he was tracked down some time later that he preferred "the wild liberty of the Red men, better than the tyranny of his own brothers." He remained with the Cherokee for nearly 3 years, and learned their language and customs. Sam was given the name Kalanu — translated meaning "The Raven" — by his surrogate father, Ooleteka, who was chief of the tribe.

Houston returned to the white man's world as a teacher in a school near Marysville. This man who wore his hair Indian fashion, with a lengthy queue hanging down his back, earned $8 tuition from each of the 18 students — payable in thirds of cash, corn, and cloth. The money offered some relief, for Sam had accumulated debts to his family and local merchants while living with the Cherokee. Sam was well-versed in the 3 R's

in addition to the classics and geography, but it was his qualities as a speaker that made his teaching tenure a success. The job lasted 6 months, and in 1812 he departed to resume his education at the Porter Academy.

*Military Service*

The United States had entered into a conflict with Great Britain, and, with the blessing of his mother, Sam heeded the call and enlisted in the infantry to fight in the War of 1812. He was quickly promoted to ensign, and then on December 31 to 3rd lieutenant in the 39th Regiment, which also claimed as a member David CROCKETT, who became a lifelong friend. Houston arrived at Fort Strother, Alabama, on February 13, 1814, and assisted General Andrew Jackson in the training of troops.

Gen. Jackson, Houston, and about 500 men from the 39th Regiment departed Fort Strother on March 14, and, in the company of about 500 Cherokees and 100 friendly Creeks, set out to attack a large, fortified Creek town on the Tallapoosa River at Horseshoe Bend. The "Red Sticks" as they were called were allies of the British, and had about 1000 warriors waiting behind double-walled breastworks. On March 28, Jackson ordered a cannon barrage from across the river — a distance of about 80 yards, which inflicted many casualties. Jackson's Cherokee allies swam the river and managed to appropriate enough canoes to ferry the troops across. Jackson ordered an attack, and, with one part of his force able to maneuver behind the Creek village, dispatched the remainder of his troops on a frontal assault. Sam Houston and the 39th led the charge to scale the walls of the Creek fortification. His commander, Maj. Lemuel Montgomery, was almost immediately killed atop the wall. Houston was directly behind Montgomery, and urged the men to follow him. He successfully scaled the wall, but was struck in the thigh by an arrow. He called on a comrade to remove the barbed arrow, and, after three attempts, the arrow was released — tearing flesh and gushing blood. Houston had the wound treated and intended to return to the battle, but was ordered by Jackson to remain in the rear. Meanwhile, the Creeks had retreated to the river, and were pinned down by army rifles in a natural redoubt. Jackson ordered a charge. Despite his wound, Sam Houston led the assault. He was within 5 yards of the Creek position when 2 rifle shots struck him in the right shoulder. Houston was carried unconscious to the surgeon, who was able to remove only one of the musket balls. It was presumed that Houston, with one ball remaining in his shoulder and a nasty arrow wound in his thigh, would soon die. While Houston lay on the ground waiting for the end to come, his shoulder and leg aching from the enemy arrow and musket ball, his companions set fire to the wooden redoubt and sharpshooters slaughtered the hostile Red Sticks. The Battle of Horseshoe Bend, the decisive engagement of the Creek War, had been won. Gen. Jackson singled out Houston for his gallantry during the battle, and later promoted him to 2nd lieutenant for his actions. To the surprise of many, the wounded Sam Houston had not died during the night as had been expected. He was loaded onto a litter the next day, and carried for 2 long months before arriving at his mother's house.

Doctors in Tennessee were equally pessimistic about his prognosis. Houston defied them as well, and that summer was well enough to ride. He set off for Washington, D.C., to seek more advanced medical techniques to treat his wounds. Houston decided not to remain in Washington, which had been burned to the ground by the British, but continued on to his childhood home in Virginia. It was there that relatives nursed him back to health.

Houston had intentions of remaining in the army, but was afraid that he would be dismissed due to his wound and the downsizing that was taking place. On his 22nd birthday, he sent letters to his state senator, and congressman, and Secretary of War James Monroe requesting retention. His effort was successful, and, on July 4, 1815, he reported for duty in Nashville and was subsequently sent to a post in New Orleans. Houston endured a painful operation to remove a shattered bone from his wounded shoulder, and remained confined to his barracks throughout the winter reading and writing letters. He sailed for New York City in April, 1816 — apparently for medical reasons — and reported for duty at Nashville in the fall. Houston was quartered at the Hermitage, the residence of his commander Andrew Jackson, and was initiated into the Masonic Order, whose membership boasted most of the influential men of that time. Jackson dispatched Houston in the fall of 1817 — in the prestigious position of sub-agent — with responsibility of persuading his old friends, the Cherokee, to accept a move to Arkansas Territory. Houston arrived at the Cherokee Agency near present-day Calhoun, Tennessee on December 18, and was immediately concerned about the behavior of the Indian agents who had been profiting at the expense of the Cherokee as well as selling them whisky. Houston prohibited the sale of alcohol, and by promising bribes of supplies convinced about 500 Cherokee, including his former surrogate father, Ooleteka, to emigrate. The Cherokee, however, were apprehensive, and a delegation of chiefs — accompanied by Sam Houston — travelled to Washington for talks. The Indians arrived in February, 1818, and were treated to a series of receptions and armloads of presents. Houston was at that time accused by political enemies of Andrew Jackson of preventing the Cherokees from fighting in the Seminole War in Florida, and of himself engaging in illegal slave trading. Houston had no problem refuting the charges, but the episode served to reinforce his opinion that he was not suited for the pettiness and politics of the army. On March 1, 1818, he submitted his resignation. He remained with the Indian delegation, however, and presented himself to President Monroe on March 7 wearing full Indian dress. Monroe was outraged by such behavior, and made it a point to angrily lecture Houston following the meeting.

## Politics

Sam Houston had spent 5 years in the army and had managed to cultivate many influential friends, but his future endeavors were less than settled. He briefly returned to Baker's Creek to contemplate his opportunities, and soon decided to pursue the legal profession. Sam travelled to Nashville in June, 1818 to study law in the offices of respected Judge James Trimble. Houston at this time became widely known in the social community, and had even became a member of the Dramatic Club of Nashville. The law course designed for Houston was supposed to consume the better part of a year, but in only a few months of intensive study he was prepared to take the bar examination. In early 1819, he was admitted to the Tennessee bar, and opened an office in Lebanon — about 30 miles from Nashville. Later that year, he ran for district attorney of Davidson County and easily won. Sam returned to Nashville, the county seat, and remained in office until late 1821 when monetary considerations compelled him to open his own law practice. He was named a colonel in the local militia, eventually was promoted to adjutant general, and in October, 1821

was elected major general — head of the division that comprised two-thirds of the state. Houston lived at the Nashville Inn at this point in time, which was frequented by state legislators and traveling dignitaries and became a hotbed of political activities from deals to feuds. In 1823, Houston was nominated to run for the U.S. Congress, and, with no opposition against him, garnered 100 percent of the vote and was elected to represent Tennessee's Ninth Congressional District in the Eighteenth Congress. Houston served in Washington with such historical political giants as the president, James Monroe; cabinet members John Quincy Adams and John C. Calhoun; congressmen Thomas Hart Benton, Henry Clay, Andrew Jackson, and Daniel Webster; Chief Justice of the Supreme Court John Marshall; and former presidents Thomas Jefferson, John Adams, and James Madison, who regularly commented about public affairs. Houston as a freshman congressman wisely deferred the business of the nation to his more experienced colleagues. His first term was unremarkable, other than one rousing speech — the defense of the people of *The Iliad* who had risen up against their Turkish masters — in which Houston supported Greek independence. He was reelected in 1825, and accomplished little more than helping to set the stage for the presidency of Andrew Jackson by acting as his point man in the House and responding to criticism of his mentor with vigor and effectiveness. Houston attributed his success in politics to his ability as a natural orator who could expound on any subject for hours at a time.

In 1826, he became embroiled in a matter of politics that eventually led to a duel. In nominating a candidate for postmaster in Nashville, Houston vilified a man, John P. Erwin, that happened to be the son-in-law of secretary of state Henry Clay. Erwin received the appointment, and a supporter of his, John Smith, who was unknown to Houston, challenged Houston to a duel for defaming the new postmaster. Dueling was illegal in Tennessee, and Houston replied through an emissary that for that reason he declined to participate. Meanwhile, another Erwin supporter, Gen. William White, who was well known by Houston, took up the challenge. There had been bad blood between the two men for years due to White's outspoken anti–Jackson sentiments. Houston accepted this challenge, and retired to The Hermitage, Jackson's estate, to practice. The laws in Kentucky were more lenient than those in Tennessee, and the two men met at dawn on September 21 in a location said to have been about 6 miles south of Franklin, Kentucky — but was likely in Tennessee. Gen. White shot first, and missed. Houston's bullet found its mark, and White crumpled to the ground, wounded in the groin. White survived, and the Kentucky governor called for the arrest of Houston "for having feloniously shot and wounded" the general. Tennessee authorities made no effort to arrest or extradite Houston. He was, however, suspended by his Masonic lodge for one year for fighting a duel with a fellow Mason.

At the urging of Andrew Jackson, Sam Houston ran for governor of Tennessee in 1827. He effectively justified himself when the dueling issue was raised by his opponent by declaring that he had been defending his honor. And, with the support of Jackson and the 3-term incumbent, William Carroll, who could not succeed himself, Houston easily won election. He called for internal improvements such as roads, bridges, canals, the promotion of commerce and trade, and a fund set aside for public schools. The following year, Houston traveled to New Orleans and other places to participate in the successful campaign for the election of Andrew Jackson as president.

On January 22, 1829, 36-year-old Sam Houston married 20-year-old Eliza H. Allen, the daughter of a prominent Tennessee aristocrat, at Allenwood, the family plantation on the Cumberland River. Eliza's brother had served in Congress with Houston, and Sam had frequently visited the Allen plantation. Eliza's father had vigorously encouraged his daughter to accept Houston's proposal in what could best be described as an arranged marriage. The Houstons traveled by horseback to Nashville, and set up housekeeping on the second floor of the Nashville Inn.

Governor Houston did not attend the March 4 inauguration of Jackson in Washington for reasons rumored to be marital. The marriage had been in trouble since the onset, perhaps due to the age or cultural differences — Eliza was better educated and more refined than Sam. Regardless of the particulars, Eliza left Houston in early April and returned to her father's plantation. Houston's enemies contended that it was his unjustified jealousy that caused the breakup, but neither party ever offered a reason for her departure and a divorce was later granted on grounds of abandonment. He was aware that the scandal involving the powerful Allen family would likely make him a political pariah in Tennessee. With that in mind, Houston, who had previously intended to run for reelection, submitted his letter of resignation as governor on April 16. He secluded himself in his rooms, drank heavily, and mourned his loss while contemplating his future. Sam Houston, reportedly in a state of suicidal despair, boarded a steamboat headed for the Mississippi River on April 23 and set out to locate his old Indian friends.

### Indian Trader

Houston arrived in Little Rock, Arkansas 15 days after leaving Nashville. He wrote a letter to President Jackson, not to explain his reasons for the unsuccessful marriage or his impulsive actions, but to refute rumors that he was plotting to separate Texas from Mexico with the help of western Indians. Jackson, who had heard the rumors and was indeed upset by them, wrote back: "I must have really thought you deranged to have believed you had such a wild scheme in contemplation; and particularly when it was communicated that the physical force to be employed was the Cherokee Indians! Your pledge of honor to the contrary is a sufficient guaranty that will never engage in any enterprise injurious to your country, or that will tarnish your fame."

Houston — "The Raven" — was met by Chief Ooleteka, whom he had not seen in 11 years, at Webber's Falls near the mouth of the Illinois River. The Cherokee had been relocated to this western territory that was ancient hunting ground of the Comanches, Osage and Pawnee tribes. Houston immediately became involved in Indian affairs in an effort to diffuse the threat of tribal warfare and to condemn the dealings of unscrupulous Indian agents who had been taking advantage of the Cherokee. Houston worked zealously to defend the Cherokee in these matters, and was successful in removing several Indian agents and preventing war between that tribe and the Pawnees. On October 21, 1829, Houston was granted citizenship in the Cherokee Nation. He traveled to Washington in January, 1830, and was heartily welcomed by President Jackson. Houston also was introduced at that time to Texas EMPRESARIOS David BURNET and Lorenzo de ZAVALA, who in 1836 would become the first president and vice-president of the Republic of Texas. Houston assisted the two financially strapped men in transferring their land contract to the New York-based Galveston Bay and Texas Land Company.

In what would later become a scandal, Houston was said to have received privileged information from Jackson about the removal and relocation of some Indian tribes, and embarked on a scheme to bid for rations that would be provided to immigrating Indians. His bid — as was the case with the others — was rejected as being too high, and the army was charged with feeding these tribes. He returned to the Cherokee Nation and established his home and a trading post, called the Wigwam Neosho, on the Verdigis River across from Fort Gibson. Detractors claimed that his acceptance into the Cherokee Nation had been a gambit designed to circumvent the requirement of government approval for a trading post. His initial supplies arrived in July, and included 9 barrels of alcoholic spirits, which displeased the commander of Fort Gibson. Houston, who had years before fought to keep whiskey from the Indians, grudgingly promised not to sell to Indians and likely consumed much of the stock himself.

Also that summer, Sam Houston married Tiana Rogers Gentry — known as Talahina to the Cherokees — who was the niece of Ooleteka and the daughter of a Scottish trader and a woman who was one-eighth Cherokee. Tiana had attended a missionary school in Tennessee, and brought a substantial dowry of property, livestock, and slaves.

Houston continued to speak out against the behavior of Indian agents, and from June to December, 1830 had letters published in the *Arkansas Gazette* — some under the name Tah-LohnTus-Ky — which were highly critical of the War Department and gained attention throughout the country. The Indian agents challenged Houston's accusations. His efforts were rewarded with a reorganization of the entire program but no substantial change in procedures. In spite of his advocacy, he was defeated in a bid to become a member of the Cherokee Tribal

Council in May, 1831. Houston, who had the reputation of being a drunk, was devastated by the rejection. He confronted Chief Ooletka and received a lecture about his drinking. Houston attacked the old man, but was restrained before seriously harming the chief.

In full Indian garb, Sam Houston soon boarded a steamer headed for Nashville. He spent much of the time drunk, and this behavior did not improve when he arrived at his destination. He returned to his trading post, but received word that his mother was dying and set off once more for Tennessee. He arrived in time to visit Elizabeth before she died, then headed back to the Cherokee Nation.

In December, he was an unofficial member of a Cherokee delegation to Washington and planned to go on to New York City to seek out his business connections. In April, 1832, Houston was the subject of a personal attack in a speech on the floor of Congress by William Stanbery of Ohio, a Jackson opponent. Houston's attempt 2 years earlier to gain the contract for Indian rations by using inside information was brought up in an effort to condemn Jackson. Houston confronted Stanbery on the street, and bludgeoned the congressman with a walking stick. Stanbury pointed his pistol point blank at Houston's chest, but the weapon misfired. Houston, who claimed he had struck Stanbury in self-defense only after the congressman had pulled the pistol, had given his rival a concussion, a fractured left hand, and multiple bruises on his body. Houston was arrested and brought before Congress on April 17 to be charged with assault on a congressman and contempt of Congress. It was an election year, and Jackson, who was up for reelection, protected his friend by stating that he could use "a dozen Houstons to beat and cudgel the members of Congress," and that "after a few more examples of the

same kind, members of Congress would learn to keep civil tongues in their heads." Houston went to trial on April 19 defended by lawyer Francis Scott Key, composer of "The Star Spangled Banner." On May 7, Sam Houston addressed the House in his own defense. Although nursing a terrible hangover, he demonstrated his inherent expertise as an orator and portrayed his actions as those of an innocent man protecting his reputation from a congressman who was hiding behind immunity from prosecution for libel. The eloquent speech gained him support from the public, but 4 days later the House voted 106 to 89 for a guilty verdict. Houston, however, received nothing more than a reprimand from the Speaker of the House. Stanbury pressed civil charges, and Houston was again found guilty and fined $500. The incident did much to restore Houston's tarnished reputation, and the appreciative Jackson invited Houston to live at the White House until returning west that summer.

### Texas

Sam Houston was said to have committed to a contract to be an agent for the Galveston Bay and Texas Land Company, and decided to set off for Texas to seek his fortune in real estate. That, however, may not have been the real reason for his excursion to Texas — Mexico's April 6, 1930 Law had forbidden the settling of immigrants from the United States. Houston evidently also was serving as a personal representative of President Jackson, who had always been an advocate that Texas had always been part of Louisiana Purchase. He was issued a passport on August 6, and departed in mid-September to visit territory occupied by the various Indian tribes. The mission, which he contended was simply for the purpose of fact-finding about the nature of the indigenous Indians, brought him to the Red River — the Texas border — on December 1. He arrived at Jonesborough, the first Anglo-American settlement in Texas, 10 days later. Houston moved on to Nacogdoches, and presented his credentials to the Mexican commandant. He then embarked on a 300-mile trip across Texas on the Camino Real — the Old San Antonio Road — and in early 1833 arrived in San Antonio de Bexar where he met Jim BOWIE, who had married into the prominent Veramendi family. Houston held a peace conference with local Comanche chiefs, and gained their support for another parley at Fort Gibson in the spring. He retraced his route eastward, and reported to the president from Natchitoches, Louisiana about the rich, fertile land and, more importantly, that in Houston's opinion the majority of the population favored annexation by the United States. Houston returned to San Antonio to escort the Indians, and received word that he had been elected as a delegate to the Texas Convention of 1833 in San Felipe. In April, Houston chaired the committee that drafted a Texas state constitution, which would be carried to Mexico City by Stephen F. AUSTIN. Austin would subsequently be imprisoned in that city, and would not return to Texas for more than 2 years.

Houston settled in Nacogdoches, and established a law practice. His reputation had preceded him, and he quickly had more business than he could handle. He also engaged in land speculation, and amassed holdings that included 140,000 acres in partnership with 2 other men, and 10,000 acres of his own. Sam visited his trading post in May, and closed that chapter of his life — including finding a good home for his favorite dog and the abandonment of his Cherokee wife. He then returned to his business affairs in Texas, became baptized into the Catholic

faith, and accepted citizenship in the Republic of Mexico.

Sam traveled to New York and Washington in March, 1834, and, with the April 6, 1830, Law repealed, evidently become an agent for the Galveston Bay and Texas Land Company. Houston also managed to have the $500 fine imposed by the civil court for his beating of representative Stanbury that he had failed to pay pardoned by President Jackson. He returned briefly to Texas before taking another trip to Washington. Houston apparently made statements at this time that have been construed as evidence for his ambition to annex not merely Texas but all of Mexico. He was also able to enrich his reputation as a heavy drinker by carousing all night and sleeping most of the day.

### The Texas Revolution

One week after the first shots of the TEXAS REVOLUTION were fired in the October, 1835 Skirmish at GONZALES, Sam Houston was named commander of the troops in the Nacogdoches Department under army commander in chief Stephen F. Austin, who had recently returned to Texas following his imprisonment in Mexico. Houston proclaimed: "The morning of glory is dawning upon us. The work of liberty has begun. Let your valor proclaim to the world that liberty is your birthright. We cannot be conquered by all the arts of anarchy and despotism combined. In heaven and in valorous hearts we repose our confidence. Union and courage can achieve every thing, while reason combined with intelligence, can regulate all things necessary to human happiness." Houston remained in Nacogdoches as the TEXAS REVOLUTIONARY ARMY marched against the MEXICAN ARMY. Houston attended the November TEXAS CONSULTATION OF DELEGATES, and surprisingly sided with the PEACE PARTY stance of fighting to restore the MEXICAN CONSTITUTION OF 1824 as opposed to the WAR PARTY's cry for independence. At that consultation, Austin was named to a party of commissioners who would travel to seek aid in the United States. On November 12, Houston was appointed commander in chief of the Texas Revolutionary Army with orders to raise a fighting force of men to repel the Mexican threat. He put out an urgent call to "Let each man come with a good rifle and 100 rounds of ammunition — and come soon. Our war cry is 'Liberty or Death.'" Houston emphasized this opportunity to gain property when he said, "If volunteers from the United States will join their brethren in this section (Texas), they will receive liberal bounties of land. We have millions of acres of our best lands unchosen and unappropriated." Battalions of citizen-soldiers were hastily formed and marched to Texas. Individual volunteers came from states across the country as well — including some recent arrivals from England, Scotland, Germany, Ireland.

The Texans had previously been victorious at the GOLIAD SKIRMISH and the Battle of CONCEPCION, in addition to Gonzales, and in December — in spite of Houston's orders to retreat — chased Mexican Gen. Martin Perfecto de CÓS from the Alamo in the Siege and Battle of SAN ANTONIO. The General Council, part of the TEXAS PROVISIONAL GOVERNMENT, approved an invasion of Mexico called the MATAMOROS EXPEDITION, which Houston refused to lead. This expedition, which was little more than an opportunity for several men, such as Col. Frank JOHNSON and Dr. James GRANT, to protect their illegal land holdings and for the men to plunder the Mexican countryside, was to be led by Col. James W. FANNIN. Fannin and his agents began pillaging for provisions to outfit their expedition, which included gutting the Alamo of men and supplies. Houston responded by travelling

to the various camps, and, by utilizing his great oratory power, convinced most of the men to abandon the idea. He then dispatched Jim Bowie to San Antonio with orders to evacuate and destroy the Alamo — orders that Bowie would disobey.

Houston attended the March TEXAS CONSTITUTIONAL CONVENTION in Washington-on-the-Brazos, where his selection as army commander in chief was reaffirmed. He then departed for Gonzales, where he learned the fate of the Alamo, and embarked on a retreat eastward to escape the pursuing Mexican Army which would be called the "Runaway Scrape." (See Battle of SAN JACINTO for a detailed account.) He was beset with desertions, protests and near mutinies from the officers and men, who wanted to stand and fight. At one point, Texas President David Burnet dispatched Secretary of War Thomas RUSK with a scathing message to Houston, ordering him to stand and fight. Rusk, who had the authority to relieve Houston of command if he so desired, instead joined Houston's forces and the retreat continued. On the afternoon of April 21, Houston and his army of 800 attacked 1250–1300 Mexican soldiers under the command of Gen. Antonio Lopez de SANTA ANNA on a peninsula bounded by Buffalo Bayou and Rio de San Jacinto. In the ensuing Battle of SAN JACINTO, Houston, who was severely wounded in the foot, annihilated his enemy, and in victory won independence for Texas. Santa Anna was taken prisoner, subsequently signed the Treaties of VELASCO, and the Republic of Texas was born. Houston departed in May for New Orleans in order to seek medical treatment for his injury.

*Texas Politics*

Sam Houston returned to Texas and the adulation of its people. On September 5, 1836 an election was held for president of the Republic of Texas. The results: Houston, 5,119 votes; Henry SMITH, 743; Stephen F. Austin, 587. Houston had attained 79 percent of the vote to become the first popularly elected president of Texas, and took the oath of office on October 22 in Columbia, the new seat of government. His term in office was rather uneventful, other than: he managed to send Santa Anna safely back to Mexico against great opposition; secured recognition of the Texas Republic by the United States; but failed to convince President Martin Van Buren to consider annexation by the United States. Houston's Cherokee wife, Tiana Rogers, died in 1838, and was buried in the national cemetery at Fort Gibson.

Houston was forbidden by the constitution to succeed himself, and on December 10, 1838, attended the inauguration of Mirabeau LAMAR. He established a law practice in Houston, and served as representative from San Augustine County to the Fourth and Fifth Congresses.

Sam Houston met 20-year-old Margaret Moffette Lea on a trip to Alabama, and the couple were married on May 9, 1840, at the home of her parents. Sam and Margaret would have 8 children born between 1843 and 1860, and his religious wife would manage to successfully temper his drinking.

Houston ran for the presidency of Texas in 1841, and was elected. He inherited a national debt that was estimated at more than $7 million; quelled Indian problems by negotiating treaties; and endured the threat of a Mexican invasion. When he left office in 1844, the condition of the republic was much improved. He was elected senator from Texas, and arrived in Washington in March, 1846 to serve for almost 14 years from the Twenty-ninth through the Thirty-fifth Congress. He was offered a generalship during the Mexican War, but declined. He became an advocate of the Know-Nothing Party, and,

while still in the senate, ran for governor of Texas in 1857 on that platform but was defeated. He was, however, elected governor two years later, and voiced his opposition to secession in the debates that would lead to the Civil War. At the outbreak of that war, Houston refused to swear allegiance to the Confederacy, and was deposed as governor.

### Death

Houston refused an offer by President Abraham Lincoln to dispatch Union troops in an effort to help him keep his office. Although branded a traitor, he quietly retired to his farm in Huntsville. In the summer of 1863, Houston went to bed with a severe chill. On July 26, he uttered the words, "Texas. Texas. Margaret," and died at the age of 70.

The city of Houston, Texas was named in his honor. The Sam Houston Memorial Museum Complex has been established in Huntsville, Texas on 15 original acres that were owned by Houston. The museum features personal effects belonging to Houston as well as items captured from Santa Anna at the Battle of San Jacinto. A 66-foot statue of Houston, the world's tallest of an American hero, stands in Huntsville. Many other places throughout Texas, including a national forest, have been named in his honor.

**HOWELL, William D.** (1791–March 6, 1836) NEW ORLEANS GREYS; Alamo defender from Massachusetts. Howell, who was a medical doctor, arrived in Texas on November 21, 1835, and participated in the Siege and Battle of SAN ANTONIO. It is not known whether or not he was serving as a rifleman or a surgeon for the garrison when he was killed in the ALAMO BATTLE.

# J

**JACKSON, Thomas** (?–March 6, 1836) Private, GONZALES RANGING COMPANY; Alamo defender from Ireland. Jackson arrived in DeWitt's Colony, Texas in the spring of 1831, and was a member of the original "Old Eighteen" who defended the town cannon in the GONZALES SKIRMISH. He entered the ALAMO MISSION with his unit on March 1, 1836, and was serving as a rifleman when he was killed in the ALAMO BATTLE. Jackson was married to the sister of fellow Alamo defender George W. COTTLE.

**JACKSON, William Daniel** (1807–March 6, 1836) Private, TEXAS REVOLUTIONARY ARMY; Alamo defender from Kentucky. Jackson participated in the Siege and Battle of SAN ANTONIO, and was serving as an artilleryman in Capt. William CAREY's artillery company when he was killed in the ALAMO BATTLE.

**JAMESON, Green B.** "Benito" (1807–March 6, 1836) Major, TEXAS REVOLUTIONARY ARMY; Alamo defender from Kentucky. Jameson was a lawyer who arrived in San Felipe, Texas in 1830 to establish a practice. He participated in the Siege and Battle of SAN ANTONIO, and remained to serve as chief engineer charged with overseeing fortifications at the ALAMO MISSION. Jameson was the personal messenger of Col. James BOWIE to the Mexicans on the first day of the ALAMO SIEGE. He met with Gen. Antonio Lopez de SANTA ANNA's aide-de-camp, Col. Juan ALMONTE, seeking an honorable solution to the standoff, but was given his answer by Col. Don José Batres who demanded nothing less than an unconditional surrender. Jameson returned to the Alamo, and was subsequently killed in the ALAMO BATTLE.

**JENNINGS, Gordon C.** (1780–March 6, 1836) 1st Corporal, TEXAS REVOLUTIONARY ARMY; Alamo defender from Pennsylvania. This father of four came to Texas from Missouri in 1835. He participated in the Siege and Battle of SAN ANTONIO, and was serving as a noncommissioned officer in Capt. William CAREY's artillery company when he was killed in the ALAMO BATTLE. Jennings holds the distinction of being the oldest Alamo defender at age 56. His brother, Charles, was captured and executed in the Surrender and Massacre at GOLIAD.

**JIMENES, Damacio** (aka "Ximenes"; ?–March 6, 1836) Private, TEXAS REVOLUTIONARY ARMY; Alamo defender from Texas. Jimenes participated in the Siege and Battle of SAN ANTONIO, and was serving as a rifleman when he was killed in the ALAMO BATTLE.

**JOE** (ca. 1815–?) Slave. Alamo SURVIVOR. Joe was born a slave, and accompanied his owner, Col. William TRAVIS, to the ALAMO MISSION in February, 1836. He was a combatant with a rifle alongside his master early in the ALAMO BATTLE, but sought refuge in a room after Travis was killed. Joe secreted himself in that room until near the end of the battle when a voice in accented English asked, "Are there any Negroes here?" Joe stood. "Yes, here's one," he replied. He was instantly accosted by Mexican soldiers, and was slightly wounded by a gunshot and a bayonet by the time a Mexican officer drove away his men. This officer took Joe prisoner. Joe was later presented to Gen. Santa Anna who made the slave watch a parade of Mexican troops, which was intended to impress Joe to the extent that he would warn the Americans about the strength and might of the Mexican Army. Joe did later boast that he witnessed more than 8,000 troops, which was an inaccurate total. Santa Anna then released him as a gesture meant to indicate that Mexico was a friend to all slaves in Texas, that they could be free and even enlist in the Mexican Army should they run away from their masters. He travelled with Susannah DICKINSON and Santa Anna's servant to Gonzales. Joe later recounted his eyewitness observations to Texas officials, stating that other Blacks, whom he could not identify other than a man named "John" had been inside the Alamo during the siege and battle—including one dead woman. He also reported seeing the dead body of David CROCKETT lying at his position, which contradicts Mexican claims that Crockett surrendered and was later executed (see CROCKETT, David for more). Joe became the property of John Rice Jones as part of Travis's estate, but escaped and was said to have visited his former master's family in Alabama to tell them his account of the battle. He soon disappeared, but possibly could be buried in an unmarked grave near Brewer, Alabama.

**JOHN** (?–March 6, 1836) Freedman or slave. Little is known about this man identified only as "John" on casualty lists. It has been theorized that he was a slave, according to testimony from Col. William TRAVIS' slave, JOE, who claimed that other Blacks were present in the ALAMO MISSION during the ALAMO SIEGE and BATTLE.

**JOHNSON, Francis White** "Frank" (October 3, 1799–April 8, 1884) Colonel, TEXAS REVOLUTIONARY ARMY. This native of Leesburg, Virginia, moved to Tennessee with his family when he was 13. Johnson worked as a surveyor in Alabama in 1817, moved on to Augusta, Illinois, to teach school and run a grocery store, and in 1824 worked in the lead mines near Herculaneum, Missouri.

He became ill in 1826 while floating a cargo of produce down the Mississippi River, and decided that a trip to Texas might improve his health. Johnson and his cousin traveled to DeWitt's Colony in 1827 and to San Antonio in 1828. Johnson secured work as a surveyor in the Ayish District in 1829, and became *alcalde* (mayor) of San Felipe de Austin the following year. He was a captain in the volunteers during the 1832 Battle of ANAHUAC, and was a delegate to that year's convention. Johnson was appointed adjutant and inspector general of the army, and served at the 1835 Siege and Battle of SAN ANTONIO. During the assault on San Antonio, he commanded one detachment of volunteers and assumed command of the entire force when Ben MILAM was killed. In January, 1836, Johnson, along with Col. James W. FANNIN and Dr. James GRANT, was involved with organizing the MATAMOROS EXPEDITION which was designed to invade Mexico. It was apparently Johnson's plan that the General Council approved, which caused turmoil between that body and Governor Henry SMITH, who opposed the idea, and led to a government in disarray. While foraging the countryside for horses and supplies to outfit the expedition, Johnson and 50 men were attacked by MEXICAN ARMY troops commanded by Gen. José URREA on February 27 at San Patricio. The Mexicans killed 16 and captured 24—Johnson and 4 others escaped. Johnson made it to Goliad where he informed Fannin that Urrea had executed all the prisoners, which was not true. This information confirmed Fannin's decision to abort a mission to provide aid to the Alamo garrison which was under siege. Johnson was a land speculator following the Revolution, and spent much of his time recording Texas history. He was in Aguas Calientes, Mexico, researching when he died in 1884 at the age of 84. His body was later interred in Texas.

**JOHNSON, Lewis** (1811–March 6, 1836) Private, TEXAS REVOLUTIONARY ARMY; Alamo defender from Wales. Johnson had been residing in Nacodoches, Texas when he participated in the Siege and Battle of SAN ANTONIO. He was likely serving as an artilleryman with Capt. William CAREY's artillery company when he was killed in the ALAMO BATTLE.

**JOHNSON, William** (?–March 6, 1836) Private, TEXAS REVOLUTIONARY ARMY; Alamo defender from Pennsylvania. This Philadelphian was likely serving as an artilleryman in Capt. William CAREY's artillery company when he was killed in the ALAMO BATTLE.

**JOHNSON, William P.** (?–March 27, 1836) Sergeant, TEXAS REVOLUTIONARY ARMY; COURIER from the Alamo. Johnson was dispatched by Col. William TRAVIS as a messenger to Goliad on February 23, 1836, the first day of the ALAMO SIEGE. He remained in Goliad, and was subsequently executed in the Surrender and Massacre at GOLIAD.

**JONES, John** (1810–March 6, 1836) First Lieutenant, NEW ORLEANS GREYS; Alamo defender from New York. Jones arrived in Texas with his unit on November 21, 1835, and participated in the Siege and Battle of SAN ANTONIO. He was serving as an officer in Capt. William BLAZEBY's infantry company when he was killed in the ALAMO BATTLE.

# K

**KELLOGG, John Benjamin** (1817–March 6, 1836) Private, GONZALES RANGING COMPANY; Alamo defender from Kentucky. Kel-

logg was married to Sidney Gaston, the divorced sister of fellow Alamo defender John GASTON. Her former husband, Thomas R. MILLER, who was also an Alamo defender, was said to have lost Sidney to Kellogg. The three men from Gonzales, however, rode together and entered the ALAMO MISSION with their unit on March 1, 1836. They were all killed in the ALAMO BATTLE.

**KENNEY, James** (1814–March 6, 1836) Private, TEXAS REVOLUTIONARY ARMY; Alamo defender from Virginia. Kenny, who had been residing at Washington-on-the-Brazos, was serving as a rifleman when he was killed in the ALAMO BATTLE. His riding whip is on display at the Alamo.

**KENT, Andrew** (ca. late 1790s–March 6, 1836) Private, GONZALES RANGING COMPANY; Alamo defender from Kentucky. This farmer departed Missouri and settled in Gonzales, Texas with his wife and five children. He entered the ALAMO MISSION with his unit on March 1, 1836, and was serving as a rifleman when he was killed in the ALAMO BATTLE.

**KENTUCKY MUSTANGS** This 45-man volunteer unit, comprised of one company of Kentucky Rifleman as well as some Tennessee volunteers, was commanded by Capt. Burr H. Duval. It was garrisoned at Goliad with Col. James W. FANNIN, and reportedly only 8 from its ranks survived the Surrender and Massacre at GOLIAD.

**KERR, Joseph** (1814–March 6, 1836) Private, TEXAS REVOLUTIONARY ARMY; Alamo defender from Louisiana. Joseph Kerr and his brother, Nathaniel, came to Texas from Lake Providence as members of the Louisiana Volunteers for Texas Independence. His brother unexpectedly died on February 19, 1836, and Kerr entered the ALAMO MISSION four days later — on the first day of the ALAMO SIEGE. He was serving as a rifleman when he was killed in the ALAMO BATTLE.

**KIMBELL, George C.** (aka "Kimble"; 1803– March 6, 1836) Captain, GONZALES RANGING COMPANY; Alamo defender from Pennsylvania. Kimbell settled in Gonzales by way of New York and opened a hat factory in partnership with fellow Alamo defender Almeron DICKINSON. His wife was pregnant with twins when as commanding officer he led his unit into the ALAMO MISSION on March 1, 1836. He was serving in that capacity when he was killed in the ALAMO BATTLE. Kimble County, Texas was named in honor of his sacrifice.

**KING, William Philip** (October 8, 1820– March 6, 1836) Private, GONZALES RANGING COMPANY; Alamo defender from Texas. King, one of 9 children who lived 15 miles north of Gonzales, persuaded commanding officer George KIMBELL to let him serve in the volunteer military unit in place of his father. He entered the ALAMO MISSION with that unit on March 1, 1836, and was serving as a rifleman when he was killed in the ALAMO BATTLE. King, at age 15, holds the distinction of being the youngest Alamo defender.

# L

**LAMAR, Mirabeau Buonaparte** (August 16, 1798–December 19, 1859) Colonel, TEXAS REVOLUTIONARY ARMY; first secretary of War, second vice-president, and third president of the Republic of Texas. Lamar was born near Louisville, Georgia, and was raised on his father's plantation near Milledgeville.

He was educated at Milledgeville and Eatonville, and became an expert horseman and fencer, enjoyed books and writing verse, and painted in oils. He became partner in a general store at Cahawba, Alabama in 1819, and 2 years later became publisher of the Cahawba *Press*. Lamar returned to Georgia in 1823 to become secretary to Governor George M. Troup. On January 21, 1826, he married Tabitha Jordan, who soon became ill with tuberculosis. Lamar resigned as Troup's secretary, and moved with his wife and daughter in 1828 to Columbus, Georgia, to become editor of the Columbus *Enquirer*. The following year, he was elected to the state senate, but withdrew from the race for re-election when his wife died in August, 1830. He ran unsuccessfully for a seat in the U.S. Congress in both 1832 and 1834. Lamar sold his interest in the *Enquirer* in 1835, and followed his friend James W. FANNIN to Texas. Lamar immediately declared himself in favor of Texas independence, travelled to Georgia to settle his affairs, and returned to Texas. He enlisted as a private in the TEXAS REVOLUTIONARY ARMY while it was retreating eastward in what is known as the "Runaway Scrape" in prelude to the Battle of SAN JACINTO. This retreat was highly unpopular among Gen. Sam HOUSTON's officers and men, who were itching to fight, and Lamar fueled these fires by offering a plan to take command and lead the troops himself without delay against the Mexicans. Houston ordered several graves dug, and warned his troops that anyone who volunteered to follow Lamar would be shot. Private Lamar prudently dropped his fanciful idea. On April 20, the evening before the battle, Lamar was a member of a small force commanded by Col. Sidney SHERMAN that embarked on a reconnaissance of enemy lines. Sherman disobeyed direct orders from Houston, and attacked the Mexicans with intentions of capturing their cannon. Sherman and his men were forced to dismount and re-load their weapons, and became trapped when the Mexicans charged. That attack was repelled by the Texans, but the Mexicans charged again. Secretary of War Thomas RUSK was one of those hemmed in by the assault until Mirabeau Lamar drove his stallion into a Mexican horseman to open a pathway to escape. Lamar also saved the life of another comrade when he shot a Mexican soldier who was bearing down on the defenseless Texan. Col. Sherman was relieved of command, and Gen. Houston promoted *Private* Lamar to colonel in command of the cavalry for his distinguished actions. The next day at the commencement of the battle, his regiment was positioned on the extreme right of the assault line. Ten days following that battle, he was named Secretary of War in the cabinet of President David BURNET, and was outspoken in his opinion that Mexican dictator Antonio Lopez de SANTA ANNA should be executed. One month later, Lamar was appointed major general in command of the Texas Army. His tenure was brief. The troops, who were loyal to Sam Houston, refused to accept him, and he quickly resigned the position. In September, 1836, Lamar was elected vice-president of the new Republic of Texas in the first ever nationwide election. A collector of historical data, Lamar spent the following year pursuing that endeavor, writing poetry, and studying Spanish before traveling to Georgia to publicize Texas. He returned to Texas in December, 1837, founded the Philosophical Society of Texas, a scholarly society, and found himself the candidate of the anti–Houston forces for president of Texas in 1838. He won in a landslide when the other two candidates, Peter W. Grayson and James Collinsworth, both committed suicide before election day. The highlight of his presidency was his plan to establish public education. Land was set aside to support

public schools and 2 universities — a system that remains partially in effect in present-day Texas. Lamar retired in 1841 to his home in Richmond, Texas, traveled extensively in the ensuing years, and served as a lieutenant colonel in the Mexican War. He became United States minister to Nicaragua and Costa Rica in 1857, and died of a heart attack at age 61 two months after returning home in 1859. The town of Lamar, Texas, and Lamar County, Texas, were named in his honor.

**LEWIS, William Irvine** (June 24, 1806–March 6, 1836) Private, TEXAS REVOLUTIONARY ARMY; Alamo defender from Virginia. Lewis had departed his home in Philadelphia, Pennsylvania to visit a friend in North Carolina when he impulsively decided to travel to Texas and volunteer for service. He was serving as a rifleman when he was killed in the ALAMO BATTLE. Lewis' mother, Mary Irvine Lewis, had a premonition of her son's death at their home in Philadelphia. Mrs. Lewis awoke from a troubling dream — two weeks before she would be told of her son's death — that portrayed William surrounded by smoke and flame. She later wrote a letter to the *Telegraph and Texas Register* (published on October 21, 1840) pleading for some momento of her son. A stone from the Alamo was sent to honor her request.

**LIGHTFOOT, William J.** (aka "John W. Lightfoot"; 1811–March 6, 1836) 3rd Corporal, TEXAS REVOLUTIONARY ARMY; Alamo defender from Virginia. Lightfoot participated in the Siege and Battle of SAN ANTONIO, and was serving as a noncommissioned officer with Capt. William CAREY's artillery company when he was killed in the ALAMO BATTLE.

**LINDLEY, Jonathan L.** (February, 1814–March 6, 1836) Private, GONZALES RANGING COMPANY; Alamo defender from Illinois. Lindley was the eldest of 11 children from a family that departed Sangamon County, Illinois and settled in Montgomery, County, Texas, in 1833. He had been working as a land surveyor and had accumulated a section of land near Gonzales by the time he participated in the Siege and Battle of SAN ANTONIO in late 1835. Lindley arrived at the ALAMO MISSION with his unit on March 1, 1836, and was serving as an artilleryman in Capt. William CAREY's artillery company when he was killed in the ALAMO BATTLE.

**LINN, William** (?–March 6, 1836) Private, NEW ORLEANS GREYS; Alamo defender from Boston, Massachusetts. Linn arrived in Texas with his unit on November 21, 1835, and participated in the Siege and Battle of SAN ANTONIO. He was serving as a rifleman in Capt. William BLAZEBY's infantry company when he was killed in the ALAMO BATTLE.

**LOCKHART, Byrd** (1782–1839) Captain, GONZALES RANGING COMPANY; Alamo COURIER from Virginia or Missouri. Lockhart, a widower, arrived in DeWitt's Colony, Texas with his mother, sister, and two children on March 20, 1826, and worked as a surveyor. He resided in Gonzales, Texas, where he was involved in politics and from where he served as a scout at the outbreak of the TEXAS REVOLUTION. He participated as a private along with his son, Byrd, Jr., in the Siege and Battle of SAN ANTONIO. In early February, 1836, he was named commissioner and charged with the duty of raising volunteers for the Gonzales Ranging Company, and was mustered into service on February 23, 1836 — the first day of the ALAMO SIEGE. It is unknown precisely when Lockhart arrived at the ALAMO MISSION or

when he departed, but there is evidence that he, in the company of Andrew SOWELL, were dispatched to Gonzales for the purpose of buying supplies. Evidently, the two couriers were unable to return prior to the ALAMO BATTLE. Lockhart later became captain of a spy company. The town of Lockhart, Texas, was named in his honor.

**LOSOYA, Toribio** (1808–March 6, 1836) Private, SEGUIN'S CAVALRY COMPANY; Alamo defender from Texas. Losoya participated in the Siege and Battle of SAN ANTONIO, and was serving as a rifleman when he was killed in the ALAMO BATTLE.

# M

**McCAFFERTY, Edward** (?–March 6, 1836) Lieutenant, TEXAS REVOLUTIONARY ARMY; Alamo defender from parts unknown. Little is known about this resident of Refugio County, Texas, who was killed in the ALAMO BATTLE.

**McCOY, Jesse** (1804–March 6, 1836) Private, GONZALES RANGING COMPANY; Alamo defender from Gyrosburg, Tennessee. This former town sheriff immigrated to Texas by way of Missouri, and arrived in DeWitt's Colony March 9, 1827, as one of the original settlers. McCoy entered the ALAMO MISSION with his unit on March 1, 1836 and was serving as a rifleman when he was killed in the ALAMO BATTLE.

**McDOWELL, William** (1794–March 6, 1836) Private, TENNESSEE MOUNTED VOLUNTEERS; Alamo defender from Mifflin County, Pennsylvania. McDowell travelled to Texas from Tennessee with fellow Alamo defender John P. REYNOLDS in 1835. The two men founded a settlement in Tennessee called Mifflin after their home county in Pennsylvania. They were sworn into the service in Nacogdoches on January, 14, 1836, and arrived in San Antonio on February 8. McDowell was serving as a rifleman in Capt. William HARRISON's company when he was killed in the ALAMO BATTLE.

**McGEE, James** (?–March 6, 1836) Private, NEW ORLEANS GREYS; Alamo defender from Ireland. McGee arrived in San Antonio with his unit on November 21, 1835, and participated in the Siege and Battle of SAN ANTONIO where he was wounded. If not incapacitated by his wound, he was serving as a rifleman in Capt. William BLAZEBY's infantry company when he was killed in the ALAMO BATTLE.

**McGREGOR, John** (1808–March 6, 1836) 2nd Sergeant, TEXAS REVOLUTIONARY ARMY; Alamo defender from Scotland. This resident of Nacogdoches, Texas participated in the Siege and Battle of SAN ANTONIO, and received a section of land for his service. McGregor played the bagpipes, and during the ALAMO SIEGE he and David CROCKETT kept the spirits of the men high with their bagpipe and fiddle duels. He was serving as a noncommissioned officer in Capt. William CAREY's artillery company when he was killed in the ALAMO BATTLE.

**McKINNEY, Robert** (1809–March 6, 1836) Private, TEXAS REVOLUTIONARY ARMY; Alamo defender from Tennessee. McKinney came to Texas by way of New Orleans, and was serving as a rifleman when he was killed in the ALAMO BATTLE.

**MAIN, George Washington** (1807–March 6, 1836) Lieutenant, TEXAS REVOLUTIONARY

ARMY; Alamo defender from Virginia. Main was severely wounded during the Siege and Battle of SAN ANTONIO. For that reason, it is unlikely that this officer serving with Capt. Robert WHITE's infantry company was able to perform his duties when he was killed in the ALAMO BATTLE.

**MALONE, William T.** (August 13, 1817–March 6, 1836) Private, TEXAS REVOLUTIONARY ARMY; defender from Athens, Georgia. Malone was residing with his parents in Alabama when one night he got drunk, and, rather than face his father, fled to New Orleans, Louisiana. His father traveled to that city to look for his son, but by that time Malone had departed for Texas. He participated in the Siege and Battle of SAN ANTONIO, and was serving as an artilleryman with Capt. William CAREY's artillery company when he was killed in the ALAMO BATTLE. Malone wrote home once from Texas, and, according to the family, his mother carried the letter with her until it was in shreds.

**MARSHALL, William** (1808–March 6, 1836) Private, NEW ORLEANS GREYS; Alamo defender from Tennessee. This Arkansas resident arrived in San Antonio with his unit on November 21, 1835, and participated in the Siege and Battle of SAN ANTONIO. He was serving as a rifleman in Capt. William BLAZEBY's infantry company when he was killed in the ALAMO BATTLE.

**MARTIN, Albert** ( January 6, 1808–March 6, 1836) Captain, TEXAS REVOLUTIONARY ARMY; Alamo COURIER and defender from Providence, Rhode Island. Martin arrived in Texas by way of Tennessee and New Orleans, and settled in Gonzales in May, 1835. He was a member of the "Old Eighteen," the original defenders who had protected the town cannon in the GONZALES SKIRMISH, and was said to have personally buried the disputed cannon. He later participated in the Siege and Battle of SAN ANTONIO. On the first day of the ALAMO SIEGE, February, 23, 1836, Martin was dispatched by Col. William TRAVIS to parley with the invading Mexican Army. His entreaty to Col. Juan ALMONTE was met with the demand that the Alamo defenders surrender unconditionally. The next day, Martin was the courier who carried to Gonzales the heroic message penned by Travis addressed "To the People of Texas and all Americans in the world," which was a plea for volunteers. He was perhaps chosen for duty as courier due to a severe injury to his foot suffered in a wood-cutting accident that had left him less than able-bodied as a fighting man. Martin, however, returned to the Alamo with the relief force from Gonzales on March 1, 1836, and was killed in the ALAMO BATTLE.

**MARTIN, Wiley** (1776–April 26, 1842) Captain, TEXAS REVOLUTIONARY ARMY. This native of Georgia was a school teacher and store clerk before enlisting in the army in 1805. He served as a scout, and was promoted to captain for his gallantry in the War of 1812 Battle of Horseshoe Bend. He subsequently killed a man in a duel, resigned his commission, and came to Texas in 1823 as one of Stephen F. AUSTIN's "Old Three Hundred" original colonists. Martin participated in the disturbance at Anahuac that led to the 1832 Battle of VELASCO, was a member of the 1832 and 1833 conventions and the 1835 TEXAS CONSULTATION OF DELEGATES. He joined Gen. Sam HOUSTON's army on the March, 1836 "Runaway Scrape" retreat across Texas and, when he refused to retreat any further, was dispatched with a company of men to guard against the MEXICAN ARMY

advancing toward Richmond. Martin failed in that mission, and quit the army in disgust in order to assist families fleeing the Mexicans. Following the revolution, he served as chief justice of Fort Bend County, and was elected to the Sixth Congress.

**MATAMOROS EXPEDITION** In early 1836 there was a proposal by some Texas volunteers about carrying the war into Mexico — specifically an expedition against the port city of Matamoros (pop. 12,000). This effort was later abandoned, but caused political turmoil within the Texas government and depleted the ALAMO GARRISON of men and supplies prior to the ALAMO SIEGE and ALAMO BATTLE.

*Chronology of the Texas Revolution*

- June 29, 1835: Battle of ANAHUAC
- October 2, 1835: GONZALES SKIRMISH
- October 3, 1835: MEXICAN CONSTITUTION OF 1824 officially voided
- October 9, 1835: GOLIAD SKIRMISH
- October 28, 1835: Battle of CONCEPCION
- November 3, 1835: TEXAS CONSULTATION OF DELEGATES
- November–December, 1835: Siege and Battle of SAN ANTONIO
- **January–February, 1836: The MATAMOROS EXPEDITION**
- February 23–March 5, 1836: The ALAMO SIEGE
- March 1, 1836: TEXAS CONSTITUTIONAL CONVENTION
- March 2, 1836: TEXAS DECLARATION OF INDEPENDENCE
- March 6, 1836: The ALAMO BATTLE
- March 20–27, 1836: Surrender and Massacre at GOLIAD
- April 21, 1836: Battle of SAN JACINTO
- May 14, 1836: Treaties of VELASCO

This plan for an invasion of Mexico was first approved by the TEXAS CONSULTATION OF DELEGATES on November 13, 1835, with the belief that it would advance the cause of

Texas statehood. Matamoros, it was thought, was home to many Mexican liberals who opposed General Antonio Lopez de SANTA ANNA and would align themselves with the Texans. Sam HOUSTON was chosen to lead the expedition, but declined. Jim BOWIE was then selected, but orders never reached him. In early January, 1836, the General Council issued orders for Col. Francis (Frank) JOHNSON, who had presented the idea, and Dr. James GRANT to organize the expedition. Both Houston and Governor Henry SMITH were opposed to the plan in part because the intention of its proponents was primarily to plunder the countryside for spoils and protect land claims in other states. Grant had ulterior motives for wanting this expedition — his shady land dealings with the corrupt legislature in Saltillo were at stake. Grant busily prepared for the expedition by pillaging the ALAMO MISSION garrison at San Antonio, taking with him two-thirds of the defense force — about 200 men — and most of the food, medical supplies, and ammunition. Colonel James NEILL, commander at San Antonio, informed Governor Smith that his garrison had been critically weakened, and would be unable to defend itself. An attack by the MEXICAN ARMY was imminent, Neill stated, and begged for aid. Smith was outraged, and angrily protested to the legislative council — whom he called "Judases" and "scoundrels" — for approving the expedition at the expense of San Antonio. On January 20, the General Council deposed Governor Smith, and placed Col. James W. FANNIN in charge of the expedition. Smith dissolved the council, which in turn impeached him. Sam Houston may have been commander-in-chief of the TEXAS REVOLUTIONARY ARMY, but Fannin, who was not a volunteer but a regular army officer, took his orders from the council. Houston believed that Fannin was betraying his country with this undertaking, and decided to

take his case directly to the volunteers. In mid–January, he travelled to the places where volunteers were massing, and intensely lobbied in an effort to convince the men that this expedition was not only dangerous but foolish. Houston, who was exceedingly charismatic as well as respected, succeeded in dissuading many of them from participating. Those who remained with Fannin refused to let reason diminish their lust for the wealth and adventure that awaited them in Matamoros. In addition to the Alamo, the presidio at Goliad also had been stripped of men and supplies, which left the interior of Texas virtually defenseless. On February 12, Col. Fannin grudgingly admitted that a 300 mile march to Matamoros without proper supplies and more troops was unrealistic. His army was certain to be outnumbered by the huge Mexican Army that was (correctly) rumored to be presently on the march north for the purpose of seeking revenge for its defeat in the Siege and Battle of SAN ANTONIO. Fannin reluctantly retired to Goliad, his ambitions of a glorious expedition for the time being postponed. Meanwhile, Col. Johnson and Dr. Grant with perhaps 100 men between them continued to forage the countryside for horses and supplies for the expedition. At 3 A.M. on February 27, Johnson's unit of about 50 men was attacked by Mexican Gen. José URREA at San Patricio — 16 volunteers were killed, and 24 captured. Johnson and 4 others escaped, and made their way to Goliad to inform Fannin that the captives had been executed by Urrea, which was not true. The information, however, served to reinforce Fannin's resistance to ride to the aid of the Alamo. Gen. Urrea also caught up with Dr. Grant's 15-man detachment on March 2 at Agua Dulce Creek, and killed them all. Fannin had gathered more than 400 volunteers that in mid–March also fled from Gen. Urrea's forces. Most of these volunteers that Fannin had recruited for the Matamoros Expedition would later that month be executed with their commander in the Surrender and Massacre at GOLIAD.

**MELTON, Eliel** (1798–March 6, 1836) Lieutenant, TEXAS REVOLUTIONARY ARMY; Alamo defender from Georgia. Melton had come to Texas in 1830, and was a merchant in Nashville-on-the-Brazos. He participated in the Siege and Battle of SAN ANTONIO, and remained to serve as quartermaster for the ALAMO MISSION garrison. According to Alamo survivor Susannah DICKINSON, Melton tried to escape when Mexican soldiers overran the walls during the ALAMO BATTLE. He jumped from the palisade, but was chased down and killed.

**MEXICAN ARMY** The Mexican Army that marched to engage the Texans in the TEXAS REVOLUTION consisted of about 6,500 men, and was commanded by the Mexican dictator and president, General Antonio Lopez de SANTA ANNA. The entourage that set off for Texas in late January, 1836 also included 21 artillery pieces and 6 gun carriages; 1,800 pack mules; 200 hundred oxen-drawn carts; 33 huge four-wheeled wagons; and hundreds of smaller vehicles owned by merchants who tagged along and preyed upon the soldiers by charging outrageous prices for inferior goods. Most of the soldiers had been forced into service by conscription, a draft known as the *sorteo*, which was little more than an act of kidnapping. Press gangs would arrive in a town unannounced and target vagrants, prisoners, and unmarried men for "recruitment." Some of these recruits were Mayan Indians from the Yucatan — many of whom had been taken bound in chains — and most recruits were uneducated and impoverished. For this reason, many men deserted, and when caught

would face execution by order of Santa Anna. The Mexican soldier was issued 2 pairs of shoes, a canteen, cartridges, flint, and a musket (please see WEAPONS OF THE MEXICAN ARMY for more). Cavalry uniforms were comprised of blue trousers with a scarlet side-seam; a scarlet pigeon-tailed jacket with green lapels, epaulets, frontpiece, and scarlet or green collars; and a tanned cowhide cap with chinstrap, wood plume, goat pelt crest and large brass shield. Infantrymen wore blue trousers with scarlet side-seams; blue pigeon-tailed jacket with scarlet cuffs, epaulets and collar; and a black leather helmet with a green, white, and red plume. Infantrymen wore a lighter uniform in summer, and new recruits were often issued only white linen trousers and shirt. Officers, of course, were provided more gaudy attire. Santa Anna, for example, would wear gray trousers; a blue pigeon-tailed jacket, scarlet frontpieces, gold embroidered cuffs, and a high collar embroidered with a golden palm and olive and laurel leaves, golden epaulets; a blue sash around his waist; black riding boots with spurs; and a black, two-cornered, crescent-shaped hat with an upturned brim which was lined with gold lace and topped with green, white, and red ostrich feathers. Officers of a lesser rank had less gold embroidery and wore different colored sashes according to rank. Army recruits were trained to march in formation, learn the chain of command, handle firearms, and shown basic tactics. In addition, these men were required to learn 70 different bugle calls that were used as field commands. On the march to Texas in early 1836, the army was spread out over 200 miles. Medical attention was virtually non-existent — there were *no* qualified doctors and *no* medical supplies. Many fell out ill from dysentery, diarrhea, hypothermia, or a spotted itch, or were injured in accidents or brawls among themselves, or incapacitated by foot blisters. By the time they reached Texas, the Mexicans were running out of food and many uniforms were in shreds or found to be inadequate for the winter weather. It was not unusual for the troops to bring along their families, and this caused more burden with respect to food, shelter and, most important to Santa Anna, speed of movement. Oddly enough, the army was not accompanied by a chaplain or Catholic priest. Following their victory in the ALAMO BATTLE, the army was desperately low on food and supplies, and, by order of Santa Anna, took to plundering the countryside and stealing whatever suited their fancy from the colonists on their march eastward. The Mexican soldier could be considered poorly trained and suffering from morale problems, but was more disciplined than the TEXAS REVOLUTIONARY ARMY simply because of the threat of severe punishment for any infraction of the rules. These men were frequently forced to charge the cannon's mouth and sustained an excessive amount of casualties due to the brutal disregard of their commander, Gen. Santa Anna. Notable officers include: ALMONTE, Juan; CASTRILLÓN, Manuel; CÓS, Martin; FILISOLA, Vincente; RAMÍREZ Y SESMA, Joaquín; GAONA, Antonio; URREA, José.

## MEXICAN CONSTITUTION OF 1824
(aka Federal Constitution of 1824) The repeal of this constitution on October 3, 1835 compelled Texans to fight for its restoration, and eventually to seek independence from Mexico.

### Chronology of the Texas Revolution

- June 29, 1835: Battle of ANAHUAC
- October 2, 1835: GONZALES SKIRMISH
- **October 3, 1835: MEXICAN CONSTITUTION OF 1824 officially voided**
- October 9, 1835: GOLIAD SKIRMISH
- October 28, 1835: Battle of CONCEPCION
- November 3, 1835: TEXAS CONSULTATION OF DELEGATES
- November–December, 1835: Siege and Battle of SAN ANTONIO
- January–February, 1836: The MATAMOROS EXPEDITION
- February 23–March 5, 1836: The ALAMO SIEGE
- March 1, 1836: TEXAS CONSTITUTIONAL CONVENTION
- March 2, 1836: TEXAS DECLARATION OF INDEPENDENCE
- March 6, 1836: The ALAMO BATTLE
- March 20–27, 1836: Surrender and Massacre at GOLIAD
- April 21, 1836: Battle of SAN JACINTO
- May 14, 1836: Treaties of VELASCO

The Constituent Congress of Mexico adopted this liberal constitution on October 4, 1824 after gaining independence from Spain in 1821 and the abdication of Emperor Iturbide in 1823. The president of that congress was Lorenzo de ZAVALA, who would become the first vice-president of Texas. This constitution was loosely based on the United States Constitution and the Spanish Constitution of 1812. It provided for the former Spanish provinces to become a federation of sovereign states; a president and vice-president would be elected for four-year terms by the legislative bodies of each state; and power distributed from two houses of congress. But, instead of sanctioning freedom of religion, this document established the Roman Catholic church as the official religion — supported by the public treasury. Judicial authority was vested in an 11-judge Supreme Court and attorney general, as well as lower superior courts. The constitution also forbade slavery, which the Texans were engaged in, and permitted the president to arrest anyone who was deemed a threat to the safety of Mexico. The provision stated that a region with less than 80,000 inhabitants could not aspire to statehood, which brought about the passage of the April 6, 1830, Law which cut off immigration to Texas.

Stephen F. AUSTIN conferred with the framers of the Constitution, and Erasmo Seguin, father of Juan SEGUIN, represented Texas at the constitutional assembly. States were permitted to adopt individual constitutions with respect to executive, legislative, and judicial affairs, but they were required to be in harmony with the national constitution. The document was passed by the congress without a vote of the people.

Meanwhile the Mexican government in 1832 was embroiled in a power struggle. The Texans sided with the liberal Federalists led by Antonio Lopez de SANTA ANNA as opposed to the Centralist dictatorship of President Anastacio Bustamante. The federal government was finally overthrown by Santa Anna, who became dictator with a centralist government. In spite of minor disagreements with the Mexicans — including the 1832 Battle of VELASCO and the 1833 arrest of Stephen F. Austin — Texas enjoyed improved relations with Mexico during 1833 and 1834. Laws were repealed that prohibited only native-born Mexicans from retail merchandising; Texan representation in the 12-man state congress was increased from 1 seat to 3; the English language was recognized for official purposes; there was more tolerance toward religious worship; trial by jury was established; and land was made easier to acquire.

In early 1835, however, Santa Anna began dissolving the congress, disbanding state legislatures and deposing governors, and installed a puppet congress and began passing laws to undermine the federal structure established by the Constitution of 1824. The final dictate came when Texas was combined with the state of Coahuila, which diminished the Texan's voice in governmental affairs. Texas would be required to pay taxes and customs duties without proper representation, and would be governed from Mexico City. Rampant land speculation and corrup-

tion in Coahuila, which had been going on for some time, also came to the attention of Santa Anna at that time. The governor and the state legislature at Saltillo were dishonest, and had been selling thousands of acres of land at scandalously low rates to undesirables, which troubled even those legal settlers who feared that their land rights eventually could be threatened. Santa Anna dispatched troops in June, 1835 to put a stop to this corruption by arresting known land speculators, the governor, and suspending civil government in favor of martial law. These actions were propagandized by the WAR PARTY— those Texans promoting independence — as intolerable acts that would lead to martial law and the confiscation of land in Texas.

On October 3, 1835 — the day after the Skirmish at GONZALES—the Constitution of 1824 and Federalism were replaced by a centralized system of government called the *Siete Leyes* that gave ultimate power to dictator Santa Anna.

By voiding the Constitution of 1824 and setting up a powerful central government, Santa Anna impelled the Texans to rebel against Mexico and seek resolution of their grievances. Santa Anna, who had in 1824 been a primary promoter of the Constitution, would now fight against those who were defending their rights under that document to remain a Mexican state. The TEXAS CONSULTATION OF DELEGATES in November, 1835 voted to establish a TEXAS PROVISIONAL GOVERNMENT based "upon the principles of the Constitution of 1824." Those volunteers who died in the March 6, 1836 ALAMO BATTLE were fighting not for independence but for restoration of the Constitution of 1824. In fact, the design on the flag said to have been raised over the ALAMO MISSION during the ALAMO SIEGE bore the red, white and green colors of the

was called Emmett's Rebellion; his father fought in the Battle of New Orleans; and his grandfather was with George Washington at Valley Forge. Parker arrived in Texas in November, 1835 by way of Natchez, Mississippi, and settled in Vehlein's Colony. He was serving as a rifleman when he was killed in the ALAMO BATTLE.

**PARKS, William** (1805–March 6, 1836) Private, TEXAS REVOLUTIONARY ARMY; Alamo defender from Rowan County, North Carolina. Parks participated in the Siege and Battle of SAN ANTONIO, and was serving as a rifleman with Capt. Robert WHITE's infantry company when he was killed in the ALAMO BATTLE.

**PATTON, William Hester** (1808–June 12, 1842) Captain, TEXAS REVOLUTIONARY ARMY; COURIER from the Alamo. This merchant and surveyor commanded a company of volunteers during the Siege and Battle of SAN ANTONIO. He was then ordered by Gen. Sam HOUSTON to Velasco as assistant quartermaster general to assist troops arriving by sea, but may not have ever served in that capacity. Patton was dispatched by Col. William TRAVIS as a courier from the ALAMO MISSION shortly before the siege began on February 23, 1836. He served as aide-de-camp to Houston during the Battle of SAN JACINTO, and remained in the army as quartermaster general until August, 1837. Patton represented Bexar (San Antonio) County in the second congress of Texas, and was murdered on June 12, 1842, by a band of Mexicans.

**PEACE PARTY** This term characterized those Texas colonists who accepted living under the provisions of the MEXICAN CONSTITUTION OF 1824 and opposed those rebels

who promoted Texas independence. In October, 1835 after Mexican dictator Antonio Lopez de SANTA ANNA had annulled the Mexican constitution, these Texans argued at the TEXAS CONSULTATION OF DELEGATES in favor of fighting to restore the Mexican constitution rather than fighting for independence. With future WAR PARTY proponent Sam HOUSTON's encouragement, the convention voted for the Peace Party's stance on the issue. New arrivals to Texas, however, embraced the War Party stance, and, following the invasion of Santa Anna's army, many who had argued for peace were now alarmed that their rights were sufficiently threatened and revolution was the only answer (see also TEXAS REVOLUTION).

**PERRY, Richardson** (1817–March 6, 1836) Private, TEXAS REVOLUTIONARY ARMY; Alamo defender from Texas. Perry was a resident of Brazos County, Texas, when he participated in the Siege and Battle of SAN ANTONIO. He was serving as an artilleryman in Capt. William CAREY's artillery company when he was killed in the ALAMO BATTLE.

**POLLARD, Amos** (October 29, 1803–March 6, 1836) Regimental surgeon, TEXAS REVOLUTIONARY ARMY; Alamo defender from Ashburnham, Massachusetts. Pollard was raised in Surry, New Hampshire, and studied medicine at Vermont Academy in Castletown, Vermont. He practiced in New York City until leaving for Texas by way of New Orleans. He settled in Gonzales, and participated in both the GONZALES SKIRMISH and the Siege and Battle of SAN ANTONIO as a private. Pollard remained at the ALAMO MISSION, and was appointed regimental surgeon by Stephen F. AUSTIN in October, 1835. He was killed in the ALAMO BATTLE while treating the wounded in his hospital on the second floor of the long barracks. Pollard's portrait was painted before his immigration to Texas, and a copy of his likeness is presently on display at the Alamo.

# R

**RAMÍREZ Y SESMA, Joaquín** General, MEXICAN ARMY. Ramírez y Sesma was enroute to assist Gen. Martin Perfecto de CÓS in San Antonio when Cós surrendered after the December, 1835 Siege and Battle of SAN ANTONIO. He waited for Cós in Laredo, and both units then accompanied the main force of the Mexican Army commanded by General Antonio Lopez de SANTA ANNA on its march to San Antonio in February, 1836. On February 22, Ramírez y Sesma was ordered by Santa Anna to command a unit of cavalry and race for San Antonio, which, unknown to the Mexican dictator, would have effectively cut off the Texans from the Alamo since they were celebrating George Washington's birthday in town. Ramírez y Sesma, who was known as a timid and irresolute commander, instead halted outside of town behind the Alazan hills and waited for Santa Anna's arrival the following day. The Alamo held only 10 men during the birthday celebration, and, had Ramírez y Sesma obeyed orders to the letter, he could have seized the mission and perhaps the slaughter at the Alamo might have been averted. He participated in the ALAMO SIEGE and BATTLE, and on March 11 was ordered to San Felipe and Anahuac by way of Harrisburg. Texas Gen. Sam HOUSTON became aware of Ramírez y Sesma's movements from Alamo survivor Susannah DICKINSON, which compelled him to embark on his unpopular "Runaway Scrape" retreat from Gonzales to east Texas. Ramírez y Sesma and his men plundered their way across Texas, stealing everything from furniture to liquor from the abandoned homes of the colonists. He had received orders to join the left flank of Gen. José URREA's force when he encountered resistance at Beason's Ford on the Colorado River. Gen. Houston and 700 men had crossed the flooded Colorado River on March 19 to bivouac at Beason's Ford, and Ramírez y Sesma arrived two days later on the west bank of the river some 2 miles above the camp of the Texans. The two armies were aware of the presence of each other but remained patiently in place, both hesitant to attack without better knowledge regarding the strength of their enemy. Houston received messages ordering him to proceed to Harrisburg and provide protection for the government. Houston mulled his options. If he attacked Gen. Ramírez y Sesma across the river and lost, the war would be lost. If he defeated Ramírez, he would still have to contend with Santa Anna and his large force. Houston was aware that his men believed that this was the place to stand and fight in order to protect the settlements to the east from facing an invasion of the Mexican Army. On March 26, however, the 5th day of the standoff with Ramírez y Sesma, Houston ordered a retreat. Ramírez y Sesma received a message ordering him to rendezvous with the other Mexican detachments at Fort Bend, and was on his way when Santa Anna was defeated at the April 21 Battle of SAN JACINTO. Ramírez y Sesma then returned to Mexico with the army under the command of Gen. Vincente FILISOLA in accordance with provisions of the Treaties of VELASCO.

**REYNOLDS, John Purdy** (March 7, 1806–March 6, 1836) Private, TENNESSEE MOUNTED VOLUNTEERS; Alamo defender from Cedar Springs, Mifflin County, Pennsylvania. Reynolds studied medicine at Jefferson Medical College in Philadelphia, and was in practice for 7 years. Together

with fellow Alamo defender William MC-
DOWELL, he had founded a settlement in
Tennessee called Mifflin after their home
county in Pennsylvania. The two men travelled from Tennessee to New Orleans, were
sworn into service in Nacogdoches on January 14, 1836, and arrived at the ALAMO
MISSION in San Antonio on February 9.
There is no mention of Reynolds serving as
a doctor at the Alamo. He apparently was
serving as a rifleman in Capt. William HAR-
RISON's company when he was killed in the
ALAMO BATTLE. His childhood friend and
cousin by marriage, David CUMMINGS, was
also an Alamo defender who perished in the
battle.

**ROBERTS, Thomas H.** (?–March 6, 1836)
Private, TEXAS REVOLUTIONARY ARMY;
Alamo defender from parts unknown. Lit-
tle is known about this man who was serv-
ing as a rifleman when he was killed in the
ALAMO BATTLE.

**ROBERTSON, James Waters** (February
18, 1812–March 6, 1836) Private, TEXAS REV-
OLUTIONARY ARMY; Alamo defender from
Tennessee. Robertson arrived in Texas by
way of Louisiana, and participated in the
Siege and Battle of SAN ANTONIO. He was
serving as a rifleman when he was killed in
the ALAMO BATTLE.

**ROBINSON, Isaac** (1808–March 6, 1836)
4th Sergeant, TEXAS REVOLUTIONARY ARMY;
Alamo defender from Scotland. Robinson
participated in the Siege and Battle of SAN
ANTONIO, and was serving as a noncommissioned officer with Capt. William CAREY's
artillery company when he was killed in the
ALAMO BATTLE.

**ROBINSON, James W.** (1800–October,
1857) Lieutenant governor, TEXAS PROVI-
SIONAL GOVERNMENT. This native of Indiana practiced law in that state, and in 1820
married Mary Isdell. In 1832, Robinson deserted his wife and young son, and moved
to Arkansas. He arrived in Texas that year,
settled in Nacogdoches, and in 1835 received title to land in Joseph Vehlein's colony.
Robinson was a delegate to the November,
1835 TEXAS CONSULTATION OF DELEGATES,
and was elected lieutenant governor. When
Governor Henry SMITH became embroiled
in a dispute with the General Council,
Robinson was named governor but with the
government in disarray was unable to adequately serve in that office. He enlisted in
the TEXAS REVOLUTIONARY ARMY in March,
1836, and served as a private at the Battle
of SAN JACINTO. He became a member of
the Supreme Court in 1836 while residing
in Gonzales. Robinson was captured in a
skirmish at San Antonio in September, 1842,
and taken to Mexico as a prisoner. He began
a correspondence with Antonio Lopez de
SANTA ANNA, which led to his release to
carry terms of an armistice to Sam HOUS-
TON. He moved to San Diego, California, in
1850, and served as district attorney from
1852–1855 and school commissioner in 1854.
He was involved in the promotion of a railroad when he died in San Diego at the age
of 57.

**ROSE, James M.** (1805–March 6, 1836)
Private, TENNESSEE MOUNTED VOLUNTEERS;
Alamo defender from Ohio. Rose was the
nephew of President of the United States
James Madison. He was sworn into service
at Nacogdoches on January 14, 1836, and
arrived in San Antonio with his unit on February 8. Rose was serving as a rifleman when
he was killed in the ALAMO BATTLE.

**ROSE, Louis** "Moses" (aka "Ross"; May 11, 1785–1850) Private, TEXAS REVOLUTIONARY ARMY; Alamo escapee from Laferee, Ardennes, France. Rose claimed to have been a noncommissioned officer who fought under Napoleon Bonaparte during the invasions of Russia and Italy, although that has never been verified. He immigrated to Nacogdoches, Texas around 1826, and took up farming as well as working in sawmills and as a teamster. Rose sold his property in 1835, and volunteered to fight for Texas independence. He participated in the Siege and Battle of SAN ANTONIO, and accompanied James BOWIE to the ALAMO MISSION. Rose was present during the ALAMO SIEGE, but, according to some reports, fled before the MEXICAN ARMY attacked. The story is told that on the night before the ALAMO BATTLE (March 5, 1836), Col. William TRAVIS drew a line across the dirt with his sword. Those who pledged to remain and fight were requested to step across the line; those who wanted to leave could remain where they stood. Louis Rose was apparently the only man in the ALAMO GARRISON who refused to step across the line. He was said to have slumped to the dirt and covered his face with his hands. Rose then gathered his belongings, and jumped over the wall to flee for his life. (See TRAVIS, William for more.) Weeks later, he arrived nearly dead at the Zuber home in Grimes County. He had been forced to pass through large patches of prickly pear, and his feet and legs had been savaged by the thorns. Zuber extracted the thorns as best he could with a pair of forceps, and Rose eventually healed. He was asked for the remainder of his life why he had abandoned his comrades. His consistent reply apparently was: "By God, I wasn't ready to die." Rose was forever after branded a coward and deserter. He opened a meat market in Nacogdoches, and perhaps due to his surly and combative attitude became involved in a number of violent altercations. He was the most despised man in town because of his admitted cowardice. When an attempt was made on Rose's life, the known offender was not prosecuted. On one occasion, Rose threatened a man in his shop with a shotgun, and on another he slashed a man who had complained about the quality of the meat Rose stocked. He eventually sold his shop, drifted from Texas to Natchitoches, Louisiana, and died in 1850. In 1975, it was reported that his unmarked grave had been identified by the discovery of a bed of cactus — which is not indigenous to that state — sprouting in an overgrown pine brake near Logansport, Louisiana. It was deduced that the cactus had grown from some of the thorns that had been imbedded in Rose's legs.

**RUSK, Jackson J.** (?–March 6, 1836) Private, TEXAS REVOLUTIONARY ARMY; Alamo defender from Ireland. This resident of Nacodoches, Texas was serving as a rifleman when he was killed in the ALAMO BATTLE.

**RUSK, Thomas Jefferson** (December 5, 1803–July 29, 1857) General, TEXAS REVOLUTIONARY ARMY; First Texas Secretary of War; chief justice of the Texas Supreme Court; United States Senator. Rusk was a large man with sandy-hair and blue eyes, the son of a stonecutter who had worked on the South Carolina plantation of statesman John C. Calhoun, who sponsored Rusk's law studies. Rusk moved to Clarksville, Georgia to practice law in 1825, and two years later married Mary Cleveland. He traveled to Nacogdoches, Texas in 1835 while searching for some men who had swindled him in a business association with miners and land speculators, and decided to stay. Rusk organized a company of volunteers later that year, and marched to participate in the Siege and Battle of SAN ANTONIO, but departed before the fighting had begun. He was appointed inspector general of the army on December 14, 1835, and was a delegate to the March, 1836 TEXAS CONSTITUTIONAL CONVENTION, where he became known as a peacemaker between the various factions. At that convention, he was a signer of the TEXAS DECLARATION OF INDEPENDENCE, and appointed Secretary of War in President David BURNET's cabinet. Following the ALAMO BATTLE and the Surrender and Massacre at GOLIAD, Rusk was dispatched with a message from President David BURNET to army commander Sam HOUSTON, who was in the process of retreating across Texas. Burnet was critical of this "Runaway Scrape" as it has been called, and ordered Houston to stand and fight. Rusk at that time was given authority to replace Houston if necessary. Instead, Rusk joined Houston—a man he came to admire—on his tactical retreat, and fought by his side in the victorious April 21, 1836 Battle of SAN JACINTO. Rusk should be commended for his effort— albeit futile—to restrain the troops from committing atrocities in that battle. He did manage to take personal control of a group of prisoners surrendered by Col. Juan ALMONTE, and protected them from being harmed. Rusk reluctantly assumed command of the army from the wounded Gen. Houston following that battle, and served in that capacity until October when he accepted Houston's offer to become his Secretary of War. Rusk was asked to run for president of Texas in 1838 when Houston's term was over, but refused. He was elected chief justice of the Texas Supreme Court in December, 1838, and served in that capacity until June, 1840. At the request of President Mirabeau LAMAR, he commanded troops that defeated Cherokee Indians who had been conspiring with the Mexicans in the July, 1839 Battle of Neches near present-day Tyler, Texas, which led to a falling out with Hous-

ton. The men finally reconciled in 1844, and became firm friends. Rusk was named president of the Texas convention that convened on July 4, 1845, and accepted terms of annexation by the United States, and later completed a state constitution. In 1846, upon the admission of Texas as a State in the Union, Rusk and Sam Houston were elected to the United States Senate. Rusk was re-elected in 1851 and 1857, and served in that office as well as President pro tempore of the Senate. Unable to bear the grief after the death of his wife, he committed suicide on July 29, 1857, in Nacogdoches, and was buried in Oak Grove Cemetery. Rusk County, Texas, and the town of Rusk, Texas, was named in his honor.

**RUTHERFORD, Joseph** (1798–March 6, 1836) Private, TEXAS REVOLUTIONARY ARMY; Alamo defender from Kentucky. Rutherford was a resident of Nacogdoches, Texas when he participated in the Siege and Battle of SAN ANTONIO. He was serving as an artilleryman in Capt. William CAREY's artillery company when he was killed in the ALAMO BATTLE.

**RYAN, Isaac** (March 1, 1805–March 6, 1836) Private, TEXAS REVOLUTIONARY ARMY; Alamo defender from St. Landry Parish, Louisiana. Ryan participated in the Siege and Battle of SAN ANTONIO, and was serving as a rifleman with Capt. Robert WHITE's infantry company when he was killed in the ALAMO BATTLE.

# S

**SAN ANTONIO, Siege and Battle of** (Siege: October 29, 1835–December 4, 1836; Battle: December 5–10, 1835) (This engagement has been referred to in many reference works as the "Siege and Battle of Bexar" in reference to San Antonio's Spanish name— San Antonio de Bexar or simply Bexar. For purposes of easier geographic understanding, this siege and battle will be referred to in this entry and related entries as having taken place in San Antonio.) This siege and battle was waged at San Antonio, Texas, between about 300–500 Texas Volunteers and about 1,400 Mexican soldiers, and resulted in the surrender of the Mexicans.

### Chronology of the Texas Revolution

- June 29, 1835: Battle of ANAHUAC
- October 2, 1835: GONZALES SKIRMISH
- October 3, 1835: MEXICAN CONSTITUTION OF 1824 officially voided
- October 9, 1835: GOLIAD SKIRMISH
- October 28, 1835: Battle of CONCEPCION
- November 3, 1835: TEXAS CONSULTATION OF DELEGATES

- **November–December, 1835: Siege and Battle of SAN ANTONIO**
- January–February, 1836: The MATAMOROS EXPEDITION
- February 23–March 5, 1836: The ALAMO SIEGE
- March 1, 1836: TEXAS CONSTITUTIONAL CONVENTION
- March 2, 1836: TEXAS DECLARATION OF INDEPENDENCE
- March 6, 1836: The ALAMO BATTLE
- March 20–27, 1836: Surrender and Massacre at GOLIAD
- April 21, 1836: Battle of SAN JACINTO
- May 14, 1836: Treaties of VELASCO

Mexican dictator General Antonio Lopez de SANTA ANNA had dispatched General Martin Perfecto de CÓS, his brother-in-law, to San Antonio, Texas, in the summer of 1835 with orders to expel American settlers and arrest those rebels who were stirring up re-

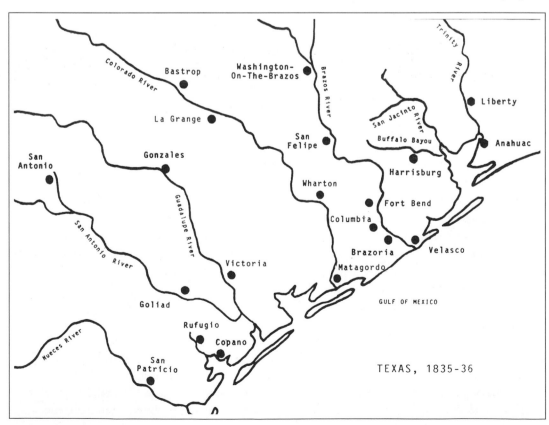

TEXAS, 1835-36

bellion in Texas. The news of this build-up of Mexican forces was a call to arms for the Americans who inhabited Texas and considered their futures jeopardized by the action. Three hundred volunteers under the command of Stephen F. AUSTIN set out on October 13, 1835 from Gonzales — about 70 miles distant — with quixotic ambitions of removing the 1,400 Mexican Army troops that were occupying San Antonio.

The volunteers, incidentally, had been hauling the cannon with its banner inscribed "Come and take it" that had been the subject of contention in the October 2 GONZALES SKIRMISH. Unfortunately, the squeaking wheels that had been made from cottonwood tree trunks contributed to the 6-pounder becoming a nuisance, and the cannon was scuttled and buried at Sandy Creek.

On October 28, Col. James BOWIE and Capt. James W. FANNIN led a scouting party of 92 men that was attacked and defeated a force of 400 Mexican soldiers — killing 60 and losing only one man — south of San Antonio in the Battle of CONCEPCION.

The volunteers then proceeded to surround San Antonio, but it was deemed that an immediate assault against such overwhelming odds would be tantamount to suicide. The Texans settled in to wait. Col. William TRAVIS took it upon himself to burn large expanses of grass to deny forage for enemy horses, and, with the assistance of scout Erastus "Deaf" SMITH, procured nearly 300 tamed horses.

The prolonged wait stretched throughout the better part of the month of November, and the morale of the volunteers suffered. Food was in short supply, and their clothing was inadequate for the cold weather. Large numbers of the volunteer force that had swelled to nearly a thousand deserted, claiming that their traditional 30-day military obligation had ended. The few minor skirmishes, which amounted mostly to sniping at sentries, did little to promote enthusiasm for fighting.

Two companies of volunteers that called themselves the NEW ORLEANS GREYS — many of whom were emigrants from Europe — arrived in late November from Louisiana, and were appalled at the lax atmosphere in the camp and the easy-going soldiering they observed. Roll calls were ignored in favor of roasting meat over a fire; soldiers were half-dressed in formation; and tents and huts were placed without military alignment. For this reason, few orders were issued or obeyed. The Greys, however, participated in artillery practice at the expense of the ALAMO MISSION masonry; and, in impromptu displays of bravado, the volunteers would charge into accessible areas of the city, steal food, and retreat before the Mexicans, who were notoriously poor marksmen, could react.

Austin learned in mid-November that the TEXAS CONSULTATION OF DELEGATES had chosen him for duty with a commission that would travel to the United States to appeal for aid. Col. Edward BURLESON was chosen as temporary commander, much to the disappointment of Jim Bowie, who believed that he deserved the honor. Austin departed on November 25. William Travis also departed at about this time to travel to San Felipe and appeal for a commission to the rank of colonel.

The day following Austin's departure, scout Deaf Smith observed the approach of a packtrain guarded by Mexican soldiers. The volunteers were convinced that the packtrain contained a large payroll in gold or silver, and that the troops were reinforcements for the beleaguered command of General Cós. In what would become known as the "Grass Fight," 100 volunteers with artillery under the command of Jim Bowie charged the muletrain about a mile from town, and engaged in a running battle. The Mexicans retreated as they fought, and in the end lost about 50 men killed before the remainder made it safely into town. The volunteers suffered only 2 men wounded, and had captured about 70 head of horse. But, much to the chagrin of the volunteer army, the pack-train contained nothing but grass as forage for the horses and cattle. The incident, although a great success in military terms, served to lower morale and further the resolve of those who wanted to return home.

A council of war was held. The field officers overruled Burleson, who wanted to stay, and voted to abandon the siege and withdraw the volunteers to Goliad to wait out the winter, a decision that was met with mixed feelings by the men. Before the withdrawal commenced, however, several men who had been held prisoner in town by the Mexicans escaped and made their way to the camp of the volunteers. Two of these men, Sam Maverick and local merchant John W. SMITH, offered vital information that compelled some volunteers to reconsider breaking the siege. It was confirmed that the Mexicans were low on food, supplies, and ammunition, and there was much discontent among the troops. In addition, the Mexican position was not as well fortified as first thought, and Maverick and Smith provided maps of strategic interest. Burleson, however, was still hesitant to attack.

Veteran plainsman and land speculator Ben MILAM, who had been arrested by Gen. Cós that summer and had escaped, as well as Col. Frank JOHNSON, were disgusted with the decision to wait. On December 4, Milam confronted what remained of the volunteer army. He scratched a line in the dirt, and called out, "Who'll go with old Ben Milam into San Antonio?" The response was mostly positive, and about 300 men crossed his line to volunteer. Those who had not volunteered to attack were urged by Burleson to remain in camp to serve as reinforcements and rear

guard. By morning the volunteer force that had committed to accompany Ben Milam into San Antonio had diminished to somewhere between 210–240, the others perhaps nagged by second-thoughts or chased away by the bone-chilling norther that had passed through during the night. Despite the desertions, the assault commenced as planned before dawn.

While Col. Burleson remained in camp with those he had coaxed into remaining as a reserve unit, Milam commanded one unit and Johnson the other on an assault of San Antonio. A detachment of volunteers laid down a base of fire, which was enthusiastically returned by the Mexicans. The main force swept across the cornfields and penetrated the town proper. Mexican artillery rained down balls and grapeshot, which caused the rebels to seek cover in nearby houses. The two divisions of New Orleans Greys became confused, and one fired upon the other. Several men fell from friendly fire before this grievous mistake could be corrected.

The street battle continued on a house to house basis for two days. The withering fire from the Mexican cannons kept the volunteers pinned down, but slowly but surely the ragtag army proceeded to gain ground. Gen. Cós, in an act of bravado, raised a red flag from the belfry of the San Fernando Church to signify no mercy.

On the third day, Ben Milam, the man who had initiated the mutiny that led to the armed confrontation, was shot in the head and died instantly. This loss perhaps inspired the volunteers to fight on with even more determination. Col. Frank Johnson was elected to replace Milam as commander of these volunteers.

The Mexicans were not accustomed to street warfare, and Cós gathered his troops inside the fortified ALAMO MISSION. But their resolve was weakening — nearly 200 had deserted. The volunteers relentlessly battered the Alamo walls with cannon balls, and on December 9, Cós raised the white flag. At that time, a total of about 150 Mexicans had been killed.

By 2 A.M. the following morning, Col. Burleson had negotiated terms of the Mexican surrender. Gen. Cós would turn over to the Texans all public property, money, arms and ammunition, and supplies in San Antonio, and agree to never fight against Texans again or to interfere with the restoration of the MEXICAN CONSTITUTION OF 1824. In return, Cós and his troops would be permitted to retreat south of the Rio Grande River with only enough arms and ammunition sufficient enough to protect themselves against possible Indian attack.

Some members of the New Orleans Greys moved into the Alamo while the volunteers who had gathered in Gonzales to march to San Antonio in late October — their quixotic intentions now realized — disbanded and returned to their homes and farms. The last remaining Mexican troops in Texas marched away south for the time being, humiliated by an army of untrained volunteers.

**SAN JACINTO, Battle of** (April 21, 1836) This battle was fought between about 800 Texas Volunteers under the command of General Sam HOUSTON and about 1,250–1,300 MEXICAN ARMY troops under General Antonio Lopez de SANTA ANNA. The actual firefight lasted about 18 minutes, and resulted in victory for the Texans, who not only won the battle but in doing so gained their independence from Mexico. The Mexicans lost about 600 killed, and likely about that same number captured — including Gen. Santa Anna. (Houston's official report lists 630 killed; 208 wounded; and 730 cap-

tured). The Texans lost 2 dead and between 23 and 34 wounded — of whom 6 would later die.

*Chronology of the Texas Revolution*

- June 29, 1835: Battle of ANAHUAC
- October 2, 1835: GONZALES SKIRMISH
- October 3, 1835: MEXICAN CONSTITUTION OF 1824 officially voided
- October 9, 1835: GOLIAD SKIRMISH
- October 28, 1835: Battle of CONCEPCION
- November 3, 1835: TEXAS CONSULTATION OF DELEGATES
- November–December, 1835: Siege and Battle of SAN ANTONIO
- January–February, 1836: The MATAMOROS EXPEDITION
- February 23–March 5, 1836: The ALAMO SIEGE
- March 1, 1836: TEXAS CONSTITUTIONAL CONVENTION
- March 2, 1836: TEXAS DECLARATION OF INDEPENDENCE
- March 6, 1836: The ALAMO BATTLE
- March 20–27, 1836: Surrender and Massacre at GOLIAD
- **April 21, 1836: Battle of SAN JACINTO**
- May 14, 1836: Treaties of VELASCO

Following his March 6, 1836, victory in the ALAMO BATTLE, Santa Anna devised a three-pronged strategy to rid Texas of the remainder of the ragtag volunteer army. Gen. José Francisco URREA would march up from the south with 1,400 men; Gen. Antonio GAONA would sweep across the north with about 700 troops; and Santa Anna with Gen. Joaquín RAMÍREZ Y SESMA would lead about 1,200 troops directly through the center of Texas.

At that same point in time, Sam Houston, commander in chief of the TEXAS REVOLUTIONARY ARMY, had departed the TEXAS CONSTITUTIONAL CONVENTION at Washington on the Brazos with the promise that he would assemble as large an army as possible and make a stand against the advancing

Mexicans. He headed west to Gonzales where he found about 375 men and learned about the fate of the Alamo. He immediately sent a messenger to notify Col. James W. FANNIN, who was at Goliad with about 400 men, to make a hasty retreat to Victoria on the Guadalupe River. Houston then dispatched scouts, including Erastus "Deaf" SMITH, to confirm the defeat of the Alamo. The scouts found Alamo survivor Susannah DICKINSON along the road on the afternoon of March 13, and escorted her to Gonzales where she recounted the particulars of the tragedy. She also informed them that a detachment of 700 Mexican troops under Gen. Ramírez y Sesma was on its way to Gonzales — pillaging the countryside as it went.

Houston realized that his small, poorly-equipped army could not defend the town, but that supplies and reinforcements could be obtained in the more populous region to

the east. On the night of March 13, Gonzales was evacuated, and Houston, his troops, and the civilian refugees set out for the Colorado River which would serve as a barrier between his force and that of Santa Anna. This mass exodus became known as the "Runaway Scrape" as thousands of men, women, and children in the path of the advancing Mexican Army headed east.

The roads were muddy which made the march difficult. Grain was in short supply, and the prairie grass was insufficient to support a large number of horses. Houston ordered that only those men who had been assigned the task of warning settlers along the way be mounted. This caused some to desert and return home rather than give up their precious mounts. Those who voluntarily walked made the sacrifice in the name of patriotism. In spite of the desertions, the army picked up new recruits along the way,

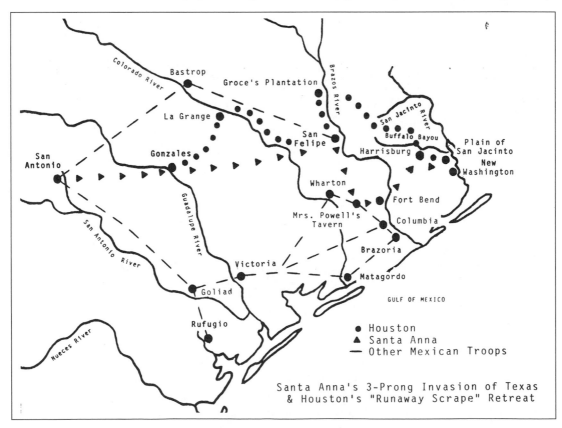

Santa Anna's 3-Prong Invasion of Texas
& Houston's "Runaway Scrape" Retreat

and, by the time Houston crossed the flooded Colorado River on March 19 to bivouac at Beason's Ford, his ranks had swelled to about 700 men.

The Mexican Army detachment under Gen. Ramírez y Sesma — now about 1,200 in size — pursued Houston, and on March 21 had arrived on the west bank of the river some 2 miles above the camp of the Texans. The two armies were aware of the presence of each other but remained patiently in place, both hesitant to attack without better knowledge regarding the strength of their enemy. Houston received messages informing him that the newly elected Texas government had fled from Washington on the Brazos to Harrisburg, and he was ordered to proceed to that city to provide protection. At the same time, news arrived that Col. Fannin and his men had been captured by Gen. Urrea, which meant that Houston could not depend on reinforcements. (See Surrender and Massacre at GOLIAD for more about the fate of Fannin and his men.)

The future of Texas now depended on the decisions made by Sam Houston. If he attacked Gen. Ramírez y Sesma across the river and lost, the war would be lost. If he defeated Ramírez y Sesma, he would still have to contend with Santa Anna and his large force. Houston was aware that his men believed that this was the place to stand and fight in order to protect the settlements to the east from facing an invasion of the Mexican Army. On March 26, the 5th day of the standoff, Houston stunned his men by ordering a retreat. The disgruntled troops marched 30 miles straight in the rain until finally halting the following day on the Brazos River near San Felipe. Houston staved off a mutiny by those who refused to retreat any farther by dispatching one detachment of 120 men under Capt. Moseley BAKER to a defensive position at San Felipe and about 100 men under Capt. Wiley MARTIN to the

crossing at Fort Bend, 30 miles downstream. Houston then led the remainder of his miserable army through the driving rain until on March 31 they arrived and bivouacked on the west bank of the Brazos River near Mill Creek across from Groce's Plantation. Houston sent out scouting patrols, and began the formidable task of attempting to transform his men — whose number now fluctuated daily due to arrivals and desertions but remained at about 800 — into some semblance of an army. Gen. Houston also was kept busy squelching rumors that had him retreating across the Sabine River into the United States in order to avoid the enemy. The fires of mutiny were fueled by the arrival in camp of Mirabeau Buonaparte LAMAR, a newspaper publisher from Columbus, Georgia and recent arrival in Texas who would later become the third president of the Republic. Lamar romanced a plan to the troops that would have him taking command and attacking Santa Anna without delay. Houston defiantly ordered several graves dug, and warned his troops that anyone who volunteered to follow Lamar would be shot. Lamar prudently dropped his fanciful idea. Another ugly situation arose when the troops held an informal election and chose Col. Sidney SHERMAN to replace Houston as commander. Houston threatened court-martials and executions, and that notion was promptly forgotten. Blame for these episodes of discontent must be placed in part on Sam Houston. He was uncommunicative to the point of not even discussing potential strategy with his officers, opting to make decisions on his own, and, if necessary, personally suffer the consequences.

His officers and men were not the only ones impatient with Houston's hesitancy to fight. President David BURNET dispatched Secretary of War Thomas RUSK to personally deliver an angry message that read in part: "Sir, the enemy are laughing you to scorn. You must fight them. You must retreat no further. The country expects you to fight." Rusk also had the authority to remove Houston as commander, if necessary. Houston remarked that Burnet's government not only had been the first to run but had run the farthest. Apparently Rusk liked what he heard from Houston, and chose to remain with the general. The two would later become close friends, and serve together in the United States Senate.

On April 2, Houston obtained the services of a steamboat. John E. Ross, captain of the *Yellow Stone*, agreed — for a handsome reward of sizable land grants — to stand by and, if necessary, ferry the Texas army across the flood-swollen Brazos River. The *Yellow Stone*, which had been built for the fur trade, could easily accommodate 500 men.

Meanwhile, Santa Anna and his army arrived at San Felipe on April 7, and found the town burned to the ground. Captains Baker and Martin had made certain that anything of use to the Mexicans had been destroyed. Baker then retreated across the Brazos River, and fired on the Mexicans when they attempted to cross in rafts. Santa Anna was anxious to fight, and sent messages to his generals in the field to move with their nearly 2,000 troops to Fort Bend where he would meet them with 750 men from Gen. Ramírez y Sesma's detachment. Capt. Baker had already departed Fort Bend, and Santa Anna decided to rest his troops east of there at a tavern owned by Mrs. Elizabeth Powell. Scouting patrols had reported the location of Houston's men as well as that of the Texas government at Harrisburg — 30 miles from Fort Bend. Santa Anna sent an order for Ramírez y Sesma to bring up his troops, and on the morning of April 11 resumed his march toward Fort Bend with intentions of going on to capture the enemy government. Santa Anna easily captured the ferry at Fort Bend — about 50 miles downriver from Houston's

headquarters — when Col. Juan ALMONTE, who spoke fluent English, tricked the slave who manned the ferry into coming across to pick them up.

One report suggests that Mrs. Powell's son, Joseph, understood Spanish, and unknown to Santa Anna had eavesdropped on the Mexicans. He was said to have reported to Sam Houston on April 12 with details of Santa Anna's plan. Houston was ecstatic. If Santa Anna had only 750 troops at his disposal, the two armies would be on equal terms with respect to number of men. Powell's report was confirmed by other scouts, and, at 10 A.M., Houston moved his army across the Brazos on the *Yellow Stone*. The steamboat later encountered some resistance above Fort Bend, and was compelled to run a gauntlet of Mexican troops that lined either bank before steaming away to safety in the Gulf of Mexico.

Santa Anna reached Harrisburg to learn from a trio of newspaper printers that the Texas government had fled by steamer to New Washington, 20 miles away. A company of dragoons under the command of Col. Juan Almonte was immediately dispatched with orders to capture President Burnet. The printers also offered information that Houston would likely try to defend Lynch's Ferry, about 15 miles east of Harrisburg on the San Jacinto River. Santa Anna understood the logic to that strategy. Houston would attempt to block the Mexican Army from advancing through the rest of Texas. If Santa could arrive there first, Houston's army would be trapped. On April 16, Santa Anna burned Harrisburg to the ground, and marched off, his destination first New Washington then Lynch's Ferry.

Houston and his troops were 45 miles from Harrisburg, and halted for the night at a fork in the road marked by what was known as the Which Way Tree — one direction led to Harrisburg and Santa Anna;

the other to Louisiana and away from a confrontation. The troops, Capt. Baker in particular, demanded to know which direction Houston intended to take, and threatened mutiny should he decide to retreat. He ignored them until the morning when he directed them down the road leading toward Harrisburg, a move that raised the spirits of the men.

By this time, Col. Almonte and his dragoons were approaching New Washington where President Burnet and his cabinet were about to board the schooner *Flash* anchored in Galveston Bay. Mike McCormick, a scout, galloped to the dock just ahead of the dragoons to inform Burnet about the presence of the Mexicans. Burnet, his wife, and several cabinet members hurriedly stepped into a rowboat and were only several yards offshore on Galveston Bay when Almonte's men arrived. Although the Texans were well within rifle range, the chivalrous Col. Almonte ordered his men to hold their fire because there was a lady in the boat. Burnet rowed out to the schooner, and the Texas government escaped to Galveston. Almonte did at that time capture large food stores from warehouses in New Washington.

Santa Anna was not pleased with news of the escape when he arrived on April 18, but his primary target was Houston and the Texas army which he planned to trap at Lynch's Ferry—10 miles away. He sent dispatches to Generals Urrea and Gaona ordering them to come forward, then retired to a nearby plantation to reportedly indulge himself in opium and a mulatto girl named Emily.

Houston arrived at Buffalo Bayou across from the ruins of Harrisburg at about noon on the 18th. It was apparent to Houston that Santa Anna had been there and had then departed for parts unknown after torching the town. The Mexican dictator's movements did not remain unknown for long. Scout Deaf Smith swam the river on his horse and cap-

tured a special courier who was carrying dispatches addressed to Santa Anna from the main force at Fort Bend. The leather saddlebag that contained the messages had the name "William Barret TRAVIS" stamped into it, and the courier was fortunate that Houston interceded on his behalf to save him from death at the hands of the angry Texans. The dispatches revealed Santa Anna's position at New Washington with 750 troops, and that 500 reinforcements would be arriving soon at Lynch's Ferry.

Houston added to his army at this time two 6-pounder cannons — called the "Twin Sisters." The cannons had been delivered by the *Flash*, the same schooner that had carried the Texas government to safety.

The following day, Houston formed his troops, mounted his white stallion, and erased any doubt about his intention to fight Santa Anna and his confidence of victory by delivering a stirring speech that promoted the battle cries: "Remember the Alamo! Remember Goliad!" Some versions of events indicate that Col. Sidney Sherman coined the famous battle cry.

Houston's inspired army crossed Buffalo Bayou to the Harrisburg side on rafts, and remained secreted in the woods until nightfall when they marched. They approached Lynchburg on the San Jacinto River just before daylight on April 20, and took control of Lynch's Ferry. Patrols were deployed, and the army camped in the nearby woods facing a mile-wide open grassy field enclosed by stands of trees. Behind them was a thick forest of live oak and Spanish moss that skirted Buffalo Bayou, which was about 300 feet wide and 15 feet deep. The San Jacinto River and Lynch's Ferry lay to their left with marsh extending for a mile where the river formed a small basin called Peggy Lake.

At the same time that Houston's men were taking their positions at Lynch's Ferry, Santa Anna was moving his army in that direction after burning the town of New Washington. When the Mexican Army arrived at the ferry, Santa Anna, who had been alerted by his patrols, was surprised that the Texans were already in place. The general hastily deployed his men on the far side of the field facing his enemy who were hidden among live oaks draped with Spanish moss, giant magnolias, hyacinths, and rhododendrons.

Mexican artillerymen immediately began firing their one piece of artillery, a brass 12-pounder, into the woods where Houston's men hid. *Deguello*, the bone-chilling bugle calls that signaled no quarter, no mercy, no prisoners, accompanied an advance by the Mexican infantry. The Texans answered with grape and canister shot from their two 6-pounder Twin Sisters cannons that were positioned about 10 yards from the treeline in the field. The Mexican soldiers retreated into the woods and opened up with musket fire, but the shots fell short. Both sides suffered a few casualties — the most notable Col. James NEILL, who was shot in the hip, and his counterpart Capt. Fernando Urizza, who was wounded by grapeshot.

Just before sunset, Col. Sidney Sherman and 85 cavalrymen rode out on a recon-

naissance of enemy lines. Sherman, however, defied Houston and disobeyed orders by attacking a Mexican position with intentions of capturing a cannon. Sherman and his men came under fire, and were forced to dismount to reload their weapons while Mexicans soldiers charged. That attack was repelled, but the Mexicans charged again and trapped the Texans. Secretary of War Thomas Rusk was one of those hemmed in by the assault, and was saved when Private Mirabeau Lamar drove his stallion into a Mexican horseman to open a pathway for

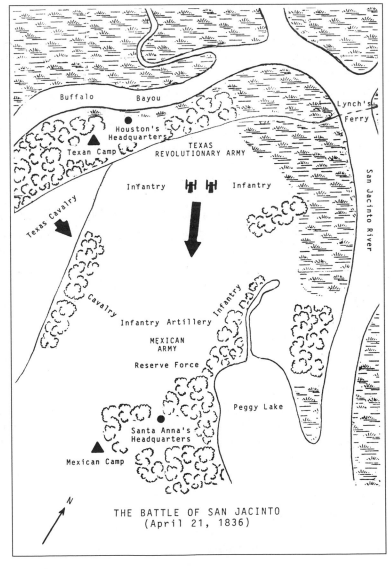

THE BATTLE OF SAN JACINTO
(April 21, 1836)

his comrades to escape. Lamar also saved the life of another Texan when he shot a Mexican soldier who was bearing down on the defenseless man. The impulsive action by Col. Sherman resulted in the loss of 2 men wounded and several horses killed. Sherman was relieved of command, and Gen. Houston subsequently promoted *Private* Mirabeau B. Lamar to colonel in command of the cavalry in recognition of his distinguished actions.

Santa Anna ordered that camp be made, and the two armies faced each other across the plain of San Jacinto for the remainder of the day. Santa Anna had hoped to provoke the Texans into leaving their cover, but Houston, once more plagued by troops anxious to fight, had his grumbling men hold their positions. Santa Anna personally directed his men during the night while they fortified their positions with a 5-foot high breastworks of baggage, pack saddles, packing cases, sacks of beans, and dirt and tree branches. The general was confident that he had Houston's men trapped with their backs to the bayou, and could order an assault at his leisure that would destroy the Texans. But he would wait for the arrival of Gen. Cós and his men before initiating an attack.

The Texans were prepared to fight at dawn and the Mexicans expected an attack, but Sam Houston slept until 8 A.M., his first sound sleep in days. At 9 A.M., about 500–550 reinforcements under Gen. Cós arrived to bolster the Mexican force to about 1,250–1,300. Santa Anna was now reassured that he greatly outnumbered Houston, and could attack whenever he chose. The president-general ordered that rifles be stacked and the men relax while he enjoyed a siesta. Oddly enough, Santa Anna had neglected to place sentries forward of his line.

Houston, who continued to be nagged by officers itching for a fight, strolled among his men and inquired of them whether or not

they wanted to fight. There was no question about it. The Texans wanted to fight. Houston told them to get their dinners and afterward he would lead them into battle. He then dispatched Deaf Smith with orders to destroy Vince's Bridge — recently crossed by Gen. Cós's men — which would cut off all means of escape for either army. Houston consulted his officers about strategy for the attack, asking them whether they should cross the field and attack or wait for Santa Anna to attack. These men, who had hounded Houston for days for his indecision, could not themselves decide on a course of action but were of the opinion that a frontal assault across the open field would be too risky. Houston dismissed them, and at 3:30 P.M. ordered the men to prepare for an attack — a frontal assault across the open field.

The Texas army emerged from the woods to form a line 900 yards long. Col. Edward Burleson's First Infantry Regiment was situated in the center, the artillery commanded by George W. HOCKLEY on Burleson's right, and on the extreme left was former cavalry commander Sidney Sherman's Second Infantry Regiment. Secretary of War Thomas Rusk would ride with Sherman on Houston's blind side for the purpose of reporting to the general once the attack was underway. Col. Mirabeau Lamar's cavalry took a position on the far right wing to provide a distraction and prevent escape in that direction.

It was 4:30 P.M. when Major General Sam Houston astride his horse, Saracen, rode the length of the line to silently inspect his troops. He halted about 30 yards in front of Burleson's First Regiment, and ordered, "Trail Arms! Forward!" The ground was wet and soft after the heavy rain, and the Texas army advanced with almost no sound. One man described it: "We marched upon the enemy with the stillness of death." Halfway across, the Texas musicians — 3 fifes and a drum — began playing "Will You Come to the Bower?" which was a popular, off-color ballad that became the Texas national anthem for that day.

Houston had his men creep forward to within about 200 yards of the enemy when, with a sweep of his campaign hat, signaled for the cannons to fire. Unknown to the Texans, the Mexican camp was totally unprepared for an attack. They were in fact asleep, their rifles stacked, apparently without sentries or patrols. General Antonio Lopez de Santa Anna was also in deep slumber — likely opium-induced — beneath the shade of a tree. Some reports claim Santa Anna at that moment was also distracted by the presence of his mulatto girl, Emily.

The silence was shattered by the roaring cannons, and grape and canister — mostly razor-sharp chopped horseshoes — rained down on the surprised Mexicans. The Texans edged forward, their collective voice rising above the din to cry, "Remember the Alamo! Remember Goliad!" The Mexican soldiers scrambled to retrieve their rifles or horses, and bodies darted about in panic and confusion.

When the line of Texans, now about 1,500 yards long, was within 60 yards of the enemy camp, scout Deaf Smith appeared on his horse and rode up and down the formation shouting over and over, "Vince's Bridge is down! Fight for your lives!" The men now knew that any avenue of retreat had been cut off, and they must fight and win. There could be no thought of surrender. To surrender meant death at the hands of Santa Anna, who had executed so many of their comrades.

Houston ordered his men to halt and fire then advance, but the frustration and anger that had built up within them exploded and they rushed forward howling and screaming their battle cry at the startled Mexicans. It

was fortunate for them that the Mexicans had been caught unaware. Had they been positioned at their barricades ready to fight, the Texans would easily have been cut to ribbons. A thick fog of black smoke quickly shrouded the field to reduce visibility to only a few yards as the Texans pressed the attack.

Sam Houston was 40 yards from the Mexican breastworks when his white stallion, Saracen, was struck in the chest at least five times — possibly by shrapnel from the Mexican cannon or a volley of musket fire — and the general was sent sprawling. At the same time, Lamar's cavalry had engaged those Mexican cavalrymen who had been able to mount for the fight, and loose horses were frantically dashing about the field. Houston accepted a replacement from one of his men, and was almost immediately struck just above the ankle by a 5-ounce musket ball and was thrown from his horse. The copper ball had shattered both bones in his right leg, but he ignored the painful wound and quickly lifted himself onto another mount and charged his enemy.

The Texans had reached the Mexican barricade, which was barely 5-feet high and poorly constructed with packing cases and pack saddles, and engaged the Mexican soldiers with rifles smoking and long-bladed knives in hand. Meanwhile, Sherman's regiment came forward to strike a second blow into the enemy breastworks. That action routed the Mexicans into an every-man-for-himself retreat — many without rifles that remained stacked and had been abandoned. The Texans chased the fleeing soldiers down, shooting, stabbing, clubbing, and yelling, "Remember the Alamo! Remember Goliad!" Peggy Lake and a tidewater bayou, which was too deep to hastily wade across, waited behind the Mexican camp. The soldiers were trapped there bunched up, and were shot down by the frenzied Texans.

Individual skirmishes soon replaced the full-scale assault. Gen. Sam Houston, his boot filling with blood, rode down the fleeing Mexicans, the saber in his hand a windmill as he slashed his way through the woods. Deaf Smith was thrown from his exhausted horse, and landed at the feet of Mexican lieutenant who brandished a saber. Smith drew his pistol, but it misfired. A fellow scout, John Nash, trampled the enemy officer with his horse while Smith wrestled away the man's saber and killed him with it. John Robbins tumbled from his excited horse into the waiting arms of a Mexican officer. Another Mexican soldier brought his lance to bear on Robbins, but, instead of running Robbins through, he discarded the lance and fled on Robbins' horse. Robbins then drove his Bowie knife into the officer's throat.

Gen. Santa Anna quickly realized that it was too late to consider any military strategy to turn the battle in his favor. But he also was aware that more than 2,500 fresh troops were waiting at Fort Bend — 45 miles away. He mounted a big black stallion owned by Col. Juan Bringas, and, with a group of his officers, raced away.

Houston estimated that only 18 minutes had expired from the time the Texans opened fire until they had secured the Mexican camp. The battle was for all intents and purposes over, but that did not stop the killing. The Texans were completely out of control, and began a bloody slaughter of their vulnerable enemy that was reminiscent of the bloodlust exhibited by the Mexican soldiers at the Alamo. Officers ordered the men to stop the carnage, but to no avail. Mexican Gen. Manuel Fernandez Castrillón attempted to surrender, but, against the orders of Secretary of War Thomas Rusk, was shot at point-blank range by Texas volunteers.

Col. Juan Almonte realized that the battle was lost and the only way to save his own life was to assemble a sizeable group of his troops and surrender to the Texans. Almonte rounded up about 400 men, and surrendered en masse. Rusk personally escorted these prisoners to prevent them from becoming victims of atrocities by the angry Texans. The men were so intent on indiscriminate killing that Gen. Houston feared that had only a small number of Mexican reinforcements arrived, they could have wiped out the entire disorganized Texas army. Houston, who was in great pain from his serious leg wound, observed Almonte's group of prisoners, and believed them to be Mexican reinforcements. "All is lost!" he cried. "My God, all is lost!"

Houston regained his senses, and was finally able to recruit enough men to guard the Mexican prisoners to protect them from others intent on more killing. The plain of San Jacinto became silent at twilight — when it became too dark to adequately chose targets.

The Mexicans lost about 600 killed and likely about that same number captured. (Houston's official report lists 630 killed; 208 wounded; and 730 captured). The Texans lost 2 dead and between 23 and 34 wounded — of whom 6 would later die. The battle of San Jacinto may have been decisively won by the Texans — the war, however, could conceivably still be lost if Santa Anna could successfully reach his troops at Fort Bend. Houston dispatched patrols to search for the Mexican dictator.

Santa Anna had separated himself from his officers in an effort to elude detection. He had become disoriented in the darkness, and spent the night hiding in tall grass by a bayou. In the morning, he happened upon a deserted house and changed some of his clothing. Not long after, he stumbled into a search party of Texans who were not aware of his identity but, given his linen shirt and jeweled studs, believed him to be an officer. Any hope of remaining incognito was dashed when Santa Anna was returned to the other prisoners, who greeted him with cries of "El Presidente!" He was immediately taken to Sam Houston.

Santa Anna was extremely agitated, and requested his usual medication. A dose of opium — either from his captured medicine box or from a supply on hand — was brought to him, and his nerves were quickly settled.

The Mexican general did not at that point plead for his life to be spared, but attempted to reason with Houston. He explained that he expected generosity inasmuch as Houston had conquered the "Napoleon of the West." Houston reminded Santa Anna about his atrocities at the Alamo and Goliad, which served to create a great deal of fear in the man who had ordered the cold-blooded executions of hundreds, perhaps thousands, of Texans. Santa Anna feebly argued that it had been the Mexican government that had ordered the executions. Houston refused to listen to any more, and interrupted to remind Santa Anna that *he was* the Mexican government. After further discussion and negotiation, Santa Anna agreed to order his remaining troops to leave Texas in trade for his life. (See Treaties of VELASCO for more.)

The Texans spent the following afternoon plundering the bodies of the dead Mexicans. Capt. Juan SEGUIN located a war chest owned by Santa Anna, and the booty of about 7,000 pesos — of the 12,000 that it was rumored to have held — was divided up among the men.

At present-day Deer Park, Texas, the site of the battlefield has been marked by a 570-foot monument constructed of reinforced concrete faced with Texas fossilized buff limestone. The San Jacinto Museum of Texas History is located at the base of the shaft, which displays historic exhibits. Visitors can view "Texas Forever! The Battle of San Jacinto," a 35-minute multi-image history of Texas presentation that utilizes 42 projectors.

The Patrick cabin, a replica of the cabin in which the peace treaty was drawn up after the Battle of San Jacinto, is also on display at Deer Park.

**SANTA ANNA, Antonio Lopez de** (February 21, 1794–June 20, 1876) General, commander-in-chief, MEXICAN ARMY; president and dictator of Mexico. He stood 5 feet 10 inches in height, which was quite tall for a Mexican, and in his prime was lithe and athletic.

### Birth and Early Years

Santa Anna was born in Jalapa, Mexico. His Castillian father was a mortgage broker and sub-delegate for the Spanish province of Vera Cruz, and his mother was said to have been of Creole stock, a Mexican of pure Spanish blood, but might have also had a trace of Indian blood. He briefly attended school, but was labeled "quarrelsome," and it was eventually arranged for him to work as a clerk for a merchant in Vera Cruz. This position as a "counter jumper," as he called it, was not to Santa Anna's liking. In June, 1810, his family connections obtained him an appointment — illegally since he was underage — as a first class cadet in the prestigious *Fijo de Veracruz* Regiment of Infantry in the Royal Army of New Spain. He was part of a 500-man expedition in early 1811 that was dispatched north toward the Texas frontier to fight Indians and pacify the eastern provinces. Santa Anna immediately impressed his commander, Joaquín de Arredondo, with his ability to withstand the rigors of the arduous marches and his obvious love of campaigning, which made him an example to his comrades. He was rewarded with a transfer to the cavalry. The government troops swept through the countryside, wantonly killing, terrorizing innocents, destroying property, and often torturing their prisoners. It became evident at that time that he was immune to the butchery around him. Santa Anna learned these lessons well, and revelled in the bloodshed. On August 29, he was struck by an arrow in the left arm — his first combat wound. On February 6, 1812, Santa Anna was promoted to second lieutenant, and on October 7 gained the rank of first lieutenant. At that time, he began commanding small detachments of troops. On one occasion, Santa Anna claimed to have defeated 320 Indians with only 30 troops in his unit. In April, 1813, an army of FILIBUSTERS — traders, land speculators, and other foreigners with potential revolutionist interests — had taken San Antonio by force and issued a declaration of Texas independence. The 1,800-man royalist army was ordered to march north in June, 1813 to remove these filibusters. The army arrived in mid-August, and engaged about 850 filibusters, Indians, and Tejanos in the Battle of Medina. In the initial stages of the engagement along the Loredo Road near the Medina River, more than 600 filibusters — most of them Americans — were killed by Gen. Arredondo's army. Another 150 were captured and subsequently executed. Lt. Santa Anna was awarded a decoration for his gallantry under fire during the battle. This began an effort to remove all Americans and liberal Mexicans from Texas. Deserters were shot, their wives and children made slaves, and their property seized. The army marched to San Antonio and captured that city while executing another 200 Americans. It was during this campaign that young Santa Anna learned the rudiments of dealing with invaders that he would employ during the TEXAS REVOLUTION — defeat the enemy army on the field, execute all prisoners, and terrorize civilians. The army remained in San Antonio — at the ALAMO MISSION — for nearly 2 months while forcing the locals to serve as slaves for their every need.

In late, 1814, Santa Anna was transferred to Vera Cruz, and was assigned the duty of keeping trade routes leading to the interior safe from marauding rebels and outlaws. He was so successful that he was promoted to captain in October, 1816. Santa Anna continued to serve in that capacity, and by 1821 was a veteran campaigner who had distinguished himself time and time again. He received such citations as the Shield of Honor and Certificate of the Royal and Distinguished Order of Isabella the Catholic, and a promotion to the rank of lieutenant colonel.

### Mexican Revolution

In early 1821, Agustín de Iturbide, a Mexican-born Spaniard, called for Mexico's independence from Spain. Santa Anna and his royalist troops were confronted by Iturbide's rebel army at Orizaba in March. He fortified his men in the Carmen Convent, and engaged in battle. After several successful forays in which he surprised his enemy and captured vital supplies in addition to killing a number of them, Santa Anna found himself surrounded. Instead of attacking, the rebels made entreaties to the respected soldier about joining their force. To everyone's surprise, Santa Anna agreed on the spot to change his allegiance. He was given the rank of full colonel by Iturbide, and embraced the cause of independence with the same zeal that had gained him the reputation as a respected officer in the royalist army.

Santa Anna marched to Córdoba, and united with troops under Lt. Col. José Joaquín de Herrera to force that city to surrender. He then moved in early April to Alvarado — about 45 miles south of Vera Cruz — and was saved from a battle when cries for independence could be heard among the troops garrisoned there. Santa Anna returned to Córdoba when informed that loyalist troops had besieged the city. His former comrades retreated, and Santa Anna vigorously pursued them. On May 28, Santa Anna attacked his hometown of Jalapa, and within hours had captured the city as well as artillery, muskets, stores of powder, and secured a "loan" to feed and clothe the rebels. He was subsequently vilified by the leaders of his hometown, either on account of his loyalty to the rebels, the forced loan, or his insistence at being recognized as the Military Governor of the State of Vera Cruz.

Santa Anna was given the formidable task of capturing Vera Cruz, which was the most fortified city in Mexico due to the billions in treasure that had been transferred in and out of the port over the years. He issued a proclamation to his men that read in part: "Comrades! You are going to put an end to the great work of reconquering our liberty. You are going to plant the eagle of the Mexican empire, humiliated three centuries ago on the plains of the Valley of Otumba, on the bank of the humble Tenoya, where the Castillian flag was first unfurled. The soul of Quauhpopoca, burned alive in the great square of Mexico City, because he avenged the iniquitous act of Juan Escalante, pleads for justice; and the victims of the horrible massacre of Cholula, whose cries have startled two worlds, filling both with horror, will not be satisfied unless you restore to your oppressed native land the liberty which they lost." Santa Anna reached the outskirts of Vera Cruz on June 27, and was met by reinforcements. Two days later, he chased away parties of royalists that had been destroying buildings and other emplacements outside the city walls that could provide cover for the rebels. On July 7, 1821, Santa Anna attacked his old friend from the Royalist Army, Gen. José Dávila. The assault did not go well — the rebel troops broke and ran when confronted by Spanish regulars, and sustained 30 killed and about 80 taken

prisoner. Santa Anna personally directed the retreat across a vulnerable position in which he constantly exposed himself to the fire of his enemy and was the final one to gain safety. The royalists did not pursue the rebels, and Santa Anna dispatched troops to guard the Jalapa road in an effort to prevent communication to the interior. He then fell back to Córdoba, and finally to Puebla where he met with Gen. Iturbide. It was determined that Vera Cruz would be left alone during the yellow fever season, and Santa Anna would proceed to Perote and remove the royalists that manned the old fort.

On July 30, however, the newly-appointed Spanish Viceroy, Gen. Juan O'Donojú, arrived in Vera Cruz aboard the warship *El Asia*. The Viceroy was shocked to find the port under siege, and requested a meeting with Santa Anna, who responded for an interview on August 5. The meeting resulted in an arrangement whereby the Viceroy would meet with Iturbide at Córdoba. On August 23, Santa Anna escorted O'Donojú to the conference with Iturbide. The following day, an accord known as the Plan of Iguala or Treaty of Córdoba was reached, with Santa Anna claiming participation in the proceedings. By October 7, both Perote and Mexico City had surrendered, and Santa Anna was on his way to Vera Cruz. Santa Anna ordered Dávila's surrender, but his former friend defied him by moving his men from the city to an impregnable castle on an island named San Juan de Ulloa in the bay. Santa Anna was prepared to take the city by force when the Town Council, which was aware of Santa Anna's penchant for brutality, petitioned Iturbide to send some other officer to accept their surrender. Col. Manuel Rincón was dispatched, and negotiated the surrender on October 27. Santa Anna and his men occupied the town, but Rincón remained as governor to ensure the town's safety — and Santa Anna's conduct.

Inturbide promoted Santa Anna to brigadier general, and he was hailed a hero by all the citizens of Mexico — except perhaps one. Iturbide apparently distrusted his new general, and ordered him to leave the city and for the time being relax from his labors.

## Rebellion

In 1822, Iturbide declared himself emperor of Mexico. Santa Anna journeyed to the National Capitol, and, bolstered by his rank and acclaim as a hero of the revolution, immersed himself in the upper echelon of the social scene. At this time, the dashing young general began courting the emperor's 60-year-old sister, Doña Nicolasa. He returned to Jalapa as Military Commander where his difficulties with the people in his home town intensified. Santa Anna's heavy handedness was reported through channels to Iturbide, who ignored the complaints and reiterated his support for his commander. In the meantime, Gen. Santa Anna cultivated his relationship with Iturbide by writing letters to the emperor that were filled with flattery and pledges of his loyalty — the sincerity of which must be questioned. The fact that Iturbide had declared himself emperor, the rightful occupant to the Throne of Montezuma, was highly unpopular with much of the populace — including Santa Anna. Iturbide, however, responded to the flattery by bestowing the Order of Guadalupe on his brigadier general. The award, which was established to gain support from the upper classes, had different grades of eminence. Santa Anna, instead of receiving the grand cross normally given to archbishops, bishops, and generals, was awarded a cross "*de numero*," designating the second order, a minor insult.

Santa Anna was known to frequently dally with various women, but, upon returning to the Capitol, decided to seek the hand of Iturbide's elderly sister. The emperor, who now called himself Emperor Augustin I, informed his subordinate in no uncertain terms —*amarga burla* (sneering sarcasm)— that he would never condone such a union. The humiliating rejection served to further diminish Santa Anna's loyalty to Iturbide and the new empire.

Despite the complaints from the City Council of Jalapa about Santa Anna's actions, Iturbide appointed him Military Commander of Vera Cruz in September, which gained him political control over the province. Santa Anna devised a plan to dislodge the Spanish who remained in San Juan de Ulloa, the fortified castle on an island in the bay, and were disrupting trade. The new captain general of the province, José Antonio de Echávarri, was ordered to cooperate with Santa Anna, and arrived on October 25. Santa Anna told Echávarri that he intended to trick the Spaniards into believing that the city would be surrendered to them. Their landing forces would then be ambushed and the depleted castle attacked and captured. Echávarri realized that it was he who had been tricked when the enemy landing forces arrived and there were no Mexican troops to support him. He narrowly escaped with his life. The indignant captain general reported this betrayal to Iturbide. Conflicting evidence, however, suggests that Santa Anna could have wanted his rival dead, or that Echávarri could have wanted to vilify Santa Anna for his own purposes, or that the plan had simply failed. Santa Anna states in his autobiography that the Spaniards had attacked the city without provocation, and had been beaten back in a triumph he described as "glorious for the defenders of the plaza." Iturbide initially promoted the two men, but immediately set off for Jalapa to personally deal with the allegations aimed at Santa Anna.

Iturbide arrived in Jalapa to inform Santa Anna that he was so important to the government that he was to be transferred at once to Mexico City. In truth, the emperor wanted Santa Anna, whose ambitions and treachery were a source of worry, to be located where he could keep his eye on him. During this meeting, Santa Anna made the mistake of seating himself, and was severely rebuked by the Captain of the Guard, who told him that "no one sits down in the presence of the emperor."

Santa Anna, who was offended by this indignity and the absolutism of Iturbide's power, made several excuses about tending to his affairs before he could travel to the Capitol. He later claimed that this meeting confirmed his resolve to restore his country to true freedom, and rode for Vera Cruz to form an army. He gathered about 400 men, and to the delight of the people, who evidently preferred Santa Anna over Iturbide, proclaimed liberty. He dispatched his troops to strategic locations, appropriated funds, and began to cultivate the populace. Santa Anna aligned himself with Miguel Santa María, who had recently been dismissed by Iturbide as the Minister of the Republic of Colombia. The minister set to work drafting a plan that would establish the Republic of Mexico. This December 6, 1822, manifesto guaranteed safety and citizenship to all native-born Spaniards and naturalized Spaniards and foreigners. Santa Anna then installed Manuel Felix Fernandez — who called himself Guadalupe Victoria — a well known rebel, as the official leader of the rebellion. Santa Anna wrote a letter to Iturbide promising to form a government with a constitution based on religion, independence, and union, and offered the emperor a "distinguished place in the nation" once he had renounced the crown.

Emperor Iturbide heard about Santa Anna's actions on his return trip to Mexico City. He declared his former general a traitor, and ordered that his property be confiscated. Amnesty was offered to those who would desert the rebellion, and troops were dispatched to the coast.

Meanwhile, Francisco Lemaur, the commander of the Spanish troops that remained fortified on San Juan de Ulloa, the island in the bay, negotiated an armistice with Guadalupe Victoria, and pledged to support the rebels in their fight.

The first engagement of the rebellion occurred at Plan del Río, between Vera Cruz and Jalapa, when Santa Anna met Iturbide's troops and captured a detachment of grenadiers. He freed the officers and added the men to his own army. At daybreak on December 21, he attacked Jalapa. The newly-acquired grenadiers quickly deserted, and his own men became trapped inside San José Church — where Santa Anna had been baptised — and finally surrendered. Santa Anna fled for his life. He reported to Victoria in Puente del Rey, and urged that they escape to the United States. Victoria refused, stating, "You can set sail when they show you my head." He sent Santa Anna to Vera Cruz with orders to fortify that position.

Political dissension in Mexico City was closing in on Emperor Iturbide. The Plan of Casa Mata, first proposed by Santa Anna which would guarantee a Republican form of government, was published on February 1, 1823 and was quickly endorsed by the army and the several city councils. Discussions commenced between Iturbide's commissioners and the rebels within Mexico City, but ended without an agreement. Iturbide called for a new congress in an effort to salvage his government, but the idea was rejected by the military coup. On February 19, Emperor Iturbide — Augustin I — abdicated his throne, and was exiled to Italy. The following month, the rebel army marched into Mexico City to liberate the Capitol. Santa Anna, however, was not called upon as a leader of this new government, but was simply an army officer with some measure of popularity. He briefly served as President of the Provincial Junta of Vera Cruz, but continued to carry on the revolution and was eventually sent to the Yucatan as Military Governor.

The Constituent Congress of Mexico adopted a liberal constitution on October 4, 1824. The president of that congress was Lorenzo de ZAVALA, who would become the first vice-president of Texas. This MEXICAN CONSTITUTION OF 1824 was loosely based on the United States Constitution and the Spanish Constitution of 1812. It would be the repeal of this constitution by Santa Anna in 1835 that would compel the colonists in Texas to fight for its restoration and eventually seek independence from Mexico. Free elections were held for the first time, and Guadalupe Victoria was elected president. Congress passed a decree that sentenced Iturbide to death should he return to Mexico. The former emperor, unaware of the decree, landed on Mexican shores on July 14, 1824, and was shot to death 5 days later.

Santa Anna's tenure in the Yucatan was rife with local disputes, and an unfulfilled plan to invade Cuba and add it to the Mexican Republic. He was eventually reassigned to Vera Cruz, and resigned as both Civil and Military Governor on April 25, 1825, and retired to his hacienda of Manga de Clavo, which was located on the road from Jalapa to Vera Cruz.

At some unknown point in time — likely before 1825 — Santa Anna married Doña Inés Garcia, the daughter of a prominent Spaniard who was described as a virtuous woman lacking physical beauty. Two boys (Manuel and Antonio, who died at age 5) and two girls (Maria Guadalupe and Maria del Car-

men) were born to the couple. Santa Anna would dabble in politics and live the life as a country gentleman for the next several years.

### Victor of Tampico

In 1828, Santa Anna was once more in charge of the government of Vera Cruz when Gen. Vicente Guerrero waged a bitter battle for president of Mexico against Secretary of War Manuel Gómez Pedraza. Santa Anna had supported Guerrero, but Pedraza won in a disputed election. Gómez Pedraza retaliated against Santa Anna, whom he considered a threat, by ordering a court-martial. Santa Anna took refuge with about 40 men in a fortress in Perote — 40 miles from Jalapa, and was declared an outlaw. He repelled an assault of government troops, and fled that position to fight a running battle for 200 miles away to Oaxaca. Gómez Pedraza was soon overthrown by Guerrero, and, in appreciation for his support, Santa Anna resumed his duties as Governor of Vera Cruz.

The Spanish, who had been closely watching the political climate in Mexico, decided in July, 1829 to reconquer that country. On July 16, when the Spaniards landed close to Tampico — 250 miles north of Vera Cruz — Santa Anna, without receiving authorization, mobilized a local militia of 2000 men, commandeered every ship in the port, and set sail. His actions were later criticized as reckless for leaving the port unguarded, but he had a penchant for favoring boldness over prudence.

The Spanish, meanwhile, had underestimated their mission. Three-thousand troops had set out from Cuba, but 400 were soon lost in a shipwreck. In addition, the Spaniards had unknowingly landed at Tampico during the height of yellow fever season. By the time Santa Anna arrived at Tampico, the

Spanish were losing many men daily to the disease and had divided their forces to seek a healthier location.

While en route, Santa Anna received word from the Congress that his actions had been authorized, which saved him from having a potential victory tarnished. After a couple of weeks of sporadic fighting in which Santa Anna once more distinguished himself with his ability to command under fire, the Spanish raised the white flag on August 22. Santa Anna had defeated mighty Spain, and had overnight became a national hero.

President Guerrero interrupted a performance at the theatre to make the announcement: "Mexicans, I am going to give you some splendid news which will fill your hearts with rejoicing. Brigadier Santa Anna has forced Barradas to surrender in Tampico, he has conquered him, saving the honor of the nation. As a just recompense I am going to send him this general's belt which I am wearing, in order that he shall put it on with all solemnity and as a just reward in his camp and before his soldiers." The performance was not resumed as the crowd joyously ran into the streets to spread the good news.

Santa Anna later wrote: "As is customary in Mexico, applause to the victor, ovations on all sides. The General Congress saw fit to give me the title of *Benemerito de la Patria* (Well deserving of the Native Land); the government promoted me to the rank of General of Division, sending me the insignia to be conferred upon me. Some legislatures gave me swords of honor and the people called me the Victor of Tampico."

The name of the city of Tampico was officially changed to Santa Anna de Tamaulipas. The victor sent two captured Spanish standards and a flag to Mexico City, which were placed on the balcony of the National Palace for all to see. Santa Anna returned to Vera Cruz where he received his most enthusiastic reception, and a ball was held in

his honor. Even the townspeople of Jalapa changed their opinion about their native son, and paid him great homage.

### Politics

Vice-President Anastasio Bustamante decided to overthrown the regime of President Guerrero in late 1829, a move to which Santa Anna was opposed. He marched his army toward Mexico City with intentions of aiding the president, but Guerrero had by then fled to his estate and accepted defeat. Congress then conferred the presidency upon Bustamante. Santa Anna responded by submitting a letter of resignation as Governor of Vera Cruz, and retired to his country estate.

While in his self-imposed exile, former president Guerrero was charged with treason and executed on February 14, 1831. Santa Anna had been offered a position under the new administration, but declined. Instead, in the following year he became embroiled in local politics that became national. He was asked by the corrupt garrison commander at Vera Cruz to lead a movement that had grievances against Bustamante, and cautiously accepted. Santa Anna assumed control of the highly profitable customs house at Vera Cruz, and offered President Bustamante his assistance in mediating the disagreement that had been initiated by the local garrison. Bustamante responded by dispatching the army. Santa Anna answered by stating in a letter that the grievances were not with the president, but with a cabinet officer and if he were removed the controversy would be settled. Bustamante refused to negotiate. Santa Anna formed an army of about 300 cavalry, and on February 24 attacked and captured a government convoy 15 miles from Vera Cruz. His booty from the capture included munitions and a substantial amount of cash. He then marched his enlarged army, and, on March 3, engaged in the Battle of Tolumé where his men were devastated by a superior force — over 450 were killed and wounded. Santa Anna retreated back to Vera Cruz, assembled additional troops, and prepared for an assault. The Mexican Army laid siege to the town, but was forced to retreat from constant artillery barrages. More and more local governments began to side with the rebels, and on May 17 the cabinet officers resigned. Santa Anna entered into negotiations that demanded the removal of President Bustamante and the reinstatement of old rival Manuel Gómez Pedraza. Bustamante placed himself in charge of the army, and Santa Anna prepared his troops for war. Santa Anna marched toward Mexico City, and engaged in a number of successful skirmishes that encouraged Bustamante to open negotiations. An agreement to end hostilities was reached on December 11, 1832. Gómez Pedraza would serve as president until April 1, 1833. Elections would be held to chose new state legislatures that would then select the new president.

### President of Mexico

Santa Anna immediately positioned himself as the front-runner for the presidency. He issued a proclamation on January 19 that read in part a plea for: "Indulgence with mistakes of opinion, an end to hatreds, and the erasure from memory of the word 'vengeance.' Thus you will attain the object of your desires and sacrifices, long and happy days for the republic, durable happiness for all. If my dedication and sacrifices for liberty are worth anything, respond to my pleas. My whole ambition is restricted to beating my sword into a plowshare. If any hand should gain disturb the public peace and constitutional order, do not forget me. I shall return at your call, and we shall again show the world that the Mexican Republic will not tolerate tyrants and oppressors of the people." In the presidential election by the Congress, Santa Anna received 16 of the 18 votes cast. Santa Anna, however, chose to turn over his duties to Vice-president Valentín Gómez Farías, and retired to his hacienda allegedly to recuperate from the rigors of campaigning.

In the meantime, the Mexican State of Coahuila-Texas had held a convention. A constitution which called for Texas — which was populated mostly by anglo–Americans — to become an independent state as well as other petitions were drafted, and Stephen F. AUSTIN was chosen to deliver them to Mexico City. Austin arrived in Mexico City in July, and was forced to wait until November 5 until the "recuperating" Santa Anna finally received him. Austin was successful in persuading the repeal of the April 6, 1830, immigration law and other requests, but Santa Anna refused to recognize Texas as a state. Austin started home December, but, on a January, 1834 stopover in Saltillo, was arrested on suspicion of attempting to incite insurrection in Texas and returned to Mexico City. A letter sent by Austin in October, 1833 to the predominately Mexican city council in San Antonio had surfaced in Mexico City, and contained statements such as, "The fate of Texas depends on itself and not upon this government," and "The country is lost if its inhabitants do not take its affairs into their own hands." Austin would be held until July, 1835 when a general amnesty law was passed.

The new president, who was not known to be faithful to his wife, was said to have during this period of time freely indulged himself in the pleasures of the local girls — many of whom became pregnant. In one instance, one of his dissatisfied lovers appropriated the medals from his uniform — the Order of Guadalupe; the Order of Charles III, and cross of Tampico — and bestowed the awards on local peons in the slums. Santa Anna was compelled to pay thousands of pesos for the return of his precious medals.

Vice-president Gómez Farías began an aggressive agenda of reforms which included literacy and social benefits, but had also diminished the role of the army and the church. These radical changes did not set well with the people of Mexico who had always been bound to the dictates of the church. When popular opinion swayed against Gómez Farías and resulted in protests, Santa Anna, who had initially supported his vice-president, finally assumed control of his government in April, 1834. Gómez Farías was expelled, and the liberal Congress and liberal governors were replaced with conservatives. He established a centralist government that, by January 1835 with a hand-picked Congress comprised of members of the army and clergy, revoked powers that states had always enjoyed under the MEXICAN CONSTITUTION OF 1824. Santa Anna had for all intents and purposes become dictator of Mexico.

This caused dissent in many areas of Mexico, particularly in the state of Zacatecas. In May, Santa Anna marched his army to quell this uprising. His 3,500 troops battled a militia of 13,000, and in less than 2 hours had captured the city of Zacatecas in a stoke of brilliant military strategy. Casualty estimates range from several hundred to more than 2,500 rebels and civilians killed; Santa Anna lost less than 100 killed. The government soldiers then pillaged, raped, and destroyed property — the English and United States citizens were singled out for the worst treatment.

## Texas Revolution

Another area of the country that was staging a minor insurrection was Coahuila-Texas, and Santa Anna saw no reason not to quell the brewing discontent in that northern state. He found his excuse to send troops when rampant land speculation and corruption in Saltillo, which had been going on for some time, came to his attention. He dispatched his brother-in-law, Gen. Martin Perfecto de CÓS, in June to put a stop to this corruption by arresting known land speculators, the governor, and suspending civil government in favor of martial law. These actions were propagandized by the WAR PARTY — those Texans promoting independence — as intolerable acts that would lead to martial law and the confiscation of land in Texas.

Santa Anna also decided in that spring of 1835 that the customhouses and garrisons in Texas that had for all practical purposes been abandoned in 1832 would be reopened and duties would be collected. This led to an incident at Anahuac, the legal port for Galveston Bay, that would ignite the TEXAS REVOLUTION. When merchants protested unfair collection of duties and were arrested, William B. TRAVIS rallied a small group of armed force and on June 29 in the Battle of ANAHUAC forced the Mexican garrison to surrender. The colonists had second thoughts about the rash act by Travis, and letters of apology were sent but did not mollify the Mexicans. Public opinion, however, swayed in Travis' favor when Santa Anna ordered Gen. Cós to march for Texas and arrest Travis and other rebels. This edict evoked concerns of martial law and military occupation, and the Texans considered it unthinkable to turn their people over to a military tribunal rather than have them tried by a jury of peers. Santa Anna also at that time threatened the enforce the ban on slavery, which outraged slave holders. Committees began to form all across Texas to protest Santa Anna's actions. The colonists departed their farms and homes and rallied to repel the advancing Mexicans. The "Lexington and Concord" of the Texas

Revolution took place in the town of Gonzales when troops at San Antonio ordered that town to give up their cannon. On October 2, in the Skirmish at GONZALES, the volunteers attacked 100 Mexican troops, killing 1 and forcing the remainder to retreat. The first shots of the Texas Revolution had been fired. The day following that action, Santa Anna formally voided the provisions of the Mexican Constitution of 1824, and the colonists were now at the mercy of this dictator. On October 9, in what was called the Skirmish at GOLIAD, the Texans captured a small Mexican garrison which prevented the Mexicans from obtaining supplies and reinforcements by sea. On October 28, a scouting party of about 90 men commanded by Col. Jim BOWIE and Capt. James FANNIN was attacked by 400 Mexican troops. In the Battle of CONCEPCION, the volunteers killed about 60 Mexicans, while losing only 1 man — the first killed in the revolution. Bolstered by their victory, the volunteer army surrounded Cós's 1,400- man army in San Antonio and, hesitant to attack the superior enemy, settled in to wait. The Siege and Battle of SAN ANTONIO finally culminated in Cós's surrender on December 10. Cós and his men were sent back to Mexico where they rendezvoused in late December with Santa Anna, who had personally taken charge his army of 6,000 and was marching to put down this uprising in Texas.

Santa Anna arrived in San Antonio on February 23, 1836, and, following a 13-day siege, captured the ALAMO MISSION and killed all its defenders on March 6 (see ALAMO SIEGE and ALAMO BATTLE). He graciously freed some SURVIVORS — women, children, and a slave — before resuming his march through Texas. He then designed a three-pronged strategy to destroy the TEXAS REVOLUTIONARY ARMY, and, while he marched east, one detachment under Gen. José URREA swept toward Goliad and cap-

tured 500 men. Santa Anna, who had decreed that no prisoners would be taken, ordered the execution of these men (see -Surrender and Massacre at GOLIAD). On April 20, Santa Anna and about 850 troops who had been chasing the 800-man Texas army commanded by Gen. Sam HOUSTON, found their enemy at San Jacinto. Gen. Cós arrived the following day with 500–600 reinforcements, and Santa Anna settled in to wait for further troops before attacking. Houston, however, surprised the Mexicans that afternoon. In the Battle of SAN JACINTO, Houston soundly defeated the Mexicans. Santa Anna lost about 600 killed and likely about that same number captured — but Santa Anna was not one of them. He had escaped, and attempted to reach his troops at Fort Bend. Houston dispatched patrols to search for the Mexican dictator. Santa Anna spent the night hiding in tall grass by a bayou. In the morning, he happened upon a deserted house and changed some of his clothing. Not long after, he stumbled into a search party of Texans who were not aware of his identity but, given his linen shirt and jeweled studs, believed him to be an officer. Any hope of remaining incognito was dashed when Santa Anna was returned to the other prisoners, who greeted him with cries of "El Presidente!" He was immediately taken to Sam Houston.

Santa Anna was extremely agitated, and a dose of opium — to which he was addicted — was brought to him. The Victor of Tampico did not at that point plead for his life to be spared, but attempted to reason with Houston. He explained that he expected generosity inasmuch as Houston had conquered the "Napoleon of the West." Houston reminded Santa Anna about his atrocities at the Alamo and Goliad, which served to create a great deal of fear in the man who had ordered the cold-blooded executions of hundreds, perhaps thousands, of Texans. Santa Anna feebly argued that it had been the Mexican government that had ordered the executions. Houston refused to listen, and interrupted to remind Santa Anna that *he was* the Mexican government. After further discussion and negotiation, Santa Anna agreed to order his remaining troops to leave Texas in trade for his life.

On May 14, 1836, Texas President David BURNET negotiated two treaties with Santa Anna — one public and one secret. Among other provisions, the Treaties of VELASCO established Texas as an independent republic; declared that Santa Anna would not again take up arms against Texas; and ordered the Mexican Army to retire south of the Rio Grande River. The secret treaty was designed to receive a pledge from Santa Anna that he would influence Mexico to recognize Texas independence and accept the provisions of the public treaty; and that he would encourage the Mexican cabinet to favorably receive a Texas mission; and work toward a commerce treaty. In return, Santa Anna and his army would be spared. Santa Anna willingly signed the treaties.

There was much hue and cry to execute Santa Anna, but, instead — mainly through the efforts of Sam Houston — he was sent to Washington, D.C., in November. On January 26, 1837 the Mexican dictator culminated his visit by attending a dinner party hosted by President Andrew Jackson and his entire cabinet. Santa Anna was finally returned to Mexico in mid-1837 aboard a U.S. battleship provided by Jackson.

*Politics and War*

Santa Anna lived in retirement for a year before serving in the defense of Mexico against the French in 1838. His troops repelled an assault on Vera Cruz in December, and forced the enemy to retreat. He lost a leg in the engagement which was called the Party War, a misfortune that restored his somewhat sullied reputation. A state funeral was held for the lost leg, and a monument was raised over the burial site.

He was once more the leader of the Centralists, and served as president and virtual dictator from October, 1841 to June, 1844. A new revolution deposed him, and he was exiled to Havana, Cuba, but was recalled as provisional president in July, 1846 during the war with the United States. He had apparently made a secret agreement with President James Polk, and was said to have fought less than aggressively against the Americans. His 20,000-man army was defeated by Gen. Zachary Taylor in the Battle of Buena Vista in February, 1847 and in the Battle of Cerro Gordo by Gen. Winfield Scott. He resigned the presidency on April 5, 1848, and retired to Jamaica and on to Venezuela. He was recalled once more in 1853, and served as president for a year, but fled to Cuba during the revolution in 1855. He moved on to Venezuela and the island of Saint Thomas, and during his absence was tried and condemned in Mexico and his property was confiscated. He returned in 1864 during the French occupation, but was refused entry. He tried again in 1867, but was exiled to the United States. Following the amnesty of 1874, he returned for good and died in near poverty in Mexico City at the age of 80.

**SCURLOCK, Mial** (May 25, 1803 or 1809– March 6, 1836) Private, TEXAS REVOLUTIONARY ARMY; Alamo defender from Chatham County, North Carolina. Scurlock arrived in San Augustine, Texas by way of Tennessee and Mississippi in the company of his brother and their slaves in 1834. He participated in the Siege and Battle of SAN ANTONIO, and was serving as a rifleman when he was killed in the ALAMO BATTLE.

**SEGUIN, Juan Nepomuceno** (October 27, 1806–1890) Captain, SEGUIN'S CAVALRY COMPANY; Alamo COURIER from San Antonio, Texas. Seguin's ancestors first settled in San Antonio in 1722. His father, Erasmo, was mayor of that city in 1821, and greeted Stephen F. AUSTIN on his first trip to Texas. Juan Seguin was appointed political chief of the San Antonio district in 1834, and was an outspoken critic of the policies of Antonio Lopez de SANTA ANNA. Seguin raised a small cavalry company of Tejano (a native Mexican living in Texas) volunteers to fight against the MEXICAN ARMY at the outbreak of the TEXAS REVOLUTION, thus labelling him a traitor in the eyes of his countrymen. He was in fact interested in forming a country that would be independent of both Mexico and the United States. His unit participated in the Battle of CONCEPCION and the Siege and Battle of SAN ANTONIO. Seguin was commissioned captain in the TEXAS REVOLUTIONARY ARMY in January 1836, and entered the ALAMO MISSION with about 25 of his men on February 23, 1836 — the first day of the ALAMO SIEGE. On February 25, Seguin was chosen to carry a message from Col. William TRAVIS requesting reinforcements. Seguin and his orderly, Antonio CRUZ Y AROCHA, departed the Alamo and directed their horses down the Gonzales road. They were immediately challenged by a Mexican outpost. Seguin coolly conversed with the Mexicans, then, seizing the opportunity, the two men spurred their horses and raced away. The startled Mexicans fired at them, but to no avail. The message was on its way. Seguin raised another group of men in Gonzales, but was unable to return before the ALAMO BATTLE. Following that battle, Seguin's company served as rear guard for the army on Gen. Sam HOUSTON's "Runaway Scrape" retreat across Texas. His unit evacuated families, and prevented the Mexican Army from crossing the Brazos River and striking the Texans. Seguin was commander of a company in the 2nd regiment when he provided vital information about the movements of Gen. Santa Anna in prelude to the Battle of SAN JACINTO. His unit served ably in that battle, and afterward Seguin located a chest belonging to Santa Anna that contained more than 12,000 dollars in silver pesos, which was divided up among the soldiers. He was promoted in May, 1836 to lieutenant colonel, and charged with protecting San Antonio until a proper government could be restored. About a year after the Alamo Battle, Seguin gathered some of the exposed ashes and bones that remained from the cremated bodies of the Alamo defenders, and placed them in a coffin. Over the coffin he draped a Texas Republic flag, and upon that a rifle and sword. The coffin lay in state in the San Fernando Church until on February 27, 1837 a military procession buried the ashes with honors in a peach orchard. That act led to rumors of apparitions that are said to haunt the Alamo grounds to this day. (See DISPOSITION OF ALAMO DEAD for more.) Seguin served in the Texas Senate from 1838–1840, and was elected mayor of San Antonio in 1841. The hordes of Anglo adventurers that had descended upon San Antonio caused much trouble for Seguin and his countrymen. Assaults and robberies were commonplace — mostly against the Mexicans — and Seguin's power was a matter of resentment. His popularity was soon crippled by false rumors that he was aiding Mexican forces — likely brought on by his views that were in opposition to recent Texas settlers. With his life in jeopardy, Seguin fled to Mexico in 1842 to join relatives in Saltillo. He was imprisoned by the Mexicans in Laredo, and freed by Santa Anna when he promised to assist with an invasion of San Antonio. The "invasion" amounted to little more than a parade by Mexican troops through the main square. The act by Seguin appeased some of his countrymen, but also served to brand him a traitor to two nations. One month later, he returned to Mexico and lived there until 1848 when he came back to Texas. He died in Nuevo Laredo, Texas, and his remains were later reinterred in Seguin, Texas, a city on the Guadalupe River near San Antonio named for him by surveyor Ben McCulloch, who was a gunner at the Battle of San Jacinto.

**SEGUIN'S CAVALRY COMPANY** This company of Tejano volunteers — native Mexicans residing in Texas — comprised of local men who were loyal to Texas, was formed by rancher Capt. Juan SEGUIN at the outbreak of the TEXAS REVOLUTION. The unit participated in the Battle of CONCEPCION and the Siege and Battle of SAN ANTONIO, and about 25 of them entered the ALAMO MISSION on February 23, 1836 — the first day of the ALAMO SIEGE. On February 25, Seguin and his orderly Antonio CRUZ Y AROCHA departed the Alamo as COURIERS, and did not return in time for the ALAMO BATTLE. Following that battle, the company served as rear guard for the army. They evacuated families, and prevented the Mexican Army from crossing the Brazos River and striking the Texans. Seguin's company provided vital information about the movements of Gen. Antonio Lopez de SANTA ANNA's army that directly led to victory in the Battle of SAN JACINTO, a battle in which the company distinguished itself. Known members of this unit that were killed in the Alamo Battle include: ABAMILLO, Juan; BADILLO, Juan; DE LA GARZA, Alexandro; ESPARZA, Gregorio; FUENTES, Antonio; LOSOYA, Toribio; and NAVA, Andres.

**SEWELL, Marcus L.** (1805–March 6, 1836) Private, GONZALES RANGING COMPANY;

Alamo defender from England. This shoemaker who had been residing in Gonzales, Texas, entered the ALAMO MISSION with his unit on March 1, 1836, and was serving as a rifleman when he was killed in the ALAMO BATTLE.

**SHERMAN, Sidney** (July 23, 1805–August 1, 1873) Colonel, TEXAS REVOLUTIONARY ARMY. This native of Malboro, Massachusetts was orphaned at 12 years of age along with 9 siblings. Sherman worked as a clerk in a Boston mercantile company in 1821, and the following year opened his own business which soon failed due to lack of capital. He moved to New York, and in 1831 to Cincinnati, Ohio. Across the river from the latter city at Newport, Kentucky, Sherman established a company that was the first to make cotton bagging by machinery and the first west of the Allegheny Mountains to manufacture sheet lead. He was captain of a company of militia, and at the outbreak of the TEXAS REVOLUTION sold his cotton bagging company to outfit a 52-man unit that departed for Texas on December 31, 1835, to join the fighting. The volunteer company was delayed in Nacogdoches when Sherman became ill, but finally presented themselves in San Felipe during the March, 1836 TEXAS CONSTITUTIONAL CONVENTION. Although delegates to the convention had already been chosen, Sherman's associates evidently bullied officials into permitting them to vote. Sherman then headed west toward the Alamo, and rendezvoused with Gen. Sam HOUSTON in Gonzales in mid-March. He was appointed lieutenant colonel in Col. Edward BURLESON's regiment, and participated in Houston's controversial "Runaway Scrape" retreat across Texas in prelude to the Battle of SAN JACINTO. When the army made camp on the west bank of the Brazos river across from Groce's plantation in early April to await the

Mexicans, he was given command of a 60-horse cavalry unit. The troops, who had accused Houston of cowardice for running away and had acted mutinous and defiant throughout the forced march, decided to depose Houston in favor of Sherman. Houston responded by posting notices threatening court-martials and possible executions, and the uprising was quickly quelled. At sunset on the evening prior to the April 21, 1836, Battle of San Jacinto, Sherman and 85 cavalrymen were dispatched to reconnoiter the Mexican lines. In direct defiance of orders from Houston, he charged the enemy in an action which resulted in the wounding of two men and the loss of several horses. Houston removed Sherman from command and replaced him with Mirabeau B. LAMAR. During the battle, Sherman was placed in charge of the 2nd infantry regiment on the extreme left flank of the assault line, and remained back under cover to reinforce the initial attack. The Texans had charged the Mexican lines when Sherman's regiment burst from the edge of the woods and tore into the disorganized enemy. It has been reported that in the slaughter that ensued, Sherman's men committed some of the worst ATROCITIES. Sherman has been credited with coining the battle cry, "Remember the Alamo!" His troops carried the only flag at San Jacinto — one that featured a sword-wielding Goddess of Liberty with a banner hanging from the blade that was inscribed: "Liberty or Death." Following the battle, Sherman acted as president of a board of officers charged with distributing captured Mexican property to the soldiers. He reportedly took more than his share — the choice items — which caused some grumbling and resentment among the troops. He was soon dispatched to the United States by President David BURNET to recruit additional soldiers. Sherman returned to Texas later that year with his wife, Catherine, and settled on a bluff overlooking the San Jacinto

battlefield he called Mount Vernon before moving in 1839 to Cresent Place on San Jacinto Bay. He represented Harris County at the Seventh Congress of the Republic, and in 1843 was elected major general of the militia. Sherman moved to Harrisburg after Texas was annexed by the United States, and engaged in land sales. At that time, he organized a company and built the first railroad in Texas — the Buffalo Bayou, Brazos, and Colorado — that ran from Harrisburg to the Brazos River. A series of mishaps — a rescue from a steamer that had burst its boilers; a sawmill owned in partnership that burned down; and the destruction of his home by fire — compelled Sherman to send his family back to Kentucky while he moved into his railroad office. That office was subsequently destroyed by fire. During the Civil War, he was appointed commandant of Galveston until he was incapacitated by illness and retired to his home on San Jacinto Bay. After losing one son to illness, another son in the Battle of Galveston, and his wife in 1865, Sherman lived his remaining years in poverty and as an invalid until his death in 1873 at the age of 68. Sherman County, Texas, and the city of Sherman, Texas, in Grayson County were named in his honor.

**SHIED, Manson** (1811–March 6, 1836) Private, TEXAS REVOLUTIONARY ARMY; Alamo defender from Georgia. Shied was a carpenter residing in Brazoria, Texas, when he participated in the Siege and Battle of SAN ANTONIO. He was serving as an artilleryman in Capt. William CAREY's artillery company when he was killed in the ALAMO BATTLE.

**SIMMONS, Cleveland Kinlock** (June 8, 1815–March 6, 1836) First Lieutenant, TEXAS REVOLUTIONARY ARMY; Alamo defender from Charleston, South Carolina. Simmons arrived in Texas in the company of fellow

Alamo defender Richard W. BALLENTINE aboard the schooner *Santiago* in January, 1836. He was serving as an officer in Capt. John FORSYTH's cavalry company when he was killed in the barracks in the ALAMO BATTLE.

**SLAVERY IN TEXAS** The first slave in Texas arrived with a Spanish expedition in 1528, and was subsequently captured and enslaved by Indians — along with his master. This man named Estavan, a Black Moor of Azamor in Morocco, learned the language and customs of his captors, escaped, and eventually led a Spanish expedition in search of Indian treasure. Other slaves who had been shipwrecked along the coast or had descended from Blacks in Spanish settlements joined those runaways from the United States to became freemen and members of communities across Texas. In 1792, there were 34 Blacks and 414 mulattos in Texas among the native population of nearly 3,000. When immigrants from the United States began arriving in the early 1820's, a great number of slaves were brought into Texas. At this time, there were instances where Blacks who were married to whites were freed and became members of the settlements — albeit not favorably accepted. The Mexican government, which had overthrown Spanish rule in 1821, as well as the church favored the emancipation of slaves, but those laws were usually ignored by the Texans. The Imperial Colonization Law of 1823 recognized slavery, but outlawed the slave trade and decreed that slaves born in Texas would be freed at the age of fourteen. Austin's Colony at that point in time had a population of 443 slaves and 1,347 whites. The Texas state constitution of 1827 recognized existing slavery, and permitted slaves to be brought into the state for 6 months following its adoption but provided that none born thereafter

could be enslaved. The following year, however, the Mexican government for all intents and purposes legalized the slave trade by ruling that a slave could "change" his or her master "if the new master would indemnify the old." Slaves became "servants" under contracts rather than being considered enslaved. On September 15, 1829, the Mexicans issued a proclamation to end slavery throughout the nation. Texas, however, protested, and was granted an exemption from the decree. This threat of abolishing slavery, however, served to cause the colonists to question the loss of future rights. The April 6, 1830 Law, which severely limited immigration from the United States, permitted existing slavery but abolished further introduction. In 1832, the state legislature limited servant contracts to 10 years. The Battle of VELASCO in 1832 was preceded by the Mexican garrison commander at Anahuac using slave labor for public works without any compensation to the owners. At that time, rumors circulated among colonists that the Mexicans intended to incite a slave rebellion, but no such incident occurred. A white abolitionist named Benjamin Lundy, and Nicholas Drouett, a mulatto and retired Mexican Army officer, sought permission to establish a colony for free blacks in the 1830s, but, in spite of Mexico's approval, opposition by Texans ended the plan. Mexican Col. Juan ALMONTE on his fact-finding trip to Texas in 1834 estimated that there were about 1,000 slaves and 9,000 colonists. Almonte was authorized to advise slaves that they could invoke protection under the April 6, 1830, Law, and thereby gain freedom. It is unknown if his entreaties were at all successful. A number of Blacks — both freemen and slaves — served in the TEXAS REVOLUTION. The most notable are Samuel McCullough, who was wounded during the GOLIAD SKIRMISH; Thomas Stephens, who participated in the Siege and Battle of SAN

ANTONIO; and JOE, the slave owned by Col. William B. TRAVIS who survived the ALAMO BATTLE. Joe claimed to have observed other Blacks in the Alamo — likely slaves of other officers such as Jim BOWIE — including one woman and a man named JOHN who were killed during the Mexican assault. Joe was presented to Mexican Gen. Antonio Lopez de SANTA ANNA following that battle, and, before being set free, was urged to tell other slaves that they would be free men in Mexico and could even serve in the army. Word of this informal emancipation proclamation by Santa Anna was viewed as an economic and social threat by Texas slave owners, and renewed worries of the Mexicans inciting slaves to rebel. During Sam HOUSTON's retreat across Texas to flee the pursuing Mexican Army in prelude to the Battle of SAN JACINTO, which became known as the "Runaway Scrape," thousands of civilians, men, women, and children trailed along behind the army. The property owned by some of these people was left in the care of their slaves, many of whom viewed the action as a chance to escape and did so. Others were freed by the Mexican Army as it moved through the countryside chasing Houston. It might be noted that Col. James W. FANNIN who was executed in the Surrender and Massacre at GOLIAD was said to have made huge profits from the illegal trafficking of African slaves, which did not set well with many of the troops he commanded. The institution of slavery was made legal in the constitution drawn up at the TEXAS CONSTITUTIONAL CONVENTION of 1836, but the trade in African slaves was outlawed as piracy. The slave population in 1836 when Texas gained its independence has been estimated at about 5,000. Ten years later, the figure had increased to about 39,000.

**SMITH, Andrew H.** (1815–March 6, 1836) Private, TEXAS REVOLUTIONARY ARMY; Alamo defender or deserter from parts unknown. There has been some confusion about whether or not this man was a deserter or was in fact killed in the ALAMO BATTLE. In a January, 1836 letter to Governor Henry SMITH, Col. William TRAVIS listed an "Andrew Smith" as one of six men who had deserted. Andrew Smith, however, has been included on the rolls of those killed. Four men named "Smith" are listed as casualties, and, since that is a common name shared by others who were in the service if Texas, it would be reasonable to assume that he could have been confused with another with the same last name.

**SMITH, Charles S.** (1806–March 6, 1836) Private, TEXAS REVOLUTIONARY ARMY; Alamo defender from Maryland. Smith arrived in Texas by way of Louisiana in October, 1835, and participated in the Siege and Battle of SAN ANTONIO. He was serving as an artilleryman in Capt. William CAREY's artillery company when he was killed in the ALAMO BATTLE.

**SMITH, Erastus** "Deaf" (April 19, 1787– November 30, 1837) Scout, TEXAS REVOLUTIONARY ARMY. This native of Duchess County, New York, immigrated with his parents to Mississippi Territory near Natchez in 1798. A childhood disease was responsible for his defective hearing, which inspired his nickname. He visited Texas in 1817 but soon departed and returned in 1821 while in poor health and made his home in the San Antonio vicinity. Smith traveled around that territory and restored his health while learning the language and customs of the Mexicans. In 1822, he married Guadalupe Ruiz Duran, and the couple had 4 children. At the outbreak of the TEXAS REVOLUTION, Smith was neutral until denied access to his family in San Antonio by Mexican soldiers. He immediately enlisted in the army, and due to his knowledge of the area and expertise was assigned duty as a scout. Smith dressed like a Mexican, and it was said that due to the hearing problem his other senses — eyesight and intuitiveness in particular — were sharpened beyond that of any other scout. His first action came at the Battle of CONCEPCION on October 28, 1835 and, when the troops subsequently surrounded San Antonio, he accompanied Col. William TRAVIS on a successful horse gathering expedition. Smith was the one who discovered the Mexican wagon train that initiated the "Grass Fight" during the Siege and Battle of SAN ANTONIO. Smith then served as a scout for Sam HOUSTON, who relied on him more than any other scout, and was dispatched from Gonzales in mid March, 1836 to learn the fate of the Alamo. Along the way, he encountered Alamo survivor Susannah DICKINSON on the road, and escorted her party back to Gonzales where she related tales of horror from the ALAMO BATTLE and a warning that 700 Mexican troops were following her. Smith accompanied Gen. Houston on his "Runaway Scrape" retreat to east Texas in prelude to the Battle of SAN JACINTO. At Buffalo Bayou across from the ruins of Harrisburg on April 18, he swam the river on his horse and captured a Mexican courier with vital information detailing the plans of Santa Anna. Prior to Houston's assault on Santa Anna's position at San Jacinto on April 21, Smith was dispatched to destroy Vince's Bridge, which would cut off escape for either army. When the attacking Texans were within 60 yards of the enemy camp, Smith rode up and down the formation shouting "Vince's Bridge is down! Fight for your lives!" During the battle, he was thrown from his horse, and landed at the feet of a Mexican lieutenant who brandished a saber. Smith drew his pistol, but it misfired. A fellow scout, John Nash, trampled the enemy officer with his horse while Smith

wrestled away the man's saber and killed him with it. Mexican General Martin Perfecto de CÓS had fled on foot when the Mexican troops were routed. Smith captured the general — whose identity was unknown to him — near a deserted farm near the Brazos late on April 23. He told his captive that he had been looking for Gen. Cós who had once offered $1000 for Smith's head. Smith vowed to cut off Cós's head and send it to Mexico if he should happen to find the general. Cós was returned to San Jacinto, and, much to Smith's surprise, identified. Smith, however, took no action against the prisoner. Smith served as the captain of a company of rangers following the revolution before retiring to Richmond, Fort Bend County where he died and was buried at age 50. Deaf Smith County was named in his honor.

**SMITH, Henry** (May 20, 1788–March 4, 1851) First American governor of Texas. This native of Kentucky was married 3 times and the father of 9 children. He immigrated to Brazoria County, Texas in 1827, and farmed as well as taught school. He participated in the 1832 Battle of VELASCO where he was severely wounded. In 1833, Smith was elected *alcalde* (mayor) of Brazoria and later a delegate to the Texas convention. The following year, he was named the political chief of the Department of the Brazos, which demonstrated that Mexican officials believed him to be no threat. That opinion might have changed in 1835 when he was chosen to serve on the Columbia Committee of Safety and Correspondence and was elected to represent his district at the TEXAS CONSULTATION OF DELEGATES. Smith supported the WAR PARTY, those colonists urging independence from Mexico, but the convention voted for the PEACE PARTY stance to restore the MEXICAN CONSTITUTION of 1824 that at the time was being picked apart by

Mexican dictator Antonio Lopez de SANTA ANNA. At that consultation, a TEXAS PROVISIONAL GOVERNMENT was chosen, and Smith was elected governor. Smith saw his election as a mandate for independence, which caused turmoil within the government. This strife between Smith and the General Council came to a boiling point when a plan for an invasion of Mexico, called the MATAMOROS EXPEDITION, was approved by the council in January, 1836. Both Sam HOUSTON and Governor Smith were opposed to the plan in part because the intention of its proponents, which included Col. Frank JOHNSON, Dr. James GRANT, and Col. James FANNIN, was primarily to plunder the countryside for spoils and protect their land claims in other states. Preparation for the expedition began by pillaging the ALAMO MISSION garrison at San Antonio, taking two-thirds of the defense force — about 200 men — and most of the food, medical supplies, and ammunition. Colonel James NEILL, commander at San Antonio, informed Smith that his garrison had been critically weakened, and would be unable to defend itself. An attack by the MEXICAN ARMY was imminent, Neill stated, and begged for aid. Smith, who rarely compromised and was by no means a diplomat, was outraged. He angrily protested to the legislative council — whom he called "Judases" and "scoundrels" — for approving the Matamoros Expedition at the expense of San Antonio. The council had approved the plan against the governor's wishes, and repeatedly passed measures over the veto of Smith. Smith dissolved the council in a flurry of insults, which caused them on January 20, 1836, to impeach Smith and declare the office of governor vacant. Lieutenant Governor James W. ROBINSON was inaugurated as acting governor. Smith fought the action by refusing to deliver up the archives and accepting mail addressed to the governor, which for all intents and purposes made the government inefficient until the TEXAS CONSTITUTIONAL CONVENTION in March, 1836. Smith was not a member of that convention, and was not nominated for any post. Perhaps in an effort to vindicate himself, Smith ran for the presidency of the Republic of Texas in September, 1836. He later had a change of heart, and asked that his name be withdrawn. The results: Houston, 5,110 votes; Smith, 743; and Stephen F. AUSTIN, 587. Smith was appointed secretary of treasury in Houston's cabinet, but had trouble attending to his duties due to a lack of money. He was elected to the United States House of Representatives in 1840, and served on the finance committee for one term before retiring. In 1849, Smith was struck with gold fever, and set out for California. He prospected the gold fields for 2 years, but found nothing and died in a mining camp in Los Angeles County at the age of 62.

**SMITH, John William** "El Colorado" (March 4, 1792–January 12, 1845) Merchant; mayor; Texas Congress senator; Alamo COURIER from Virginia. This civil engineer, carpenter, and shopkeeper who had resided in San Antonio since 1831 was captured by Mexican troops during the Siege and Battle of SAN ANTONIO. He later escaped, and provided vital information to the Texas volunteers that was instrumental in their successful assault. Smith, in the company of Dr. John SUTHERLAND, rode out on February 23, 1836, to confirm the presence of Mexican troops beyond the Alazan Hills outside of town which signaled the beginning of the ALAMO SIEGE. On that day, he accompanied Sutherland, who had been dispatched as a courier, to Gonzales. He returned to the ALAMO MISSION as the guide for the GONZALES RANGING COMPANY on March 1, 1836, and was sent out once more on March 3 as a courier in search of reinforcements. Smith was on his way back from San Felipe on March 6 with 25 volunteers, but was too late to participate in the ALAMO BATTLE. He was a 3-time mayor of San Antonio — a bitter rival of Juan SEGUIN — and was representing Bexar County in the Texas Congress in Washington-on-the-Brazos at the time of his death from pneumonia.

**SMITH, Joshua G.** (1808–March 6, 1836) Sergeant; TEXAS REVOLUTIONARY ARMY; Alamo defender from North Carolina. Smith had been residing in Bastrop, Texas when he was serving as a noncommissioned officer in Capt. John FORSYTH's cavalry company and was killed in the ALAMO BATTLE.

**SMITH, William H.** (1811–March 6, 1836) Private, TEXAS REVOLUTIONARY ARMY; Alamo defender from parts unknown. Smith, a resident of Nacogdoches, Texas, participated in the Siege and Battle of SAN ANTONIO. He was serving as an artilleryman in Capt. William CAREY's artillery company when he was killed in the ALAMO BATTLE.

**SMITHERS, Launcelot** (1800–August 11, 1842) Private; TEXAS REVOLUTIONARY ARMY; Alamo COURIER. Smithers arrived in Texas from Alabama in 1828, and worked as a horse trader in San Antonio and provided medical care to the Mexican garrison. He accompanied the MEXICAN ARMY as an intermediary during the GONZALES SKIRMISH, and was taken prisoner by the Texans. He was ordered to repair a house in Gonzales that had sustained damage in the fighting. On November 2, 1835, he was severely beaten by rampaging white mercenaries who were terrorizing the countryside. Susannah DICKINSON, whose husband, Almeron, was in San Antonio at the time, had asked Smithers to accompany her home for protection. He agreed, and was subsequently dragged into the street and assaulted by men who beat him "to a poltice." (See ATROCITIES for more.) Smithers arrived in San Antonio sometime before the ALAMO SIEGE, and departed, perhaps without orders, on the afternoon of February 23 — the first day of the siege — to spread the alarm in Gonzales. He later carried the heroic message requesting reinforcements entrusted to Albert MARTIN by Col. William TRAVIS from Gonzales to San Felipe. Smithers served as city treasurer of San Antonio from 1839–1840, and mayor pro-tempore for less than a month in 1841 in the absence of Juan SEGUIN. He was killed by Mexican troops at Sutherland Springs on September 11, 1842.

**SOWELL, Andrew Jackson** ( June 27, 1815–January 4, 1883) Private, TEXAS REVOLUTIONARY ARMY; Alamo COURIER from Davidson County, Tennessee. Sowell came to Texas with his parents and family by way of Missouri, and settled in Gonzales in 1829 where four years later he and his brothers raised the first corn grown by white men in Guadalupe County. He participated in the GONZALES SKIRMISH, the Battle of CONCEPCION, and the Siege and Battle of SAN ANTONIO. Sowell was at some point dispatched from the ALAMO MISSION as a courier in the company of Byrd LOCKHART for the purpose of obtaining supplies. The two men were detained in Gonzales, and did not return before the ALAMO BATTLE. Early casualty lists incorrectly included his name. Sowell later was a Texas Ranger; served in the Confederate Army in the Civil War; and counted Kit Carson among his friends when he worked as a scout.

**STARR, Richard** (1811–March 6, 1836) Private, NEW ORLEANS GREYS; Alamo defender from England. Starr arrived in San Antonio with his unit on November 21, 1836, and participated in the Siege and Battle of SAN ANTONIO. He was serving as a rifleman in Capt. William BLAZEBY's infantry company when he was killed in the ALAMO BATTLE.

**STEWART, James E.** (aka "Stuart"; 1808–March 6, 1836) Private, TEXAS REVOLUTIONARY ARMY; Alamo defender from England. Little is known about this volunteer who was serving as a rifleman when he was killed in the ALAMO BATTLE.

**STOCKTON, Richard L.** (1817–March 6, 1836) Private, TENNESSEE MOUNTED VOLUNTEERS; Alamo defender from Essex County, New Jersey. Stockton was sworn into service in Nacogdoches on January 14, 1836, and arrived in San Antonio with his unit on February 8. He was serving as a rifleman in Capt. William HARRISON's company when he was killed in the ALAMO BATTLE.

**SUMMERLIN, A. Spain** (1817–March 6, 1836) Private, TEXAS REVOLUTIONARY ARMY; Alamo defender from Tennessee. Summerlin came to Texas by way of Arkansas and had been residing with his parents and family in Nacogdoches when he participated in the Siege and Battle of SAN ANTONIO. He was serving as a rifleman in Capt. Robert WHITE's infantry company when he was killed in the ALAMO BATTLE.

**SUMMERS, William E.** (1812–March 6, 1836) Private, GONZALES RANGING COMPANY; Alamo defender from Tennessee. Summers, a Gonzales resident, entered the ALAMO MISSION with his unit on March 1, 1836, and was serving as a rifleman when he was killed in the ALAMO BATTLE.

## SURVIVORS OF THE ALAMO BATTLE

Although all 188 Texas volunteers who defended the ALAMO MISSION were likely killed in the ALAMO BATTLE, Mexican officers hurried to rescue noncombatants from death at the hands of their blood-crazed troops. Gen. Antonio Lopez de SANTA ANNA had defeated his enemy in battle, and now desired to demonstrate his generosity. Following a tour of the battlefield and a laudatory speech to his assembled troops, Santa Anna had these civilian survivors brought to him for interrogation from the Alamo chapel where they had been held after the battle. The first to see Santa Anna was Juana ALSBURY, Jim BOWIE's sister-in-law, her infant son and her sister, Gertrudis NAVARRO, all of whom had been rescued from being harmed by Mexican troops by an officer who had been checking rooms for noncombatants. Santa Anna, who was sipping coffee on the north side of the Plaza, briefly asked about their roles with the Texans. Their response apparently satisfied him. The general gave them each a blanket and two pesos and released them. Senora Ana Salazar ESPARZA, the wife of Alamo defender Gregario ESPARZA, and her four children were then presented to Santa Anna. The general reminded her that, unlike her husband, her brother-in-law was a loyal Mexican soldier. He then gave the grieving woman two pesos and a blanket and she was released to return to her home in nearby San Antonio to mourn the loss of husband. The next to be interviewed was Susannah DICKINSON, wife of Alamo defender Almeron DICKINSON, who, along with her daughter Angelina, also had been found by an officer in a chapel room where she had taken refuge. This officer had prevented the soldiers from attacking her, but she was nonetheless struck in the right calf by an errant bullet upon reaching the courtyard. A Mexican surgeon had tended to her wound, and she was presented to Santa Anna. The general was said to have been immediately attracted to 15-month-old Angelina, and decided that he would adopt the child and take her to Mexico with him to be raised like a princess. Susannah refused permission. Col. Juan AL-MONTE, the interpreter, interceded on Susannah's behalf and convinced Santa Anna to drop the notion. Susannah was given a blanket and two pesos, and set free. She limped away on the road toward her home in Gonzales — possibly with Santa Anna's Black servant, Ben, as escort. Santa Anna then welcomed JOE, William TRAVIS's slave, and decided to use the young man for propaganda purposes. The general told Joe to spread word about the wrath of his powerful army. He then freed Joe, and encouraged him to go forth and tell other slaves that Mexico was a friend to them, a place where they could live in freedom and even serve in the army. Joe politely declined the offer to join the military, and hurried to catch up with Susannah Dickinson on the road to Gonzales. Some of the Mexican women and children that were freed have been tentatively identified as Dona Petra Gonzales; Trinidad Saucedo; Concepcion Losoya and her son, possibly the mother and brother of Alamo defender Toribio LOSOYA; Juana Melton, wife of Alamo defender Eliel MELTON; and a Mrs. Victoriana and her daughters. The presence of Senora Candelaria, the Mexican folk healer who was said to have treated Jim Bowie, has been disputed over the years. The Texas State Legislature, however, awarded her an Alamo survivor pension in 1899. A total of at least a dozen noncombatants were released.

Evidence exists that suggests that one Alamo defender, Henry WARNELL, escaped at some point during battle, and, although badly wounded, managed to make his way to Nacogdoches or Port Lavaca where he died 3 months later. Warnell's name appears on the role of those killed in the battle, and

his son was awarded a grant of land in 1860 for his father's service at the Alamo after filing a claim with the General Land Office. This possible escape coincided with that of another unnamed man, perhaps in the company of Warnell or another unnamed man, who were said to have also arrived in Nacogdoches in late March. The fate of those two men remains unknown. (See also CROCKETT, David for events surrounding his alleged survival; COURIERS DISPATCHED DURING THE ALAMO SIEGE; and ROSE, Louis, for more about the man who allegedly escaped just prior to the battle.)

**SUTHERLAND, Dr. John** (May 11, 1792–April 11, 1867) Private, TEXAS REVOLUTIONARY ARMY; Alamo COURIER from Danville, Virginia. Sutherland, whose father was an army officer who served with George Washington, was a bank president in Decatur, Alabama when he studied an alternate form of medicine based on vegetable compounds, red peppers, steam, and the like. He moved to Texas and joined the volunteer army in December, 1835. He became a resident of San Antonio — living with the Almeron DICKINSON family — and assisted Dr. Amos POLLARD, the garrison doctor. Sutherland, in the company of merchant John W. SMITH, rode out on February 23, 1836, to confirm the presence of Mexican troops beyond the Alazan Hills outside of town which signaled the beginning of the ALAMO SIEGE. His horse fell on the muddy road while returning to town, and Sutherland sustained an injury to his leg. Later that day, he was dispatched by Col. William TRAVIS as a courier. He again joined up with John Smith, and the two men made their way out of town to Gonzales. Sutherland was unable to return before the ALAMO BATTLE. He settled in Egypt, Texas, in 1837 to practice medicine, and in 1840 moved to Wilson County, where the sulfur springs were known as Sutherland Springs and Sutherland became postmaster. In 1860, he wrote about his experiences in a book titled *The Fall of the Alamo* (San Antonio: Naylor Press, 1936). Sutherland states in this book that he was one of the final messengers from the Alamo before the battle, which is likely not true, and therefore casts shadows of doubt over the authenticity of his account.

**SUTHERLAND, William DePriest** (August 10, 1818–March 6, 1836) Private, TEXAS REVOLUTIONARY ARMY; Alamo defender likely from Alabama. This nephew of John SUTHERLAND studied medicine at LaGrange College in Tuscumbia, Alabama before arriving in San Antonio, Texas in September, 1835. Sutherland resided with the local land commissioner, José Antonio Navarro, and was intent upon learning Spanish. He enlisted in the cavalry in late 1835, and was serving as a rifleman when he was killed in the ALAMO BATTLE.

# T

**TAYLOR, Edward** (1812–March 6, 1836) Private, TEXAS REVOLUTIONARY ARMY; Alamo defender from Tennessee. Taylor worked with his brothers, George TAYLOR and James TAYLOR, picking cotton on the Dorsett farm in Liberty, Texas before joining the army. He was serving as a rifleman when he was killed in the ALAMO BATTLE.

**TAYLOR, George** (1816–March 6, 1836) Private, TEXAS REVOLUTIONARY ARMY; Alamo defender from Tennessee. Taylor worked with his brothers, Edward TAYLOR and James TAYLOR, picking cotton on the Dorsett farm in Liberty, Texas before joining the army. He

was serving as a rifleman when he was killed in the ALAMO BATTLE.

**TAYLOR, James** (1814–March 6, 1836) Private, TEXAS REVOLUTIONARY ARMY; Alamo defender from Tennessee. Taylor worked with his brothers, Edward TAYLOR and George TAYLOR, picking cotton on the Dorsett farm in Liberty, Texas before joining the army. He was serving as a rifleman when he was killed in the ALAMO BATTLE.

**TAYLOR, William** (1799–March 6, 1836) Private, TEXAS REVOLUTIONARY ARMY; Alamo defender from Tennessee. Taylor, a resident of Little River Community (present-day Milam County), was serving as a rifleman when he was killed in the ALAMO BATTLE.

**TENNESSEE MOUNTED VOLUNTEERS** This group of about 18 who volunteered to fight for Texas independence was formed from those men drifting around Nacogdoches, Texas, in late 1835 and early 1836. Most of the unit—which included 3 lawyers and 2 doctors—were descendants of soldiers who had served in the Revolutionary War, but its most famous member was *Private* David CROCKETT, whose appearance in Texas was the subject of much excitement and official welcomes. Despite the name, only about half the group had come from Tennessee, the remainder being from other states. Additionally, most were not mounted, and had walked to Nacogdoches. The group, under the command of Capt. William HARRISON, was sworn into service in that city on January 14, 1836. The men—minus a few who had dropped out along the way—arrived in San Antonio on February 8, 1836, and during the ALAMO SIEGE were assigned the defense of the wooden palisade that ran from the chapel to the low barracks along the south wall of the ALAMO MISSION. The entire unit was killed at that position during the ALAMO BATTLE. Known members include: AUTREY, Micajah; BAILEY, Peter; BAYLISS, Joseph; CAMPBELL, Robert; CLOUD, Daniel; CROCKETT, David; FAUNTLEROY, William; HARRISON, William; McDOWELL, William; REYNOLDS, John; ROSE, James; STOCKTON, John; THOMAS, B. Archer M.; THOMSON, John; and WASHINGTON, Joseph.

**TEXAS CONSTITUTIONAL CONVENTION** (March 1–17, 1836) The General Council had passed on December 14, 1835, over Governor Henry SMITH's veto, an act calling for the governor and council to be supplanted by a constitutional convention for the purpose of establishing a government independent of Mexico. Fifty-nine delegates from counties across Texas, who had been elected on February 1, convened on March 1, 1836 in an unfinished blacksmith building at Washington on the Brazos — about 35 miles upstream from San Felipe. 52 delegates were from the United States — 12 were natives of Virginia; 10 from North Carolina; 9 from Tennessee; 6 from Kentucky; 4 from Georgia; 3 from Pennsylvania; 3 from South Carolina; 3 from Mexico; 2 were Texas natives, both from San Antonio; 2 from New York; and 1 each from Massachusetts, Mississippi, New Jersey, England, Ireland, Scotland, and Canada — 45 from the South, 7 from the North. Only 10 delegates had lived in Texas more than 6 years; 2 had arrived in Texas in 1836; and only 1 had been an original member of Austin's colony.

*Chronology of the Texas Revolution*

- June 29, 1835: Battle of ANAHUAC
- October 2, 1835: GONZALES SKIRMISH
- October 3, 1835: MEXICAN CONSTITUTION OF 1824 officially voided
- October 9, 1835: GOLIAD SKIRMISH
- October 28, 1835: Battle of CONCEPCION
- November 3, 1835: TEXAS CONSULTATION OF DELEGATES
- November–December, 1835: Siege and Battle of SAN ANTONIO
- January–February, 1836: The MATAMOROS EXPEDITION
- February 23–March 5, 1836: The ALAMO SIEGE
- **March 1, 1836: TEXAS CONSTITUTIONAL CONVENTION**
- March 2, 1836: TEXAS DECLARATION OF INDEPENDENCE
- March 6, 1836: The ALAMO BATTLE
- March 20–27, 1836: Surrender and Massacre at GOLIAD
- April 21, 1836: Battle of SAN JACINTO
- May 14, 1836: Treaties of VELASCO

The outlook for the future at this point in time was quite grim. Thousands of MEXICAN ARMY soldiers had recently invaded Texas. At that moment, Col. José URREA with his army was moving toward Goliad (see Surrender and Massacre at GOLIAD), and the 188 defenders inside the ALAMO MISSION, 150 miles away, were under siege by Gen. Antonio Lopez de SANTA ANNA and at least 2,000 troops with more on the way (see ALAMO SIEGE and ALAMO BATTLE). Washington on the Brazos was without troops and defenseless. Yet, these men assembled in this new town with but one muddy street in a building under construction that required cloth to be stretched across the windows to keep out the cold wind for the purpose of breaking free of the tyranny that had been a constant threat to their lives. Col. William TRAVIS's first dispatch from the Alamo had reached that town the day before, and some delegates had suggested postponing the convention and going to the aid of these trapped men. After some debate, however, it was determined that the business of replacing the ineffective provisional government with a more permanent one was more important (see TEXAS PROVISIONAL GOVERNMENT for more).

Richard Ellis of Pecan Point (present-day Red River County), who had served as a member of the Alabama constitutional convention and supreme court, was elected convention president. George C. Childress was elected chairman of a committee to draft the TEXAS DECLARATION OF INDEPENDENCE. Childress presented the completed document to the delegates on March 2, and it was unanimously adopted. The delegates then set to work drafting a constitution for their new nation.

Alamo COURIER Lancelot SMITHERS, who had carried Col. Travis's famous Alamo "Victory or Death" message from Gonzales, arrived in San Felipe on March 3. Word of that drifted to the floor of the convention, and debate about the fate of the Alamo was the main topic. But news that Col. James FANNIN was evidently marching from Goliad with reinforcements encouraged them to believe that the Alamo was in no immediate danger.

On March 4, Sam HOUSTON was named "Commander in Chief of all land forces of the Texan Army, both regulars, volunteers, and militia, while in actual service."

Another message from Col. Travis arrived on the morning of March 6 in the care of courier John W. SMITH, and read in part: "We have contended for ten days against an enemy whose numbers are variously estimated from fifteen hundred to six thousand men. I hope your honorable body will hasten on reinforcements, ammunitions and provisions to our aid so soon as possible ... God and Texas — Victory or Death."

Unknown to those attending the convention, Travis and his comrades were already dead. Patriotic fever, however, swept through the convention with the receipt of this plea for help, and one delegate made a motion that the convention adjourn and rush to the aid of those defenders. Major General Houston, however, argued against the motion by stating that inasmuch as most of their problems had been derived from disorganization, the establishment of a new nation should have priority. Houston then departed for Gonzales to assemble his army, and promised that if at all possible he would march to the Alamo. Houston privately was of the opinion that the Alamo likely had already fallen, and rode to Gonzales, arriving on March 11 (see SAN JACINTO, Battle of for more).

A constitution for the nation of Texas, based for the most part on the United States Constitution as well as those of several states, was adopted at midnight on March 16. Some similar features included: legislative powers were granted to a Congress comprised of a Senate and a House of Representatives; the president assumed power similar to that of the U.S. president; judicial powers were vested in a Supreme Court. Some features unique to this document include: the term of the president would be 3 years (the first president serving only 2 years); the president could not succeed himself; the president could not command the army unless approved by Congress; each head of a family was granted a certain amount of land; ordained ministers could not hold office; SLAVERY was legalized.

Twenty-three counties were created: Austin had its county seat at Belleville. Bastrop had its seat at Bastrop. Bexar at San Antonio. Brazoria at Angleton. Colorado at Columbus. Goliad at Goliad. Gonzales at Gonzales. Harris at Harrisburg (its name changed to Houston on December 26, 1839). Jackson at Edna. Jasper at Jasper. Jefferson at Beaumont. Liberty at Liberty. Matagorda at Bay City. Milan at Cameron. Nacogdoches at Nacogdoches. Red River at Clarksville. Refugio at Refugio. Sabine at Hemphill. San Augustine at San Augustine. San Patricio at Sinton. Shelby at Center. Victoria at Victoria. Washington at Brenham.

The final act of this convention was to elect government officials. David BURNET won the *ad interim* presidency over Samuel P. Carlson by a vote of 29 to 23. In a display of the unity of the Texas people, Lorenzo de ZAVALA, former president of the Mexican Congress, former governor of the state of Mexico, former treasury minister, former Mexican minister to France, who became an opponent of Santa Anna, was elected *ad interim* vice-president. Samuel P. Carlson was elected secretary of state; Bailey Hardeman, secretary of the treasury; Thomas J. RUSK, secretary of war; Robert Potter, secretary of the navy; and David Thomas, attorney general. These officials were sworn in at 4 A.M. on March 17, and the convention was adjourned soon after. The newly elected government immediately fled to Harrisburg, 100 miles to the east, to escape the advancing Mexican Army (see SAN JACINTO, Battle of for more).

## TEXAS CONSULTATION OF DELEGATES (1835) This convention, the third in recent years (see TEXAS REVOLUTION for others) was convened at San Felipe on October 16, 1835, for the purpose of forming a TEXAS PROVISIONAL GOVERNMENT, but soon adjourned for lack of a quorum due to many members participating in the Siege and Battle of SAN ANTONIO. The convention reconvened on November 3 with 58 of 98 eligible delegates from 12 municipalities attending.

### Chronology of the Texas Revolution

- June 29, 1835: Battle of ANAHUAC
- October 2, 1835: GONZALES SKIRMISH
- October 3, 1835: MEXICAN CONSTITUTION OF 1824 officially voided
- October 9, 1835: GOLIAD SKIRMISH

- October 28, 1835: Battle of CONCEPCION
- **November 3, 1835: TEXAS CONSULTATION OF DELEGATES**
- November–December, 1835: Siege and Battle of SAN ANTONIO
- January–February, 1836: The MATAMOROS EXPEDITION
- February 23–March 5, 1836: The ALAMO SIEGE
- March 1, 1836: TEXAS CONSTITUTIONAL CONVENTION
- March 2, 1836: TEXAS DECLARATION OF INDEPENDENCE
- March 6, 1836: The ALAMO BATTLE
- March 20–27, 1836: Surrender and Massacre at GOLIAD
- April 21, 1836: Battle of SAN JACINTO
- May 14, 1836: Treaties of VELASCO

Dr. Branch T. Archer from Brazoria, a former member of the Virginia legislature, was elected president of the Consultation. The primary issue facing these delegates was whether Texas would fight for independence from Mexico or remain loyal to Mexico and endeavor to restore the MEXICAN CONSTITUTION OF 1824 that had been picked apart by SANTA ANNA. Two differing factions debated their positions for 3 days — the WAR PARTY wanted to fight for independence; and the PEACE PARTY chose to support the Constitution, although condemning the dictatorship of Antonio Lopez de SANTA ANNA. The Consultation voted on November 6, and, by a tally of 33 to 15, the Peace Party's stance was adopted; they would fight to restore the Mexican Constitution of 1824. The vote was said to have been greatly influenced by Sam HOUSTON who, to the surprise of many, sided with the Peace Party. The decision of the majority became known as the DECLARATION OF NOVEMBER 7, 1835. The delegates then designed a vague constitution, termed the Organic Law, which set down the organization and powers of the elected Texas Provisional Government. Henry SMITH was elected governor; James W.

ROBINSON, lieutenant governor; Stephen F. AUSTIN, Branch T. Archer, and William H. Wharton were designated emissaries to the United States, and would depart to appeal for volunteers and funds. Sam Houston was appointed commander of all troops of the newly created TEXAS REVOLUTIONARY ARMY, except for those presently engaged in San Antonio which would be led by Col. Edward BURLESON. Houston was authorized to raise an army which would consist of 1,120 men and 150 rangers. That attempt failed, and the army never had more than 100 regulars during the revolution.

The Consultation adjourned on November 14, and was scheduled to reassemble on March 1, 1836 (see TEXAS CONSTITUTIONAL CONVENTION).

## TEXAS DECLARATION OF INDEPENDENCE (March 2, 1836) This Declaration drawn up and approved at the TEXAS CONSTITUTIONAL CONVENTION at Washington on the Brazos proclaimed Texas to be independent of Mexican rule — superseding a preliminary proclamation known as the DECLARATION OF NOVEMBER 7, 1835.

### Chronology of the Texas Revolution

- June 29, 1835: Battle of ANAHUAC
- October 2, 1835: GONZALES SKIRMISH
- October 3, 1835: MEXICAN CONSTITUTION OF 1824 officially voided
- October 9, 1835: GOLIAD SKIRMISH
- October 28, 1835: Battle of CONCEPCION
- November 3, 1835: TEXAS CONSULTATION OF DELEGATES
- November–December, 1835: Siege and Battle of SAN ANTONIO
- January–February, 1836: The MATAMOROS EXPEDITION
- February 23–March 5, 1836: The ALAMO SIEGE
- March 1, 1836: TEXAS CONSTITUTIONAL CONVENTION

- **March 2, 1836: TEXAS DECLARATION OF INDEPENDENCE**
- March 6, 1836: The ALAMO BATTLE
- March 20–27, 1836: Surrender and Massacre at GOLIAD
- April 21, 1836: Battle of SAN JACINTO
- May 14, 1836: Treaties of VELASCO

The Texas Declaration of Independence was written by George C. Childress, a recent arrival from Tennessee, who based the document on the principles written sixty years earlier by Thomas Jefferson for America's Declaration of Independence. The Declaration was unanimously adopted without amendment in less than one hour. Some notable signers included: Sam HOUSTON; former U.S. Congressmen from North Carolina Robert Potter and Samuel Carson; former member of the Mexican Congress Lorenzo de ZAVALA; two framers of state constitutions, Richard Ellis and Martin Parmer; James Collinsworth, future chief justice of the Texas Supreme Court; and Thomas J. RUSK, secretary of war during the TEXAS REVOLUTION. There were no printing presses available, so clerks wrote out the document by hand while a copy was sent across the Sabine River to the United States for mass production and distribution to the public.

The text of the Texas Declaration of Independence:

When a government has ceased to protect the lives, liberty and property of its people, from whom its legitimate powers are derived, and for the advancement of whose happiness it was instituted, and so far from being a guarantee for the enjoyment of those inestimable and unalienable rights, becomes an instrument in the hands of evil rulers for their oppression: When the Federal Republican Constitution of their country, which they have sworn to support, no longer has a substantial existence, and the whole nature of their government has been forcibly changed without their consent, from a restricted federative republic, composed of sovereign states to a consolidated central military depostism in which every interest is disregarded but that of the army and the priesthood — both the eternal enemies of civil liberty, the ever-ready minions of power, and the usual instruments of tyrants:

When long after the spirit of the constitution has departed, moderation is at length so far lost by those in power that even the semblance of freedom is removed, and the forms, themselves, of the constitution discontinued; and so far from their petitions and remonstrances being regarded, the agents who bear them are thrown into dungeons; and mercenary armies sent forth to force a new government upon them at the point of a bayonet: When, in consequence of such acts of malfeasance and abdication, on the part of the government, anarchy prevails, and Civil Society is dissolved into its original elements. In such a crisis, the first law of nature, the right of self-preservation — the inherent and unalienable right of the people to appeal to first principles and take their political affairs into their own hands in extreme cases enjoins it as a right towards themselves and a sacred obligation to their posterity to abolish such government and create another in its stead, calculated to rescue them from impending dangers, and to secure their future welfare and happiness.

Nations, as well as individuals, are amenable for their acts to the public opinion of mankind. Statement of a part of our grievance is, therefore, submitted to an impartial world, in justification of the hazardous but unavoidable step now taken of severing our political connection with the Mexican people, and assuming an independent attitude among the nations of the earth.

The Mexican government, by its colonization laws, invited and induced the Anglo-American population of Texas to colonize its wilderness under the pledged faith of a written constitution that they should continue to enjoy that constitutional liberty and republican government to which they had been habituated in the land of their birth, the United States of America. In this expectation they have been cruelly disappointed, in as much as the Mexican nation has acquiesced in the late changes made in the government by General Antonio Lopez de SANTA ANNA, who,

having overturned the constitution of his country, now offers as the cruel alternative either to abandon our homes, acquired by so many privations, or submit to the most intolerable of all tyranny, the combined depotism of the sword and the priesthood.

It has sacrificed our welfare to the State of Coahuila, by which our interests have been continually depressed through a jealous and partial course of legislation carried on at a far distant seat of government by a hostile majority, in an unknown tongue; and this to, notwithstanding we have petitioned in the humblest terms, for the establishment of a separate state government, and have, in accordance with the provisions of the national constitution presented to the General Congress a republican constitution which was, with just cause, contemptuously rejected.

It incarcerated in a dungeon, for a long time, one of our citizens, for no other cause but a zealous endeavor to procure the acceptance of our constitution and the establishment of a state government.

It has failed and refused to secure on a firm basis, the right of trial by jury, that palladium of civil liberty, and only safe guarantee for the life, liberty, and property of the citizen.

It has failed to establish any public system of education, although possessed of almost boundless resources (the public domain) and although it is an axiom in political science, that unless a people are educated and enlightened it is idle to expect the continuance of civil liberty, or the capacity for self-government.

It has suffered the military commandants stationed among us to exercise arbitrary acts of oppression and tyranny; thus trampling upon the most sacred rights of the citizen and rendering the military superior to the civil power.

It has dissolved by force of arms, the State Congress of Coahuila and Texas, and obliged our representatives to fly for their lives from the seat of government; thus depriving us of the fundamental political right of representation.

It has demanded the surrender of a number of our citizens and ordered military detachments to seize and carry them into the interior for trial; in contempt of the civil authorities, and in defiance of the laws and the constitution.

It has made political attacks upon our commerce, by commissioning foreign desperadoes, and authorizing them to seize our vessels, and convey the property of our citizens to far distant ports for confiscation.

It denies us the right of worshipping the Almighty according to the dictates of our own conscience, by the support of a national religion calculated to promote the temporal interest of its human functionaries rather than the glory of the true and living God.

It has demanded us to deliver up our arms, which are essential to our defense, the rightful property of freemen, and formidable only to tyrannical governments.

It has invaded our country by sea and by land, with intent to lay waste our territory and drive us from our homes, and has now a large mercenary army advancing to carry on against us a war of extermination.

It has, through its emissaries, incited the merciless savage, with the tomahawk and scalping knife, to massacre the inhabitants of our defenseless frontiers.

It hath been, during the whole time of our connection with it, the contemptible sport and victim of successive military revolutions, and hath continually exhibited every characteristic of a weak, corrupt, and tyrannical government.

These and other grievances, were patiently borne by the people of Texas until they reached that point at which forbearance ceases to be a virtue. We then took up arms in defense of the national constitution. We appealed to our Mexican brethren for assistance. Our appeal has been made in vain. Though months have elapsed, no sympathetic response has yet been heard from the interior. We are, therefore, forced to the melancholy conclusion that the Mexican people have acquiesced in the destruction of their liberty and the substitution therefore of a Military Government — that they are unfit to be free and incapable of self-government.

The necessity of self-preservation, therefore, now decrees our eternal political separation.

We therefore, the delegates with plenary powers, of the people of Texas, in solemn convention assembled, appealing to a candid world for the necessities of our condition, do hereby resolve and declare that our political connection with the Mexican Nation has forever ended; and that the people of Texas do now constitute a free sovereign and independent republic, and are fully vested with all the rights and attributes which properly belong to independent nations; and conscious of the rectitude of our intentions, we fearlessly and confidently commit the issue of the decision of the Supreme Arbiter of the destinies of Nations.

RICHARD ELLIS, *President*

Test:

H. S. KIMBLE, *Secretary*

## TEXAS PROVISIONAL GOVERNMENT

The plan for a provisional government — known as the Organic Law — was drawn up in November, 1835 at the TEXAS CONSULTATION OF DELEGATES (1835). It provided for the members of the consultation to elect a governor, lieutenant governor, and a General Council comprised of one member from each municipality in Texas. The instrument, however, had failed to clearly define the powers of these offices, which would soon render the government powerless. The General Council, which for the most part had PEACE PARTY tendencies and favored restoration of the MEXICAN CONSTITUTION OF 1824 as stated in the DECLARATION OF NOVEMBER 7, 1835 rather than seek independence, oddly enough elected WAR PARTY (independence) advocates Henry SMITH of Brazos as governor and James W. ROBINSON of Nacogdoches lieutenant governor. This provisional government began by creating the framework of a government, establishing a post office, an army and a navy, appointing judges, prohibiting the residence of free Blacks in Texas, passing several ineffective tax laws, and dispatching emissaries — including Stephen F. AUSTIN — to the United States to seek aid, but was soon beset with internal discord. Hostility between the council and governor Smith arose over differences of opinion, such as the governor's insistence for an immediate declaration of independence, and came to a head over the proposed MATAMOROS EXPEDITION, a plundering invasion of Mexico, that the council had approved. The council had the desire to cooperate with Mexican liberals in that city who were opposed to dictator Antonio Lopez de SANTA ANNA, and for that reason had approved the invasion plan against the governor's wishes — in addition to repeatedly passing other measures over Smith's veto. Smith dissolved the General Council in a flurry of personal insults, which caused the council on January 20, 1836, to impeach Smith and declare the office of governor vacant. Lieutenant Governor Robinson was then inaugurated as acting governor. Smith fought the action and remained in possession of the archives, which for all intents and purposes made the Texas government inefficient and without leadership until the TEXAS CONSTITUTIONAL CONVENTION in March, 1836. A total of 39 men served at one time or another on the General Council, and normally 14 or 15 members would attend meetings. This figure dropped to only 2 participants by the end of February, 1836, and the council as well as the Texas Provisional government had for all intents and purposes ceased to exist.

**TEXAS REVOLUTION** (1835-1836) This conflict between American colonists residing in the state of Coahuila-Texas in the Country of Mexico and the Mexican government, was waged in a series of skirmishes and battles that resulted the establishment of the independent Republic of Texas.

### Pre-Revolution

(For preceding events see TEXAS SETTLEMENT BY AMERICANS.) The roots of revolution grew from basically the identical grievances that had initiated the American Revolution — a tyrannical government imposing its will over colonists settled within its territory. The first real incident of distrust and anxiety between Mexico and Texas came on September, 15 1829, when the government abolished SLAVERY in Mexico. Texas soon after received an exemption from this decree, but some colonists were of the opinion that their interests could be threatened in the future due to Mexico's intention of gradually banning slavery in Texas. The following year, the Mexican government, concerned about the growing colonization of Texas by Americans, passed the April 6, 1830, Law, which ended *EMPRESARIO* contracts for the settlement of land by immigrants from territories adjacent to Mexico — meaning the United States. Then in 1831, army troops were dispatched to establish a presence intended to maintain the integrity of the Mexican territory of Texas from its anglo-influence, and at the same time open customhouses at certain ports to collect duties. The Texans desired free trade with the United States, and these restrictions encouraged them to take to smuggling. The colonists, who for the most part had accepted the provisions of the MEXICAN CONSTITUTION OF 1824, began to challenge Mexican authority.

There was also the question of roots. The Texans were primarily southern Protestants who had been required to pledge themselves to the Catholic Church; and most considered themselves superior — racially, politically, and morally — to those who held authority over them, which predictably fostered resentment. In other words, the colonists harbored the desire of establishing an American country within Mexico. President Andrew Jackson shared this opinion of Mexico's inferiority, and wanted to add Texas to the United States. In mid-1832, Sam HOUSTON made his way to Texas, and was rumored to be an unofficial representative of Jackson on a confidential mission to discern if the colonists favored annexation. Houston, who was said to have reported that annexation was indeed favored — which may or may not have been true — returned to Texas and established a law practice and engaged in land speculation.

The first major armed conflict during this pre-revolution period was the result of drastic actions taken by Col. John (Juan) Bradburn, who commanded the Mexican garrison at Anahuac. In late 1831, Bradburn arrested a man he claimed had violated the April 6, 1830 Law. He abolished a settlement, confiscated the settler's land, and, among other indignities, imposed martial law. Some colonists — including William B. TRAVIS— protested, and were also arrested. A group of 160 colonists marched on the garrison to free the prisoners, but, aware that they were outgunned, backed off for the time being but called for reinforcements. The colonists gathered at Turtle Bayou, and, in what were called the Turtle Bayou Resolutions, pledged to support Mexican rule and loyalty to the Mexican Constitution of 1824 but repudiated President Anastasio Busamente in favor of Antonio Lopez de SANTA ANNA. Meanwhile, volunteers from Brazoria responded, and while en route to Anahuac were intercepted by Mexican soldiers from the garrison at Velasco. In the ensuing June 26, 1832, Battle of VELASCO, 10 colonists and 5 Mexican soldiers were killed, but the Mexicans were forced to surrender and abandon their garrison. In the meantime, the Mexican commander from Nacogdoches negotiated with the colonists in Anahuac, which resulted in the Anahuac garrison being closed and the troops returned to Mexico. In August, the Nacogdoches garrison was also run out of Texas by colonists determined to rid the country of Mexican troops. Customs duties collected in Texas amounted to very little from that point in time until Santa Anna

reopened the customhouses in the spring of 1835.

The colonists feared retribution for their rash acts, but fortunately for them Santa Anna was at that moment leading a rebellion against President Bustamante, and both political leaders were preoccupied with that conflict. An expedition of 400 soldiers under the command of Col. José Antonio Mexia, who was loyal to Santa Anna, did march to Texas. In his company, however, was Stephen F. AUSTIN, who was returning from the legislature in Saltillo, and had alerted the colonists and perhaps influenced the colonel along the way. The colonists greeted Col. Mexia in Brazoria with a lavish dinner and grand ball. Mexia accepted the explanation that they had not been fighting against the Mexican Constitution but against Col. Bradburn, who was a Bustamante loyalist.

The Texans held a convention in October, 1832, which was attended by 58 delegates from 16 districts, and presided over by Stephen Austin. In addition to local business, such as Indian affairs and the organization of a militia, the convention petitioned the Mexican government to repeal the April 6, 1830, Law that had cut off immigration; requested a 3-year extension to the tariff exemption on necessities; and asked for the right to establish Texas as a separate state in the Mexican confederation. Mexican authorities ignored the convention, and the petitions were never presented.

The Texans held a second convention on April 1, 1833, in San Felipe. William H. Wharton was elected president of this convention that was attended by only about one-third of those who had attended the previous year. The delegates repeated the concerns of the first convention, including a constitution for a new state that Sam Houston helped draft which was loosely based on the United States Constitution. Stephen Austin was chosen to deliver the petitions and constitution to Mexico City. By this time, Santa Anna had overthrown Bustamante and won the presidency. Austin arrived in Mexico City in July, and presented the petitions to vice-president Valentín Gómez Farías. Santa Anna at that time was "recuperating" from his political victory at his estate, and remained unavailable to Austin until November 5. Austin was successful in persuading the repeal of the April 6, 1830, immigration law and other requests, but Santa Anna refused to recognize Texas as a state. Austin started home December, but, on a January, 1834 stopover in Saltillo, was arrested on suspicion of attempting to incite insurrection in Texas and returned to Mexico City. A letter sent by Austin in October, 1833 to the predominately Mexican city council in San Antonio had surfaced in Mexico City, and contained statements such as, "The fate of Texas depends on itself and not upon this government," and "The country is lost if its inhabitants do not take its affairs into their own hands." Austin would be held until July, 1835 when a general amnesty law was passed.

Surprisingly, Texas enjoyed improved relations with Mexico during 1833 and 1834. Laws were repealed that prohibited only native-born Mexicans from retail merchandising; Texan representation in the 12-man state congress was increased from 1 seat to 3; the English language was recognized for official purposes; there was more tolerance toward religious worship; trial by jury was established; and land was made easier to acquire. In 1835, however, when Santa Anna began replacing liberal officials with a centralist form of government many of these freedoms were revoked. Widespread discontent ensued in Coahuila-Texas among the American colonists, many of whom began calling for independence. In May, 1835, Santa Anna had defeated rebels in the state of Zacatecas, and saw no reason not to quell the brewing discontent in Texas. He found his excuse to send troops when rampant land speculation and corruption in that state, which had been going on for some time, came to his attention. The governor and the state legislature at Saltillo were dishonest, and had been selling thousands of acres of land at scandalously low rates to undesirables, which troubled even those legal settlers who feared that their land rights eventually could be threatened. Santa Anna dispatched an army commanded by his brother-in-law, Gen. Martin Perfecto de Cós, in June, 1835 to put a stop to this corruption by arresting known land speculators, the governor, and suspending civil government in favor of martial law. The governor fled north toward Texas, but was captured. Other Texans, including Ben MILAM, later the hero of the Siege and Battle of SAN ANTONIO, were also arrested. Jim BOWIE managed to elude capture. These actions were propagandized by the WAR PARTY—those Texans promoting independence—as intolerable acts that would lead to martial law and the confiscation of land in Texas. This threat, whether real or imagined, became one factor that encouraged Texans, the majority of whom still favored peace, to openly rebel against Mexico.

### Revolution

### Chronology of the Texas Revolution

- June 29, 1835: Battle of ANAHUAC
- October 2, 1835: GONZALES SKIRMISH
- October 3, 1835: MEXICAN CONSTITUTION OF 1824 officially voided
- October 9, 1835: GOLIAD SKIRMISH
- October 28, 1835: Battle of CONCEPCION
- November 3, 1835: TEXAS CONSULTATION OF DELEGATES
- November–December, 1835: Siege and Battle of SAN ANTONIO
- January–February, 1836: The MATAMOROS EXPEDITION

- February 23–March 5, 1836: The ALAMO SIEGE
- March 1, 1836: TEXAS CONSTITUTIONAL CONVENTION
- March 2, 1836: TEXAS DECLARATION OF INDEPENDENCE
- March 6, 1836: The ALAMO BATTLE
- March 20–27, 1836: Surrender and Massacre at GOLIAD
- April 21, 1836: Battle of SAN JACINTO
- May 14, 1836: Treaties of VELASCO

Santa Anna also decided in that spring of 1835 that the customhouses and garrisons in Texas that had for all practical purposes been abandoned in 1832 would be reopened and duties would be collected. This led to an incident at Anahuac, the legal port for Galvestown Bay, that would ignite the revolution. Several merchants in Anahuac protested to the Mexican commander, Capt. Antonio Tenorio, that the collection of duties was rife with corruption, and should be more fairly collected. Tenorio replied by jailing them. In what became known as the Battle of ANAHUAC, lawyer William Travis raised a company of 25 armed men, and, on June 29, marched to Tenorio's headquarters and ordered the Mexicans to leave. The commander complied and surrendered his 44 troops, but the rash act by Travis did not set well with many of the townspeople, who feared repercussions. Letters of apology were sent to Tenorio and his superiors, but did not mollify the Mexicans. Public opinion, however, swayed in Travis' favor when Santa Anna ordered his arrest and that of other rebels. This edict evoked concerns of martial law and military occupation, and the Texans considered it unthinkable to turn their people over to a military tribunal rather than have them tried by a jury of peers. The Mexican dictator also threatened to enforce the ban on slavery, which outraged slave holders. Committees began to form all across Texas to protest Santa Anna's actions. The

various factions among the colonists found common ground with their own particular grievances toward Santa Anna, and for all practical purposes revolution in Texas became a distinct possibility.

The PEACE PARTY made overtures toward Gen. Cós, who had remained south of Texas, and requested a meeting with him to solve their differences. Cós refused to grant them an audience until after the agitators had been turned over to him. The Mexican general became more adamant with his demand following a Fourth of July speech delivered in San Felipe by Robert "Three-legged Willie" Williamson, so nicknamed for his wooden leg, who has been called the "Patrick Henry of the Texas Revolution." Williamson, whose name was included on the list of those targeted for arrest said in part: "Let us no longer sleep at our posts; let us resolve to prepare for War — and resolve to defend our country against the danger that threatens it. Liberty or Death should be our determination and let us one and all unite to protect our country from all invasion — and not down our arms so long as a soldier is seen in our limits."

Cós viewed this speech and others of its kind to be inflammatory, and therefore dashed any hope of conciliation. He decided to march to Texas and arrest Travis and the other rebels.

The colonists had formed in each precinct Committees of Safety and Correspondence — organizations that kept people in the state aware of current developments that concerned them — with a Central Committee held over from the 1833 convention that served as a clearing house to disseminate information. Committees such as these had been formed during the American Revolution by Samuel Adams, and made organized resistance possible. William Wharton had called for another convention, and word was spread through the Texas committees. Each jurisdiction was permitted to elect and send 5 delegates to this consultation in Washington-on-the Brazos on October 15. Stephen Austin arrived home from Mexico in September, and was guest of honor at a testimonial dinner in Brazoria on September 8. He agreed that a consultation was in order, and accepted the chairmanship of the Central Committee of Safety of San Felipe, which for all practical purposes made him the leader of the revolution.

The first battle on the high seas between Mexico and the Texans occurred on September 1, 1835, when the Mexican schooner *Correo*, which had been seizing cargo and ships around Velasco, fired upon the *San Felipe*, an armed schooner owned by Thomas F. McKinney. Following a 2-hour battle, the *Correo* was captured and later transported to New Orleans.

Meanwhile, the colonists were aware that Gen. Cós and his troops were on their way to Texas, and, like the "Minutemen" of the American Revolution, departed their farms and homes and rallied to repel the advancing Mexicans. (See TEXAS REVOLUTIONARY ARMY for more.)

In an unrelated engagement, the "Lexington and Concord" of the Texas Revolution was about to take place in the town of Gonzales. Col. Domingo de Ugartechea, the commander of Mexican troops at San Antonio, ordered the town of Gonzales to hand over its 6-pounder cannon that had been provided 4 years earlier for protection from Indians. The townspeople refused, and once more, word went out for volunteers. When Lt. Francsico Castaneda and 100 Mexican soldiers approached Gonzales, they were faced with about 160 armed men waving a flag that proclaimed "Come and Take It." On October 2, in the Skirmish at GONZALES, the volunteers attacked the Mexican troops, killing 1 and forcing the remainder to retreat back to San Antonio. The first

shots of the Texas Revolution had been fired.

At this point in time, this was not a revolution designed to gain independence, rather a fight to restore the MEXICAN CONSTITUTION OF 1824, the provisions of which Santa Anna had picked apart in the preceding months and officially voided entirely on October 3, the day following the action at Gonzales. The colonists were now at the mercy of the whims of this tyrannical dictator in Mexico City, and members of the two unofficial parties debated their future in earnest.

One company of Texas volunteers commanded by Capt. George M. Collinsworth, detoured on their way to intercept Gen. Cós at San Antonio, and, on October 9, captured a small Mexican garrison at Goliad. They also captured vital provisions and prevented the Mexicans from obtaining supplies and reinforcements by sea. (See Skirmish at GOLIAD for more.)

In the meantime, about 300–500 volunteers had assembled at Gonzales in preparation for the march to San Antonio. Stephen Austin was summoned and reluctantly accepted command of the ragtag force. On October 12, the newly-formed volunteer army set off to meet Gen. Cós and the 1,400 troops that waited in San Antonio.

On October 28, a scouting party of about 90 men commanded by Col. Jim Bowie and Capt. James FANNIN were attacked by 400 Mexican troops. In the Battle of CONCEPCION, the volunteers killed about 60 Mexicans, while losing only 1 man — the first Texan killed in the revolution. Bolstered by their victory, the volunteer army surrounded San Antonio and, hesitant to attack the superior enemy, settled in to wait. (See Siege and Battle of SAN ANTONIO for more.)

The TEXAS CONSULTATION OF DELEGATES, scheduled for October 15, had to be postponed due to the lack of quorum — the missing men had marched with the army. On November 3, 1835, the consultation finally convened in San Felipe. The primary issue facing these delegates was whether Texas would fight for independence from Mexico or remain loyal to Mexico and endeavor to restore the Mexican Constitution of 1824. A vote was taken — which became known as the DECLARATION OF NOVEMBER 7, 1835 — and it was decided that they would fight to restore the Mexican Constitution. The delegates then designed a vague constitution, and elected a TEXAS PROVISIONAL GOVERNMENT consisting of a General Council, governor and lieutenant governor. Sam Houston was appointed commander of all troops of the newly created army except for those presently engaged in San Antonio, which would be led by Edward Burleson because Stephen Austin had been relieved of command to be part of a commission that would travel to the United States to seek aid. The Consultation adjourned on November 14.

Rallies in support of Texas began sweeping across the United States. Money, provisions, and small military units had formed and began arriving in Texas to assist their brethren. Many of these men had joined up to seek adventure, but others had their sights set on obtaining the grants of Texas land that had been offered for their service. (See UNITED STATES SUPPORT FOR TEXAS REVOLUTION.)

Cold weather and boredom was taking its toll on the volunteers who were camped around San Antonio. Many had become impatient with the hesitancy to assault the town, and returned home. It was finally decided that the entire force would abandon the siege and retire to Gonzales. When several Americans had escaped from the town with word that ammunition was low and the Mexican troops were demoralized, Ben MILAM decided to take matters into his own hands. He rallied the troops by drawing a line in the dirt and asking, "Who will follow old Ben Milam into San Antonio?" The response was overwhelming, and on December 5, about 300 Texans began a house to house fight that forced Gen. Cós to remove his troops into the ALAMO MISSION. The volunteers sniped at the soldiers and battered the mission walls with cannon shot. On December 10, Cós raised a white flag and surrendered his 1,100 troops — nearly 200 had deserted. Cós promised to never again fight against the Mexican Constitution of 1824, and was paroled with his troops to return to Mexico. (See Siege and Battle of SAN ANTONIO for more.)

The Texans were under the mistaken impression that they had won the war. The provisional government called for another convention to be convened on March 1, 1836, that would form a permanent government. The provisional government, however, was falling apart. The final blow came at the suggestion that the Texans undertake an offensive military operation into Mexico called the MATAMOROS EXPEDITION, which would invade the city of Matamoros. Governor Henry SMITH and army commander Sam Houston vehemently opposed this operation, but the General Council in San Felipe supported it. When Houston refused to led the expedition, Col. James Fannin was chosen. Fannin and his associates, Col. Frank JOHNSON and Dr. James GRANT, plundered the garrison at the Alamo of men and provisions, and began organizing their force at Goliad. Governor Smith called on the council to disband, and they in turn voted to replace him with lieutenant governor James W. ROBINSON. Eventually through the efforts of Sam Houston, who influenced many men not to participate, coupled with the lack of supplies, the idea of a Matamoros Expedition was for the time being postponed. It had, however, served to render the government of Texas impotent.

The presence of Mexican ships — both armed and transport — that continued to cruise the coast compelled the Texas government in January, 1836 to purchase 4 naval vessels: the 60-ton *Liberty*; the 125-ton *Independence*; the 125-ton *Invincible*; and the 125-ton *Brutus*, which had 8 guns and was placed in the command of Charles E. Hawkins, who was commissioned to the rank of commodore of the Texas Navy. These ships maintained a blockade along the Texas coastline, and on several occasions intercepted Mexican vessels and captured valuable cargo including munitions intended for the Mexican Army.

Santa Anna had no intentions of permitting the Texans to get away with their rebellious acts. He was of the opinion that the colonists were intent on separating from Mexico and gaining independence. In January, he formed his army and marched toward Texas, eventually crossing the Rio Grande on February 16. He had been encouraged to march for San Felipe, but decided that his destination would be San Antonio in order to avenge Gen. Cós's recent defeat.

The president-general and his army arrived in San Antonio on February 23, and quickly occupied the town. There were, however, about 150 Texas volunteers, commanded by William Travis and Jim Bowie, holed up inside the Alamo Mission. Rather than immediately attack, Santa Anna decided to wait for the remainder of his army, which had become strung out along his pathway north. An artillery bombardment of the mission commenced, and several troops assaults were ordered, but, for the most part, it was simply a waiting game until the Texans surrendered or Santa Anna became impatient and decided to root out his enemy. (See ALAMO SIEGE for a day-by-day account.)

Meanwhile, Santa Anna had dispatched a detachment of 1,400 troops under the command of Gen. José URREA toward Goliad.

On February 27 at San Patrico — 50 miles south of Goliad — Urrea and 100 cavalrymen came upon Col. Frank Johnson and 50 men who were out attempting to capture wild horses for the ill-fated Matamoros Expedition. Urrea attacked, and killed 16 Americans and captured 24. The prisoners were sent to Matamoros and eventually released, but Johnson, who escaped with 4 others, spread the word that his men had been executed. That disturbing news reached Col. Fannin in Goliad and acted to justify his decision to abort an impending mission to rescue the Alamo. On March 2, Urrea set an ambush at Agua Dulce Creek, and annihilated a 15-man force under Dr. James Grant.

Word that the Alamo was under siege had reached the delegates arriving in Washington-on-the-Brazos for the TEXAS CONSTITUTIONAL CONVENTION. Many were of the opinion that they should forgo the convention and rally to the aid of the Alamo defenders. Sam Houston convinced them that at the moment the most important business for the future of Texas was to form a permanent government to replace the ineffective provisional government. On March 1, 1836, the convention was called to order. The TEXAS DECLARATION OF INDEPENDENCE was presented as a completed document to the delegates on March 2, and it was unanimously adopted. The delegates then set to work drafting a constitution for their new nation. Col. William Travis's famous "Victory or Death" message arrived on March 3, but the mistaken news that Col. James Fannin was marching from Goliad with reinforcements encouraged them to believe that the Alamo was in no immediate danger. On March 4, Sam Houston was named "Commander in Chief of all land forces of the Texan Army, both regulars, volunteers, and militia, while in actual service."

On the morning of March 6, Santa Anna attacked the Alamo. In a battle that lasted approximately 90 minutes that has been considered among the most dramatic and heroic in history, 1,800–2,100 Mexican troops overwhelmed and killed about 188 Texas volunteers and captured the Alamo Mission. The Mexican Army lost about 500–600 killed and an undetermined amount of others wounded. (See ALAMO BATTLE for a detailed account.)

Another message from Col. Travis pleading for reinforcements and supplies arrived in Washington-on-the-Brazos that morning. Patriotic fever once more swept through the convention, but Houston quelled the hysteria by departing for Gonzales to assemble his army with the promise that if at all possible he would march to the Alamo.

A Constitution for the nation of Texas, based for the most part on the United States Constitution as well as those of several states, was adopted at midnight on March 16. The following day, government officials were elected with David BURNET as president and Lorenzo de ZAVALA, former president of the Mexican Congress, vice-president. The convention was adjourned that day, and the government fled to Harrisburg to escape the advancing Mexican Army.

Santa Anna did not take time to gloat over his victory — albeit costly — at the Alamo, but set to work designing a three-pronged strategy to destroy the remainder of the Texas army. Gen. José Urrea would continue to move up from the south with 1,400 men; Gen. Antonio GAONA and 700 troops would head north; and Santa Anna would led 1,200 men through the center of Texas.

Gen. Houston, who had arrived in Gonzales on March 11, was aware that his enemy was on the move, and sent a message to Col. James Fannin at Goliad ordering the immediate abandonment of that post. Fannin vacillated, and delayed his retreat. Finally, with a wagon train and 400 troops, he set out on March 19, but was only 6 miles from Goliad when his detachment was surrounded by Gen. Urrea's troops. Fannin, although wounded, held off the Mexicans for 2 days inside a square of wagons, but finally surrendered. The captured volunteers were marched back to Goliad, and held prisoner for 8 days. On Palm Sunday, March 27, Fannin and most of his men — as well as others who had been captured — were executed by order of Santa Anna. (See Surrender and Massacre at GOLIAD for more.)

Gen. Houston realized that the Mexican Army would be after his small force, and decided that he would retreat to the east and make a stand where it was more populated. On a forced march, known as the "Runaway Scrape," that caused protests from his officers and men, he worked his way back to the west bank of the Brazos River and camped to wait for Santa Anna. After learning that Santa Anna had only 750 troops, Houston chose a place called Lynch's Ferry near Lynchburg on the San Jacinto River to make a stand. On April 20, he secreted his 800 men in the woods, and, as expected, the Mexicans arrived. Santa Anna quickly deployed his troops in a wooded position on the far side of an expansive prairie directly across from Houston's men. The Mexican army dug in while the Texans waited. At about 9 A.M. on the following day, April 21, 500–550 Mexican reinforcements arrived to boost Santa Anna's troop total to about 1,250–1,300. That afternoon, Houston made the decision to attack. His timing could not have been better. The Mexicans were asleep, and had not bothered to post sentries. The Texans swept across the plain of San Jacinto, and in a bloody firefight that lasted only about 18 minutes the Mexicans lost about 600 killed and likely that same number captured. Houston lost about 8 dead and 23–34 wounded. Santa Anna escaped, but was captured the following day and delivered to Houston.

The headquarters of the Texas government had moved to Velasco, and on May 14, 1836, President David Burnet negotiated two Treaties of VELASCO with Santa Anna — one public and one secret — in that city. The public treaty, among other provisions, established Texas as an independent republic. The secret treaty was designed to receive a pledge from Santa Anna that he would influence Mexico to recognize Texas independence and accept the provisions of the public treaty. In return, Santa Anna and his army would be spared. Mexico's dictator willingly signed the treaties, but his action was immediately annulled by the Mexican government due to Santa Anna's status as a prisoner under duress.

In spite of Mexico's refusal to accept the treaties, Texas had for all intents and purposes won its independence. The Republic of Texas had been born.

**TEXAS REVOLUTIONARY ARMY** This military unit that fought in the TEXAS REVOLUTION was composed of primarily untrained militia and volunteers who resided in Texas, as well as those mercenaries, known as an auxiliary corps, who journeyed to Texas from the United States when the revolution commenced in the fall of 1835.

The first organized military units in Texas were militias formed in the early 1820s by Stephen F. AUSTIN in order to protect his colony from hostile Indians and outlaws. Those volunteer companies initially had been established for defensive purposes, but soon began raiding Indian encampments — at the encouragement of Mexican authorities. These mounted units that called themselves "ranging companies" were the precursors of the Texas Rangers. In 1830, when members of the so-called WAR PARTY, such as William TRAVIS, rebelled against Mexican customhouses, volunteers — like the "Minutemen" of the American Revolution — responded to the call to arms and left their farms and homes to come to the aid of their comrades. This practice continued throughout the early stages of the Texas Revolution. Settlers in the vicinity of Gonzales rallied to raise a local militia to protect their cannon from seizure by the Mexicans in the October, 1835 Skirmish at GONZALES, which has been called the "Lexington and Concord" of the Texas Revolution. These local militia units, which were designed to consist of all able bodied men between the ages of 16 and 56, were well-meaning but untrained and often lacked serviceable weapons (see WEAPONS OF THE ALAMO DEFENDERS for more). The November, 1835 TEXAS CONSULTATION OF DELEGATES authorized a regular army consisting of 1,120 men and a ranger unit of 150, but the effort to raise a regular army failed — less than 100 men could be recruited. Capt. Juan SEGUIN raised a small company of local Mexicans (Tejanos) who were loyal to Texas called SEGUIN'S CAVALRY COMPANY, and joined the fight for independence. The makeup of the Texas Revolutionary Army dramatically changed in the fall of 1835 from local volunteer militia units to a more hard-core mercenary army when word that Mexican dictator Gen. Antonio Lopez de SANTA ANNA had dispatched troops to arrest Texas rebels and quell the growing seeds of revolution. Rallies were held across the United States to raise money and volunteers to fight for Texas independence. Army Commander in chief Sam HOUSTON put out an urgent call to "Let each man come with a good rifle and 100 rounds of ammunition — and come soon. Our war cry is 'Liberty or Death.'" Houston emphasized this opportunity to gain property when he said, "If volunteers from the United States will join their brethren in this section (Texas), they will receive liberal bounties of land. We have millions of acres of our best lands unchosen and unappropriated." Mercenaries from the United States — the auxiliary corps of volunteers — who enlisted for the duration of the war would receive 1,280 acres; a 6-month enlistment guaranteed 640 acres; half that time, 320 acres. Battalions of citizen-soldiers were hastily formed and marched to Texas — the ALABAMA RED ROVERS; MOBILE GREYS; NEW ORLEANS GREYS; TENNESSEE MOUNTED VOLUNTEERS; the GEORGIA BATTALION; and the KENTUCKY MUSTANGS. Many of these bands of mercenaries were simply seeking adventure; others joined for the free land promised for their service. Individual volunteers came from states across the country as well — including some recent arrivals from England, Scotland, Germany, Ireland. A great number of the men who would fight and die for Texas independence were new arrivals to Texas who had attended a Texas meeting and departed their homes for a chance to share the wealth that awaited them in Texas. (See UNITED STATES SUPPORT FOR THE TEXAS REVOLUTION.) There were, of course, those cynics in the U.S. who perceived the revolution as nothing more than a land grab and the opportunity to spread SLAVERY. President Andrew Jackson, who had long coveted Texas, responded to the criticism of these mercenaries by saying that "Americans had a lawful right to emigrate and to bear arms." These diverse groups that came to Texas were by no means unified as an army. Many deserted, or refused to obey orders from officers, and each individual group acted autonomously without any central command. Some of these newcomers rampaged across the countryside — stealing, beating innocent people, raping Mexican women, and quartering themselves in the homes of those they had chased off. (See ATROCITIES COMMITTED DURING THE TEXAS REVOLUTION for more.) Needless to say, the resident Texans resented, disliked, and disapproved of most of the volunteers from the

states. In order to appease these soldiers of fortune, a scheme was dreamed up by Col. Frank JOHNSON, Dr. James GRANT, and Col. James W. FANNIN that called for rewarding these volunteers by plundering Mexico. In January, 1835, Fannin began organizing the MATAMOROS EXPEDITION, but it was eventually postponed due to the lack of supplies. Gen. Sam Houston was plagued with objections and near mutinies by recent arrivals from the states on his march to engage Santa Anna in the Battle of SAN JACINTO, which gained Texas independence. That was not to imply that every volunteer from the states was a barbarian. There were those who arrived in Texas with good intentions, and of those volunteers who were killed in the ALAMO BATTLE many were newcomers who could have heeded Travis's call to escape yet chose to remain and fight (see ALAMO GARRISON for more). The great majority of Fannin's troops who were executed in the Surrender and Massacre at GOLIAD were also newcomers. The question of whether or not the Texans could have defeated Santa Anna's forces relying solely on a volunteer army comprised of settlers is debatable. The most effective fighting of the revolution, however — at the Siege and Battle of SAN ANTONIO and the Battle of SAN JACINTO — was accomplished mainly by Texas residents, those militia "Minutemen" who fought to gain their freedom against a tyrannical government. Following that battle, the locals returned to their homes, and the Texas army was almost entirely comprised of volunteers from the United States. Those men, which numbered perhaps 2,500, were furloughed the following year when there were no funds in the government treasury to pay them.

## TEXAS SETTLEMENT BY AMERICANS

The first Americans came to Texas from Louisiana in the late 18th century while that land was ruled by Spaniards who had arrived nearly 300 years earlier. There were at that time few inhabitants other than a scattering of colonial settlements, Apache and Comanche Indians, and small religious communities founded by Catholic priests for the purpose of converting the Indians to Christianity. The Americans worked for the most part as horse traders who at times provided the Indians a market for horses stolen from Spanish posts. The presence of these intruders or FILIBUSTERS as they were known — traders, land speculators, and others with potential revolutionist interests — was a matter of great concern to Spanish authorities who had ordered Texas off limits to all Americans. President James Madison urged Americans to stay out of Texas, but his words did little to discourage the adventurers who had heard about the rich soil, dense forests, and natural harbors in this wilderness. Frontiersmen brazenly ventured into this land of opportunity; many settling permanently in northeast Texas in present-day Red River County.

Meanwhile, this movement into Texas was contemplated in more rational and enterprising terms by a man named Moses AUSTIN. This Missourian was the prosperous owner of real estate, a lead mine, and a bank in St. Louis — until 1819 when a financial panic wiped him out. Moses was deeply in debt, but not without ideas about how to regain his lost fortunes. He was aware that American colonization of Texas was only a matter of time, and that the Spanish would perhaps be receptive to a plan for an orderly settlement. This plan called for the Spanish to permit controlled immigration of responsible Americans who would then swear allegiance to the King of Spain and therefore be duty bound to protect their interests in Texas against the intrusion of illegal Americans. Austin would act as EMPRESARIO — the promoter of a colony — and

by assisting the Spanish in their dilemma would in the process restore his financial stability. Part of the panic that had ruined Austin was due to wild land speculation. The U.S. government had moved to tighten restrictions by demanding payment for land in full rather than allowing four years, and were now charging $1.25 an acre — a premium price in such hard times. Moses Austin would charge less per acre and offer generous payment terms to lure those Americans who would be willing to pledge their allegiance to Spain.

Moses's son, Stephen F. AUSTIN, who had studied law and served six years in the Missouri House of Representatives, declined to participate in his father's plan. He drifted from Missouri to New Orleans to began work as a low-paid assistant to the editor of a newspaper while seeking to establish a law practice.

Despite the misgivings of his son, Moses arrived in San Antonio, Texas on December 23, 1820, and presented himself to Governor Antonio de Martinez. The governor refused to receive the American, but by chance Moses encountered an old acquaintance, Baron de Bastrop. This self-appointed baron interceded on his friend's behalf by presenting Austin's Spanish passport. Austin explained to the governor that he was a former Spanish subject who had moved to Spanish Missouri in 1798, and was now prepared to renew his allegiance. He claimed to represent 300 families who were sympathetic to Spain and wanted to establish a permanent settlement in Texas to raise cotton, corn and sugar. Martinez was impressed with Austin's plan, and pledged to endorse his application. The application was approved by the provincial deputation in Monterey on January 17, 1821.

Moses Austin returned to Missouri, and word of the approval of the petition granting him 200,000 acres of land reached him in May, 1821. He immediately informed his son about the good news. Stephen remained apprehensive about the situation, but did agree to accompany his father on his next scheduled trip to Texas. That trip never occurred; Moses Austin died of pneumonia on June 10. Moses had on his death bed, however, begged his wife to tell Stephen that it was his wish that his son carry on with the plan to colonize Texas. Stephen could not refuse such a request.

In the company of a small group of Americans, Stephen Austin arrived in Texas on July 21, 1821. This was not by any means a half-hearted effort on his part to patronize his father's dying request, rather a commitment that he later explained by stating: "I bid an everlasting farewell to my native country, and adopted this, and in so doing I determined to fulfill rigidly all the duties and obligations of a Mexican citizen."

Austin travelled to San Antonio, and was favorably received by Governor Martinez, who recognized him as heir to his father's commission. Austin set out to explore the country, and on September 20 discovered in an area 175 miles southeast of San Antonio in the rich river bottoms of the Colorado and Brazos Rivers what he described in his journal as "a most beautiful situation for a town or settlement. The country back of this place for about 15 miles is as good in every respect as a man could wish for, land all first rate, plenty of timber, fine water." This particular place had access to the gulf, enjoyed abundant rainfall, and would make for fertile farmland. Austin's plan was to allot 640 acres of land to each man, with additional acreage for a wife and children. The town of San Felipe de Austin would be established on a bluff in the midst of this grant estimated at 11 million acres — about 18,000 square miles.

Austin went to Natchitoches, Louisiana, and found that news of his enterprise had travelled fast. Nearly a hundred inquiries from anxious would-be settlers awaited him. He dispatched a former business associate, Josiah H. Bell, to deal with those early birds. Austin then travelled in November to New Orleans in an effort to raise operating capital. He signed over half interest in his colony for $4000 to an acquaintance, Joseph H. Hawkins, a lawyer who had represented Kentucky in Congress. Austin purchased the schooner *Lively*, and loaded it with tools, household goods, and other essential provisions as well as 18 settlers. The crew of the *Lively* was instructed to shove off and wait for him at the mouth of the Colorado River. Austin would meet them there after travelling overland and then guide the schooner to his colony.

In November, 1821, the first settler of the colony, Andrew Robinson, had arrived to establish a ferry on the Brazos River at Washington on the Brazos. Others soon arrived, including the three Kuykendall brothers — Abner, Joseph, and Robert — and their families who came from Arkansas. Joseph Kuykendall and Daniel Gilleland moved west on the La Bahia Road to start the first settlement on the Colorado near present-day Columbus. Thomas Boatright called the stream where he settled on January 1, 1822 "New Year's Creek." William Kinchloe of Louisiana was given an extra section of land and a town lot in exchange for building a mill on the Colorado. Southern planter and lumberman Jared E. Groce also came to the colony in January with fifty wagons laden with supplies and 90 slaves. Groce would later become the largest cotton grower and one of the largest stock raisers in Texas.

Meanwhile, the *Lively* had mistaken the Brazos for the Colorado, and had run aground on Galveston Island. Unknownst to Austin, the immigrants returned to New Orleans and the entire cargo was lost, which was a huge financial setback. Perhaps worse yet was the potential loss of supplies for the colony during the first several months. The settlers refused to eat the corn they had brought for planting, and were said to have subsisted primarily on meat from turkey and deer. Jared Groce provided some relief by sharing from the large quantity of supplies that he had imported.

Stephen Austin searched for the *Lively* until March when he decided to report to Governor Martinez in San Antonio. He was shocked to learn from the governor that the officials at Monterey had refused to recognize his claim to his father's grant. The Mexican government, which had staged a revolution in 1821 and gained independence from Spain, was presently formulating its own colonization policy for Texas. That meant that the 8 families already in place and the 150 or so men preparing for the arrival of their families could be legally considered trespassers. Martinez suggested Austin go to Mexico City and reapply for legal title to the land.

Austin disguised himself as a beggar to avoid the attention of bandits, and, after a 1,200 mile journey, arrived in Mexico City on April 29, 1822. Austin wrote to his concerned colonists: "I arrived in the City of Mexico in April, without acquaintances, without friends, Ignorant of the language, of the Laws, the forms, the dispositions and feelings of the government, with barely the means of paying my expenses for a few months. Added to all this I found the City in an unsettled state, the whole people and country still agitated by the revolutionary convulsion, public opinion vacillating — Party spirit raging."

This political turmoil thwarted Austin's efforts to initiate a general colonization law which would legalize his settlement. The Federalists favored his cause while the Centralists were opposed. Finally in January, 1823 the Centralist Emperor of Mexico, General Agustin Iturbide, approved Austin's petition and signed a colonization law. A new Mexican Congress, however, soon overturned that law. Austin refused to give up. He learned fluent Spanish, and made friends of politicians and other influential aristocrats while continuing to press for colonization. On April 11, 1823, his patience and diplomacy paid off when the Congress approved his request for a colony by passing the Imperial Colonization Law. Oddly enough, at the same time the Congress voided the law, which made Austin the sole recipient of its provisions. The terms were generous — most settlers would receive 4,605 acres of land; taxes were waived for 6 years; Austin was permitted to charge his settlers 12 and one-half cents per acre to cover his costs; and he was personally awarded 100,000 acres. Austin was appointed Civil Commandant of the colony, and his father's old friend Baron de Bastrop was made land commissioner. Conditions set forth by the Mexican government required that each settler convert to Roman Catholicism and become a Mexican citizen.

Austin returned to his colony in August, 1823 to discover that all was not well. In fact, the colony was on the brink of collapse. A severe drought had ruined the first corn crop that had been planted the previous April, and Karankawa Indians had continually attacked the settlers and had killed many of them. Some colonists had abandoned their prime locations and returned to the United States. Austin assured those who had remained during his 17-month absence that his contract had been validated by Mexican authorities, and spelled out the new, favorable terms. Austin's grants were divided into two separate units. Those engaged in farming would receive 177 acres, those raising stock would receive a square league — about 4,428 acres — and each plot would be situated so that, if possible, it had frontage on the water for access to inexpensive river transportation. Property owners would be required to abide by the provisions of the law set forth above by the Mexican government, as well as occupy and improve the land within 2 years of the receipt of a deed. Slaves born to those already present would be freed upon reaching their 14th birthday. He then formed a militia to deal with the Indians, and set down additional rules and regulations to guide the colony. Austin's colony had issued 272 titles to land by September, 1824, and 25 more thereafter. These 297 original families who had settled along the Brazos, Colorado, and Bernard Rivers, spanning a territory from present-day Navasota, Brenham, and La Grange to the coast became known as the OLD THREE HUNDRED.

The Mexican Congress enacted the National Colonization Law in August, 1824, which opened up Texas to additional settlers. EMPRESARIOS soon began establishing new settlements under the Mexican law, and more and more Americans flocked to this promised land. Thousands of newcomers arrived in east Texas to establish farms, cotton plantations, and cattle ranches.

One particular *empresario*, Haden Edwards, received a grant in 1825 of more than 300,000 acres in eastern Texas, some of which already had been settled. Edwards, against the advice of Stephen Austin, ordered these people off his land. The settlers complained to the President of Mexico, and while Edwards was visiting the United States, his contract was revoked and he was ordered to leave the country. His brother, Benjamin, however, called for a revolt against Mexico, and in what became known as the Fredonia Rebellion, rallied about 30 colonists, seized an old fort near Nacogdoches, and proclaimed it the "Republic of Fredonia." On January 28, 1827, 250 Mexican troops accompanied by about 100 militia members from Austin's colony, set out to expel Edwards from the country. When the expedition arrived at "Fredonia," they found it de-

serted. Benjamin Edwards had fled to the United States. The Fredonian affair did, however, serve to create further suspicions in the minds of Mexican officials about whether or not the U.S. had intentions of adding Texas as a state.

Immigration from the United States was dealt a blow by the Mexican government by a decree on April 6, 1830. It had been determined by Gen. Manuel Mier y Teran on a fact-finding mission in 1828 that Mexican influence in Texas had greatly diminished and was being replaced by an American-based culture. The American population stood at about 16,000, which outnumbered the Mexican population by a ratio of four to one. In addition, more than a dozen villages with brick stores and frame houses had been established, a few well on their way to becoming towns. Austin's town of San Filipe had a population of about 200, with 50 houses and businesses such as 2 general stores and a blacksmith shop. The Colonization Law of April 6, 1830, was passed by the Mexican legislature and for all intents and purposes forbade immigration from the United States. In a move aimed directly at Americans, Article 11 of the decree stated in part: "Citizens of foreign countries lying adjacent to the Mexican territory are prohibited from settling as colonists in the states or territories of the Republic adjoining such countries," and suspended *empresario* contracts not yet fulfilled. The Mexican government dispatched troops throughout the state to collect taxes for the first time and to enforce the closed border policy. These troops were eventually run out of the country by irate Texans opposed to interference with trade. (See TEXAS REVOLUTION for more.)

At the same time, a cholera epidemic arrived from New Orleans and swept through east Texas. Some towns — including Velasco and Brazoria — were severely affected by this disease and many lives were lost.

Settlers in the colonies prospered between 1832 and 1834, and were for the most part content about their relationship with Mexico. That government had not levied taxes, or demanded strict adherence to the Catholic faith. Mexican presence and authority had virtually disappeared, and eastern Texas was free to engage in activities, such as smuggling and immigration, that would later become a matter of contention. New arrivals, a combination of farmers, ranchers, planters, merchants, adventurers, and land speculators, were pouring into the region in great numbers — many leaving behind a sign on their door that simply read "GTT" — Gone to Texas. These newcomers, however, were more intolerant than the present residents and hesitant to give up rights they had enjoyed as Americans — such as freedom of religion — and were opposed to this tyranny to which they had been forced to pledge allegiance in order to receive land. Stephen Austin, who remained loyal to Mexico and made an effort to maintain harmony, nevertheless recognized the roots of revolution as more and more settlers of a defiant and aggressive nature poured into Texas.

Mexican Army Colonel Juan ALMONTE recognized this trend when he toured Texas in 1834. At that time, he conducted a headcount and estimated that there were perhaps 20,700 Americans (in addition to 600–700 slaves) and 4,000 Mexicans — a five to one ratio. Almonte, who had mingled easily with the people because he spoke fluent English, also recommended on his return to Mexico that troops be promptly dispatched to quell the rebellious attitude of the populace. Otherwise, he prophetically assessed, Texas would be lost to Mexico.

In June, 1835, the first incident of the TEXAS REVOLUTION took place at Anahuac, and Texas was torn between fighting to remain a state of Mexico or gain independence. The call to arms brought many more peo-ple — mostly mercenaries and adventurers — to journey to Texas.

With the establishment of the Republic of Texas, that ratio rose to ten to one as more than a thousand American and European settlers per day entered the territory. Immigrants were offered 1,280 acres of land free of charge; a single man received 640 acres. By the time Texas had joined the United States in 1847, the population had risen from about 35,000 in 1836 to an astounding 140,000. This figure leaped to over 600,000 in 1860, with 9 out of 10 of these immigrants coming from the U.S.

**THOMAS, B. Archer M.** (1818–March 6, 1836) Private, TENNESSEE MOUNTED VOLUNTEERS; Alamo defender from Logan County, Kentucky. Thomas travelled to Texas in the company of fellow defenders Peter BAILEY, Daniel CLOUD, William FAUNTLEROY, and Joseph WASHINGTON. The five men enlisted with their small unit, which was under the command of Capt. William HARRISON, in Nacogdoches on January 14, 1836, and arrived in San Antonio on February 8, 1836. Thomas was serving as a rifleman when killed in the ALAMO BATTLE.

**THOMAS, Henry** (1811–March 6, 1836) Private, NEW ORLEANS GREYS; Alamo defender from Germany. Thomas arrived in San Antonio with his unit on November 21, 1835, and participated in the Siege and Battle of SAN ANTONIO. He was serving as a rifleman in Capt. William BLAZEBY's infantry company when he was killed in the ALAMO BATTLE.

**THOMPSON, Jesse G.** (1793–March 6, 1836) Private, TEXAS REVOLUTIONARY ARMY; Alamo defender from Arkansas. This resident of Brazoria, Texas, was serving as a rifleman when he was killed in the ALAMO BATTLE.

**THOMSON, John W.** (1807–March 6, 1836) Private, TENNESSEE MOUNTED VOLUNTEERS; Alamo defender from North Carolina. Thomson was a medical doctor who arrived in Texas by way of Tennessee in late 1835. He was mustered into service in Nacogdoches on January 14, 1836, but apparently travelled to the ALAMO MISSION on his own rather than with his unit. It is not known whether or not he served in the capacity of surgeon during the ALAMO SIEGE and BATTLE. He was listed as a rifleman when he was killed in the Alamo battle.

**THURSTON, John M.** (aka "Mountjoy Luckett Thurston" and "Thruston"; April 17, 1812–March 6, 1836) Second Lieutenant, TEXAS REVOLUTIONARY ARMY; Alamo defender from Pennsylvania. Thurston arrived in Texas by way of Kentucky, and was appointed 2nd Lt. on December 21, 1835. He was serving as an officer in Capt. John FORSYTH's cavalry company when he was killed in the ALAMO BATTLE.

**TRAMMEL, Burke** (aka "Tommel"; 1810–March 6, 1836) Private, TEXAS REVOLUTIONARY ARMY; Alamo defender from Ireland. Trammel participated in the Siege and Battle of SAN ANTONIO, and was awarded a section of land for his service. He was serving as an artilleryman in Capt. William CAREY's artillery company when he was killed in the ALAMO BATTLE.

**TRAVIS, William Barret** "Buck" (August 9, 1809–March 6, 1836) Colonel, Texas Cavalry; Alamo commander from Edgefield County, South Carolina. Travis was about 6 feet tall, weighed 175 pounds, had a fair complexion, blue-gray eyes, and curly auburn hair.

*Birth and Early Life*

Travis's ancestry and the circumstances surrounding his birth are difficult to document. His family possibly immigrated to Jamestown Island or Williamsburg, Virginia perhaps as early as 1637. His father, Mark Travis, Sr., was a farmer in Edgefield County, South Carolina, when on January 1, 1808, he married Jemima Stallworth. William was said to have been born around August 9, 1809 near Red Banks, Edgefield County, South Carolina, one of 9 or 10 children and the eldest son. Other accounts suggest that William was born in North Carolina, and another claims that he was a foundling adopted by the Travis family. Regardless, he would have been schooled at home in both basic subjects and religion — his father was a "Missionary Baptist." At some point in time, he attended Red Banks District school (perhaps aka Sparta Academy) where it is possible he became acquainted with fellow Alamo defender James B. BONHAM— some claim they were cousins. Bonham, however, enjoyed a higher social standing than Travis, which could have prevented them from socializing together in later years. Mark Travis, however, apparently had become quite prosperous by the time he moved his family to a farm in Conecuh County, Alabama, somewhere between 1818 and 1820.

Travis graduated from school, and then taught in Monroeville and Claiborne, Alabama while studying law at Claiborne in the offices of Judge James Dellett. He married Rosanna Cato, one of his pupils, on October 26, 1828, and was admitted to the bar in 1829. He gave up teaching, opened his own law office, established a home, joined the Masonic Lodge, was adjutant of the militia, and on August 8, 1829, a son, Charles

Edward, was born. The marriage, for some unknown reason — perhaps infidelity on one or the other's part — did not work out. One rumor, likely incorrect, reported that Travis had killed his wife's lover and blamed a slave for the act. Regardless, in early 1831— with Rosanna expecting their second child, Susan Isabelle, date of birth unknown — Travis signed over his considerable assets to his wife and, in the company of his slave, JOE, departed for Texas.

*Texas*

Travis travelled to Texas by way of New Orleans, and arrived in Nacogdoches by wagon. He moved on to Anahuac, and in April 1831, listing himself as a widower, registered for land. Travis set up a law practice — first alone then in partnership with Patrick C. Jack. It was here that Travis in 1832 had a hand in instigating a pre-revolution incident fueled by friction between the colonists and Mexico that became known as the Battle of VELASCO. Col. John Bradburn, the tyrannical Mexican commander at Anahuac, for no apparent reason arrested an *EMPRESARIO*, abolished his settlement, and confiscated the colonists' land. When this action was protested, Bradburn established martial law and arrested several outspoken colonists which included Travis and his partner Patrick Jack. This act inspired 160 townspeople, led by Jack's brother, to march on the garrison to demand their release. They arrived to find the two men shackled to the floor, and Bradburn threatening to kill them if there was any sign of aggression. Travis bravely called for them to shoot, allegedly saying he would "rather die a thousand deaths than permit this oppressor to remain unpunished." The colonists, who were outgunned, wisely backed off for the time being. Bradburn than arrested more colonists. Although the radical stance of Travis and his

companions was not supported by most colonists, neither was the threat of their execution by Mexicans. The call went out for artillery and more men, which began forming in Brazoria. The Mexican commander at Nacogdoches, arrived to negotiate with the colonists. He freed Travis, Jack, and the other prisoners, and made other concession which included the removal of the Anahuac customhouse. Word of the truce did not reach the volunteers that were en route to Anahuac, and they were intercepted by the Mexican garrison at Velasco. A battle ensued, which resulted in 10 colonists killed and 11 wounded, and 5 Mexican soldiers killed and 16 wounded. The Mexicans, however, ran out of ammunition and abandoned that post as well.

Meanwhile, Travis was creating a reputation for himself as a prosperous businessman with an engaging, flamboyant manner, and that of a heavy gambler, flashy dresser — white hat and red pantaloons — and perhaps most of all, a womanizer. He meticulously noted each conquest in his diary, but his womanizing may have ended or at least slowed in late 1833 when he made the acquaintance of Rebecca Cummings, who managed her brother's inn at Mill Creek. Rebecca would become his "fiancée" since he was still married to Rosanna.

Travis's business continued to grow, and he become an outspoken member of the WAR PARTY. He encouraged the colonists to set up their own government independent of Mexico. When Santa Anna unexpectedly reopened the customhouse at Anahuac in early 1835, Travis and his allies were once again subject to duties that they believed were unjust.

At about the same time, Travis was confronted by his wife, who had travelled to Texas and demanded that he either live with her or grant her a divorce. Travis agreed to a divorce, but requested and was given custody of his son, Charles. Rosanna Travis returned to Alabama and eventually remarried.

### Texas Revolution

Travis become embroiled in another confrontation with Mexican authorities when in June, 1835 the new commander of the customhouse, Capt. Antonio Tenorio, was accused of unfairly levying taxes. In what became known as the Battle of ANAHUAC, (June 29) Travis raised a company of 25 men, marched on Tenorio's headquarters, and gave the Mexicans 15 minutes to leave. The commander complied and surrendered his 44 troops, but the rash act by Travis did not set well with many of the townspeople, who were afraid of repercussions. Letters of apologies were sent to Tenorio and his superiors. Public opinion, however, swayed in Travis' favor when Santa Anna ordered his arrest, which evoked visions of martial law and military occupation in addition to indiscriminate arrests. Committees began to form all across Texas to protest Santa Anna's actions. The Mexican president responded to this call to arms by dispatching his brother-in-law, Gen. Martin Perfecto de CÓS and an army of regular troops to Texas to arrest dissidents and quell the uprising, which included halting shady land dealings by the legislature in Saltillo. For all practical purposes, the TEXAS REVOLUTION had begun.

The first shots of the revolution were fired in the GONZALES SKIRMISH on October 2, the day before Santa Anna officially voided the MEXICAN CONSTITUTION OF 1824. One week later in the GOLIAD SKIRMISH, the volunteer Texas army captured the small Mexican garrison in that town, which effectively prevented the Mexicans from receiving provisions or troops by sea.

William Travis joined the army scouting service and soon became chief of the recruiting service at San Felipe. The small TEXAS REVOLUTIONARY ARMY of about 500 men had by this time marched to commence the November-December Siege and Battle of SAN ANTONIO, which was intended to rid Texas of the 1,400 Mexican soldiers garrisoned in that town. Travis proceeded to San Antonio, and continued his scouting activities, which included burning the prairie to deny forage for Mexican horses. He also captured 300 head of horses and 5 prisoners from a Mexican camp on November 10. Some accounts have suggested that Travis distinguished himself during the battle of San Antonio, but most report that he had grown impatient with the siege and travelled to San Felipe in late November in order to pressure Governor Henry SMITH into appointing him a lieutenant colonel. Travis succeeded in gaining an appointment to that rank in late December, and was ordered to raise a cavalry and ride for San Antonio.

### The Alamo

Travis arrived at the ALAMO MISSION in San Antonio with 20–30 men — including his slave, Joe — on February 3, 1836. In his possession was a lock of Rebecca Cummings' hair and a ring given to him by her. He reported to commander Col. James NEILL, and soon discovered that there was a dispute over command of the small garrison between Neill and Jim BOWIE. An election was held on February 12 to select a commander, and Bowie, who was extremely popular with the men, easily won. Col. Neill immediately found an excuse to leave — illness in his family has been cited — and rode out of the Alamo the day following the election. Neill apparently had designated Travis as his successor, which prompted a dispute between Travis and Bowie. Travis began firing off letters to San Felipe complaining about Bowie's high-handedness, drunkenness and general bad behavior. Bowie was said to have turned San

Antonio into one giant party, a drunken orgy designed to demonstrate his power over both his men and the civilians to the point of martial law. Apparently Bowie and Travis managed to negotiate a tentative truce between them. On February 14, a letter was dispatched to Governor Smith that stated in part: "By an understanding of today Coln J. Bowie has the command of the volunteers of the garrison, and Col. W. B. Travis of the regulars and volunteer cavalry. All general orders and correspondence will henceforth be signed by both until Col. Neill's return."

This joint command would be tested when on February 23, Santa Anna and his army approached San Antonio to begin the ALAMO SIEGE. Travis immediately retired to his headquarters room located along the west wall, and began writing messages requesting reinforcements from Goliad and Gonzales. Santa Anna arrived in town and ordered that a red flag — the Mexican symbol for no mercy — be hoisted from the belfry of San Fernando Church. Travis, without consulting Bowie, fired the 18-pounder cannon. The cannonball fell harmlessly in town, but served as a message of defiance. Bowie considered the impulsive action by Travis a waste of cannon shot and a threat to possible negotiation, and, without consulting Travis, dispatched a messenger, Green B. "Benito" JAMESON, to town to explore an honorable truce. He had in his own manner of defiance ended his note with the salutation "God and Texas" after crossing out "God and the Mexican Federation." This insult irritated Santa Anna, and he responded through an aide that there would be no terms other than unconditional surrender. Travis was angered that Bowie would send a message signed only by Bowie and without consulting him. He dispatched his own emissary, Albert MARTIN, who received more or less the same reply.

The feud between Travis and Bowie was settled in the wee hours of February 24 when Bowie became incapacitated with an unknown illness — some claim that his drinking binges had caught up with him. Bowie at that time surrendered his authority to Travis, and was carried to a small room in the low barracks where he was attended to by a Mexican folk healer.

That night, Travis sent out Albert Martin with a message addressed "To the People of Texas & all Americans in the world." This letter appealing for help has been considered one of the most heroic in American history.

Travis wrote:

Fellow Citizens & Compatriots:

I am besieged by a thousand or more of the Mexicans under Santa Anna. I have sustained a continual bombardment and cannonade for 24 hours & have not lost a man. The enemy have demanded a surrender at discretion; otherwise, the garrison is to be put to the sword if the fort is taken. I have answered the summons with a cannon shot, & our flag still waves proudly from the walls. *I shall never surrender or retreat.* Then, I call on you in the name of liberty, of patriotism & every thing dear to the American character, to come to our aid with all dispatch. The enemy are receiving reinforcements daily & will no doubt increase to three or four thousand in four or five days. If this call is neglected, I am determined to sustain myself as long as possible & die like a soldier who never forgets what is due his own honor & that of his country.

*VICTORY OR DEATH.*

Travis continued to dispatch messages in the ensuing days, but, other than 32 men who arrived from Gonzales on March 1, his pleas went unheeded. (See COURIERS DISPATCHED FROM THE ALAMO for more.) These messages have given researchers valuable information about conditions inside the Alamo and the conduct of the defenders during the siege.

On March 3, with the Mexican army creeping closer and the bombardment intensifying, Travis sent a message to the convention at Washington-on-the-Brazos, then scribbled notes to his fiancée, Rebecca Cummings, and a close friend, Jesse Grimes. His final letter was addressed to David Ayers, who was boarding Travis's son Charles. "Take care of my little boy," he wrote. "If the country should be saved, I may make him a splendid fortune; but if the country should be lost and I should perish, he will have nothing but the proud recollection that he is the son of a man who died for his country." These messages as well as those written by many of the other defenders were taken out at midnight by John W. SMITH.

According to Mexican sources, on the evening of March 5, the day before the ALAMO BATTLE, Travis allegedly dispatched from the Alamo a Mexican woman who lived in San Antonio as an intermediary in a effort to seek terms for a possible surrender. The surrender attempt, if it indeed happened, was rejected.

## The Line in the Dirt

On that night of March 5, Travis was said to have assembled the entire garrison in a single file and stood before them. He was an effective public speaker, and it was evident that he had rehearsed his speech. In a voice brimming with passion and choked with the emotion of the moment, he told his men that there would be no reinforcements at this late hour, and presented the choices that faced them — they could surrender, or try to escape, or, if those options were unacceptable, they could stay and fight. He vowed that it was his intention to stay and fight even if every one of them chose to attempt an escape or surrendered.

Travis then dramatically drew his sword, and scratched a line in the dirt as he walked from one end of the compound to the other. Those volunteers who chose to stay and fight, he declared, should step across that line. Those who had chosen to stay could remain where they stood. Within moments, every man in the garrison had crossed the line — except one. Louis ROSE. Rose ignored the glares of his comrades, gathered his belongings, and disappeared over the wall.

The question of whether or not Travis actually drew this line has been a matter of controversy and debate throughout the ensuing years. The story first came to light in 1873 from William Zuber, whose parents had taken in a nearly dead Louis Rose following his escape. Rose was allegedly illiterate, and Zuber's parents had not documented the tale in any manner. In fact, it was questioned as to whether or not a "Louis Rose" had even been in the Alamo at all. Therefore, the idea that Travis had performed such a dramatic act was dismissed as myth until other accounts — slightly differing versions — surfaced from SURVIVORS OF THE ALAMO BATTLE Susannah DICKINSON and Enrique ESPARZA. Mrs. Dickinson's statement read in part: "On the evening previous to the massacre, Colonel Travis asked the command that if any desired to escape, now was the time, to let it be known, and to step out of ranks. But one stepped out. His name to the best of my recollection was *Ross* (Rose?). The next morning he was missing." The discrepancy in spelling could have been attributed to the fact that Dickinson could neither read or write. Also, there is no mention of a line being drawn. The matter of Rose's presence at the Alamo was also given life in 1939 by an office worker by the name of R. B. Blake who found in the Nacogdoches County Courthouse the testimony of Louis Rose in a land claim request from the heirs of Alamo defender John BLAIR. Rose stated in that document that he had left the Alamo on March 3. The date is 2 days short of

Travis's alleged act (it can be presumed that calendars were in short supply on the frontier), but does verify that there was indeed a Louis Rose in the Alamo who left at some point during the siege. This same Louis Rose, as evidenced by his known biography, was subsequently vilified wherever he went following his admitted cowardice at the Alamo. Zuber, however, later claimed that he had made up much of his story — which brings us back to the credibility of Susannah Dickinson, who was not the least bit interested in her historical significance as a witness to the siege and battle.

Travis's action, however, was not without recent precedent. In December, 1835, Ben MILAM at the Siege and Battle of SAN ANTONIO had used the same tactic of drawing a line in the dirt to solicit volunteers to attack the Mexican Army. Travis had likely already departed San Antonio by that time, but Milam's gesture became quite well known — later portrayed in a posthumous play about Milam — and it is conceivable that Travis was aware of it, perhaps from some of the Alamo defenders who had crossed Milam's line. In fact, the act of crossing a line to indicate support — voting with their feet — had been used for some time on the frontier. The question posed by Travis was not one that a simple "yea" or "nay" would suffice as an answer. His dramatic speech called for dramatic action.

Did Travis draw the line? No proof exists to confirm that he did not.

After his speech, Travis, perhaps seeking some respite from his gloomy thoughts, paid a visit to Susannah Dickinson and her daughter Angelina, who huddled in the chapel. In a gesture that could be interpreted as a premonition of his death and a desire to in some manner be remembered, he removed from his finger the gold cat's eye ring that had been a gift from his fiancée Rebecca Cummings.

He then tied the ring on a string and looped it around little Angelina's neck.

### Death

On the morning of March 6, William Travis was in his room sleeping when roused by officer of the day and second in command Capt. John BAUGH with word that the Mexican Army was attacking. Armed with a sword and a shotgun, Travis and Joe immediately dashed to the north parapet. Within a matter of minutes, the Mexicans had become a confused mass that had assembled beneath the north wall. Travis leaned over that wall, aimed his shotgun point-blank into the mass of Mexican soldiers, and fired both barrels. He had raised the weapon to reload when a bullet struck him in the head. Travis reeled backward and tumbled down the dirt embankment. He landed in a sitting position, his sword clutched in his hand, and remained there stunned until dying a few minutes later. William Travis, the man who had vowed "Victory or Death," was likely the first American casualty of the battle. Joe fled to seek refuge in one of the rooms, and survived the battle. Gen. Martin Perfecto de CÓS allegedly later forced Joe to identify the body of his master. Cós then drew his sword and brutally mutilated the face and limbs of Travis.

There have been a number of stories — some more outrageous than others — alleging that Travis either committed suicide, surrendered, or died in some other location. No evidence exists, however, that contradicts the above account of his death.

William Travis will be remembered as perhaps the most gallant figure associated with the Alamo due to his unwavering courage and heroic messages urging aid from his fellow Texans. His diary offers an interesting peek into the activities of a man who accounted for every aspect of his life — including legal transactions; gambling winnings and losses; pennies given to children; bushels of corn; and even sexual conquests. (For a more detailed account of Travis's actions at the Alamo See ALAMO SIEGE and ALAMO BATTLE.)

**TUMLINSON, George W.** (1814–March 6, 1836) Private, GONZALES RANGING COMPANY; Alamo defender from Missouri. This resident of Gonzales participated in the Siege and Battle of SAN ANTONIO. He was at his home when the ALAMO SIEGE began, and entered the ALAMO MISSION with his unit on March 1, 1836. He was serving as an artilleryman in Capt. CAREY's artillery company when he was killed in the ALAMO BATTLE.

**TYLEE, James** (1795–March 6, 1836) Private, TEXAS REVOLUTIONARY ARMY; Alamo defender from New York. Tylee, who was married and residing in Texas, was serving as a rifleman when he was killed in the ALAMO BATTLE.

# U

**UNITED STATES OFFICIAL REACTION TO THE TEXAS REVOLUTION** Laws had been passed over the years that made it a crime for American citizens to mount military expeditions into foreign countries. The first of these laws, the Neutrality Act of April 24, 1800, imposed the penalty of a $1000 fine and up to 3 years imprisonment for enlistment into the service of a foreign country, and up to $3000 for aiding or mounting an armed expedition. The Neutrality Act was amended in 1817 to include territories such as Texas, but this had not slowed the efforts of FILIBUSTERS to embark on efforts to spark revolution in Texas

that had begun as early as the late 1700's. At the outbreak of the TEXAS REVOLUTION in 1835, the official position of the United States was one of neutrality. And, when the Mexican government protested about the bands of mercenaries from the United States that were invading Texas (see UNITED STATES SUPPORT FOR TEXAS INDEPENDENCE), Secretary of State John Forsyth formally warned U.S. district attorneys in a number of states to prosecute these offenders under neutrality laws. The mercenaries, some of whom were aided by local district attorneys, dodged this law by calling themselves "emigrants" and their weapons "hollow-ware." President Andrew Jackson, who secretly coveted Texas, was honored with a salute by a unit of Texas volunteers in Nashville. When asked by an outraged dignitary about his willingness to ignore this lawbreaking, Jackson replied "That Americans had a lawful right to emigrate and to bear arms." The press in the North protested these violations of law, and condemned those Americans such as Sam HOUSTON who encouraged armed support from the United States. The South, however, had pulled together in their belief that SANTA ANNA must be defeated. In other words, the country was split along the same lines that caused the division that led to the Civil War a quarter of a century later. Even as Gen. Antonio Lopez de Santa Anna's troops marched into Texas, official entreaties by Jackson's minister to sell Texas to the United States were being made in Mexico City. Jackson refused to grant Stephen F. AUSTIN's request that he demonstrate support for the Texas Revolution and supply troops and provisions, which would have been politically unacceptable and might have sparked an unwanted war with Mexico. He did, however, in an move designed to perhaps intimidate Mexico, dispatch U.S. Army troops under the command of Gen. Edmund Gaines along the Sabine River with official orders —

in accordance with a U.S.-Mexican treaty — to prevent Indian activities that originated in the U.S. from spilling over into Mexico. The Mexicans protested this troop build-up, but were ignored. Some evidence indicates that Sam Houston might have been attempting to coax the U.S. troops across the river into Texas by heading east with his "Runaway Scrape" in prelude to the Battle of SAN JACINTO. Certain Texans attempted to lure Gaines and his troops across the border by warning of an alliance between Indians and Mexicans that was preparing to attack innocent refugees. Gaines had observed refugees fleeing Texas, but there was no evidence that Indians were involved, much less an uprising that would permit him to take action. The Indians were in fact frightened by this conflict, and had fled to the prairie to escape being attacked themselves. Gaines did receive authorization to enter Texas as far as Nacogdoches, but those orders arrived 4 days after the Texans had won independence at San Jacinto.

**UNITED STATES SUPPORT FOR TEXAS REVOLUTION** The TEXAS REVOLUTION was financed in part by money and supplies from donors in the United States. Many Americans also volunteered to bear arms for the cause of independence, and traveled to Texas with the promise of land grants for their service. The largest chunk of money — about $150,000 — came in the form of loans negotiated by a commission headed by Stephen F. AUSTIN — much of it from land speculators. "Texas Meetings," fueled by events in that Mexican state, were commonplace in many cities across the United States in the fall of 1835. Patriotic Americans, many of whom had heeded the call for freedom in the American Revolution 50 years earlier, wanted to assist their brethren with men, money, arms and supplies. Letters written by Sam HOUSTON and other Texans, and editorials in newspapers inspired crowds to pack theaters and meeting halls nationwide to discuss this quest for liberty that was taking place in Texas. Macon, Georgia collected $3,150; Nashville's Henry Hill donated $5,000; $396.50 was offered from theatergoers in Natchez, Mississippi; Mobile, Alabama raised $1,500; cannon and kegs of powder in addition to more over $10,000 was loaded aboard a schooner in New Orleans for shipment to Texas. The bulk of war supplies came from New Orleans, much of it from the firm of William Bryan and Company, which shipped rifles, lead, powder, clothing, and other vital provisions. Recruiting stations were established in Louisville, Cincinnati, and New Orleans. More than 2,000 people gathered at New York's Tammany Hall to proclaim loyalty to Texas. Mexican dictator Antonio Lopez de SANTA ANNA was burned in effigy in Philadelphia. But most of all it was men with a taste for adventure who heeded Sam Houston's urgent call to "Let each man come with a good rifle and 100 rounds of ammunition — and come soon. Our war cry is 'Liberty or Death.'" Some of these volunteers were motivated by the noble cause of freedom, but others realized that grants of rich Texas land were in the future of those who fought for the cause. Houston emphasized this opportunity to gain property when he said, "If volunteers from the United States will join their brethren in this section (Texas), they will receive liberal bounties of land. We have millions of acres of our best lands unchosen and unappropriated." Mercenaries from the United States — called auxiliary volunteers — who enlisted for the duration of the war would receive 1,280 acres; a 6-month enlistment guaranteed 640 acres; half that time, 320 acres. Battalions of citizen-soldiers were hastily formed. In Mobile, Alabama, James BONHAM and Capt. Burke assembled the

MOBILE GREYS, and Bonham was charged with personally delivering to Sam Houston a resolution of support; Capt. Jack Shackleford recruited his ALABAMA RED ROVERS; the TENNESSEE MOUNTED VOLUNTEERS boasted David CROCKETT as a member; in New Orleans, Capt. Thomas Breece formed 2 companies of the NEW ORLEANS GREYS; others included the GEORGIA BATTALION from Georgia and Alabama, and the KENTUCKY MUSTANGS from Kentucky and Tennessee. Individual volunteers came from states across the country — including some recent arrivals from England, Scotland, Germany, Ireland. A great number of the men who would fight and die for Texas independence at the Alamo and at Goliad were new arrivals to Texas who had attended a Texas meeting and departed their homes for a chance to share the wealth that awaited them in Texas (see TEXAS REVOLUTIONARY ARMY).

**URREA, José Francisco** (1797–August, 1849) General, MEXICAN ARMY. This 4th-generation military officer was raised in the state of Durango. He joined his father in the army, and supported Agustín de Iterbides' plan for Mexican independence, But both men came under fire by backing the Republicans which led to his father's exile and José's dismissal from the service in 1827. He reentered the army in 1829, and, under the tutelage of Antonio Lopez de SANTA ANNA rose to the rank of general. Urrea participated in the May, 1835 Battle of Zacatecas when Santa Anna — in an action that firmly established him as military dictator of Mexico — defeated a fortified army of 13,000 with 3,500 troops in less than 2 hours. Urrea was elected governor of Durango in September, 1835. In January, 1836, while Santa Anna moved to San Antonio, Urrea's 1,200 infantrymen were sent to Matamoros with orders to march along the coast into Texas by way of Refugio and Goliad to serve as the army's right wing. He added to his command the services of 300 Mayans from the Yucatan, and departed Matamoros on January 18. On February 27, 1836 some 50 miles south of Goliad at San Patricio, the general and 100 cavalrymen came upon Col. Frank JOHNSON and 50 men who were out foraging for horses and supplies for the ill-fated MATAMOROS EXPEDITION. Urrea attacked at 3 A.M. in a driving rainstorm, and killed 16 Americans and captured 24. The prisoners were sent to Matamoros and eventually released, but Johnson, who escaped with 4 others, spread the word that his men had been executed. That disturbing news reached Col. James FANNIN in Goliad and acted to further justify his decision to abort an impending mission to rescue the Alamo. Urrea then turned his attention to the rebel garrison at Goliad. On the way, the Mexican general set an ambush at Agua Dulce Creek, and on March 2 annihilated a 15-man force under Dr. James GRANT. On March 14, Urrea surrounded another rebel force of 200 men under Col. William Ward, who had been dispatched by Fannin to help evacuate colonists' families in the Refugio vicinity. Urrea killed 16 and captured 31. That same day, Gen. Sam HOUSTON, who was aware that Urrea was on the move, sent a message to Col. Fannin at Goliad ordering him to immediately abandon that post. On March 16, Urrea captured one of Fannin's messengers and learned about the plans to fall back to Victoria. About that point in time, Urrea also relented to the wishes of his officers, and obeyed Santa Anna's standing orders to execute all "pirates" as the mercenaries were called. Urrea removed himself from camp while about 30 of his 50 prisoners were executed. The remaining 20 prisoners were determined to be either Mexicans or colonists, and were released. Fannin had vacillated, and delayed his retreat with a wagon train and 400 men until March 19. Urrea was hot on his trail, and Fannin was only 6 miles from Goliad when the Mexicans surrounded the wagon train in an open prairie near Coletto Creek. The wagons were formed into a square, and the volunteers made a stand. Mexican charges were repelled throughout the afternoon with moderate casualties sustained on both sides. At nightfall, the two sides suspended hostilities. Bodies of dead Mexicans littered the prairie — about 50 killed and 140 wounded. The rebels had to that point suffered 7 killed and 50 wounded, including Col. Fannin who was wounded in the thigh. Urrea's artillery opened up at daybreak. Fannin understood that it would only be a matter of time until they would be overrun by the superior force, and raised the white flag. Gen. Urrea personally visited the rebel camp to accept Fannin's surrender. The prisoners were marched back to Goliad. Urrea was uncertain about the disposition of these prisoners. Santa Anna had ordered that all prisoners without exception be executed, but Urrea could not comprehend the killing in cold blood of such a large number of people. Therefore, he permitted the wounded to be treated, and put the healthy to work building rafts and repairing fortifications that had earlier been destroyed. He even gained an admiration for Col. Fannin, whom he believed was a gentleman and a man of great courage worthy of being spared. Meanwhile, Urrea's men had caught up with Col. William Ward and about 120 men who had eluded capture for a week after being attacked. These men were transported to Goliad, and, along with other small detachments, brought the total number of prisoners to about 500. Santa Anna was incensed when informed that Gen. Urrea had not already followed orders and executed his prisoners. He dispatched a messenger with a letter to Urrea that read in part:

I have been surprised that the circular of the said supreme government has not been fully complied with in this particular; *I therefore order, that you should give immediate effect to said ordinance in respect to all foreigners* who have yielded to the force of arms, having the audacity to come and insult the republic, to devastate with fire and sword, as has been the case in Goliad, causing vast detriment to our citizens; in a word, shedding the precious blood of Mexican citizens, whose only crime has been their fidelity to their country. I trust that, in *reply* to this, you will inform me that *public vengeance has been satisfied by the punishment of such detestable delinquents.*

Gen. Urrea — who had departed Goliad for Victoria — replied to Santa Anna with an request for clemency. The plea, however, failed to change his commander's mind. Santa Anna wrote out an order in triplicate, and had it delivered to Col. José Nicolas Portilla, who was in direct command of the Goliad prisoners. Even as Portilla received this order from Santa Anna, Gen. Urrea sent him a message from Victoria telling him to treat the prisoners well and have them continue rebuilding the fort. On Palm Sunday, March 27, the prisoners were told they were to be released. Instead, they were marched in three separate columns away from camp, and, other than perhaps 60 or so who escaped, were executed by firing squads. Urrea — like most other Mexican officers — was shocked by the carnage. (See GOLIAD, Surrender and Massacre at for a detailed account.) Urrea's force continued east, and, amazed by the unfamiliar and interesting items found on the Anglo farms — such as candle wax, white sugar, bitter chocolate, cigars, tailored clothes — the soldiers began pillaging goods. The army confiscated liquor as well, and the troops became undisciplined and resorted to brawling to the extent that some were killed. Houses were burned, slaves were liberated, and colonists — branded "tories" for their support of Mexico — turned in local traitors, who were then taken prisoner. Urrea was on his way from Matagorda to Fort Bend where the Mexican units had been ordered to rendezvous when Santa Anna was defeated in the Battle of SAN JACINTO on April 21, 1836. Following Santa Anna's surrender, Urrea urged the army's second in command, Gen. Vincente Filisola, to disobey orders to retreat and instead attack the rebels to free the prisoners. Filisola refused. Urrea may not have been so adamant had he known that Santa Anna had offered Gen. Houston that he would be pleased once he returned to Mexico City to make an example of Urrea for the massacre at Goliad. In early 1837, Urrea was in command of the main body of troops at Matamoros while 8,000 others were poised just across the Rio Grande River from Texas, but the Mexican Army was too disorganized to invade and mount a campaign. Urrea became military commander of Sonoroa and Sinaloa, and, in a series of federalist revolts in 1837, 1839, 1840, and 1841, endeavored but failed to reestablish the MEXICAN CONSTITUTION OF 1824. He had surrendered in June, 1839, but escaped, was captured and escaped again before being recaptured to end the coup attempts. In 1841, when Santa Anna regained power, Urrea was appointed governor and commanding general of Sonora (1842–1844). He provoked a 3-year civil war in that state against both the central government and Yaqui and Mayo Indians, which ended with Urrea being stripped of his command by the new national government. Urrea served with Santa Anna against the United States in the Mexican War, and died in Durango of cholera at the age of 52.

# V

**VELASCO, Battle of** (June 26, 1832) (For events preceding and following this battle please see TEXAS REVOLUTION.) This prerevolution incident — likely the first involving bloodshed between Texas and Mexico — was fueled by outrageous acts by a Mexican garrison and customhouse commander. The result was a brief battle, and the withdrawal of Mexican troops from the state of Coahuila-Texas.

A customhouse and military post had been established by the Mexicans at Anahuac in 1831 for the purpose of enforcing the collection of duties. The garrison was comprised of about 120 *presidarios*— convict soldiers — under the command of Col. John (Juan) Davis Bradburn, a Kentucky-born mercenary who had gone to Mexico in 1817. Bradburn outraged the merchants in Texas with a number of inconvenient demands, but his most outrageous act was his incorrect interpretation of the April 30, 1830, Law, which stated that due to excessive American influence in Texas, *EMPRESARIOS* from states or territories adjacent to Texas were prohibited from settling — meaning the United States. He decided that *empresario* Francisco Madero had violated that law — which was not the case — and arrested Madero, abolished his settlement of Liberty and confiscated the colonists' land. Bradburn then placed the area under martial law, impressed supplies for his garrison, and used slave labor for public works. When this action was protested, Bradburn arrested several outspoken colonists, including William TRAVIS and his law partner Patrick C. Jack. Travis's crime was writing anonymous letters threatening that an armed force of colonists would march against Bradburn. The arrests compelled Jack's brother, William, to rally about 160 townspeople and march on the garrison to demand the release of the prisoners. They arrived to find the two men shackled to the floor, and Bradburn threatening to kill them if there was any sign of aggression. Travis bravely called for them to shoot, allegedly saying he would "rather die a thousand deaths than permit this oppressor to remain unpunished." The colonists, who were outgunned, wisely backed off for the time being. Bradburn than arrested more colonists, and, although the radical stance of Travis and his WAR PARTY was not supported by most colonists, neither was the threat of their execution by Mexicans. The colonists gathered at Turtle Bayou, and, in what were called the Turtle Bayou Resolutions, pledged to support Mexican rule and loyalty to the MEXICAN CONSTITUTION OF 1824 but repudiated President Anastasio Busamente in favor of Antonio Lopez de SANTA ANNA in their struggle for power over Mexico. The call went out for artillery and more men, and a force of volunteers began forming in Brazoria. In the meantime, Mexican Colonel José de las Piedras, commander of the Nacogdoches garrison, arrived in Anahuac to parlay with the colonists. He courteously listened to their grievances against Col. Bradburn, and agreed to free the prisoners, remove Bradburn, endeavor to restore the confiscated property, and end martial law. In fact, the customhouse at Anahuac was abandoned and those troops returned to Mexico. Word of Piedras' magnanimous action had not reached those colonists who were en route by boat to Anahuac. On June 26, 1832, at the mouth of the Brazos River at Velasco—80 miles from Anahuac—they were intercepted by the Mexican garrison there, which was commanded by Col. Domingo de Ugartechea. The ensuing battle resulted in 10 colonists killed and 11 wounded, and 5 Mexican soldiers killed and 16 wounded. The Mexicans, however, ran out of ammunition, were forced to surrender, and withdrew to Matamoros. All customhouses in Texas remained closed until reopened in 1835 by Santa Anna.

**VELASCO, Treaties of** (May 14, 1836) These treaties—one public and one secret—which ended hostilities between Texas and Mexico and brought about the Republic of Texas, were signed in Velasco by Texas *ad*

*interim* President David BURNET and Mexican dictator Antonio Lopez de SANTA ANNA.

*Chronology of the Texas Revolution*

- June 29, 1835: Battle of ANAHUAC
- October 2, 1835: GONZALES SKIRMISH
- October 3, 1835: MEXICAN CONSTITUTION OF 1824 officially voided
- October 9, 1835: GOLIAD SKIRMISH
- October 28, 1835: Battle of CONCEPCION
- November 3, 1835: TEXAS CONSULTATION OF DELEGATES
- November–December, 1835: Siege and Battle of SAN ANTONIO
- January–February, 1836: The MATAMOROS EXPEDITION
- February 23–March 5, 1836: The ALAMO SIEGE
- March 1, 1836: TEXAS CONSTITUTIONAL CONVENTION
- March 2, 1836: TEXAS DECLARATION OF INDEPENDENCE
- March 6, 1836: The ALAMO BATTLE
- March 20–27, 1836: Surrender and Massacre at GOLIAD
- April 21, 1836: Battle of SAN JACINTO
- **May 14, 1836: Treaties of VELASCO**

The Texas army had been victorious in the April 21, 1836 Battle of SAN JACINTO, and established *de facto* independence in so doing. Mexican president Santa Anna on April 22 entered into an armistice with Gen. Sam HOUSTON which ended the fighting between Texas and Mexico pending formal negotiations. Meanwhile, the headquarters of the Texas government moved to Velasco, and on May 14, 1836, President *ad interim* David Burnet negotiated two treaties with Mexican dictator Antonio Lopez de Santa Anna—one public and one secret—in that city. The public treaty established Texas as an independent republic; declared a permanent end to hostilities between Texas and Mexico, and that Santa Anna would not again take up arms against Texas; ordered the MEXICAN ARMY to retire south of the Rio

Grande River; provided for the release of Texas and Mexican prisoners; property confiscated by the Mexicans would be restored; and that the boundary between the two countries would be established in a later treaty, but Texas would not extend beyond the Rio Grande. The secret treaty, which would be executed when provisions of the public treaty had been fulfilled, was designed to receive a pledge from Santa Anna that he would influence Mexico to recognize Texas' independence and accept the provisions of the public treaty; and that he would encourage the Mexican cabinet to favorably receive a Texas mission; and work toward a commerce treaty. In return, Santa Anna and his army would be spared.

Santa Anna willingly signed the treaties, but his action was immediately (May 20) annulled by the Mexican government. It was pointed out that Santa Anna was a prisoner of war and in that capacity could not speak for Mexico. In addition, according to international law a captive under duress could not be held accountable for his actions. The Texans argued that until removed from office, Santa Anna was dictator of Mexico not merely a constitutional president and did not require any other approval. This was proven by the fact that Santa Anna's orders were obeyed by Gen. Vincente FILISOLA when told to retire south of the Rio Grande. In addition, Santa Anna had revoked the MEXICAN CONSTITUTION OF 1824, which left Mexico without a proper constitution and all power in the hands of the dictator. Santa Anna's signature was the signature of Mexico. In other words, as stated by Mexican historian, José de Vasconcelos, Mexico was "without any other authority than the strong boot of the soldier." And that soldier was clearly Santa Anna or his assignees — one of whom was Gen. Filisola.

The Mexican Army led by second in command Gen. Filisola received by messen-

ger Santa Anna's order to retire south of the Rio Grande while already in retreat. It was decided by the Texas government, however, to ensure validity, that Gen. Filisola, who was not a prisoner, should also sign the treaty. To accomplish that, Col. Benjamin F. Smith and Capt. Henry Teal were dispatched, and on May 26, 1836 at the stream of Mugerero secured the signatures of Filisola and two subordinates, Gen. Eugenio Tolsa and Col. Agustin Amat. Filisola was criticized for signing the treaty, but was simply obeying the orders of his superior, Santa Anna, as well as — and perhaps more importantly — discretionary powers granted him by the Minister of War in Mexico City, Gen. José Maria Tornel y Mendivil. Tornel was the dominant member of Santa Anna's government, and was more concerned with the disposition of President Santa Anna and the prisoners than the loss of Texas. Filisola later justified his actions by stating "...only in a war where no quarter was to be given, by an especial and positive order from the government, could I be prohibited the exchange of prisoners. And to what else did I compromise myself in recognizing that treaty (of Velasco) than to retreat and exchange prisoners... Mexico had lost it (Texas) forever, due to the anxiety and indiscretion of the general-in-chief (Santa Anna), who wasn't content with only punishment...but who wanted to exterminate them (the Texans) forever." Filisola later faced a court-martial, but was exonerated of any wrongdoing.

This dispute over Texas independence and the boundary between the two countries would be a matter of contention until the Treaty of Guadalupe Hidalgo in 1848.

# W

**WALKER, Asa** (1813–March 6, 1836) Private, TEXAS REVOLUTIONARY ARMY; Alamo

---

defender from Tennessee. Walker arrived in Texas in November, 1835. Upon reaching Washington-on-the-Brazos, Walker was compelled to write to a Mr. Gant with a confession. It seems that Walker had borrowed, without consent, an overcoat and gun belonging to Gant, and had left behind his clothing as collateral. Walker participated in the Siege and Battle of SAN ANTONIO, and was listed as being in the hospital following that battle. If healthy, he was serving as a rifleman with Capt. Robert WHITE's infantry company when he was killed in the ALAMO BATTLE. Walker's cousin, Jacob WALKER, also perished in the Alamo battle.

**WALKER, Jacob** (May, 1799–March 6, 1836) Private, TEXAS REVOLUTIONARY ARMY; Alamo defender from Rockridge County, Tennessee. Walker, the father of four children who was residing in Nacogdoches, Texas, participated in the Siege and Battle of SAN ANTONIO and was awarded a section of land for his service. He was serving as an artilleryman in Capt. William CAREY's artillery company in the ALAMO BATTLE. Susannah DICKINSON later stated that toward the end of the battle, Walker attempted to take refuge with her in the baptistry. Four Mexican soldiers shot him, then, while he was still alive, hoisted his body on their bayonets like a bale of hay on a pitchfork several times until he died in convulsions. He was the brother of famous mountain man Joe Walker, and the cousin of Alamo defender Asa WALKER.

**WAR PARTY** This term characterized those Texans who were determined that Texas should gain independence from Mexico at a time when most colonists accepted living under the provisions of the MEXICAN CONSTITUTION OF 1824. Most of these hard core rebels were not idealists who envisioned freedom for freedom's sake, rather were lawyers and land speculators who realized the profits that could be made from a free Texas. Early proponents of independence included William TRAVIS and his law partner, Patrick Jack; Jim BOWIE; Ben MILAM; Frank JOHNSON; Robert "Three-legged Willie" Williamson; and William and John Wharton. Most of the Texas colonists in pre-revolution times were for peaceful relations with Mexico, and were irritated by the actions of these "War Dogs" as they called them. In June, 1832, Travis and Jack instigated a minor rebellion against a Mexican garrison to protest duties and arrests of protesters that resulted in the Battle of VELASCO, which eventually swayed some colonists to their way of thinking when Mexico threatened military tribunals. Texas prospered during the following 2 years, and Mexico relaxed some of the more restrictive provisions of the constitution. But that attitude changed in early 1835 when Mexican dictator Antonio Lopez de SANTA ANNA reopened customhouses to collect duties and land speculation became rampant with corruptness. Travis instigated another protest in June, 1835 for reasons similar to his previous effort that resulted in the Battle of ANAHUAC, which edged more colonists closer to revolution. But this time, Santa Anna, who had been embroiled in politics in Mexico City in 1832, ordered the arrest of Travis and other rebels and land speculators. Then in October, 1835 Santa Anna tightened his grip on Texas by annulling the Mexican constitution. The rebellious Texans argued at the TEXAS CONSULTATION OF DELEGATES in favor of fighting for independence but, with future War Party proponent Sam HOUSTON voting against them, the convention chose to fight for the restoration of the Mexican constitution rather than independence. New arrivals from the United States, however, embraced the War Party stance, and, when Santa Anna invaded Texas in late 1835, the elements were in place for most colonists to accept revolution (see also TEXAS REVOLUTION; PEACE PARTY).

**WARD, William B.** (1806–March 6, 1836) Sergeant, TEXAS REVOLUTIONARY ARMY; Alamo defender from Ireland. Ward, who had earned the reputation as a heavy drinker, was said to have been stone sober when he was killed in the ALAMO BATTLE while serving as an artilleryman.

**WARNELL, Henry** (aka "Warnal," "Wornell," and "Wurnall"; 1812–June, 1836) Private, TEXAS REVOLUTIONARY ARMY; Alamo defender from Arkansas. This jockey and hunter departed his home in Arkansas after his wife died giving birth to a healthy baby boy. He had left the infant in the care of friends, and became a resident of Bastrop, Texas in January, 1835. He participated in the Siege and Battle of SAN ANTONIO, and served as an artilleryman with Capt. William CAREY's artillery company during the ALAMO SIEGE. Some evidence exits that Warnell escaped from the Alamo — either alone or in the company of another man — on the morning of the ALAMO BATTLE, but died in June at Nacogdoches of wounds sustained either during the battle or on his flight across the prairie. (See SURVIVORS OF THE ALAMO BATTLE for more.) Warnell's son was awarded a grant of land in 1860 for his father's service at the Alamo after filing a claim with the General Land Office.

**WASHINGTON, Joseph G.** (aka "James Morgan"; 1808–March 6, 1836) Private, TENNESSEE MOUNTED VOLUNTEERS; Alamo defender from Logan County, Kentucky. Washington travelled to Texas in the company of fellow defenders Peter BAILEY, Daniel CLOUD, William FAUNTLEROY, and B. Archer

M. THOMAS. The five men enlisted with their small unit, which was under the command of Capt. William HARRISON, in Nacogdoches on January 14, 1836, and arrived in San Antonio on February 8, 1836. During the ALAMO SIEGE, Washington was serving as a rifleman when he was killed in the ALAMO BATTLE.

**WATERS, Thomas** (1812–March 6, 1836) Private, NEW ORLEANS GREYS; Alamo defender from England. Waters arrived in San Antonio with his unit on November 21, 1835, and participated in the Siege and Battle of SAN ANTONIO. He was serving as an artilleryman with Captain William CAREY's artillery company when he was killed in the ALAMO BATTLE.

**WEAPONS OF THE ALAMO DEFENDERS** Most rifles carried into the Alamo by the defenders were of the flintlock variety left over from the Revolutionary War or the War of 1812, and in a condition that compelled a Texas blacksmith named Noah Smithwick to remark: "I fixed up many an old gun that I wouldn't have picked up in the road." The flintlock could fire only one round at a time then required reloading. The basic steps to reloading were complex, and required expertise and a steady hand. When the trigger was squeezed, the charge was ignited by sparks produced by a spring-actuated cock striking a piece of flint against a vertical, pivoted striking place (frizzen). Flame and smoke exploded in all directions, and, after a fraction of a second, the ball was driven up and out of the barrel. The typical single-shot muskets with a proper supply of gunpowder could shoot with relative accuracy to about 50–70 yards. The Pennsylvania or Kentucky long rifle could accurately fire about twice that distance — or up to 200 yards in the hands of a sharpshooter like

David CROCKETT. Pistols, which were highly inaccurate except at close range, required the same loading procedures. Some defenders carried shotguns — including Col. William TRAVIS — but these were looked down upon by the farm boys who scorned anything but a rifle for hunting. Many of the volunteers also carried knives — Jim BOWIE and some members of the NEW ORLEANS GREYS had the famous Bowie knife. The Alamo defenders who lined the walls, when aware that Santa Anna's attack was imminent, had 3 or 4 loaded rifles at their disposal and could therefore rapid fire. It was doubtful, however, that these muzzle-loaders ordinarily remained loaded for long periods of time. The charge in the frizzen could be ruined by dew, rain, or humidity, and the men would occasionally fire their weapons and reload to ensure proper discharge if needed. The Alamo had 14–18 artillery pieces, but lacked trained crews, and, in fact, likely could not spare enough men to man the guns. These muzzle-loading cannons required five men apiece: a loader, a rammer, a thumbstall, a gunner, and a powder monkey. Therefore, 18 pieces of artillery would require about 90 men — half the total of the garrison. Artillery ammunition, in addition to cannon balls which were scare, was made from cutting chain, iron bars, and horseshoes into grapeshot. The known positions of the Alamo's 14–18 guns were as follows: the 18-pounder, the heaviest piece which could throw a solid iron ball more than half a mile, was located at the south end of the plaza's west wall and pointed west toward San Antonio; a battery of three 12-pounders were situated in rough embrasures atop the 12 foot high dirt ramp at the apse of the chapel — the center one aimed east, those on the flanks north and south; four 4-pounders pointed south from the unwalled side of the courtyard where the main gate was located; at least one 8-pounder was situated at the western end of the north wall; two 8-pounders in the center of the north wall; two 6-pounders protecting the porte-cochere pointing south; one 12-pounder in the center of the western wall; one or two 8-pounders were possibly located in the plaza in the event the Mexicans managed to breach the walls.

**WEAPONS OF THE MEXICAN ARMY AT THE ALAMO** Most Mexican soldiers carried a British surplus smooth-bore flintlock musket, known as the India pattern, and affectionately called "Brown Bess." This musket had a 39-inch barrel, fired a .753-caliber ball about 70–100 yards with any accuracy, and carried a socket bayonet with a triangular 17-inch blade. Mexico had obtained thousands of these heavy, old fashioned blunderbusses left over from the days of Waterloo that the British had manufactured and condemned. The cavalry carried these weapons as well as a one-and-a-half inch thick wooden lance and a sword or saber slung from a waistbelt. Some infantrymen carried a British Baker flint ignition gun with a 30-inch barrel. The Mexican soldiers were notoriously poor shots, in part due to the mule-like kick of the Brown Bess and their habit of undercharging their shot to compensate for the recoil which affected both range and accuracy. Mexican artillery consisted of at least 21 cannons and howitzers — including 2 12-pounders that were their largest. Santa Anna tended to rely on his 9-pounders that could fire 2 rounds of solid shot per minute and reach a distance of 1,400 yards. Mexican artillery kept up an incessant barrage of the Alamo, but until the final days failed to cause much damage. The position of these guns just before the battle: one 6-cannon battery emplacement was within 250 yards of the Alamo to the north; two 9-pounders had been placed just across the river in San Antonio, 400 yards to the west; one battery was 300 yards away to the south in La Villita; another 1000 yards to the south at the powder house; another 800 yards northeast on the ditch; and one battery at the old mill, 800 yards north.

**WELLS, William** (August, 16, 1798–March 6, 1836) Private, TEXAS REVOLUTIONARY ARMY; Alamo defender from Hall County, Georgia. Wells was serving as a rifleman when he was killed in the ALAMO BATTLE.

**WHITE, Isaac** (?–March 6, 1836) Sergeant, TEXAS REVOLUTIONARY ARMY; Alamo defender from Alabama or Kentucky. This noncommissioned officer was a married man with one daughter when he was killed in the ALAMO BATTLE.

**WHITE, Robert** (1806–March 6, 1836) Captain, TEXAS REVOLUTIONARY ARMY; Alamo defender from parts unknown. White, who made his home in Gonzales, participated in the Siege and Battle of SAN ANTONIO. He was promoted to Captain on February 4, 1836, and was serving as commanding officer of an infantry company when he was killed in the ALAMO BATTLE.

**WILLIAMSON, Hiram James** (aka "H. S. Williamson"; 1810–March 6, 1836) Sergeant major, TEXAS REVOLUTIONARY ARMY; Alamo defender from Philadelphia, Pennsylvania. This resident of Washington-on-the-Brazos, Texas, participated in the Siege and Battle of SAN ANTONIO. He was the highest ranking enlisted man — garrison sergeant major — when he was killed in the ALAMO BATTLE.

**WILLS, William** (?–March 6, 1836) Private, VOLUNTEER ARMY OF TEXAS; Alamo defender from parts unknown. This farmer from Brazoria County, Texas was serving as a rifleman when he was killed in the ALAMO BATTLE.

**WILSON, David L.** (1807–March 6, 1836) Private, TEXAS REVOLUTIONARY ARMY; Alamo defender from Scotland. Wilson had been residing in Nacogdoches, Texas when he volunteered for service and was killed in the ALAMO BATTLE while serving as a rifleman.

**WILSON, John** (1804–March 6, 1836) Private, TEXAS REVOLUTIONARY ARMY; Alamo defender from Pennsylvania. Wilson was serving as a rifleman when he was killed in the ALAMO BATTLE.

**WOLFE, Anthony** (aka "Wolf," "Wollf," and "Woolf"; February 17, 1782–March 6, 1836) Private, TEXAS REVOLUTIONARY ARMY; Alamo defender from England. Wolfe came to America with his sons, Benjamin and Michael, following the death of his wife and settled in the Louisiana-Texas territory. He spoke various Native American dialects, and served in the capacity as interpreter and emissary to the Wichita Indians in 1818, and Indian agent to the Cherokees in 1822. Wolfe was residing in Nacogdoches at the time he entered the ALAMO MISSION in early 1836 accompanied by his two sons, and served as an artilleryman in Captain William CAREY's artillery company. There are differing stories regarding the death of Wolfe and his two sons in the ALAMO BATTLE. One account was related by Enrique Esparza, son of Alamo defender Gregorio ESPARZA. Enrique testified that one of the Wolfe boys was killed beside him in the room where he huddled with his family, his body falling upon him. The elder Wolfe then grabbed the remaining boy, and both of them leaped off the high chapel wall. They were either killed by the fall or shot dead by Mexican soldiers. Susannah DICKINSON claimed that the only man to ask for quarter was named "Wolff," and he was killed on the spot. His two little boys, aged 11 and 12, were then killed, she said, and the Mexican soldiers carried the bodies out of the room on their bayonets.

**WRIGHT, Claiborne** (1810–March 6, 1836) Private, GONZALES RANGING COMPANY; Alamo defender from North Carolina. Wright joined the army in November, 1835, and participated in the Siege and Battle of SAN ANTONIO. He entered the ALAMO MISSION from his home in Gonzales with his unit on March 1, 1836, and was serving as a rifleman when he was killed in the ALAMO BATTLE.

# Z

**ZANCO, Charles** (aka "Zanor," "Lance," and "Danor"; 1808–March 6, 1836) Lieutenant, TEXAS REVOLUTIONARY ARMY; Alamo defender from Denmark. Zanco, an artist and painter who had settled in Harris County, Texas, may hold the distinction of creating the prototype of what later became the state flag of Texas. He was charged with designing a flag for his volunteer company at the outbreak of the TEXAS REVOLUTION, and chose a lone star with the word "Independence." Zanco participated in the Siege and Battle of SAN ANTONIO, and was assistant to the ordnance chief— responsible for the maintenance of all weapons — when he was killed in the ALAMO BATTLE.

**ZAVALA, Lorenzo de** (October 3, 1789–November 15, 1836) Vice-president, Republic of Texas. This liberal intellectual and Texas land speculator was born in the village of Tecoh in Yucatan, Mexico. Zavala was edu-

cated in the Seminary of Ildefonso, and became an advocate of liberal, democratic reforms. In May 1814, he was imprisoned for his beliefs at the Castle of San Juan de Ulloa. For the next 3 years, Zavala made good use of his time by studying English and medicine. He was in Madrid, Spain representing the Yucatan in the Spanish Cortes when Mexico declared its independence in 1821. He returned home and served as a member of the Mexican Constituent Congress from 1822–1826, and was president of that body during the passage of the MEXICAN CONSTITUTION OF 1824. In 1827, he was elected governor of the state of Mexico, but fled due to military unrest. He soon resumed that position, as well as that of national secretary of the treasury. In 1829, he applied for and received an *EMPRESARIO* grant to settle 500 families in Texas, but the following year — with partners David BURNET and Joseph Vehlein — transferred this contract to the Galveston Bay and Texas Land Company. He returned in 1832 as governor of the state of Mexico, then became a member of the Mexican Chamber of Deputies the following year, and in October, 1833 was appointed minister to France by President Antonio Lopez de SANTA ANNA. It was while in Paris that Zavala became disenchanted with Santa Anna and the factional politics in Mexico, and made his intentions known that he was going to settle in Texas in order to rebuild his fortune which had diminished during his political career. There is some evidence that Zavala had secretly planned as early as 1830 to incite a revolution in Texas and instill himself as president. He arrived in July, 1835 to establish a home on Buffalo Bayou near present-day Houston, and immediately established himself with the radical community but was not entirely trusted because he was a Mexican. Zavala continued to encourage rebellion against Santa Anna who he contended had lost all right to loyalty from the

Mexican people. Zavala counseled Stephen F. AUSTIN about strategies that could be used against Mexico, but his motives were likely for the purpose of aligning himself with the Mexican *federalistas* with whom he could assume power. Zavala traveled to San Felipe in late September, 1835 to assist Austin and others with planning the impending November, 1835 TEXAS CONSULTATION OF DELEGATES, for which he had been elected as a delegate from Harrisburg. He was also elected as a delegate to the March, 1836 TEXAS CONSTITUTIONAL CONVENTION, and became a signer of the TEXAS DECLARATION OF INDEPENDENCE. At that convention, in a show of unity of Texans of both Mexican and Anglo-Saxon heritage, Zavala was elected

*ad interim* vice-president of the Republic of Texas. After the April 21, 1836 Battle of SAN JACINTO, his home across the bayou was used as a hospital. The body of Mexican Gen. Manuel CASTRILLÓN, an old friend from Mexico who had been killed in that battle, was removed from the battlefield and buried in the Zavala family plot. Zavala resigned his office on October 17, 1836, and shortly after that toppled from a boat into the cold water of Buffalo Bayou. He contracted pneumonia and within days had died at the age of 47. Zavala had been married twice, and was the father of 6 children. He was buried in the family plot, which later became a part of the San Jacinto State Park. Zavala County, Texas, was named in his honor.

# SELECTED BIBLIOGRAPHY

Almonte, Juan N. "The Private Journal of Juan Nepomuceno Almonte, February 1–April 16, 1836." *Southwestern Historical Quarterly* 48, no. 1 (July, 1944).

Baker, Karle W. "Trailing the New Orleans Greys." *Southwest Review* vol. 22 (April, 1937).

Barker, Eugene C. "The San Jacinto Campaign." *Southwestern Historical Quarterly* vol. 9, (1901).

_____. "Land Speculation as a Cause of the Texas Revolution." *Southwestern Historical Quarterly* vol. 10, no. 1 (July, 1906).

_____. "The Texas Revolutionary Army." *Quarterly of Texas State Historical Association* vol. 9, no. 4 (April, 1906).

_____. "The Influence of Slavery in the Colonization of Texas." *Southwestern Historical Quarterly* vol. 28 (July, 1924).

_____. *Mexico and Texas, 1821–1835*. Dallas: P. L. Turner Company, 1928.

Baugh, Virgil E. *Rendezvous at the Alamo*. New York: Pageant Press, 1960; reprinted by University of Nebraska Press, 1985.

Becerra, Francisco. *A Mexican Sergeant's Recollections of the Alamo and San Jacinto*. Austin: Jenkins Publishing Company, 1980.

Bennett, Miles S. "The Battle of Gonzales." *Texas Historical Association Quarterly* vol. 2 (1899).

Binkley, William C., ed. *Official Correspondence of the Texas Revolution*. 2 vols. New York: D. Appleton-Century Company, 1936.

_____, *The Texas Revolution*. Baton Rouge: Louisiana State University Press, 1952.

Blake, R. B. "A Vindication of Rose and His Story." In *The Shadow of History*, edited by Frank Dobie, Mody C. Boatright, and Harry H. Ransom. Austin: Texas Folk-Lore Society, 1939.

Bonham, Milledge L., Jr. "James Butler Bonham: A Consistent Rebel." *Southwestern Historical Quarterly* vol. 35, no. 2 (October, 1931).

Brogan, Evelyn. *James Bowie: A Hero of the Alamo*. San Antonio: Theodore Kunzman, 1922.

Burke, James W. *David Crockett: Man Behind the Myth*. Austin: Eakin Press, 1984.

Callcott, Wilfrid H. *Santa Anna*. Norman: University of Oklahoma Press, 1936.

Carter, Hodding. *Doomed Road of Empire*. New York: McGraw-Hill, 1963.

Castaneda, Carlos Eduardo. *The Mexican Side of the Texas Revolution by the Chief Mexican Participants*. Austin: Graphic Ideas Incorporated, 1970.

Chabot, Frederick C. *The Alamo: Mission, Fortress and Shrine.* San Antonio: The Leake Company, 1935.

Chariton, Wallace O. *100 Days in Texas — The Alamo Letters.* Plano, Texas: Woodware, 1990.

Cleaves, W. S. "Lorenzo de Zavala in Texas." *Southwestern Historical Quarterly* vol. 36 (July, 1932).

Colleti, Sarah. "Found: Alamo Traitor's Grave." *The Shreveport Times,* May 25, 1975.

Connelly, Thomas L. "Did David Crockett Surrender at the Alamo? A Contemporary Letter." *Journal of Southern History* vol. 26, no. 3 (August, 1960).

Connor, Seymour V. *Battles of Texas.* Waco: Texian Press, 1967.

Costeloe, Michael P. "The Mexican Press of 1836 and the Battle of the Alamo." *Southwestern History Quarterly* vol. 91. no. 4 (April, 1988).

Crimmins, M. L. "American Powder's Part in Winning Texas Independence." *Southwestern Historical Quarterly* vol. 52, no. 1 (July, 1948).

Crockett, David. *Col. Crockett's Exploits and Adventures in Texas.* Philadelphia: T. K. and P. G. Collins, 1836.

_____. *A Narrative of the Life of David Crockett of the State of Tennessee, written by Himself.* Lincoln: University of Nebraska Press, 1987.

Cruz, Gilberto Rafael, and James Arthur Irby, eds. *Texas Bibliography: A Manual on History Research Materials.* Austin: Eakin Press, 1982.

Davenport, Harbert. "The Men of Goliad." *Southwestern Historical Quarterly* vol. 48, no. 1 (July, 1939).

De Bruhl, Marshall. *Sword of San Jacinto: A Life of Sam Houston.* New York: Random House, 1993.

de la Pena, José Enrique. *With Santa Anna in Texas: Narrative of the Revolution.* Translated and edited by Carmen Perry. College Station: Texas A & M University Press, 1975.

De León, Arnoldo. "Tejanos and the Texas War for Independence: Historiography's Judgment." *New Mexico Historical Review* vol. 61 (April, 1986).

De Shields, James T. *Tall Men with Long Rifles: The Glamorous Story of the Texas Revolution as Told by Captain Creed Taylor.* San Antonio: Naylor Printing Company, 1935.

Derr, Mark. *The Frontiersman: The Real Life and the Many Legends of Davy Crockett.* New York: William Morrow, 1993.

Dixon, Sam Houston, and Louis Wiltz Kemp. *The Heroes of San Jacinto.* Houston: Anson Jones Press, 1932.

Douglas, Claude L. *James Bowie: the Life of a Bravo.* Dallas: B. Upshaw & Company, 1944.

Ehrenberg, Herman. *With Milam and Fannin: Adventures of a German Boy in The Texas Revolution.* Edited by Henry Smith. Dallas: Tardy Publishing Company, 1935.

Fehrenbach, T. R. *Lone Star: A History of Texas and Texans.* New York: American Legacy Press, 1985.

Filisola, General Vincente. *Evacuation of Texas.* Translated by George Louis Hammeken, edited by James M. Day. Waco: Texian Press, 1965.

_____. *The History of the War in Texas*. Translated by Wallace Woolsey. 2 vols. Austin: Eakin Press, 1985–87.

Flynn, Jean. *Remember Goliad: James W. Fannin*. Austin: Eakin Press, 1984.

Franz, Joe B. *Texas: A History*. New York: W. W. Norton & Company, 1984.

Friend, Llerena B. *Sam Houston: The Great Designer*. Austin: University of Texas Press, 1985.

Gaddy, Jerry J., comp. *Texas in Revolt: Contemporary Newspaper Accounts of the Texas Revolution*. Fort Collins, Colorado: Old Army Press, 1983.

Garver, Lois. "Benjamin Milam." *Southwestern Historical Quarterly* vol. 38, nos. 2 and 3 (1934).

Green, Michael R. "El Soldado Mexicano, 1832–1836." *Military History of Texas and the Southwest* vol. 13, no. 1.

_____. "To the People of Texas & All Americans In the World." *Southwestern Historical Quarterly* vol. 91, no. 4 (April, 1988).

Green, William E. "Remembering the Alamo." *American Heritage* vol. 37, no. 4 (June/July, 1986).

Groneman, Bill. *Alamo Defenders*. Austin: Eakin Press, 1990.

_____, *Defense of a Legend: Crockett and the de la Pena Diary*. Plano, Texas: Republic of Texas Press, 1994.

_____, and Rosenthal, Philip. *Roll Call at the Alamo*. Fort Collins: Old Army Press, 1985.

Guerra, Mary Ann Noonan. *Alamo Heroes*. Accurate Lithograph and Printing Company, 1981.

_____. *The Alamo*. San Antonio: Alamo Press, 1983.

Hardin, Stephen L. *Texas Illiad: A Military History of the Texas Revolution*. Austin: University of Texas Press, 1994.

Harris, Helen Willits. "Almonte's Inspection of Texas in 1834." *Southwestern Historical Quarterly* vol. 41, no. 3 (January, 1938).

Haythornthwaite, Philip. *The Alamo and the War of Texan Independence 1835–36*. London: Osprey Publishing, 1986.

Hogan, William R. *The Texas Republic: A Social and Economic History*. Norman: University of Oklahoma Press, 1946.

Hopewell, Clifford. *James Bowie: The Fighting Man*. Austin: Eakin Press, 1994.

Hunnicut, Helen. "A Mexican View of the Texas War." *The Library Chronicle of the University of Texas* Summer, 1951.

Huston, Cleburne. *Deaf Smith: Incredible Texas Spy*. Waco: Texian Press, 1973.

James, Marquis. *The Raven: A Biography of Sam Houston*. St. Simon, Georgia: Mockingbird Books, 1981.

Jones, Oakah L. Jr. *Santa Anna*. New York: Twayne Publishers, 1968.

Kemp, Louis Wiltz. *The Signers of the Texas Declaration of Independence*. Houston: Anson Jones Press, 1944.

Kilgore, Dan. *How Did Davy Die?* College Station: Texas A & M University Press, 1978.

King, Richard. *Susannah Dickinson, Messenger of the Alamo.* Austin: Shoal Creek Publishers, 1986.

Koury, Michael J. *Arms for Texas: A Study of the Weapons of the Republic of Texas.* Fort Collins: Old Army Press, 1973.

_____. "Cannon for Texas: Artillery in the Revolution and the Republic." *Military History of Texas and the Southwest* vol. 10, no. 2 (1972).

Lamar, Mirabeau B. "Mirabeau B. Lamar's Texas Journal." *Southwestern Historical Quarterly* vol. 64, no. 2 (October, 1980) and no. 3 (January, 1981).

Leclerc, Frederic. *Texas and Its Revolution.* Houston: Anson Jones Press, 1960.

Lofaro, Michael A. *Davy Crockett: The Man, The Legend, The Legacy, 1786–1986.* Knoxville: The University of Tennessee Press, 1985.

Long, Jeff. *Duel of Eagles: The Mexican and U.S. Fight for the Alamo.* New York: William Morrow, 1990.

Lopez, Antonio. *Santa Anna: Revolution and Republic.* Dallas: American Guild Press, 1957.

Lord, Walter. *A Time to Stand: The Epic of the Alamo.* New York: Harper & Row, 1961; reprinted by University of Nebraska Press, 1978.

Lozano, Ruben Rendon. *Viva Tejas: The Story of the Tejanos, The Mexican-Born Patriots of the Texas Revolution.* San Antonio: Alamo Press, 1985.

Matovina, Timothy M. *The Alamo Remembered: Tejano Accounts and Perspectives.* Austin: University of Texas Press, 1995.

Montaigne, Sanford H. *Blood Over Texas.* New Rochell, New York: Arlington House, 1976.

Myers, John M. *The Alamo.* Lincoln: University of Nebraska Press, 1973

Nevin, David. *The Texans.* New York: Time-Life, 1971.

Newell, Chester. *History of the Revolution in Texas.* New York: Arno Press, 1973.

Nofi, Albert A. *The Alamo and the Texas War for Independence.* New York: Da Capo Press, 1994.

Nordyke, Lewis. *The Truth About Texas.* New York: Thomas Y. Crowell, 1957.

Oakes, Stephen B., ed. *The Republic of Texas.* Palo Alto: American West Publishing Company and Texas State Historical Association, 1968.

Pohl, James W., and Stephen L. Hardin. "The Military History of the Texas Revolution: An Overview." *Southwestern Historical Quarterly* vol. 89, no. 3 (January, 1986).

Potter, Reuben M. *The Fall of the Alamo: A Reminiscence of the Revolution of Texas.* Edited by Charles Grosvenor. Hillside, New Jersey: Otterden Press, 1977.

Presley, James. "Santa Anna in Texas: A Mexican Viewpoint." *Southwestern Historical Quarterly* vol. 62, no. 4 (April, 1959).

Price, Robert *The Annals of Texas History.* Austin: Texas House, 1914.

Richardson, R. N. *Texas, The Lone Star State.* Englewood Cliffs, New Jersey: Prentice-Hall, 1981.

Sánchez Lamego, Miguel A. *The Siege and Taking of the Alamo.* Translated by Consuelo Velasco. Santa Fe: Blue Feather Press, 1968.

Santa Anna, Antonio Lopez de. *The Eagle: The Autobiography of Santa Anna*. Edited by Ann Fears Crawford. Austin: The Pemberton Press, 1967.

Santos, Richard G. *Santa Anna's Campaign Against Texas 1835–1836*. Waco: Texian Press, 1968.

Shackford, James A. *David Crockett, The Man and the Legend*. Chapel Hill: University of North Carolina Press, 1956; reprinted by University of Nebraska Press, 1994.

Sibley, Marilyn McAdams. "The Burial Place of the Alamo Heroes." *Southwestern Historical Quarterly* vol. 70, no. 2 (October, 1966).

_____. *Travelers in Texas: 1761–1860*. Austin: University of Texas Press, 1967.

Smith, Ruby Cumby. "James W. Fannin, Jr. in the Texas Revolution." *Southwestern Historical Quarterly* vol. 23, nos. 2 and 3 (1919).

Smithwick, Noah. *The Evolution of a State or Recollections of Old Texas Days*. Austin: University of Texas Press, 1983.

Sterne, Adolphus. *Hurrah for Texas!* Edited by Archie P. McDonald. Waco: Texian Press, 1969.

Sutherland, John. *The Fall of the Alamo*. San Antonio: Naylor Press, 1936.

Teer, L. P. "Was There a Coward at the Alamo?" *Frontier Times*. vol. 39, no. 6 (October/November, 1965).

Thonhoff, Robert H. *The Texas Connection with the American Revolution*. Burnett, Texas: Eakin Press, 1981.

Timmons, Walter H. *The Anglo-American Advance into Texas, 1810–1830*. Boston: American Press, 1981.

Tinkle, Lon. *13 Days to Glory: The Siege of the Alamo*. New York: McGraw Hill, 1958; reprinted by Texas A & M University Press, 1996.

Tolbert, Frank X. *The Day of San Jacinto*. New York: McGraw Hill, 1959.

Travis, William B. *Diary of William Barret Travis: August 30, 1833–June 26, 1834*. Edited by Robert E. Davis. Waco: Texian Press, 1966.

Vigness, David M. *The Revolutionary Decades, 1810–1836*. Austin: Steck-Vaughn Company, 1965.

Villasenor, Juan. *Santa Anna: Napoleon of the West*. St. Louis: Copeland Publishing, 1932.

Webb, Walter Prescott, ed. *The Handbook of Texas*. 2 vols. Austin: Texas State Historical Association, 1943.

Weber, David J. *The Mexican Frontier, 1821–1846: The American Southwest under Mexico*. Albuquerque: University of New Mexico Press, 1982.

Williams, Amelia W. "A critical Study of the Siege of the Alamo and of the Personnel of Its Defenders." *Southwestern Historical Quarterly*. vol. 36, no 3 (April, 1933) and vol. 37, no. 4 (January, 1934).

_____. "Notes on Alamo Survivors." *Southwestern Historical Quarterly* vol. 49, no. 4 (April, 1946).

Wooten, Dudley G. *A Comprehensive History of Texas, 1685–1897*. 2 vols. Dallas: Scarff, 1898.

Zuber, William Physik. *My Eighty Years in Texas*. Edited by Janis Boyle Mayfield. Austin: University of Texas Press, 1971.

# INDEX

Bold page numbers indicate the main reference, and *italic* type indicates maps